# The Mozart–Da Ponte Operas

# The
# Mozart–Da Ponte Operas

The Cultural and Musical
Background to *Le nozze
di Figaro*, *Don Giovanni*, and
*Così fan tutte*

ANDREW STEPTOE

CLARENDON PRESS · OXFORD

*This book has been printed digitally and produced in a standard design*
*in order to ensure its continuing availability*

# OXFORD
UNIVERSITY PRESS

Great Clarendon Street, Oxford OX2 6DP

Oxford University Press is a department of the University of Oxford.
It furthers the University's objective of excellence in research, scholarship,
and education by publishing worldwide in

Oxford New York

Athens Auckland Bangkok Bogotá Buenos Aires Cape Town
Chennai Dar es Salaam Delhi Florence Hong Kong Istanbul Karachi
Kolkata Kuala Lumpur Madrid Melbourne Mexico City Mumbai Nairobi
Paris São Paulo Shanghai Singapore Taipei Tokyo Toronto Warsaw

with associated companies in Berlin Ibadan

Oxford is a registered trade mark of Oxford University Press
in the UK and in certain other countries

Published in the United States
by Oxford University Press Inc., New York

© Andrew Steptoe 1988

ISBN 0-19-816221-9

for Jane

# Contents

List of Illustrations     ix

Note concerning Currency     x

A Note to the Paperback Edition     x

Introduction     1

1 The Social Context: Vienna and her Ruler     13

2 Musicians, Opera, and Audience in Mozart's Time     33

3 Mozart and Vienna     53

4 Mozart and his Personal Circle     77

5 Da Ponte and the *Buffa* Plot     98

6 *Così fan tutte* and Contemporary Morality     121

7 Mozart and *Opera Buffa*     140

8 Drama and Musical Form in *Le nozze di Figaro*     160

9 *Don Giovanni*: Musical Form and Dramatic Cohesion     185

10 *Così fan tutte*     208

Epilogue     243

Appendix     247

Bibliography     263

Index of Mozart's Works     269

General Index     271

# List of Illustrations

## Plates

### (between pages 118 and 119)

1 General view of Vienna, 1785
2 View of the inner city of Vienna, 1796
3 The Michaelerplatz, Vienna, 1783
4 Early groundplan of the Burgtheater
5 The Graben, Vienna, 1781
6 The Wien Fluss and the road to the Landstrasse
7 The gardens of the Reisenberg
8 The actor Joseph Lange
9 The soprano Nancy Storace
10 The singer Francesco Benucci
11 The stage of the Burgtheater

## Figures

| | | |
|---|---|---:|
| 1 | Mozart's Public Performances as a Soloist in Vienna, 1781–1791 | 57 |
| 2 | Overall Plan of *Don Giovanni* | 119 |
| 3 | Outline of *Così fan tutte* | 133 |
| 4 | Outline of *Le Jeu de l'amour et du hasard* | 134 |
| 5 | Circle of Fifths | 161 |
| 6 | Key Structure of Act I of *Don Giovanni* | 192 |

## Tables

| | | |
|---|---|---:|
| 1 | Performances of Operas by Four Composers at the Burgtheater between 1785 and 1791 | 46 |
| 2 | Number of Performances of Five Operas at the Burgtheater between 1784 and 1791 | 48 |
| 3 | Major Compositions Completed by Mozart between 1784 and 1791 | 71 |
| 4 | Outline of Act II Finale of *Le nozze di Figaro* | 174 |
| 5 | The Key Structure of Act I of *Così fan tutte* | 233 |
| 6 | The Key Structure of Act II of *Così fan tutte* | 234 |

# A Note concerning Currency

The units of currency operating in Austria and the Empire during this period are complicated, so for convenience most sums have been converted to Viennese gulden.

Other units are as follows:

> 1 gulden (equivalent to 1 florin) = 60 kreuzer
> 2 gulden = 1 speziesthaler (the common thaler)
> 1½ gulden = 1 reichsthaler
> 4½ gulden = 1 ducat (3 reichsthaler)
> 7½ gulden = 1 Louis d'or = 1 pistole

To complicate matters still further, 10 Viennese gulden were worth 12 Salzburg gulden. In international terms, 1 gulden was equivalent to approximately 2 English shillings, while 5 gulden could be exchanged for 1 Venetian zecchino. More information about currency in the late eighteenth century can be found in W.H. Bruford, *Germany in the Eighteenth Century* (Cambridge, 1959). Additional details concerning fluctuations in the value of different currencies can be found in Appendix F of P.G.M. Dickson, *Finance and Government under Maria Theresia 1740–1780*, ii (Oxford, 1987).

# A Note to the Paperback Edition

The publication of this edition has given me the opportunity to make a number of corrections and amendments. I am grateful to the scholars and reviewers who have noted inconsistencies and errors in the first edition, and in particular to Professor Julian Rushton from the University of Leeds for his helpful comments.

# Introduction

> I have an inexpressible longing to write another opera. . . . I
> have only to hear an opera discussed, I have only to sit in a
> theatre, hear the orchestra tuning their instruments—oh, I am
> quite beside myself at once.[1]

Mozart's passionate desire to prove himself in Italian opera—the most
popular and cosmopolitan of contemporary genres—was repeatedly frustrated by the lack of good libretti. The fragments of unfinished operas
that survive even from his maturity bear witness to Mozart's enthusiasm,
and the way in which it foundered in the absence of an inspired collaborator.[2] The first mention of Lorenzo Da Ponte in Mozart's correspondence
was inauspicious:

> Our poet here is now a certain Abbate Da Ponte. He has an enormous amount to
> do in revising pieces for the theatre and he has to write per obbligo an entirely
> new libretto for Salieri, which will take him two months. He has promised after
> that to write a new libretto for me. But who knows whether he will be able to
> keep his word—or will want to? For, as you are aware, these Italian gentlemen
> are very civil to your face. Enough, we know them! If he is in league with Salieri,
> I shall never get anything out of him. But indeed I should dearly love to show
> what I can do in an Italian opera![3]

Nevertheless, by the autumn of 1785, Da Ponte and Mozart were
working together, fashioning an opera out of Beaumarchais's notorious
*Le mariage de Figaro*. According to Da Ponte, it was Mozart who suggested the subject, but the poet himself who contrived to obtain Emperor
Joseph's consent to the adaptation, for the play was banned throughout
the Habsburg Empire. Mozart's father Leopold was far from pleased
when he learned of the plan:

> He is up to his eyes in work at his opera *Le nozze di Figaro* . . . I know the piece;
> it is a very tiresome play and the translation from the French will certainly have to
> be altered very freely, if it is to be effective as an opera. God grant that the text
> may be a success. I have no doubt about the music. But there will be a lot of
> running about and discussions, before he gets the libretto so adjusted as to suit

---

[1] Letter to Leopold Mozart dated 11 Oct. 1777. The translations of Mozart's correspondence are
taken from E. Anderson, *The Letters of Mozart and his Family*, 2nd edn. by A. Hyatt King and
M. Carolan, (London, 1966).

[2] The two major unfinished operas from Mozart's Vienna years both date from 1783. They are
*L'Oca del Cairo* (K. 422) and *Lo sposo deluso* (K. 430).

[3] Letter to Leopold Mozart dated 7 May 1783.

his purpose exactly. And no doubt according to his charming habit he has kept on postponing matters and has let the time slip by.

Leopold Mozart's letter was written on 11 November 1785, and suggests that the plan for the opera was well advanced by this time. It is surprising therefore that the first production did not take place until May 1786. Generally, Mozart completed his operas only shortly before their performance. However, he had several other enterprises in hand, including the Keyboard Concerto in E flat, K.482 (December 1785), and the brief entertainment *Der Schauspieldirektor*, which was mounted in February 1786. Two further concertos (K. 488 in A major and 491 in C minor) are dated March 1786, together with miscellaneous minor compositions. Moreover, the production of *Le nozze di Figaro* was evidently fraught with rivalry and intrigue. None of the surviving reports is impartial, so the truth of the affair is difficult to penetrate. Da Ponte considered the Director of the Burgtheater, Count Franz Orsini-Rosenberg, to be behind these machinations. He recounted how the Count attempted to destroy Act III by claiming that the Emperor had forbidden interpolated ballet scenes. During a rehearsal attended by Joseph II, the cast mimed their way through this section of the score. When the irritated Emperor discovered what was afoot, he reproved his officials and demanded complete restoration of the music.[4] On the other hand, Mozart's early biographer Niemetschek blamed the singers for frustrating the opera, asserting that they deliberately stumbled over their lines until brought to order by the Emperor. Yet a third witness was Michael Kelly, the Irish tenor who played the parts of Basilio and the Judge Don Curzio. He recalled that Mozart was 'touchy as gunpowder', and that Salieri and his faction were responsible for the delay.[5]

Michael Kelly has also left a touching account of Mozart at a rehearsal of Act I:

Mozart was on the stage with his crimson pelisse and gold-laced cocked hat, giving the time of the music to the orchestra. Figaro's song, 'Non più andrai, farfallone amoroso', Benucci gave, with the greatest animation and power of voice. I was standing close to Mozart, who, sotto voce, was repeating, Bravo! Bravo! Benucci; and when Benucci came to the fine passage 'Cherubino, alla vittoria, alla gloria militar', which he gave out with Stentorian lungs, the effect was electricity itself, for the whole of the performers on the stage, and those in the orchestra, as if actuated by one feeling of delight, vociferated Bravo! Bravo! Maestro. Viva, viva, grande Mozart. . . . The little man acknowledged, by repeated obeisances, his thanks for the distinguished mark of enthusiastic applause bestowed upon him.[6]

[4] L. Da Ponte, *Memoirs*, trans. E. Abbott, (New York, 1967), 159–61.
[5] M. Kelly, *Reminiscences*, ed. R. Fiske, (London, 1975), 130.
[6] Kelly, *Reminiscences*, p. 131.

*Le nozze di Figaro* finally made its appearance at the Burgtheater in Vienna on 1 May 1786, with the following cast:

| | |
|---|---|
| La Contessa | Luisa Laschi |
| Susanna | Nancy Storace |
| Cherubino | Dorotea Bussani |
| Marcellina | Maria Mandini |
| Barbarina | Anna Gottlieb |
| Il Conte | Stephano Mandini |
| Figaro | Francesco Benucci |
| Bartolo/Antonio | Francesco Bussani |
| Don Basilio/Don Curzio | Michael Kelly. |

It was repeated three times in May, Mozart relinquishing direction after the first two performances to the 20 year-old Joseph Weigl. Its success was reflected in the fact that keyboard reductions of the score were published by two separate firms within the space of eight weeks. The opera was given a further five times at the Burgtheater in 1786, but was eclipsed in the autumn by the appearance of Vicente Martín y Soler's *Una cosa rara*.

Fortunately, *Le nozze di Figaro* met with more enduring success when it was presented by Pasquale Bondini's company in Prague during the autumn. In January 1787, Mozart travelled to the Bohemian capital to enjoy his triumph. He stayed in the city for a month, relaying his delight at the opera's reception to Gottfried von Jacquin on 15 January:

I looked on, however, with the greatest pleasure while all these people flew about in sheer delight to the music of my 'Figaro'. . . . Nothing is played, sung or whistled but 'Figaro'. No opera is drawing like 'Figaro'. Nothing, nothing but 'Figaro'. Certainly a great honour for me!

This approbation had a tangible consequence in the shape of a commission to write a new *opera buffa* especially for Prague. Mozart turned to Da Ponte again, and it was the poet who selected *Don Giovanni*, 'a subject that pleased him [Mozart] mightily'. Da Ponte's choice was probably determined less by the appropriateness of the tale for Mozart than by the availability of a recent libretto by Giovanni Bertati.[7] For the poet was simultaneously occupied with books for Martín y Soler (*L'arbore di Diana*) and Antonio Salieri (an adaptation of the libretto entitled *Tarare* that Beaumarchais had written for Paris). Da Ponte later described writing these works in parallel, working day and night, diverted only by Tokay, snuff, coffee, and a nubile 16 year-old.

---

[7] For details of Da Ponte's debts to Bertati, see H. Abert, *Mozart's Don Giovanni*, trans. P. Gellhorn, (London, 1976); C. Bitter, *Wandlungen in den Inszenierungsformen des Don Giovanni von 1787 bis 1928* (Regensburg, 1961); and S. Kunze, *Don Giovanni vor Mozart* (Munich, 1972).

The bulk of the score was probably composed over the summer of 1787 in Vienna, and it is uncertain how much music remained to be written on Mozart's arrival in Prague at the beginning of October.[8] Certainly Da Ponte came to Prague for last-minute modifications of the libretto, and it is likely that the opera was completed by the middle of the month. Nevertheless, the first performance was delayed until Monday 29 October. Mozart explained to Gottfried von Jacquin that the opening had been held up by illness in the cast. Pasquale Bondini's company was too small to accommodate such mishaps, and even with the full complement, the roles of Masetto and the Commendatore were doubled. The first cast was as follows:

| | |
|---|---|
| Donna Anna | Teresa Saporiti |
| Donna Elvira | Caterina Micelli |
| Zerlina | Caterina Bondini |
| Don Giovanni | Luigi Bassi |
| Leporello | Felice Ponziani |
| Don Ottavio | Antonio Baglioni |
| Commendatore/Masetto | Guiseppe Lolli |

A week after the opera was presented, Mozart wrote once again to Jacquin. Although he had previously promised to deliver an account of *Don Giovanni*'s reception, he was curiously reticent in his letter, dismissing the matter in two lines,

My opera *Don Giovanni* had its first performance on October 29th and was received with the greatest applause. It was performed yesterday for the fourth time, for my benefit.

This suggests that the occasion was less of a success than Mozart had hoped, and for a time he was pessimistic about a Vienna production being mounted at all. But the opera was eventually presented at the Emperor's behest in 1788, with this cast:

| | |
|---|---|
| Donna Anna | Aloisia Lange |
| Donna Elvira | Caterina Cavalieri |
| Zerlina | Luisa Mombelli (Laschi) |
| Don Giovanni | Francesco Albertarelli |
| Leporello | Francesco Benucci |
| Don Ottavio | Francesco Morella |
| Commendatore/Masetto | Francesco Bussani |

Several modifications were made to the score for Vienna. The tenor aria 'Il mio tesoro' was replaced by 'Dalla sua pace', while the soprano

---

[8] For the arguments relevant to this issue, see J. Rushton, *W. A. Mozart: Don Giovanni* (Cambridge, 1981).

Catarina Cavalieri was given a new *scena* ('In quali eccessi, . . . Mi tradi quell'alma ingrata') as Elvira. Additional music was also composed for the prima donna Luisa Mombelli and the popular *buffo* Francesco Benucci. As Zerlina and Leporello, they were provided with a duet 'Per queste tue manine', followed by a comic recitative for Leporello, during which he tricks the peasants into releasing him from captivity.

The opera was given fifteen times during the year in Vienna, but then not again in Mozart's lifetime. For in the late summer of 1789, it was *Le nozze di Figaro* that returned to the Burgtheater repertoire, and helped revive Mozart's reputation through a series of successful performances. Two new numbers were composed for Adriana Ferrarese ('La Ferrarese'), the soprano who later played an important part in the genesis of *Così fan tutte* . She was given the part of Susanna, and insisted that the major aria ('Deh vieni non tardar') be replaced by one more suited to her own talents. Mozart obliged with 'Al desio di chi t'adora' (K. 577), while also replacing Susanna's Act II 'Venite, inginocchiatevi' with another brief aria ('Un moto di gioia,' K. 579) for Susanna. On the strength of this revival, Mozart was commissioned to write a second *opera buffa* for the Imperial theatre.

It is interesting to take stock of Mozart's status in the world of Italian opera just before the production of *Così fan tutte*. Despite the infrequency of performances in Vienna, his works were widely appreciated in the German-speaking world. During 1789 alone, *Don Giovanni* was given in Italian in Warsaw, with German versions at Frankfurt, Mannheim, Hamburg, Graz, Passau, and Brno. *Le nozze di Figaro* was played in Hannover, Frankfurt, Mainz, Bonn, and Braunschweig. Even early works such as *La finta giardiniera* (K. 196) continued to be heard throughout the Empire.

*Così fan tutte* was written during the autumn of 1789. Da Ponte provides very little information about its composition, according the work a single passing reference in his memoirs, where it is mentioned in the context of his relationship with Adriana Ferrarese:

For her I wrote the *Pastor Fido* and the *Cifra* with music by Salieri, two operas that marked no epoch in the annals of his glory, though they had great beauty here and there; and then the *School for Lovers* with music by Mozart, an opera that holds third place among the three sisters born of that most celebrated master of harmony.[9]

The opera was evidently completed by the end of the year, since it is mentioned in a letter written by Mozart to his creditor and fellow Freemason Michael Puchberg, dated 29 December 1789,

---

[9] Da Ponte, *Memoirs*, p. 185.

I invite you, you alone, to come along on Thursday at 10 o'clock in the morning to hear a short rehearsal of my opera. I am only inviting Haydn and yourself. I shall tell you when we meet about Salieri's plots, which, however, have completely failed already.

The work did indeed survive Salieri's intrigues, and was given its first performance one month later on 26 January 1790. The cast was:

| | |
|---|---|
| Fiordiligi | Adriana Ferrarese |
| Dorabella | Louise Villeneuve |
| Despina | Dorotea Bussani |
| Ferrando | Vincenzio Calvesi |
| Guglielmo | Francesco Benucci |
| Alfonso | Francesco Bussani |

It received five performances in rapid succession, then the death of Emperor Joseph on 20 February closed the theatres for several months. *Così fan tutte* was given five more times over the summer, but was subsequently dropped from the repertoire.

The three Mozart–Da Ponte collaborations have enjoyed varying reputations over the last two centuries. *Le nozze di Figaro* has generally maintained its position in the repertoire, although critical opinion has fluctuated from considering it a pretty *ancien régime* frolic to a revolutionary manifesto in which 'The Count's arbitrary and self-interested exercise of aristocratic authority is met by a popular-front alliance of three oppressed classes, namely servants, women and the young'.[10] On the other hand, both *Don Giovanni* and *Così fan tutte* have sustained considerable opprobrium, in some periods leading to considerable neglect. In each case, the risqué nature of the plot has led the opera into disrepute, and has stimulated prudish adaptations. An early critic remarked of Mozart's decision to make an opera out of *Don Giovanni*,

O that you had not wasted your spirit in this way! That your feeling had matched your imagination, and that the latter had not led you by such sordid paths to greatness! What can it profit you if your name be inscribed in diamond letters on a golden tablet—if the tablet is hung on a pillory![11]

Ruskin regarded *Don Giovanni* as

The foolishest and most monstrous of conceivable human works and subjects of thought. No such spectacle of unconscious . . . moral degradation of the highest faculty to the lowest purpose can be found in history.[12]

---

[10] B. Brophy, 'Da Ponte and Mozart', *The Musical Times*, 122 (1981), 454-6.
[11] Quoted in Abert, *Don Giovanni*. The fate of Mozart's operas in the 19th cent. has been discussed in detail in the *Mozart-Jahrbuch 1980–83*, several articles in which are devoted to this issue.
[12] Quoted in W. J. Allanbrook, *Rhythmic Gesture in Mozart* (Chicago, 1983), 364.

Even such a champion of Mozart as the actor Friedrich Schröder wrote of *Così fan tutte*:

It is a miserable thing which lowers all women, cannot possibly please female spectators, and will therefore not make its fortune.[13]

Richard Wagner's dislike of the story led him to doubt the quality of the music,

O how doubly dear and above all honour is Mozart to me, that it was not possible for him to invent music . . . for *Così fan tutte* like that of *Figaro*! How shamefully would it have desecrated Music![14]

Nevertheless, Mozart's music retained its admirers throughout the most hostile periods. George Hogarth praised *Così fan tutte* even during the early nineteenth century, when it was quite out of favour,

For in musical beauty it does not yield to any of them [the other operas]. We are not sure indeed if any of them exhibits such an exquisite union of all that is sweet and graceful in Italian melody, with the richness and depth of German harmony and instrumentation.[15]

No consensus of opinion has emerged since the composition of these works about their true nature, the composer's intentions, or his perspective on the characters and action. Curiously, *Le nozze di Figaro*, *Don Giovanni*, and *Così fan tutte* are rarely considered as a group, despite their narrative affinity, and the consistent developments in musical technique that run through them. This book is intended to provide a framework for understanding these operas, and some conclusions about Mozart's purposes in composing them. However, before the background to the operas is described, some preliminary remarks about the approach that I have taken in this study of Mozart and his music are in order.

Commentaries on opera tend to fall into one of two broad categories—the analytic and the descriptive. The musical analytic approach endeavours to explore the composer's achievement through detailed analysis of the themes, musical forms, tonality, and orchestration of each number, identifying precedents in earlier works, uncovering musical parallels, and so on. Descriptive or 'impressionistic' criticism on the other hand is ultimately an attempt to translate the musical experience into words, and to convey the feelings and sensations of the writer. In most cases, this leads to an emphasis on the libretto, since the text is inevitably more open

[13] Quoted in O. E. Deutsch, *Mozart: A Documentary Biography*, trans. E. Blom, P. Branscombe, and J. Noble, (London, 1966), 394.
[14] Quoted in A. Einstein, *Mozart: His Character—his Work*, trans. A. Mendel, and N. Broder, (London, 1971), 459.
[15] G. Hogarth, *Memoirs of the Opera* (London, 1851), ii. 190.

to verbal interpretation and argument than the music. Musical descriptions are introduced into impressionistic criticism to reinforce the commentator's view of the action; the music may be said, for instance, to convey anger, remorse, joy, and other emotions, as appropriate.

Both approaches have their adherents and critics. One of the main frustrations inherent in the musical analytic strategy is the difficulty of concluding anything about the emotional content or 'meaning' of the work. Does one know any more about the character of Don Giovanni after dissecting his music, however exhaustively? As the conductor and scholar Robert Craft has put it, 'Analyses of most composers, including Mozart, usually consist of little more than tracing resemblances—recurring melodic patterns, harmonic progressions—between one work and another.'[16] Frequently, the opera is never discussed as a whole, and no synthesis follows the analysis. A more severe dismissal of this approach has been made by that strange, acerbic composer, Kaikhosru Shapurji Sorabji,

All that infantilistic babble about 'form', 'subjects', 'development' and all the rest of the classroom claptrap, tells us less than nothing about the music: . . . It is high time to declare roundly that all that pseudo-anatomical nonsense of the text-books and the analytical programme is so much pernicious and noxious rubbish, confusing the issues and darkening counsel. It distracts attention from what matters—the music—to subordinate and subsidiary matters . . .[17]

Yet impressionistic criticism has an even greater limitation in the essentially subjective nature of the enterprise. This is illustrated by the way in which interpretations vary with the intellectual fashions and moral climate of the time in which they were written (as with the nineteenth-century strictures of *Don Giovanni* and *Così fan tutte* quoted earlier). The authenticity of the interpretation depends not on objective evidence, but upon the authority of the writer and the conviction with which the arguments are presented.[18] No one has expressed these problems more eloquently than Edward Dent, still the most readable of commentators on Mozart's operas:

All that we can do in studying the music of the past is to analyse and classify its technical characteristics. Feeling and emotion are certainly not to be denied or repudiated; but our difficulty is, not that they cannot be analysed, but that they cannot command any safe measure of agreement. Our interpretation of them is

---

[16] R. Craft, *Current Convictions* (London, 1978), 19.

[17] Quoted in D. Stevens, *Musicology* (London, 1980), 48.

[18] Anyone doubting this proposition need only collect two or three recent books on Mozart's operas, and pick some key moment, such as Elvira's first entry in *Don Giovanni*. The range of opinions about the emotions that the opening ritornello is meant to convey is bewildering: agitation, injured pride, defiant questioning, disappointed love, 'angular' fury, full-bloodedness, warm credibility, coherence, passionate rage, and extravagance from just three sources.

too individual and personal. I might possibly succeed in persuading you to agree with my own interpretation of a piece of music—I mean as regards its emotional aspect—but I have no means of convincing you by argument. I draw your attention to this difference, because in musical criticism as it is generally practised we are so much accustomed to the method of persuasion, or even to that of dogmatic assertion, that few people are really ready to give their minds to an argument based on technical and ascertainable facts. The persuasive method is to most people the more attractive . . . There are many interpretations of music in words which take high rank in the company of *belles-lettres*; but, all the same, they are unscientific and fundamentally dishonest.[19]

Perhaps this impasse can best be resolved by considering criticism in a related field. Commentators of spoken theatre, particularly Shakespeare, mulled over precisely the same difficulties many decades ago, when dry analyses of style or sources vied with brilliant but ephemeral subjective interpretations of the plays. It was realized at the turn of the century by the scholar A. C. Bradley that the two approaches were not in opposition, but needed to be integrated in order to understand the works more fully:

In the process of comparison and analysis it is not requisite, it is on the contrary ruinous, to set imagination aside and to substitute supposed 'cold reason'; and it is only want of practice that makes the concurrent use of analysis difficult or irksome.[20]

In the present day, it is virtually taken for granted that while no serious discussion of *Hamlet* can ignore contemporary views of melancholy, madness, and revenge, such information does not on its own lead to understanding of the play.

What then is required for the fuller appreciation of opera? William Witherle Lawrence identified two basic questions in his classic study of Shakespeare's problem comedies, and the same issues arise in relation to Mozart's operas:

(1) How did the author intend that these plays (operas) should be understood by his audience?

(2) How are the particular characteristics of these plays (operas) to be explained in the overall development of the author's art? Put simply, how did he come to write them?

Starting from these basic issues, I have attempted in this book to draw together the strands that seem essential for an adequate analysis of the collaborations between Mozart and Da Ponte. Firstly, the social and cultural context needs to be defined. For what sort of society were these operas written? Who went to the opera, and what expectations did the

[19] E. Dent, *The Rise of Romantic Opera*, ed.W. Dean, (London, 1976), 31.
[20] Quoted in W. W. Lawrence, *Shakespeare's Problem Comedies* (London, 1969), 40.

audience have about this form of entertainment? What music and opera did they like, and what did they hope to hear in the theatre? These questions are discussed in Chapters 1 and 2.

Secondly, Mozart's position within this society must be clarified. Mozart did not write for posterity, but for his day-to-day existence. How then did he live and what aspirations did he have? What were his intentions and hopes for his works, and for these operas in particular? Chapters 3 and 4 are devoted to these issues.

Of course, opera is a collaborative venture, and the librettist was responsible for the most accessible portion of the enterprise—the text. Lorenzo Da Ponte's attitudes must also be taken into account. Since none of the three collaborations was based on an entirely original plot, the forms in which the stories were presented tell us a good deal about Da Ponte's views of opera and the type of entertainment he set out to create. The sources of the libretti and their position within Da Ponte's own career are therefore discussed in Chapters 5 and 6.

Finally, the practicalities of opera presentation must be borne in mind. How did Mozart go about composing an opera, and how did the composer and librettist collaborate? Inevitably, the practical aspects of production—the musical resources, the availability of singers, and the staging facilities—placed constraints on the works written by Mozart. It is important to identify the influence of these factors on the final creation, and this is attempted in Chapter 7.

All this information sets the scene for the operas, but leaves the fundamental issue of Mozart's musical intentions only partly explained. The analysis of musical expression is a complex issue over which whole South American rain forests are expended.[21] The aim here is rather more modest, since I have decided not to engage in a piecemeal dissection of each musical number. Rather, I have attempted to describe the stylistic framework of the operas, and to outline how Mozart exploited his musical style for dramatic purposes. *Le nozze di Figaro* is discussed in Chapter 8, *Don Giovanni* in Chapter 9, and *Così fan tutte* in Chapter 10.

I hope that this approach does illuminate the meaning of the works. However, my intention is not to uncover the secret reasons why Mozart

---

[21] One of the most interesting discussions of musical expression to emerge over recent years is Peter Kivy's *The Corded Shell* (Princeton, 1981). Working from the premises of 18th-cent. aesthetics, he distinguishes two fundamental models: the 'contour' model, in which expressiveness derives from resemblances with the expression of emotion verbally or in behaviour, and the 'convention' model, which is based upon customary associations between musical features or gestures and particular emotions, derived through years of conventional use. Another important account of musical expression was presented by Deryck Cooke in *The Language of Music* (Oxford, 1959). Cooke attempted to derive the expressive function of different intervals and other elements of musical language from the basic principles of harmonics, and illustrated the remarkable consistency with which the components of musical vocabulary have been used by Western composers.

wrote one piece or another, nor to infer what Mozart 'really meant'. Such an enterprise would seem to imply that Mozart expressed himself inadequately. Rather, I work from the assumption that what Mozart meant is manifest in his output. To paraphrase Gilbert Ryle, the style and procedures of Mozart's music *are* the way his mind worked, and not merely imperfect reflections of secret 'mental' processes: 'Overt intelligent performances are not clues to the workings of minds; they are those workings.'[22]

---

[22] G. Ryle, *The Concept of Mind* (London, 1963), 57.

# 1

# The Social Context: Vienna and her Ruler

The appearance of Vienna in the eighteenth century was unusual for a major European city. Whereas the medieval centres of other towns were surrounded by the ordered, elegant signs of urban expansion, no building in Vienna had been erected within several hundred yards of the old walls (see Plate 1). This was a consequence of the great Turkish siege of 1683, during which the suburbs had been demolished. When Vienna was reconstructed and fortified in 1704, a wide protective glacis and rampart were built around the city (now the site of the Ringstrasse development).[1] As a result, the inner city was densely packed, while extensive suburbs grew up at a distance. The latter contained not only the factories and workshops of the new industrialization, but also the magnificent mansions and parks of the nobility and rising middle class. During the summer, the wealthy would move to these semi-rural suburbs, returning to their city residences only in the autumn.

This topography accounts for the high rents and prices of the old city, and it also provides an index to Mozart's varying fortunes in his maturity. Mozart lived in Vienna from 1781 until his death ten years later, and during that time he moved house many times. Whenever he abandoned the old city to set up residence in the periphery, it was a sign that he was in straitened circumstances. For although a house in a suburb such as Landstrasse was an asset for the well-to-do, it was a very different matter to live there from necessity. Mozart was a working artist reliant on the patronage of the rich. His livelihood depended on taking pupils and performing to the nobility, while hovering at the edges of Court society. Such a career could not be advanced by residing outside the city, and we shall see in Chapter 3 how Mozart's frequent changes of address act as a barometer of his material success.

The inner city itself was dominated by the palaces of the Imperial family and aristocracy, but much else was squeezed within its narrow walls (see Plate 2). It has been estimated that in 1795, there were 3,253 members of the nobility living in Vienna, cared for by 6,000 lackeys and 34,000 other servants. The overall population was nearly a quarter of a million, and included a considerable number of tailors, goldsmiths,

---

[1] The development of the Ringstrasse, and the debate surrounding the use of the ramparts and glacis in the nineteenth century, are detailed in 'The Ringstrasse and the Birth of Urban Modernism', by C. Schorske, in *Fin-de-Siècle Vienna: Politics and Culture* (New York, 1980).

wigmakers, and other purveyors of luxury.[2] Yet although these figures suggest crowded urban living, they convey little idea of what Vienna was actually like in the eighteenth century. Nor are the writings of the inhabitants very useful, as they recorded the exceptional rather than the commonplace, taking for granted much that interests us now. More instructive are the comments of travellers and visitors to Vienna and the Empire; these give a vivid impression of the city and society in which Mozart moved.

Take, for example, the apparently simple operation of walking in the streets. The hazards encountered in the Empire seem to have outraged the tidy-minded English, as these comments from William Howitt indicate:

Every street, almost every house, and every hour has its own appropriate, peculiar and by no means enviable smell. The pavements, with a few exceptions, are of the most nobbly and excruciating kind. There appears no evidence of any special attention to them. . . . the paves, where there are any, seem appropriated to every purpose but that of walking. If an Englishman, accustomed to his well-paved and well-regulated towns, were suddenly set down in a German town at night, he would speedily break his neck or his bones, put out an eye, or tear off a cheek.[3]

One of the most interesting visitors was Hester Lynch Piozzi, the former Mrs Thrale, who left on her continental tours shortly after her unpopular marriage to Gabriel Piozzi in 1784. Although the marriage signalled the end of her close association with the literati of Georgian London (her family and friends such as Samuel Johnson and Fanny Burney were disgusted by the match), her travel journals provide a valuable glimpse of cultured middle-class opinion. Moreover, she was in Vienna in 1786, when Mozart's popularity was at its zenith. Indeed, the Irish tenor Michael Kelly recalled meeting her one evening at the Martinez House where the poet Metastasio lived, and claims that Mozart was present as well. Mrs Piozzi formed a somewhat unfavourable impression of Vienna's appearance and salubrity:

The streets of Vienna are not pretty at all, God knows; so narrow, so ill built, so crowded . . . many wares placed upon the ground where there is a little opening, seems a strange awkward disposition of things for sale.

I have no notion that Vienna can be a very wholesome place to live in; the double windows, double feather-beds etc in a room shut without a chimney is surely ill contrived. All external air is shut out in such a manner that I am frightened . . . while the wind whirls one about in such a manner that it is displeasing to put out one's head.[4]

[2] According to the *Nouveau Guide par Vienne* (Vienna, 1792), 52,000 of these inhabitants were resident in the city itself, and the remainder in the suburbs.

[3] W. Howitt *The Rural and Domestic Life of Germany* (London, 1842).

[4] H. L. Piozzi, *Observations and Reflections made in the Course of a Journey through France, Italy and Germany* (London, 1789), ii. 309–10.

Vienna was nevertheless the centre and focus of the Empire, and compared with other regions it was well advanced. Prague for example was the second city, yet appalling squalor and poverty existed among the lower orders; the famines of 1771 and 1772 killed off some 14 per cent of the population in that region of Bohemia.[5] Hungary fared even less well, since the aristocracy stifled industrial progress in order to ensure the preeminence of the land. Prince Eszterházy, to take the most extreme case, owned 10 million acres which brought him an income of 700,000 gulden annually. He lived and built on a scale rare outside royal circles—Eszterháza alone cost 16 million gulden. At the same time, in the whole of Hungary only seven factories employing more than 100 workers existed. The northern Hungarian wine trade was in collapse following the wars with Prussia, while other regions suffered the constant threat of invasion from Turkey. Given such conditions in the provinces, it is perhaps not surprising that Vienna was a magnet for cultivated people.

Any outline of the society in which Mozart made his living must acknowledge the immense gulf separating the nobility from other classes. The traditional position of the aristocracy endowed them with such economic power, educational and social superiority, that the forces of rationalism and enlightenment encountered fierce resistance. Bruford has described the difference as follows:

From the Emperor down to the penniless widow of a ruined Reichsritter, the nobility considered themselves in fact, with rare exceptions, to be a different race from the untitled mass. There were even those who thought that in future life too they would receive differential treatment.[6]

They had huge advantages in most forms of public life. They were given preferential treatment and advanced rapidly in the army and church. The titled classes as a whole were excused from rates, taxes, and such disagreeable duties as billeting. In law too they had the advantage. Punishments were light, and imprisonment was rare even in the most serious cases:

He was not above the ordinary law, civil or criminal, but it was extraordinarily difficult for a peasant to win a case against a landlord, or for a bourgeois creditor to recover a debt from a noble debtor desirous of evading his obligation.[7]

It would be a mistake, however, to see the scions of the *ancien régime* blithely enjoying their privileged existence until forced to reality by the French Revolution and subsequent wars with Napoleon. In the first place, the aristocracy was not inviolable. People of ability could rise into the ranks of the nobility, obtaining the attendant advantages in tax, military service, and education. Indeed, the Emperor made considerable sums by

[5] C. A. Macartney, *The Habsburg Empire 1790–1918* (London, 1968), 40 ff.
[6] W. H. Bruford, *Germany in the Eighteenth Century* (Cambridge, 1959), 58.
[7] Macartney, *The Habsburg Empire*, p. 54.

selling titles, charging 20,000 gulden for the rank of Count, and 6,000 for
that of Baronet.[8] Consequently, by the late eighteenth century there were
in reality two nobilities, the old and the new.[9] The ancient, hereditary aristocracy had endured lean times in the aftermath of the Thirty
Years War, only to find themselves superseded in lucrative official positions by civil servants loyal to the Habsburgs. Yet although these bureau-
crats attained noble status, they never mixed in traditional circles, but
preferred the company of the merchant classes from which they derived.
Mozart's patrons largely belonged to the new nobility, and many of his
enlightenment beliefs were stimulated by this intellectual milieu.
Moreover, the middle class was instrumental in the massive growth of
commerce and industry during the 1770s and 1780s. Thus the Austrian
society of Mozart's maturity was characterized by tensions between the
decaying old aristocracy and a vigorous urban culture.

The main concern here is with the social consequences of these changes.
They were sensitively observed by Dr John Moore, a Scottish physician
and father of Sir John Moore of Corunna. Late in Maria Theresa's reign,
Moore travelled through central Europe in the privileged position of
companion to the Duke of Hamilton. This gave him an entrée to the most
exalted circles, and he was quick to note the discontents lurking in social
exchanges between the old class and the new.

People of different ranks now do business together with ease, . . . Yet trifling
punctilios are not so completely banished, for there is a greater separation than
good sense would direct between the various classes of subject.— . . . The
higher, or ancient families, keep themselves as distinct from the inferior, or newly
created nobility, as do these from the citizens; so that it is very difficult for the
inferior classes to be in society.[10]

The traditionalist was, however, presented with a new difficulty—that of
determining the status of other people. Men and women could no longer
be categorized on the old criteria of family reputation or upbringing.
Dress and material affluence were also misleading, since these ceased to
be definite markers of class; even the fashions of the highest nobility were
rapidly transmitted through society, becoming popular in cheaper
forms.[11] Confusion was especially marked in cities such as Vienna, where
strangers and the young tended to congregate.

These developments were viewed with bewilderment throughout

---

[8] In 1802, Schiller was raised to the nobility on the recommendation of Karl August of Weimar,
plus the payment of 428 gulden, 30 kreuzer.

[9] See E. Sagarra, *A Social History of Germany* (London, 1977), pp. 47–63.

[10] J. Moore, *A View of Society and Manners in France, Switzerland and Germany* (London,
1779), ii. 335. Moore's further claim to fame is the authorship of *Zeluco*, an influential novel much
admired by Byron.

[11] See R. Sennett, *The Fall of Public Man* (Cambridge, 1977).

Europe. In London, for example, the *Lady's Magazine* of 1784 reported this astonished response from a merchant to his wife's excursions into fashion:

When down dances my rib in white, but so bepukered and plaited, I could not tell what to make of her; so turning about, I cried, 'Hey, Sally, my dear, what new frolic is this: it is like none of the gowns you used to wear.' 'No, my dear,' crieth she, 'It is no gown, it is the chemise de la reine.' 'My dear,' replied I, hurt at this gibberish . . . 'let us have the name of your new dress in downright English.' 'Why then' said she, 'if you must have it, it is the queen's shift.' Mercy on me, thought I, what will the world come to , when an oilman's wife comes down to serve in the shop, not only in her own shift, but in that of the queen. [12]

These realignments in society had a number of important effects. The general solution to the problem of categorization was to respond to people on the basis of their appearance. Hence the immense care that men in particular took with their dress. Mozart was no stranger to this; a fashionable costume endorsed his passport into a class of society to which his origin and status did not entitle him. His mature operas, too, share this preoccupation with the sincerity of appearances. For people who set such store by appearance ran the risk of being misled, a confusion that promoted the prospects not only of the talented but also of the opportunist. The late eighteenth century was a golden age for the intrepid adventurer, particularly at Court.

Wherever there is a rich widow to be married, a pension or office to be had at Court, they are quickly on the scent. They baptise themselves, give themselves titles, re-create themselves, as often as they please, and as the matter in hand requires. What they cannot pull off as a simple nobleman they attempt as Marquis or Abbé or officer. There is no enterprise or state department between heaven and earth which they would not be prepared to take charge of, no branch of knowledge about which they cannot converse with a self-confidence that puts even scholars to confusion. With admirable adroitness, with a savoir vivre that better men might learn from them with advantage, they obtain things which honest and capable men have not the courage to desire. [13]

Baron Johann Caspar Riesbeck, a traveller whose views were generally somewhat sour, observed the same phenomenon:

Vienna swarms with literati. When a man accosts you, whom you do not know by his dirty hands for a painter, smith or shoemaker, or by his finery for a footman, or by his fine clothes for a man of consequence, you may be assured that you see either a man of letters or a tailor; for between these two classes I have not yet learned to distinguish. [14]

[12] Quoted by Sennett, *The Fall of Public Man*, pp. 68–9.
[13] A. von Knigge in 1788, quoted by Bruford, *Germany*, p. 104.
[14] J. C. Riesbeck, (sometimes spelt Risbeck), *Travels through Germany*, trans. Revd Mr Maty, (London, 1787), Vol 1, p. 286.

But if people of low status could rise through the system, it was also true that those in the highest ranks could descend from their elevated positions and mingle with the masses. No special disguise was needed, and such forays satisfied egalitarian principles as well as curiosity. Furthermore, the Emperor himself endorsed these exchanges between ranks, since they accorded with his staunch enlightenment views.

## Emperor Joseph: The Reforming Monarch

There is a remarkable parallel between the careers of Mozart and Emperor Joseph II, in that their hopes flourished and decayed over the very same years.[15] Although co-ruler with his mother from 1765, it was not until Maria Theresa died in 1780 that Joseph was able to pursue his own policies without hindrance. Only six months later, Mozart finally liberated himself from Salzburg and his father to settle in Vienna. Both men had their greatest triumphs early in the decade, and in their respective spheres enjoyed immense popularity. Mozart's failure and despair at the end of the 1780s is mirrored in Joseph's decline. The Emperor died on 20 February 1790, just a month after the première of *Così fan tutte*. The composer survived only two more years, and in doing so entered a new phase both musically and in his mental outlook.

The connection is not merely coincidental, for the climate created by Joseph's reforms enabled Mozart to develop intellectually. Likewise, the composer's later despondency was fostered by the collapse of the ideals championed by the 'enlightened despot'. Joseph was a ruler who struggled to realize the social and intellectual themes of his day without being prepared to accept their full consequences. Two aspects of his reign stand out: the atmosphere of egalitarian, advanced, and relatively free thinking promoted by his reforms, and the impact of his personal informality on his contemporaries.

Almost before his mother Maria Theresa was cold in her grave, Emperor Joseph embarked on a programme of radical legislation that delighted rationalist circles. He had long been concerned with the abuses of Catholic institutions, although devout himself:

How shameful are the cases which have recently occured in Prague: in this year's famine five or six people have actually died in the streets, and many more have fallen ill and have taken the last sacrament in the streets. . . . In this city, where there is a rich archbishop, a large cathedral chapter, so many abbeys, three Jesuit

---

[15] I have previously discussed the influence of Joseph II on Mozart in 'Mozart, Joseph II and Social Sensitivity', *The Music Review*, 43 (1982), 109–20. A recent detailed account of Joseph II's character is provided in D. Beales, *Joseph II. 1: In the Shadow of Maria Theresa, 1741–1780* (Cambridge, 1987).

palaces, so many monks, there is not a single proven case that any of these took in one of the miserable wretches who were lying in front of their doors.[16]

One of his first acts was therefore to reform the Church, suppressing rich landowning monasteries, curtailing clerical privilege, and removing numerous Saints' days from the calendar. He allowed the practice of non-Catholic faiths, and in the Toleranzedikt of 1781 ended discrimination against Lutherans, Calvinists, and the Greek Orthodox Churches. This did not please conservative elements, nor did his moves to rehabilitate the Jews. Other enlightened policies followed, with the introduction of poor relief, the prohibition of child labour, and the establishment of schools, hospitals, and asylums. Civil marriage was permitted from 1789, and the death penalty was abolished.

Joseph found it necessary to create a new central administration to carry out his plans, and his handling of the old government system was undiplomatic and authoritarian. But if the Emperor displeased the traditional aristocracy in these matters, his land reforms threatened their very livelihood. Joseph believed that with prosperity and security, the peasants would realize their potential as responsible citizens.[17] He calculated that they must be allowed to retain 50 per cent of their gross income, and his land tax of 1789 was designed to cut the revenue of many landlords substantially. The resistance to this policy contributed greatly to the drastic retractions that Joseph was forced to make in the last year of his reign.

No such disagreement was however voiced openly in the early years of the decade. The Emperor's rational approach included a relaxation in censorship and encouragement of freedom of thought that was exhilarating in the Habsburg domain. His confidence and humanitarian sufferance of opposition permitted the open dissemination of dissenting views, not only in print but in the free atmosphere of coffee-house debate. Intellectual licence became the hallmark of Viennese life during the period, and it was a quality admired by almost all visitors.

One striking illustration of the new climate was the official tolerance of Masonry, which led to a massive expansion of the movement throughout the middle classes. The Papal condemnation of the Order had never been enforced in Austria, probably because of Joseph's hostility towards Rome. By 1784, the Grand Lodge of Austria consisted of sixty-six Lodges, with eight in Vienna alone.[18] Caroline Pichler describes in her memoirs how Freemasonry became a positive fashion during the 1780s; Masonic songs were popular, while symbols were worn as charms on watch chains.

---

[16] From the Journal of Joseph II's journey through Bohemia in 1771, quoted by E. Wangermann in *The Austrian Achievement 1700–1800* (London, 1973), 100.

[17] Wangermann, *The Austrian Achievement*, p. 93.

[18] J. Chailley, *The Magic Flute, Masonic Opera*, trans. by H. Weinstock (London, 1972), 61.

Enlightenment propagandists such as Joseph von Sonnenfels and Gottfried van Swieten were Masons, along with many members of the intelligentsia.[19] Mozart was of course a committed Freemason, and amongst his circle his brother-in-law Joseph Lange, the publisher Artaria, the singer Adamberger, and several other musicians were enrolled. The Lodge presented an unparalleled opportunity for the interchange of views across social strata, and strongly affected Mozart's life and development, as will be seen in Chapter 4.

The traditional establishment soon felt threatened by these developments, and was able to introduce repressive legislation as early as December 1785. The 'Patent concerning Freemasons' required the official registration of Lodges, and allowed the police to supervise their activities.[20] Many Masons, including the renowned Ignaz Born for whom Mozart wrote *Die Maurerfreude* (K. 471), retired from active membership, and numbers fell rapidly. Mozart's own Lodge was obliged to amalgamate with less intellectual Rosicrucian Lodges. A stormy meeting was held on 20 December 1785, at which 240 of the 600 members resigned in protest.[21] Yet the Masons were still considered a threat when Leopold ascended the throne in 1790, and it was thought prudent to set up new 'loyal' Lodges.

Much of Joseph's energy seems to have been devoted to reforms that failed to have their desired effects. But these did not prevent him from being considered a champion of rationalism. The characterization was enhanced by the Emperor's personal behaviour. His modest self-effacement and lack of pomp were noted with astonishment by visitors, as John Moore confirmed to his readers in England:

You have often heard of the unceremonious and easy manner in which this great Prince lives with his subjects. Report cannot exaggerate on this head . . . This monarch converses with all the ease and affability of a private gentleman, and gradually seduces others to talk with the same ease to him. He is surely much happier in this noble condescention, and must acquire a more perfect knowledge of mankind, than if he keep himself aloof from his subjects, continually wrapt in his own importance and the Imperial fur.[22]

---

[19] Josef von Sonnenfels (1733–1817) was professor at the University of Vienna. Gottfried van Swieten (1734–1803) became one of Mozart's most important patrons, and his career typifies the rewards for talent in the enlightenment period. He was the son of Maria Theresa's physician, and came to Vienna as a child. He entered the diplomatic service, holding posts in Brussels and Paris, and was appointed ambassador in Berlin in 1771. He became President of the Commission for Education and Censorship in 1781, and from this position fostered the relaxation of censorship and the development of rational policies over several years.

[20] E.Wangermann, *From Joseph II to the Jacobin Trials* (London, 1959), 37.

[21] K.Thomson. *The Masonic Thread in Mozart* (London, 1977), 83.

[22] Moore, *A View of Society*, ii.332. It should be noted that observers from the nobility found Joseph's informality affected, and almost treasonable to the aristocratic order, see Beales, *Joseph II*, pp. 309–13.

The full impact of such behaviour can only be understood by comparison with other European monarchs of the time. Much has been written about French royalty and its haughty indifference to the lower orders, yet perhaps the most telling parallel is with George III and Queen Charlotte. They ruled the country that even in the eighteenth century was admired as a bastion of freedom and informality. Fanny Burney was employed in the Queen's suite from 1786 to 1791, and her celebrated diary is full of observations on this couple. They emerge as pleasant people, but with expectations of behaviour and deference entirely different from those of Emperor Joseph. The general pattern is reflected in Burney's surprised delight when they condescend to converse with her. Her amusing 'Directions for coughing, sneezing or moving before the King and Queen' are the height of absurdity.

In the first place, you must not cough. If you find a cough tickling in your throat, you must arrest it from making any sound; if you find yourself choking with the forbearance, you must choke—but not cough.

   In the second place, you must not sneeze. If you have a vehement cold, you must take no notice of it; . . . if a sneeze still insists upon making its way, you must oppose it, by keeping your teeth grinding together; if the violence of the repulse breaks some blood vessel, you must break some blood vessel—but not sneeze.[23]

An incident some years later indicates that this description was not entirely facetious. Fanny Burney had by this time been a close attendant of the Queen for a considerable period, and so she was asked to read a play to the royal ladies one evening. Even this intimate, family atmosphere was stultifying.

It went off pretty flat. Nobody is to comment and nobody is to interrupt; and even between one act and another not a moment's pause is expected to be made . . . Lady Courtown never uttered one single word the whole time; yet is she not one of the most loquacious of our establishment. But such is the settled etiquette.[24]

Compare this with the admiring portrait of Joseph left by the Irish tenor Michael Kelly:

He was an enemy to pomp and parade, and avoided them as much as possible; indeed, hardly any private gentleman requires so little attention as he did. He had a seat for his servant behind his carriage, and when he went abroad in it he made him sit there. I was one day passing through one of the corridors of the palace, and came directly in contact with him; he had his greatcoat hanging on his arm: he stopped, and asked me in Italian, if I did not think it was very hot; he

[23] *The Diary of Fanny Burney*, ed. by L. Gibbs, (London, 1940), 113.
[24] Burney, *Diary*, p. 265.

told me that he felt the heat so oppressive that he had taken off his greatcoat, preferring to carry it on his arm. . . . His desire was never to have any fuss made about him, or to give any trouble, which was all mighty amiable.[25]

Dr Moore came away with the same impression:

His manner, . . . is affable, obliging and perfectly free from the reserved and lofty deportment assumed by some on account of high birth. Whoever has the honour to be in company with him, so far from being checked by such despicable pride, has need to be on his guard not to adopt such a degree of familiarity as would be highly improper to use. . . . He is regular in his ways of life, moderate in his pleasures, steady in his plans and diligent in business.

One evening at the Countess Waldstein's, . . . he [said] 'all the grimace and parade to which people in my situation are accustomed from their cradle, have not made me so vain as to imagine that I am in any essential quality superior to other men; and if I had any tendency to such an opinion, the surest way to get rid of it is to mix in society, where I have daily occasion of finding myself inferior in talent to those I meet with. . . .'[26]

Perhaps Mozart's curious inertia in trying to further his career in foreign countries may be related to these unique attributes of the Emperor. Mozart had been fêted by the highest in Europe while still a child, but Joseph was the only monarch who would accord even a fraction of that dignity to an adult.

## Viennese Society in the Josephinian Decade

Since the upper strata of society centred on the Court, the tone of polite intercourse was set by the ruler. In Maria Theresa's later years, an atmosphere of severity and conscious propriety prevailed. Thus, when John Moore wrote of the possibility of illicit attachments, he concluded that

The ladies . . . are obliged to observe an uncommon degree of circumspection, as nothing is more heinous in the eyes of her Imperial Majesty. She seems to think that ladies of her court, like the wife of Caesar, should not only be free from guilt, but what is more difficult, free from suspicion, and strongly marks by her manner that she is but too well informed when any piece of scandal circulates to the prejudice of any of them.[27]

But the society for which Mozart worked was very different. Joseph's reign brought a relaxation of standards and flexibility to personal behaviour, particularly in relations between the sexes. Mozart's mature operas shared with contemporary Viennese society a preoccupation with love.

[25] M. Kelly, *Reminiscences*, ed. R. Fiske (London, 1975), 104.
[26] Moore, *A View of Society*, ii. 382 and 387.
[27] Moore, *A View of Society*, ii. 388–9.

Comments about the elegance and accomplishment of Viennese women are conspicuous in the reminiscences of both male and female visitors. Michael Kelly was not to collect his memoirs for more than a quarter of a century, yet he still recalled that

The women, generally speaking, are beautiful; they have fine complexions and symmetrical figures, the lower orders particularly. All the servant maids are anxious to show their feet (which are universally handsome), and are very ambitious of having neat shoes and stockings.[28]

Mrs Piozzi was also impressed:

The society here is charming. . . . The ladies here seem very highly accomplished, and speak a great variety of languages with facility.[29]

Even the splenetic Nathaniel Wraxall, who visited Vienna while a young man, was prepared to concede some positive points:

Vienna abounds with beautiful women . . . they are by no means deficient in external accomplishments, mental and personal; they are in general elegant, graceful and pleasing; . . . their conversation, if not improving, is rarely deficient in spirit, vivacity and animation.[30]

It is evident that among the nobility, at least, little of this charm was wasted on spouses. The role of the cicisbeo seems to have been well established, according to Baron Riesbeck:

The cicisbeos accompany the married women from their beds to church, and then lead them back again. . . . The women of this place are not like the French ones, who let their lovers languish a great while; on the contrary, they are easily gained. Their lovers are chiefly officers or high churchmen, between which orders there is constant rivalry and jealousy.[31]

Foreigners were astonished at the openness in which such infidelities took place. John Moore noticed the sad appearance of a lady one evening, and was told that the cause was the absence of her lover. On asking whether her husband knew of this 'violent passion', he was told,

Yes, he knows it, and enters with the most tender sympathy with her affliction; he does all that can be expected from an affectionate husband to comfort and soothe his wife, assuring her that her love will ware away with time. But she always declares that she has no hope of this, because she feels it augment every

[28] Kelly, *Reminiscences*, p. 100.
[29] Piozzi, *Observations*, ii. 299.
[30] N.Wraxall, *Memoirs of the Courts of Berlin, Warsaw and Vienna* (Dublin, 1799), ii. 120–1.
[31] Riesbeck, *Travels*, ii. 80. In *La Chartreuse de Parme*, Stendal noted that by the end of the eighteenth century, the role of *cicisbeo* had become so well established that the individual in question was sometimes selected by the husband's family, and his name inserted in the marriage contract.

day. - Mais, au fond, cela lui fait bien de la peine, parceque malheureusement il aime sa femme à la folie.[32]

As the writer tartly notes, 'in England, such passions are generally imputed to people as crimes'. But behaviour of this nature was typical of the nobility, and much less of the middle-class circles in which Mozart moved. The distress he showed when remonstrating at Constanze's mild flirtations indicates the emotional chasm between the composer and his aristocratic patrons and audience. As shall be seen in Chapter 4, Mozart's marriage seems to have been governed not by these conventions of aristocratic infidelity, but by the new ideals of companionship that permeated the family life of the urban intelligentsia.

Sentimental affairs may have played a major role in the entertainments of society, but they were not the sole preoccupation. Eating, gambling, conversation, dancing, and music were all pursued with varying degrees of seriousness. The social season proper began in the autumn and lasted until Lent, unlike the pattern in London and other Protestant cities. The climax came with the carnival—that prospective reward for the rigours of Lent—so from January social life built up to a hectic level. The season was extended briefly after Easter, but many wealthy families left the city for country residences or watering-places such as Baden. The Court too was dispersed in the summer, since the Emperor frequently moved his household on a more modest scale to the country palace of Laxenburg.

On a typical day in the season, dinner was held at about 2.30 p.m. Women did not appear in the morning except to go to Mass; instead they remained in private *déshabillé*, preparing their toilet and drinking coffee or chocolate. Dressing took a good deal of time, since aristocratic ladies continued to sport high coiffures, powdered hair, and much rouge. Paris was the arbiter of taste, and French the language of polite society. Mannequin dolls were dressed up in current fashions and sent to Vienna, where they acted as models for the wealthy.

Dinner itself was an affair of some magnificence, eating being a favourite pastime of the Viennese. It was considered an insult to offer less than six dishes to a member of the nobility, and the middle classes also lavished much attention on food. As Baron Riesbeck ruefully acknowledged,

What distinguishes the people of this place from the Parisians is a certain coarse pride not to be described, an insurmountable heaviness and stupidity, and an unaccountable propensity to guzzling. . . . It is certainly true that a man eats much better here than he does in Paris; and he certainly also eats a great deal more. At the common table of the people of a middling rank (such as the lower servants of the court, merchants, artists), you commonly see six or even ten dishes with two, three or even four kinds of wine.[33]

[32] Moore, *A View of Society*, ii. 340.
[33] Riesbeck, *Travels*, ii. 337.

The restaurants were also impressive; in 1781, a six-course meal was to be had for 45 kreuzer, even on a fast day. But all the feasting had a coarser side:

In some houses, the masters of which affect to live in the highest style, it is customary when an entertainment is given, to provide doses of tartar emetic, and set them in an adjoining room; thither the guests retire when they happen to be too full, empty themselves, and return to the company as if nothing had happened.[34]

Ironically, one of the most distinguished members of Austrian society displayed some of the worst behaviour when dining. Prince Wenzel Anton Kaunitz was Chancellor of State under Maria Theresa, Joseph, and Leopold II, and one of the ablest politicians of the eighteenth century. He was a connoisseur of the arts and a considerable patron. Yet he had the notorious habit of cleaning his teeth at the table after dinner. This distasteful sight was once witnessed by the diplomat, Henry Swinburne:

After dinner, the Prince treated us with the cleaning of his gums; one of the most nauseous operations I have ever witnessed, and it lasted a prodigious long time, accompanied by all manner of noises. He carries a hundred implements in his pocket for this purpose.[35]

The most convivial period of the day was after dinner, when both the nobility and middle-classes went visiting. The age had passed when such a visit was simply an excuse for cards—conversation and music now reigned. Amateur musicians flourished, and publishers hastened to supply the market not only with chamber works, but with keyboard reductions or variations on popular operatic pieces. Mozart and Hadyn wrote much of their chamber music for accomplished amateurs, with whom they often performed themselves. Haydn summed up the pleasures of these salons when he wrote to Marianne von Genzinger from his cold isolation in Eszterháza, shortly after his departure from Vienna in Feburary 1790,

Here I sit in my wilderness; forsaken, like some poor orphan, almost without human society; melancholy, dwelling on the memory of past glorious days. Yes, past alas! And who can tell when those happy hours may return? Those charming meetings? Where the whole circle have but one heart and one soul—all those delightful musical evenings, which can only be remembered and not described.[36]

The informal blend of music and cultivated conversation were features that gave Vienna a special charm during the 1780s. Nathaniel Wraxall later recalled, 'I shall always esteem the time which I have passed here

[34] Riesbeck, *Travels*, ii. 368.

[35] H.Swinburne, *The Courts of Europe at the Close of the Last Century* (London, 1841), ii. 353–4.

[36] Joseph Haydn, in *Letters of Distinguished Musicians*, trans. Lady G.M. Wallace (London, 1867), 123–4.

among the best employed as well as most pleasing moments of my life.'[37]

Later in the evening people went to the theatre or opera, although gambling and dancing were also popular. Dancing was not only a crucial social accomplishment, but one that was enjoyed at every opportunity. Michael Kelly was particularly struck by the enthusiasm of the Viennese:

The propensity of the Vienna ladies for dancing and going to carnival masquerades was so determined, that nothing was permitted to interfere with their enjoyment of their favourite amusement—nay, so notorious was it, that for the sake of the ladies in the family way, who could not be persuaded to stay at home, there were apartments prepared, with every convenience for their accouchement, should they be unfortunately required. And I have been gravely told, and almost believe, that there have actually been instances of the utility of the arrangement.[38]

The multiple dances in the Act I Finale of *Don Giovanni* are modelled on the pattern of a Viennese ball. First came a stately French dance—a minuet, pavan, or quadrille. Next was the less formal English country dance, and last of all the German dance. In this final category, the waltz had become popular by the 1770s but still took many years to attain respectability;as late as 1794, the Queen of Prusssia 'averted her eyes' whenever the waltz was danced at a Berlin Court Ball.[39]

The public gardens that characterize Vienna even today were popular with all classes. Both the Prater and the Augarten had recently been opened, and Michael Kelly vividly recollected their charms:

The Prater, . . . I consider the finest public promenade in Europe, far surpassing in variety our own beautiful Hyde Park. . . . On all sides, deer are seen quietly grazing, and gazing at the passing crowds. At the end of the principal avenue is an excellent tavern, besides which, in many other parts of this enchanting spot, there are innumerable cabarets, frequented by people of all ranks in the evening, who immediately after dinner proceed thither to regale themselves with their favourite dish, fried chickens, cold ham, and sausages; . . . and stay there until a late hour: dancing, music and every description of merriment prevail.[40]

With all these enticements, it may be wondered that there was any time for serious cultural pursuits. In fact, apart from music and opera, the arts fared poorly, and the disgust of the literati paved the way for resistance to Emperor Joseph's regime. There was little public interest in the visual arts, even though the Emperor established a school for painting

---

[37] Wraxall, *Memoirs*, ii. 118.
[38] Kelly, *Reminiscences*, p. 102.
[39] The social taxonomy of dance is discussed in detail by W. J. Allanbrook in *Rhythmic Gesture in Mozart* (Chicago, 1983).
[40] Kelly, *Reminiscences*, pp. 100–1.

and sculpture. Visitors such as Baron Riesbeck could not fail to notice this discrepancy:

The arts enjoy as little from the riches of this place as the poor do; almost all the palaces and gardens bespeak nothing but a tasteless profusion . . . Music is the only thing for which the nobility show a taste.[41]

Such was the society that emerged during Joseph II's reign, forming the background against which Mozart developed. Although there were many frivolous aspects, the picture that emerges is very different from the *ancien régime* stereotype. There was no arrogant nobility rushing heedlessly towards catastrophe, determined to squeeze the last drop of enjoyment from life. Indeed, in comparison with cities such as Venice, Vienna appears almost mild and sober. It was a society in which enlightened and controversial views were discussed, while genuine attempts were being made to put rational theories and beliefs into practice. In the last analysis, it was the combination of the serious and frivolous that made Vienna so attractive. As John Moore concluded,

I have never passed my time more agreeably than since I came to Vienna. There is not such a constant round of amusements as to fill up a man's time without any plan or occupation of his own; and yet there is enough to satisfy any mind not perfectly vacant and dependent on external objects. . . . There is no city in Europe where a young gentleman, after his university education is finished, can pass a year with so great advantage.[42]

## Revolution and Retrenchment

How convenient it would be to stop at this point. This was the society for which Mozart's comedies were intended—a world in which people were prepared to countenance new ideas while remaining alert to the pleasures that were formerly the preserve of the élite. The tone of these works matches such preoccupations precisely, and they should have struck a responsive chord in the audience. But unfortunately for Mozart and Da Ponte, this lively culture changed with unforeseen vehemence even as they worked. By the beginning of 1790, when *Così fan tutte* appeared, Vienna was a very different place.

The reasons for this reaction and the dramatic reversals of Joseph II's enlightened policy are complex and difficult to state in brief.[43] It appears that the accumulating disasters in Austrian foreign policy, together with

[41] Riesbeck, *Travels*, i. 308–9.
[42] Moore, *A View of Society*, ii. 310.
[43] See Wangermann, *The Austrian Achievement*, p. 157.

growing internal dissatisfaction with Joseph's reforms, combined to frighten the authorities. The catalyst that finally mobilized the machinery of repression was the news of revolution in France.

Although Joseph may have seen himself as a martial leader in the mould of Frederick the Great, his foreign adventures were not marked with success. Twice he tried to gain control over Bavaria, and on both occasions failed in confusion. The war with Turkey was an even greater disaster. Austria entered the campaign in 1788 not because of any threat to herself, but through the obligations of an alliance with Russia; although Joseph was required to supply only 30,000 troops, he ended up mobilizing some 200,000 men. The war was stagnant and dispiriting, despite occasional victories such as the capture of Belgrade by Marshal Loudon in 1789. Russia was preoccupied with Sweden, so offered little support as the Austrians were forced back through southern Hungary.[44] After the initial patriotic flush that spawned such nationalistic songs as Mozart's 'Ich möchte wohl der Kaiser sein' (K. 539) had worn off, the war became extremely unpopular. Recruitment drives pressed even skilled workmen, and a 7 per cent War Tax was imposed at the end of 1788. The army was mismanaged, and suffered through the harsh Croatian winters at the hands of negligent supply officers. As George Hammond, the British *chargé d'affaires* in Vienna, reported to the Foreign Office in June 1789,

The embarrassments of this Government are so great, that unless this campaign be almost miraculously successful, there seems scarcely any possibility that it will be able to prosecute another. The army, one of the finest that ever was assembled, has been mouldering away in inactivity—the internal resources are strained to the utmost pitch, and the national credit does not appear to be in any estimation abroad.[45]

Popular resentment was openly expressed; Wangermann has described an anonymous play that appeared in 1789 called *Die Kriegssteuer* (The War Tax), in which a Turkish officer is almost portrayed as a hero, displaying both generosity and humanity.[46] Nor is it any accident that Turks and other Eastern characters were provided with heroic and noble qualities in contemporary operas (such as Salieri's *Axur* of 1788).

The difficult war was accompanied by major disturbances within the Empire. Hungary led the way, for Joseph's attempts to curb the traditional autonomy of the nobility had met with fierce opposition, and open rebellion broke out in 1789. The population of the Netherlands was intolerant of the Emperor's religious and political reforms, and revolts

[44] Macartney, *The Habsburg Empire*, p. 132.
[45] Public Records Office, Foreign Office 7, Vol. 17, dated 17 June 1789.
[46] Wangermann, *The Austrian Achievement*, p. 145.

were reported during 1787, culminating in the defeat of the Austrian garrison in November 1789. Although Joseph promptly cancelled many edicts, Belgium declared as an independent state in December. The provinces of Carniola and Styria were also troubled, so that there was scarcely a corner of the Empire that could be considered completely loyal by the end of the decade.

None of these problems was attacked by the Emperor with his usual vigour, for Joseph was very ill throughout the year preceding his death, and rarely set foot in Vienna. The mood in the capital caused the authorities further alarm. For many years, Joseph had not been distressed by the public expression of hostile views, secure in the conviction that openness could only favour reform. Even in 1787, he refused to suppress a highly critical pamphlet written by the leader of the aristocratic opposition in Hungary; he considered it to be personal invective rather than a challenge to the State. But ironically, this freedom was being used by the enlightened sections of society to attack the government. The diversity of opinion available in printed form stimulated a political consciousness that could not fail in the end to question the basis of autocracy itself. Thus many of Joseph's 'rational' reforms became targets of criticism. For instance, the penal code of 1787 horrified many, since although the death penalty was abolished, cruel physical punishments were devised in its place. The lack of patronage for the arts and sciences alienated the intelligentsia, cutting Joseph off from literary support. It is notable that none of the major scientific advances of the late eighteenth century originated in Austria, and that German literature flourished only in northern States. Joseph Richter must have struck a responsive chord with his pamphlet of 1787 entitled *Why is Emperor Joseph not Loved by his People?*

It is scarcely surprising that a regime which had emerged so recently from absolutism should react with fear and harshness. The fall of the Bastille on 14 July 1789 seemed to confirm the traditionalists' worst fears. The news reached the Emperor a few days later, and, according to George Hammond,

It excited a transport of passion, and drew from him the most violent menaces of vengeance in case any insult had been, or should be offered to the person of his sister [Marie Antoinette]. The state of his own Dominions in the Netherlands must naturally have entered into his consideration . . . he immediately sent peremptory instructions to the Governor there, to employ severe and efficacious measures in punishing any appearance of sedition amongst the Flemish subjects.[47]

In contrast, the enlightened circles of Vienna greeted the fall of the

---

47 Public Records Office, Foreign Office 7, Vol. 17, dated 29 July 1789.

Bastille with undisguised delight. As the editor of the *Wiener Zeitung* wrote in May,

> In France, a light is beginning to shine which will benefit the whole of humanity. Necker has persuaded the King to leave the throne of despotism, and to set an unprecedented example which is of such a nature that all countries will have to follow it sooner or later.[48]

In October 1789, Louis XVI and his family were forcibly transported from Versailles to Paris. The incident brought to light the cruelty that could be perpetrated by the mob, for not only was the journey humiliating, but the heads of two Swiss guards were carried in triumph on the ends of pikes at the front of the procession. In the panic that followed, few paused to reflect with the sanity of Lord Gower, the British ambassador in Paris:

> If this country ceases to be a monarchy, it will be entirely the fault of Louis XVI. Blunder upon blunder, inconsequence upon inconsequence, a total want of energy of mind accompanied with personal cowardice, have been the destruction of his reign.[49]

The Austrian reaction was twofold. Joseph repealed his new laws wholesale. All the Acts referring to Hungary were revoked except for the Patents concerning religious toleration and the peasants. Most reforms in the rest of the Empire were abandoned as well, barring those relating to the law, religion, and education. It is possible that these withdrawals were intended to be only temporary, but the Emperor died in February 1790. The repeals were thus among the final actions of his career, and they evoked a cry of anguish from advanced circles throughout Europe. Herder summed up these thoughts in his *Briefe zur Beförderung der Humanität*:

> Without having known the Emperor, without ever receiving any benefit from him, I could have wept when I learnt the details of the end of his life. Nine years ago, when he came to the throne, he was worshipped like a tutelary deity, and the greatest things were expected of him, the most useful, wellnigh impossible things; and now they have laid him in the grave like a victim of time. Was there ever an Emperor, was there ever a mortal I should say, who made more strenuous efforts, who worked with greater zeal? And what a fate was that monarch's, who, confronted with death, was forced not only to renounce the aim he had set himself during his noblest years, but also to disavow, formally, the whole of his life's work, to annul it solemnly, and then to die.[50]

Together with these political retractions, a more sinister change was

---

[48] Quoted by Wangermann, *From Joseph II*, p. 24.

[49] George Gower, Duke of Sutherland, in *Paris in the Revolution*, ed. R. Tannahill, (London, 1966), 44.

[50] Quoted in M. Brion, *Daily Life in the Vienna of Mozart and Schubert*, trans. J. Stewart (London, 1961), 22.

also in progress. It was signalled by the rise of Count Johann Anton Pergen to his appointment as Minister of Police in 1789. He rapidly gained massive power through playing on the fears of the ailing Emperor. This invidious memorandum from Friedrich Schilling, Secretary at the Police Ministry, to the Emperor illustrates the technique:

Your majesty will have noticed how greatly the tone in the capital has changed in the last few years. They are no longer the long suffering people they used to be, who blindly obeyed the law without arguing, looked up to their superiors with respect, and were proud of the honour to be subjects of the German Emperor. . . . One looks in vain now for these . . . loyal and contented people.[51]

Censorship was taken over by the police, bypassing the enlightened Gottfried van Swieten. Even direct reporting of the news was unsafe, on the grounds that the information itself was inflammatory, and in July 1789 one Viennese newspaper was suspended. Pergen had direct access to the Emperor, and was permitted to employ detention without trial and *agents provocateurs* in his battle against free speech.

Repression was imposed with a speed and severity that took even the most sophisticated by surprise. The publisher Georg Wucherer was arrested after a police agent had bought a prohibited book from him. The case became famous for the flagrant disregard of the law exhibited by the authorities. Wucherer was fined and his large stock of uncensored books was pulped; this was illegal since manuscripts were commonly printed before being submitted to the censor. His banishment from the Dominions was also outside the law. The reasons behind this summary justice were secret to Pergen and the Emperor, and even the Supreme Chancellor, Count Kollowrat, was not given the details.

The Freemasons were a prime target for suppression, since Pergen was convinced that secret societies were responsible for revolutionary activities. He was not alone in this belief; in 1790 Queen Marie Antoinette warned her brother Leopold, successor to Joseph as emperor, 'Take great care over any associations of Freemasons . . . it is by means of Masonry that the monsters in this country count on succeeding elsewhere.'[52] The Lodges were put under even more pressure, and by 1793 all had closed. Such measures soon had their desired effect, and the open society of the 1780s disappeared. This was confirmed by the contemporary diarist Johann Pezzl in his *Skizze von Wien*. He reported that the lively freedom of speech in the salons of earlier years was impossible. In 1790, politics was a topic to avoid.

A cloud fell over Austria at the end of Joseph II's reign. The

---

[51] Quoted by Wangermann, *From Joseph II*, p. 35.
[52] Quoted by Thomson, *The Masonic Thread*, p. 133.

disappointment of enlightenment hopes and the frustration of rationalism contributed to the mood of Mozart's last years, and account in part for the ways in which his ambitions were modified. In this darkening atmosphere, the aims and intentions behind the collaborations with Da Ponte must have seemed quite out of place.

# 2

# Musicians, Opera, and Audience in Mozart's Time

## The Musician's Career in the late Eighteenth Century

Throughout his early years, Mozart was encouraged by his father to enter the service of a noble or princely household. Leopold Mozart believed that an appointment as kapellmeister was the surest route to security and success. The status of the musician in service was not high, but with perseverance a faithful and talented composer might reach a senior position; and for members of Leopold Mozart's generation, there were few alternatives.

The career of Karl Ditters may serve as illustration. Born in 1739, Ditters soon developed into a virtuoso violinist. He briefly pursued an independent career as a young man, and toured Italy under the patronage of Gluck. Yet on returning to Austria, Ditters found it impossible to survive as a soloist, and spent the rest of his life in service.[1] For a time he played in the orchestra of the Vienna Court Opera, but this was uncongenial. Each day there were rehearsals from 10 a.m. to 2 p.m. and with performances in the evening, no time was left for teaching or solo appearances. After serving a series of minor Courts, Ditters was appointed kapellmeister to Count Schaffgotsch, the Prince-Bishop of Breslau. Here he remained from 1769 onwards, not only flourishing as composer and musician but also making his mark on the hunting-field. He was created Baron von Dittersdorf (an honour for which he paid 1,100 gulden), and for much of his later life was occupied with non-musical duties at the Bishop's Court.

Many musicians of Mozart's own age held similar positions in aristocratic households. The Viennese composer Johann Schenk was musical director to Count Auersperg, while Joseph Schuster (1748–1812) was appointed kapellmeister to the Elector of Saxony when only 24. The Moravian brothers Paul (b.1756) and Anton (b.1761) Wranitzky were close contemporaries of Mozart, and talented composers and violinists. Both spent their lives in the employ of nobles or the Court, Anton Wranitzky being kapellmeister to Prince Lobkowitz. Quite apart from a

---

[1] The details of Karl von Dittersdorf's life and career are taken from his *Autobiography*, trans. A. D. Coleridge,(London, 1896).

reliable income, there were many material advantages to such a life. At Eszterháza, for instance, old and infirm servants received generous pensions, as did widows and orphans. Several doctors were available to tend employees, and a hospital was built for them.[2] It is no wonder that even Beethoven cherished the idea of becoming a kapellmeister in an aristocratic household or Court.[3]

Yet the benefits of security were balanced by drawbacks that would appear particularly distasteful to individuals who identified with the aspirations of the rising middle class. For most of his career, Haydn seems to have accepted his status as servant, acknowledging the social gulf that separated him from his patrons. When he performed at Eszterháza he wore livery, with white stockings and powdered hair. He was also obliged to maintain discipline among the other musicians, and to wait daily on the Prince. Frequently, musicians doubled with other roles in the household. When Dittersdorf entered the service of the Bishop of Grosswardein, the band of thirty-four consisted of a few professionals together with a valet, a confectioner, and members of the Chapter. One of the leading *buffi* in the small theatre was a cook. Mozart found such a situation abhorrent, as a letter written during the visit of the Archbishop of Salzburg's suite to Vienna in 1781 indicates:

We lunch about 12 o'clock, unfortunately somewhat too early for me. Our party consists of the two valets, that is, the body and soul attendants of his Worship, the contrôleur, Herr Zetti, the confectioner, the two cooks, Ceccarelli, Brunetti and—my insignificant self. By the way, the two valets sit at the top of the table, but at least I have the honour of being placed above the cooks. . . . A good deal of silly, coarse joking goes on at table, but no one cracks jokes with me, for I never say a word, or if I have to speak, I always do so with the utmost gravity.[4]

Other aspects of service were equally irksome. The composer was obliged to produce music on demand, and often at short notice. During his early years at Eisenstadt, Haydn was responsible for operas and concerts, the coaching of singers and instrumentalists, as well as for providing new compositions regularly. Operas were not simply performed, but cut and reorchestrated, and in some cases rewritten to suit the company. Additionally, households were generally isolated, and regular duties prevented travelling or accepting commissions for music elsewhere. Throughout the 1770s and 1780s, Haydn never undertook a professional tour outside the Eszterháza suite; he only visited Vienna in the Prince's service, and frequently had to return to Hungary before the end of the season to work

---

[2] H. C. Robbins Landon, *Haydn Chronicle and Works*, ii (London, 1978), 35.

[3] M. Solomon, *Beethoven* (London, 1978), 104.

[4] Letter to Leopold Mozart dated 17 Mar. 1781. Francesco Ceccarelli was a castrato employed by the Salzburg court from 1778. Antonio Brunetti was the konzertmeister of the Salzburg orchestra.

up the new repertoire. Likewise, when Anton Wranitzky became director of Prince Lobkowtiz's private orchestra, he spent six months of each year in Bohemia, mainly at the castles of Roudnice and Jezeri.[5] Dittersdorf lived for most of his maturity at Johannisberg in Silesia, travelling to Vienna and Berlin only on special occasions.

Practical as well as social considerations may therefore have swayed Mozart against employment as a servant-musician. After his break with Salzburg, he never made serious efforts to re-enter service, despite some lip-service to his father.[6] The reasons why Mozart's attitude diverged so markedly from that of his contemporaries are complex, being bound up with his own youthful experience and the concept of individual dignity evolving amongst the urban intelligentsia. These factors are important to our understanding of Mozart's working life and his art, and are discussed more fully in Chapter 4.

Mozart's rejection of the conventional career in service was neither so bold nor so foolish as has sometimes been suggested. It was an acknowledgement of changing circumstances, and the increasing viability of alternative patterns of work. One new possibility was to live as an instrumental virtuoso, for opportunities had increased markedly since Dittersdorf's youth. Unfortunately the life was largely peripatetic, since no city was likely to sustain interest in an individual performer for more than a few seasons. Nevertheless, keyboard virtuosi attracted wealthy pupils, so earnings from public appearances could be supplemented by teaching. Leopold Mozart advised his son on the way a travelling musician should set about business in a letter dated 27 November 1777:

First find out from your landlord who is the kapellmeister or Music Director of the place, or, if there is none, who is its leading musician. Arrange to be taken to him, or, if he is not too grand a person, ask him to call on you. You will then know at once whether giving a concert there is an expensive business. . . . In short, you must find out quickly whether something can be done or not—and you should do this on your arrival and without unpacking anything: just put on a few fine rings and so forth, in case when you call you should find a harpsichord there and be asked to perform.

Mozart followed this course during his stay at Dresden in 1789. On arriving in the city, he immediately called on the amateur musician and librettist Johann Neumann. Here he met an old acquaintance, the soprano

[5] See T. Volek and J. Macek, 'Beethoven's Rehearsals at the Lobkowitz's', *The Musical Times*, 127 (1986), 75–80.
[6] Mozart did discuss the possibility of entering the service of the Archbishop of Cologne (Archduke Maximilian) with his father, but never actively attempted to secure the position. After Leopold Mozart's death, there are no further references to the possibility of service in Mozart's correspondence. His appointment as Imperial kammermusicus in 1787 did not represent service in any real sense, as will be seen in Chapter 3.

Josepha Dušek. At Mass on the following day, he was introduced to the Elector of Saxony's Directeur des Plaisirs. That same evening, a chamber concert was arranged in the hotel, for which various musicians who happened to be passing through Dresden were recruited, (including the Eszterháza cellist Anton Kraft and the organist Anton Teyber). Josepha Dušek sang arias from *Le nozze di Figaro* and *Don Giovanni*. Next day, Mozart played a concerto for the Elector, and the day after that took part in a virtuoso tournament against the organist Hassler at the Russian Ambassador's house. He was thus able to display his talents to the leading figures in the State within a very brief time.

Other instrumentalists engaged in more leisurely tours, as in the case of Muzio Clementi. Clementi started on his first continental tour in 1780, having established some reputation in London for brilliant keyboard execution.[7] In Paris, he performed for Queen Marie Antoinette, who probably furnished him with recommendations for the German Courts. He remained in the French capital for more than a year, and his success was reflected in five separate publications of piano works. He then travelled by way of Strasbourg to Munich, where he stayed for several weeks. Clementi's intention had been to move afterwards to Berlin, but circumstances suggested that Vienna would be more profitable. The Grand Duke (later Czar) Paul was about to visit Vienna, and this state occasion would bring ample opportunities for display. Clementi therefore arrived in Vienna in November 1781, and only five days later took part in the famous virtuoso competition with Mozart. This was held before the Emperor Joseph and Grand Duchess Maria Feodorovna, and included playing at sight, improvisation on a theme set by the Emperor, and other keyboard feats. Mozart's opinion of the Italian's vapid brilliance was low ('a mere mechanicus'), and it is interesting that Clementi's later recollections endorse this view. In 1806, Clementi was questioned about Mozart's playing by one of his pupils:

'Until then I had never heard anyone perform with such spirit and grace. I was particularly astonished by an Adagio and some of his extemporised variations. . . .' When I asked Clementi if at that time he treated the instrument in his present style, he said no, adding that in the earlier period he had taken particular delight in brilliant feats of technical proficiency, especially in those passages of double notes that were not common before his time, and in improvised cadenzas.[8]

Mozart might have been well equipped for such a life, although the virtuoso's career was not without hazards. Glory and renown frequently

[7] L. Plantinga, *Muzio Clementi: His Life and Music* (London, 1977).
[8] Quoted by Plantinga, *Clementi*, p. 65.

outstripped the material rewards of playing in foreign cities. Mozart had ample evidence of this fact, as he reminded his father in November 1777:

Let me tell you, I now have five watches. I am therefore seriously thinking of having an additional watch pocket on each leg of my trousers, so that when I visit some great lord, I shall wear both watches, . . . so that it will not occur to him to present me with another one.

Similarly, Dittersdorf recalled the magnificent gift presented to him by the monks of Bologna, after he had played for the Church. It was carried in solemn procession to his lodgings, and consisted of 20 lb. of candied fruits, six white and six black pairs of silk stockings, and half a dozen Milanese silk handkerchiefs!

Another difficulty facing the travelling instrumentalist was rather more subtle. Despite public acclaim, the social status of virtuosi was low in many countries; performers did not enjoy the kind of prestige that would have allowed them to become established in respectable circles. This may have been one reason why Clementi gave up regular public appearances after 1790. The immensely popular pianist Johann Samuel Schröter (1750–1788) was only able to marry into the English gentry on condition that he abandon his career.

The profession that probably held greater appeal for Mozart was to live by composing, without entering the service of a single patron or Court. The few musicians who successfully pursued such a career did so by concentrating on the composition of Italian operas. The evolution of opera from an exclusive Court entertainment to a genre of general popularity brought an insatiable demand for new scores. Earlier in the century, these had been provided by local composers attached to particular Courts. For instance, Hasse wrote more than 100 operas for Dresden, while Jommelli satisfied most of Stuttgart's requirements. By Mozart's time, however, more extensive travelling and improved communication had led to unification of taste. Consequently, Opera Houses across Europe turned to a handful of composers with their *scrittura*.

The most consistently successful opera composer was Giovanni Paisiello. Born in 1740, Paisiello was trained at the Sant'Onofrio Conservatory in Naples, and began to write operas in 1764. He spent the next dozen years travelling through Italy, producing works in both *seria* and *buffo* styles. In 1776 he travelled to St Petersburg, and remained at the Court of Catherine the Great for eight years. Not a year passed without the composition of one or two operas, and his output of instrumental works was meagre by comparison. On his return from Russia in 1784, he paused in Vienna to write *Il rè Teodoro* to a libretto by Casti. Settling back in Naples, Paisiello produced a *seria* work (*Antigono*) for the 1785 season at the large San Carlo theatre, and a *buffa* piece (*La grotta di*

*Trofonio*) for the smaller Fiorentini. This dual pattern continued for many years, until Paisiello withdrew  from theatrical ventures, and accepted the salaried post of Maestro di Cappella to Ferdinand IV.[9]

Opera composers needed to work rapidly, and were also obliged to accept commissions from different cities. Few could survive by living and working in a single centre, since each Opera House required only one or two works a year. This can be seen in the career of the Spanish composer Vicente Martín y Soler (1754–1806), who spent most of his life writing for the stage. His opera *Una cosa rara* was the piece that eclipsed *Le nozze di Figaro* in the Vienna of 1786. Martín y Soler remained in Austria from 1785 to 1788, when he travelled on to St Petersburg. By 1794, he was in London for further collaborations with Da Ponte, later returning to Russia. Yet at the same time, he was composing operas and ballets for Naples, Lucca, Venice, Turin, and Parma. Indeed, Martín y Soler never composed more than three stage works in succession for the same Opera House, but always found it necessary to move on. The doyen of Italian composers, Giuseppi Sarti (1729–1802) travelled to Florence, Milan, Vienna, Rome, Venice, and other cities for opera commissions, and spent much of his maturity outside Italy. Even Salieri, with his influential position in Vienna as Court Composer, conductor of the Italian Opera, and later kapellmeister, composed many of his works for Italian cities or Paris. Thus Mozart would have found difficulty in reconciling this operatic career with permanent residence in Vienna.

## Mozart, Travel, and Independence

Mozart adopted none of these established musical roles, but took an independent path. He was neither in service, nor did he live as a peripatetic composer and performer. The reasons why he failed to travel more perhaps bear examination. Such a life might have been expected to appeal to him, and indeed he did project more elaborate tours. For example, when the soprano Nancy Storace and her brother were preparing to leave Vienna in 1787, they encouraged Mozart to accompany them to England.[10] Mozart hoped to lodge his children with his father, but Leopold

---

[9] For details of Paisiello's output during this period, see D. Heartz, 'Mozart and his Italian Contemporaries; *La Clemenza di Tito*', *Mozart-Jahrbuch 1978-9*, 275–93.

[10] The English soprano Nancy Storace (1765–1817) was a member of the Italian Opera in Vienna from 1784 to 1787. She appeared in a number of important premières, including those of *Una cosa rara* and *Il rè Teodoro*, and she created the role of Susanna in *Le nozze di Figaro*. More details of her career and vocal style are given in Chapter 7. Her brother Stephen (1762–1796) took lessons in composition from Mozart, and his opera *Gli sposi malcontenti* was presented at the Burgtheater in 1785.

Mozart strongly objected to the scheme, expressing his indignation to his daughter in a letter dated 17 November 1786:

You can easily imagine that I had to express myself very emphatically, as your brother actually suggested that I should take charge of his two children, because he was proposing to undertake a journey through Germany to England in the middle of the next carnival. . . . Not at all a bad arrangement! They could go off and travel—they might even die—or remain in England—and I should have to run off after them with the children.

Four years later, Salomon tried to attract Mozart to England again. Almost simultaneously, a very tempting offer came from Robert O'Reilly, the manager of the Pantheon theatre in London:

I offer you, Sir, such a position as few composers have had in England. If you are thus able to be in London towards the end of the Month of December next, 1790, and to stay until the end of June, 1791, and within that space of time to compose at least two Operas, serious or comic,. . . I offer you three hundred Pounds Sterling, with the advantage to write for the professional concerts or any other concert-hall.[11]

Mozart may also have considered a journey to the Russian Court, in the footsteps of the successful Italians. Amongst the possessions listed on his death was a *Geographical and Topographical Travel Book through All the States of the Austrian Monarchy, with the Travel Route to St. Petersburg through Poland*, published in 1789.

Yet none of these major tours was ever undertaken, and Mozart was never absent from Vienna for more than three months. Even these shorter journeys provoked feelings of loneliness and despondency, according to the composer's letters home.

If you could only look into my heart. There a struggle is going on between my yearning and longing to see and embrace you once more and my desire to bring home a large sum of money. I have often thought of travelling farther afield, but whenever I tried to bring myself to take the decision, the thought always came to me, how bitterly I should regret it, if I were to separate myself from my beloved wife for such an uncertain prospect, perhaps even to no purpose whatever.[12]

The congenial atmosphere of Vienna may have encouraged the sedentary life. An additional deterrent must have been Mozart's distinct lack of success on those journeys that he did complete in adult life. This is illustrated by the visit Mozart made to Prussia and other North German states in 1789—his failure was due less to public indifference than to his own careless and undiplomatic approach. Dittersdorf visited Prussia

---

[11] Quoted in O. E. Deutsch, *Mozart: A Documentary Biography*, trans. E. Blom, P. Branscombe, and J. Noble (London, 1966), 377–8. £300 was equivalent to some 3,000 gulden.
[12] Letter to Constanze Mozart dated 8 Oct. 1790.

around the same period, and the contrast between the two men is illuminating.

Both musicians must have travelled to the Court at Potsdam with every expectation of success. King Frederick William was an enthusiastic and liberal patron of music, and not only played the cello, but also attended concerts and operas frequently. The Court orchestra had a high reputation, and regularly received new works from Boccherini in Madrid. Dittersdorf was a model of tact, and began by composing six new symphonies especially for Berlin. These were prudently sent ahead, so that they might be rehearsed before his arrival. His tour coincided with a festive visit from the King's sister, the Princess of Orange. This occasion provided special opportunities for concerts. On reaching the city, Dittersdorf immediately became friendly with Duport and Reichardt, two of the central figures in Prussian musical life. He expressed admiration for Reichardt's compositions, and the latter became very attentive and useful. On one occasion, Dittersdorf attended the opera *Protesilao*, the first act of which had been composed by Reichardt, and the second by Naumann; he refused to declare any partiality, but praised both men lavishly.

Dittersdorf was not paid for his many appearances and performances, but his ingratiating behaviour brought dividends in the end. With Reichardt's assistance, he was able to organize a benefit performance of his oratorio *Job*. The King allowed the Berlin Kapelle, the Court musicians, and the Opera House to be used without charge, and one of the largest musical events of the period was devised, with some 230 in the chorus and orchestra. Although Dittersdorf had to pay 1,290 gulden for copying and various accessories, the concert receipts were more than 4,700 gulden. The performance was a triumph, and Dittersdorf left Prussia with an enhanced reputation, and over 2,500 gulden profit.

Circumstances were perhaps even more favourable for Mozart, since *Die Entführung* was being successfully performed at the time of his visit. Yet he made few preparations, and unlike Dittersdorf composed no special new works. He signally failed to follow Leopold Mozart's cautious advice about how to behave in foreign centres:

There must be attention and daily concentration on earning some money and you must cultivate extreme politeness in order to ingratiate yourself with people of standing.[13]

Instead, he was not able to hide his contempt for the resident musicians. Duport, whom Leopold Mozart had described as 'very conceited', insisted on speaking French. The habit annoyed Mozart, who observed that he

---

[13] Letter dated 24 Nov. 1777.

'had been long enough making German money, and eating German bread, to be able to speak the German language'. He also spoke slightingly of Reichardt's inadequate direction of the kapelle. Consequently, he was given no support by these men, and held no public concerts in Berlin. He did however play privately for the Queen, and was commissioned to write a set of quartets and simple piano sonatas. But the profits were meagre, as can be gauged from a letter to Constanze sent on 23 May 1789:

First of all, my darling little wife, when I return you must be more delighted with having me back than with the money I shall bring.

Mozart's attempt to live outside the world of aristocratic service reflected his desire for social emancipation as an artist. German writers of the next generation, such as A. W. Schlegel and E. T. A. Hoffmann, saw him as one of the earliest artists in the romantic sense, carving out a creative niche and autonomous existence in defiance of prevailing convention.[14] Yet by doing this, Mozart was obliged to rely on sources of income that were far from secure. As will be seen in the next chapter, his earnings from public concerts were irregular, and although money could be made from pupils, teaching absorbed vital composing time. Nor was the music industry organized to facilitate such a career. The system of payments rarely allowed an individual to live from compositions alone. Publishers bought works for a fixed sum, irrespective of subsequent popularity. The composer might of course publish independently, but Mozart saw problems in that too:

If I have some work printed or engraved at my own expense, how can I protect myself from being cheated by the engraver? For surely he can print off as many copies as he likes and therefore swindle me. The only way to prevent this would be to keep a sharp eye on him.[15]

Composers were seldom paid for performances either, so they received no direct benefit from the popularity of their works. This was true even of operas. In the 1780s, composers were generally paid 100 ducats (450 gulden) for a work at the Burgtheater, although exceptions were made: Paisiello was given 300 ducats for *Il rè Teodoro* in 1784, while Mozart apparently received 200 ducats for *Così fan tutte*. These were substantial fees, but the composer could expect no further payment, apart from the occasional benefit performance. Yet frequent repetitions and public praise were vital, since they stimulated commissions for new works. Mozart was thus left with the unenviable task of promoting his music without gaining tangibly from its renown. This had an influence on the

---

14 See F. Blume, 'Mozart's Style and Influence', in *The Mozart Companion*, ed. by H. C. Robbins Landon, and D. Mitchell, (London, 1965), 10–31.
15 Letter to Leopold Mozart dated 20 Feb. 1784.

nature of the music, for financial security depended on works that appealed to the public at large. The connoisseur circles of the Viennese salons might greet chamber pieces with enthusiasm, but work of this kind could not sustain Mozart's livelihood. Popular acclaim was to be had in the concert hall, and more importantly in the Opera House. Success brought offers of *scrittura* from other Houses, and an astute composer could profit further by arranging popular numbers for instrumental groups. Opera was therefore central to Mozart's survival as an independent artist. However, in order to appreciate Mozart's works in the genre, the conventions and standards of opera in contemporary Vienna must be considered.

## Opera and Popular Taste in Mozart's Vienna

When the Burgtheater first opened in the 1740s, opera was no longer a lavish baroque Court entertainment designed to enhance the glory of the reigning prince. Instead, the theatre reflected a new age, being a modest building converted from a disused *jeu de paume* (see Plate 3). It stood adjacent to the Hofburg, and although there was a private entrance for the Monarch, Maria Theresa did not own the theatre, nor were performances given at the command of the Court. An early ground plan is reproduced in Plate 4. The theatre was small, yet had several tiers, so that social distinctions were maintained. The ruler's throne, which in earlier generations had stood directly in front of the stage, was absent, and the Court were sequestered in boxes. Apart from the Court, the capacity of the theatre was only 920, including both sitting and standing places. By comparison, the theatres of Paris and London were able to accommodate more than 2,000 during this period. Complaints about the building's inadequacy, lack of distinction, and comfort abounded from its early years onwards, culminating in a major refurbishment three years after Mozart's death. Despite this, however, the Burgtheater had virtually ceased to be used for opera by the end of the century, and became the province of spoken drama.[16]

The Burgtheater was administered for many years by independent impresarios, until nationalization by Joseph II. Later he put the House at the disposal of the German Opera, at the expense of French and Italian companies. This move may have reflected an upsurge in nationalism rather than any change in the demands of the audience; a similar veto was

---

[16] For details of the Burgtheater and its development, see E. Wlassack, *Chronik des K. K. Hof-Burgtheaters* (Vienna, 1876), and more recently K. Zobel and F. E. Warner, 'The Old Burgtheater: A Structural History', *Theatre Studies*, 19 (1972/3), 19–53. Also D. Heartz, 'Nicholas Jadot and the Building of the Burgtheater', *Musical Quarterly*, 48 (1982), 1–31.

placed on Italian opera by the Elector Charles Theodore of Munich in an attempt to encourage native art. In Vienna the policy failed, although it provided Mozart with his first major opportunity in *Die Entführung*. Instead, Singspiel took firmer root in the popular suburban theatres, where Mozart's later collaborator Schikaneder was the outstanding figure.

Italian opera returned to the Burgtheater in 1783, following the demise of the German tradition, and the dismissal of a French company. According to Michael Kelly, the latter came about as follows:

One day, while they were drinking their wine, and abusing it, the Emperor passed by the salle à manager, which opened into the Royal Gardens. One of the gentlemen, with the innate modesty so peculiarly belonging to his nation and profession, jumped up from the table with a glass of wine in his hand, followed His Majesty, and said,—'sire, I have brought your Majesty some of the trash which is given us by your purveyor, by way of wine; we are all disgusted by his treatment, and beg to request your Majesty to order something better, for it is absolutely impossible for us to drink it . . .'

The King, with great composure, tasted the wine; 'I think it excellent,' said His Majesty, 'at least, quite good enough for me, though, perhaps not sufficiently high-flavoured for you and your companions; In France, I dare say, you will get much better.' He then turned on his heel, and sending immediately for the Grand Chamberlain, ordered the whole corps dramatique to be discharged, and expelled from Vienna forthwith.[17]

Joseph II's role in the management of the Opera is of some interest, since it reflects his relationship with the musicians and performers of Vienna. A large collection of memoranda addressed to the Director of the Court Theatres (Count Rosenberg) survives, documenting the Emperor's intimate concern with the day-to-day running of the Opera. He was closely involved with the hiring of principals, ensuring for example that Nancy Storace and the soprano Celesta Coltellini were offered the same terms, and that Francesco Benucci should not be paid too much.[18] When in Italy, Joseph was constantly on the look-out for new talent, and would send Rosenberg reports of likely prospects. His cordial relations with the principals are abundantly illustrated by contemporary memoirs. Perhaps the most important result of his influence was the emphasis on comic opera at the Burgtheater. In most other major cities, *opera seria* dominated the major House, while comedy was relegated to smaller theatres. Vienna alone did not conform to this pattern, primarily because of the Emperor's dislike of *seria*.

[17] M. Kelly, *Reminiscences*, ed. R. Fiske (London, 1975), 97–8.

[18] See R. Payer von Thurn, *Joseph II als Theaterdirektor* (Vienna, 1920). Francesco Benucci (*c.*1745–1824) was the leading *buffo* at the Italian Opera throughout most of Mozart's maturity. He created the roles of Figaro and Guglielmo in *Così fan tutte*, and was the first Leporello in Vienna (see Chapter 7).

Yet Joseph was not all-powerful in the theatre, and policy was ulti-mately determined by public taste. A clear instance is the fate of the singer Maria Anna Tauber, who belonged to the Eszterháza company in 1778. The Emperor was attracted by her voice at a concert of the 'Tonkünstler-Societät' (The Musician's Benefit Society), and ordered that she be given a leading role in the next production at the Burgtheater. She duly appeared in Gretry's *Lucile*, but failed to make an impression on the public, and did not secure a contract.[19] Similarly, the Emperor might commission an opera, but he could not guarantee more than a few perfor-mances, and the repertoire was largely out of his hands. Furthermore, he was frequently away from the capital, and could not take a controlling interest in the theatre all the time.

Finally, in 1788, Joseph effectively cut off the Imperial subsidy to the Italian Opera, pleading that the deficit of 80,000 Gulden was too great for the Exchequer. According to Da Ponte, this move was prompted by a letter of complaint from Celesta Coltellini. It is more likely however that the costly Turkish Wars had put extra strains on the Treasury, and that luxuries such as the theatre were the first to be axed. In fact, the Opera did not collapse, since Da Ponte organized a group of nobles to underwrite the operation; nevertheless, 1788 marked the end of the Emperor's active concern with the Italian Opera. After Leopold's accession to the throne, the Burgtheater reverted to conventional commercial management.

Some indication of the conditions and standards of performance pre-valent in late eighteenth-century Italian opera can be extracted from contemporary sources. Both the stage and auditorium were lit by cande-labra, and the candles remained burning throughout the House. The continual illumination during performances did not encourage audience concentration, and it is clear that attention was only paid to the stage intermittently. Mozart himself admitted to behaviour that would horrify present-day audiences in a letter to Gottfried von Jacquin dated 15 January 1787:

The evening surprised us sooner than you might perhaps believe. Well, it was soon time to go to the opera. We heard *Le gare generose*. In regard to the performance of this opera I can give no definite opinion because I talked a lot; but that quite contrary to my usual custom I chattered so much may have been due to . . . Well, never mind!

Many of the audience did not arrive at the theatre until after the performance had begun. In London, for example, the nobility dined at 4 p.m. or later, while the Opera commenced at 7 p.m. Since performances frequently continued until after midnight, even devotees rarely sat

[19] M. Horanyi. *The Magnificence of Eszterháza*, trans. A. Deák, (London, 1962), 111.

through an entire work.[20] Nor was the public afraid of making its presence felt in other ways. The King's Theatre in London witnessed serious riots in 1789, provoked by dissatisfaction with the season in general, and the dancers in particular. Subscribers raided the stage, destroying scenery, properties, and lighting. Michael Kelly has left an amusing account of the patrons of the Rome Opera:

> The severest critics are the Abbés who sit in the front row of the pit, each armed with a lighted wax taper in one hand, and a book of the opera in the other, and should any poor devil of a singer miss a word, they call out, 'Bravo, bestia!' . . .
>
> It is customary for the composer of an opera to preside at the pianoforte the first three nights of its performance, and a precious time he has of it in Rome. Should any passage in the music strike the audience as similar to one of another composer, they cry, 'Bravo, il ladro,'—'Bravo, you thief'; or 'Bravo Paisiello! Bravo Sacchini!' if they suppose the passage to be stolen from them, 'the curse of God light on him who first put a pen in your hand to write music!'[21]

It is evident that the audience took great interest in the politics of the theatre, and had clear expectations about the nature of the entertainment provided.[22] Public taste can best be gauged by considering what operas were actually performed during Mozart's maturity. Fortunately, full lists for the Burgtheater survive.[23] The most striking feature is that almost all the works were written by living composers, many of whom lived in or visited the city. Opera was not a resurrection of former glories, but a vital and active medium. The total number of performances for a series of musicians during Mozart's Vienna years is summarized in Table 1. Although other composers were represented in the repertoire, the individuals shown in the diagram are the most valuable for placing Mozart's experience in context.

Not surprisingly, Paisiello was solidly represented in Vienna by a number of works. Considering that opera alternated with plays at the Burgtheater and Kärntnertortheater, and that the season was limited, the figures reflect an extraordinary degree of popularity. Moreover, Paisiello was extremely prolific—during 1785 and 1786 for example, he had five different pieces in the repertoire, and the decade from 1782 saw no fewer than fifteen of his operas on the stage in Vienna. Yet even Paisiello's success was not unvarying, for none of his operas was given at

---

[20] C. B. Hogan, *The London Stage 1776–1800. A Critical Introduction* (Carbondale, Ill. 1968), p. ccxvi.

[21] Kelly, *Reminiscences*, pp. 32–3.

[22] This interest is nowhere more vividly expressed that in the conversations between Mr Dangle and Sneer in *The Critic* by Richard Brinsley Sheridan (1779).

[23] The information given here is extracted from O. Jahn, *W. A. Mozart* (Leipzig, 1859), iv, Appendix 23. More recent details are provided in O. Michtner, *Das alte Burgtheater als Opernbühne von der Einführung des deutschen Singspiels (1778) bis zum Tod Kaiser Leopold II (1792), Theatergeschichte Österreichs*, iii. 1, (Vienna, 1970).

TABLE 1.  PERFORMANCES OF OPERAS BY FOUR COMPOSERS AT THE BURGTHEATER BETWEEN 1785 AND 1791

| Composer | 1785 | 1786 | 1787 | 1788 | 1789 | 1790 | 1791 |
|---|---|---|---|---|---|---|---|
| Paisiello (1740–1816) | 46 | 31 | 37 | 18 | 0 | 32 | 41 |
| Salieri (1750–1825) | 17 | 22 | 5 | 30 | 28 | 20 | 10 |
| Martín y Soler (1754–1806) | 0 | 13 | 31 | 12 | 42 | 32 | 8 |
| Mozart (1756–91) | 0 | 9 | 0 | 15 | 11 | 25 | 3 |

the Burgtheater in 1789. This may have been fortuitous rather than a result of public satiation, with neither revivals nor new works being available. Clearly, absence from the repertoire for a season could not be considered a mark of failure.

Salieri made his mark as an opera composer with a series of works in Paris, and performance rates in Vienna may have been inflated on account of his official position. Both he and Paisiello had *seria* as well as *buffo* operas in the repertoire, and Salieri was in fact more successful with the former. Thus his *Axur*, originally composed for Paris as *Tarare* to a libretto by Beaumarchais, was given twenty-nine times in 1788. It was seen on fifteen occasions during the next season, with a further nine performances in 1790; none of Salieri's comic operas achieved such popular approval.

Vicente Martín y Soler's career is interesting in that it overlapped closely with that of Mozart. Like Mozart, he was not a native Italian, and his main support came from the Spanish faction at Court. His first work was produced in the same year as *Le nozze di Figaro*, and like Mozart he had three *opere buffe* presented at the Burgtheater. Yet throughout these years, Martín y Soler was consistently more successful, and received greater acclaim from theatre audiences. But the public did not accept works indiscriminately from him or any other composer. All experienced failures as well as triumphs. Salieri's *Il ricco d'un giorno* was presented in June 1784, and survived only six catastrophic performances, while *La fiera di Venezia* did little better in the following year. Martín y Soler's first opera for Vienna, *Il burbero di buon cuore*, made a poor showing in 1786, and was only revived in 1789 after the success of subsequent works. This version included revisions and interpolations by Mozart (two soprano arias, K. 582 and 583), but still failed to please and was soon dropped.

Mozart never achieved popular recognition as an opera composer on the scale accorded to Paisiello and Martín y Soler. Höslinger has calculated that in terms of overall number of performances between 1782 and 1791, Mozart ranked seventh in Vienna; not only Paisiello, Salieri, and Martín y Soler, but Cimarosa, Guglielmi, and Sarti were played more frequently.[24] Both *Le nozze di Figaro* and *Don Giovanni* took many years to become established in Vienna. It is ironic that 1790, almost certainly the least productive year of Mozart's maturity, saw the greatest number of Burgtheater performances. This was due to the appearance of *Così fan tutte* in the middle of a successful revival of *Le nozze di Figaro*. The fate of Mozart's individual works can best be understood by considering some typical patterns of production during this period.

Several of the more popular works of the 1780s are plotted in Table 2. *Il rè Teodoro* was written by Paisiello specially for Vienna, and was one of the operatic events of the decade. Not only was the composer present, but the libretto was written by the Abbé Casti, the arch-rival of Lorenzo Da Ponte. He was hoping to establish his claim to be Metastasio's successor, and receive the appointment of 'Ceasarean Poet'. The pattern of performance was typical for Vienna, with an initial run followed after an interval by a shorter revival. Few works remained in the repertoire for many consecutive seasons, although Paisiello's exceptional *Il barbiere di Siviglia* was seen every year from 1783 to 1788.

*La grotta di Trofonio* was one of Salieri's most vital comic works, and its plot shows important parallels with *Così fan tutte* (see Chapter 6). It had a solid run but was then dropped and not revived. Again, however, it is Martín y Soler who offers the most telling contrast to Mozart. Mozart might reasonably have expected *Le nozze di Figaro* to be retained at the Burgtheater in 1787, but it was squeezed out by the phenomenal triumph of *Una cosa rara*. Martín y Soler's opera appeared late in 1786, so its full impact developed over the following year. Da Ponte jubilantly described its success in terms that resemble Mozart's comments on *Le nozze di Figaro*, quoted in the Introduction:

The ladies in particular, who could see nothing but the Cosa rara, and dress only in the styles of the Cosa rara, believed that Martín and I were in truth two 'rare things' ourselves. We might have had more amorous adventures than had all the Knights of the Round Table in twenty years. We were the lions of the hour to the exclusion of all others. . . . Sugary love letters, presents accompanied by enigmatic verses, invitations to drives, banquets, dinners. . . .[25]

Martín y Soler did not allow the enthusiasm of the Viennese to wane. A year later, he produced *L'arbore di Diana*, and this also was highly

---

[24] See C. Höslinger, 'Mozarts Opern in den Sonnleithner Regesten', *Mozart-Jahrbuch 1978-9*, 149-53.

[25] L. Da Ponte, *Memoirs*, trans. E. Abbott (New York, 1967), 171.

TABLE 2.  NUMBER OF PERFORMANCES OF FIVE OPERAS AT THE
BURGTHEATER BETWEEN 1784 AND 1791

| Opera | 1784 | 1785 | 1786 | 1787 | 1788 | 1789 | 1790 | 1791 |
|---|---|---|---|---|---|---|---|---|
| *Il rè Teodoro* (Paisiello: première 23 Aug. 1784) | 14 | 9 | 11 | 2 | 0 | 0 | 19 | 1 |
| *Una cosa rara* (Martín y Soler: première 17 Nov. 1786) | — | — | 4 | 17 | 2 | 19 | 9 | 3 |
| *Le nozze di Figaro* (Mozart: première 1 May 1786) | — | — | 9 | 0 | 0 | 11 | 15 | 3 |
| *L'arbore di Diana* (Martín y Soler: première 1 Dec. 1787) | — | — | — | 9 | 10 | 19 | 21 | 5 |
| *La grotta di Trofonio* (Salieri: première 28 May 1785) | — | 7 | 13 | 5 | 1 | 0 | 0 | 0 |

acclaimed; it was the most popular of all Da Ponte's Vienna libretti, and was given fifty-nine times in the first four years.

It can be seen from Table 2 that ten performances in a year was a respectable achievement. *Le nozze di Figaro* did not reach this level on its first appearance, but the revival in 1789 received greater approbation. It is difficult to ascribe this delayed success to a change in public taste, since after 1791 the work disappeared again from the repertoire. Apart from the diversion of interest on to Martín y Soler's opera, more subtle disappointments may have been significant (see Chapter 8). Both Mozart's later Burgtheater productions had substantial first runs—fifteen performances for *Don Giovanni*, and ten for *Così fan tutte*—yet they then disappeared from the stage, without the customary revival after a few seasons.

The dearth of Austrian or German successes at the Burgtheater might give the impression that native composers were entirely neglected in Vienna. However, most Central Europeans did not even attempt to compete in the Italian arena, but concentrated on Singspiel. Dittersdorf, for example, stayed in Vienna for two years during this period, and his

*Doktor und Apotheker* was presented in 1786. This triumph was followed by two more Singspiele within a few months, yet he only composed a single Italian work for the Viennese stage. The indifferent reception of Mozart's works is comparable with the fate of German classical spoken drama. At Mannheim's influential National Theatre, Schiller's *Die Räuber* was shown only fifteen times between 1781 and 1788, while *Don Carlos* appeared on just three occasions. Yet performances of sentimental plays by Iffland and Kotzebue numbered 2,000 over the same period. Similarly, in Dresden, works by these two authors were seen over 470 times in the years around 1800; the plays of Goethe, Schiller, and Lessing together contributed only fifty-eight evenings.[26]

Although Vienna was the touchstone of success for Mozart, it was not the only important centre for Italian opera. Other repertoires can be examined, to see whether Mozart suffered from local prejudice in Vienna. If fact, similar tastes prevailed in many theatres. The repertoire at Eszterháza, for example, was dominated by the popular Italians.[27] The decade from 1781 saw the production of no fewer than thirteen separate works by Cimarosa, seven by Paisiello, and as many from Anfossi. So too in London, then famed for its vigorous cosmopolitan musical life—among the favoured composers were Pietro Guglielmi (1728–1804), Paisiello, and Cimarosa, each of whom had works in almost every season.[28]

It was only in the Opera Houses of Germany that Mozart received a more favourable reception, as the performances detailed in the Introduction indicate. Italian opera did not bring Mozart widespread international acclaim in his lifetime, nor did it foster immense local esteem in Vienna. In many ways, it would be easier to understand if Mozart's operas were rejected entirely. Such an attitude might be ascribed to Italian chauvinism, or to blinkered enthusiasm for the fashionable composers. Yet this was not the case; his *buffo* works were moderately successful, suggesting that the audience sampled before rejecting his offerings. In contrast, the instrumental works were greatly admired, and Mozart remained highly regarded for most of his life.

One explanation for this discrepancy is that Italian opera was judged on criteria different from those applied to other forms of composition. Innovations were accepted in instrumental works that were not permitted on the stage. The distinction can be illustrated by exploring contemporary reactions to Mozart's musical style.

---

[26] W. H. Bruford, *Theatre, Drama and Audience in Goethe's Germany* (London, 1950).
[27] See Horanyi, *The Magnificence of Eszterháza*.
[28] W. C. Smith, *The Italian Opera and Contemporary Ballet in London, 1789–1820* (London, 1955).

## Mozart and Contemporary Musical Taste

The reasons people gave for favouring the operatic style of Italian composers were comparatively consistent throughout the late eighteenth century. The appeal was based on the simplicity and beauty of settings, and
these characteristics were equated with the 'natural'. German music on
the other hand was considered complicated, a product of contrived rather
than spontaneous talent. Admirers of Italian lyricism consequently
labelled the forays of northern composers into *seria* and *buffo* as 'learned',
putting form before melody and vocal expression.[29] Paisiello expressed
these views succinctly:

In Italy, we attach value only to melody; whether by nature, or whether because
of the harmonious effects our voices and our manner of singing produce in us;
and we make use of modulations only to strengthen the expression of the work.
In Germany, however, . . . they attach little value to melody and use it only
sparingly; thus they are obliged to avail themselves of a studied harmony, in
order thereby to make up for the lack of melody and of the magic of a beautiful
voice.[30]

The contrast emerges vividly in discussions of modulation. Modulation
was tolerated only to a limited extent, and when it appeared to be 'natural'. This ruled out many of the possibilities inherent in classical sonata
development, and throughout the century, the champions of Italian style
failed to acknowledge the dramatic possibilities of form. Thus Paisiello
regarded modulation as a theatrical trick, designed to create a brief emotional *frisson*. Piccinni equated modulation based on harmonic arguments with the learned style:

To modulate, is to take a route which the ear will follow willingly. It even asks to
be led; but only on condition that when arrived at the point to which you have
conducted it, . . . it may enjoy some repose. . . . To quit a key almost as soon as
we have entered it, to become extravagant without reason or end, to proceed by
jumps and skips, . . . is to prove that the artist is ignorant of the end of his art as
well as of its principles, and that he affects a superabundance of imagination and
learning in order to conceal the want of both.[31]

A similar view was expressed by John Brown, the Scottish painter who had
a passion for Italian opera and developed an extensive taxonomy of forms
in his *Letters upon the Poetry and Music of the Italian Opera*. Indeed, he
was prepared to accept modulation only in *recitativo accompagnato*:

---

[29] The same argument had been used in the 'Querelle des Bouffons' earlier in the century. In the
late 1770s, the 'natural' style of Gluck was pitted against the mannered Piccinni.

[30] Quoted by A. Einstein, *Mozart: His Character–his Works*, trans. A. Mendel and N. Broder
(London, 1971), 116. Paisiello is however known to have praised Mozart on other occasions, and
recommended him to the Rome theatre manager Gasparoni.

[31] Quoted by G. Hogarth, *Memoirs of the Opera* (London, 1851), ii. 90.

It is in this species of song that the finest effects of the chromatic and, as far as our system of musical intervals is susceptible of it, even of the enharmonic scale, are peculiarly fit; and it is here also that the powers of modulation are most happily, because most properly, employed, by changes of the tone analogous to the variety of the matter. [32]

Hester Lynch Piozzi damned the Germans with faint praise; writing from Vienna in the 1780s, she displayed a typical cultivated English opinion:

Nor will German music much delight those who have been long accustomed to more simple melody, though intrinsic merit and complicated excellence will always deserve the highest note of praise. Whoever takes upon him to under-rate that which no one can obtain without infinite labour and study, will ever be censured, and justly, for refusing the reward due to deep research; but if a man's taste leads him to Cyprus wine, let him drink that, and content himself with commending the old hock. [33]

Mozart was a prime target for criticism of this type. Complaints were focussed primarily on his stage works, since his style was much more acceptable on the concert platform. An exchange between the Emperor Joseph II and Dittersdorf (later recorded by the latter) emphasizes the distinction. When Dittersdorf was asked by the monarch for his opinion of Mozart, he replied:

'I have never yet met with any composer who had such an amazing wealth of ideas. I could almost wish he were not so lavish in using them. He leaves his hearer out of breath; for hardly has he grasped one beautiful thought, when another of greater fascination dispels the first, and this goes on throughout, so that in the end it is impossible to retain any one of these beautiful melodies. . . .'

Joseph replied, 'He has only one fault in his pieces for the stage, and his singers have very often complained of it—he deafens them with his full accompaniment.' [34]

The same views resurface frequently. Even complimentary writers described the music as being for the discriminating only:

Nor did Mozart's music make much sensation among our public. It is for the connoisseur who knows how to unravel its refinements, rather than for the dilettante who lets himself be guided by his natural feeling, and judges only according to the first, immediate impression. [35]

Mozart's opponents and rivals dismissed his style as learned. When

---

[32] J. Brown, *Letters upon the Poetry and Music of Italian Opera* (Edinburgh, 1789), 16.

[33] H. L. Piozzi, *Observations and Reflections made in the course of a Journey through France, Italy and Germany* (London, 1789), ii. 301.

[34] Dittersdorf, *Autobiography*, p. 251.

[35] From the *Frankfurt Dramaturgische Blätter* of 1789, quoted by Deutsch, *Mozart*, pp. 340–1.

Sarti had cursorily looked over the two quartets, K. 421 and K. 465, he announced:

From these two passages we can decide that the composer, whom I do not know and do not want to know, is only a clavier player with a depraved ear; he is a sectary of the false system that divides the octave into twelve semitones.[36]

Mozart was aware that his music was complex and intellectually demanding, but hoped that it also had popular appeal. When describing three Viennese concertos (K. 413–15) to his father in a letter dated 28 December 1782, he explained:

These concertos are a happy medium between what is too easy and too difficult; they are very brilliant, pleasing to the ear, and natural, without being vapid. There are passages here and there from which the connoisseurs alone can derive satisfaction; but these passages are written in such a way that the less learned cannot fail to be pleased, though without knowing why.

Yet at the same time, he acknowledged the problem of gaining public approval:

In order to win applause one must write stuff which is so inane that a fiacre could sing it, or so unintelligible that it pleases precisely because no sensible man can understand it.

An important bar to the appreciation of Mozart's compositions was their technical difficulty. Chamber works in particular were generally assumed to be within the grasp of amateurs, and available for performance in the agreeable atmosphere of the salon without too much effort. But musicians of modest abilities were bewildered by the subtleties of Mozart's work. Only in his own hands could Mozart be confident that his music would receive its just deserts. Much of his success as a composer derived from his status as performer. It will be seen in the next chapter how many of the problems that beset Mozart in his later years resulted from the failure of his operas to provide a firm foundation of material support, once the Viennese public had lost interest in his keyboard playing.

---

[36] Quoted by A. H. King, *Mozart in Retrospect* (London, 1955), p. 5. Sarti's opinion may have seemed old-fashioned even at the time it was stated. But in the mid-eighteenth century, music that smacked of counterpoint was castigated as learned, artificial, and scholastic by admirers of the *galant*. See G. Pestelli, *The Age of Mozart and Beethoven*, trans. E. Cross, (Cambridge, 1984), 6.

# 3

# Mozart and Vienna

What provokes me most is the extent to which distinctions of rank are carried. I know perfectly well how inevitable inequalities of condition are; indeed, I myself derive advantages from them; but I would not have these institutions prove a barrier to the small chance of happiness which I may enjoy on this earth.

Goethe[1]

Our views of Mozart's years in Vienna are indelibly coloured by the series of begging letters written to his fellow Freemason, Michael Puchberg. Mozart began the correspondence in 1788 with nonchalant requests for money, but descended rapidly to urgent, pathetic appeals for amounts as small as 10 gulden. The impression of abject poverty and misery is reinforced by the fact that the composer was buried in a common grave, without even the dignity of a tombstone or monument. Yet the Viennese decade (1781–1791) was the period during which Mozart enjoyed some of his greatest triumphs, not only in the Opera House but on the concert platform. At various times he earned considerable amounts of money and lived stylishly. How can these extremes be reconciled? An explanation of this anomaly is essential for comprehending Mozart's aspirations, and his intentions in the operatic collaborations with Da Ponte.

A good starting-point for trying to place Mozart's experiences in context is an outline of his working life in Vienna.[2] Mozart was 25 years old before he finally broke with Salzburg, and he left the Archbishop's service in May 1781. Events over the previous years, including successes as a keyboard virtuoso and the commissioning of *Idomeneo* in Munich, hinted that an independent career was viable. Mozart's conviction was strengthened when he arrived in Vienna as part of the Archbishop's suite in March 1781. The favour of the nobility was unmistakable, and an appearance at a Tonkünstler-Societät concert suggested that wider audiences were also waiting.[3] Mozart described the event in a letter to his father dated 4 April:

[1] Entry dated 24 Dec. 1771 from *Die Leiden des jungen Werthers*, trans. by V. Lange (New York, 1949).

[2] I have previously discussed the financial aspects of Mozart's years in Vienna in 'Mozart and Poverty: A Re-examination of the Evidence', *The Musical Times*, 125 (1984), 196–201.

[3] The Tonkünstler-Societät (Musicians Benefit Society) held concerts in aid of indigent musicians and their families. The concerts were famed for their large scale, and most of the performers

I can say with truth that I was very well pleased with the Viennese public yesterday, when I played at a concert for the widows in the Kärntnerthor theatre. I had to begin all over again, because there was no end to the applause. Well, how much do you suppose I should make if I were to give a concert of my own, now that the public has got to know me?

Mozart was disappointed when prevented by official commitments from playing at the Countess Thun's residence a week later. He learned that the leading performers had been paid 50 ducats (225 gulden) for the concert, a sum that was half his annual salary in Salzburg. In his eagerness to escape from provincial service, Mozart ignored warnings that success as a virtuoso would only be transient. Ironically, it was the Archbishop's steward Count Arco, the same man who unceremoniously booted Mozart out of service, who predicted the course of events most accurately. According to Mozart's letter of June 2nd, the Count gave him this advice:

Believe me, you allow yourself to be far too easily dazzled in Vienna. A man's reputation here lasts a very short time. At first, it is true, you are overwhelmed with praises and make a great deal of money into the bargain—but how long does that last? After a few months, the Viennese want something new . . .

The season was almost over by the time Mozart left the Salzburg retinue, so it was too late to promote any public concerts. Nevertheless, he soon built up a small roster of pupils who helped to sustain him financially. He recruited his pupils largely from the female circles of the wealthy middle classes and new nobility. Lessons took up valuable time that might otherwise have been used for composing, so Mozart was forced into a rigorous routine:

Every morning at six o'clock, my friseur arrives and wakes me, and by seven I have finished dressing. I compose until ten, when I have to give a lesson to Frau von Trattner and at eleven to the Countess Rumbeck, each of whom pays me six ducats for twelve lessons, and to whom I go every day.[4]

A month later, Mozart altered the system of payments so as to ensure a regular income, as he told his father on 23 January 1782:

I have three pupils now, which brings me in eighteen ducats a month; for I no longer charge for twelve lessons, but monthly. I learnt to my cost that my pupils often dropped out for weeks at a time; so now, whether they learn or not, each of them must pay me six ducats. I shall get several more on these terms, but I really need only one more, because four pupils are quite enough. With four, I should have 24 Ducats . . .

---

appeared without fee. Mozart himself was refused admission to the Society because of difficulties about his birth certificate.

[4] Letter to Leopold Mozart dated 22 Dec. 1781.

The fee of 6 ducats (27 gulden) for a dozen lessons was comparatively high by contemporary standards. On the other hand, Mozart was much less expensive than Clementi, who charged one guinea (equivalent to 10 gulden) for each lesson. The wealthy ladies who came to Mozart only wanted lessons from the autumn until May or June each year. In the summer, they would move to their country estates, visit spas, or accompany the Court to Laxenburg.

It is doubtful whether Mozart realized his ambition of having four regular pupils. The number of keyboard students that can be identified is small, and there were periods (including the first half of 1790) when he had difficulties in finding any pupils at all.[5] Making the generous assumption that Mozart averaged three regular pupils, and that each had twelve lessons a month for six months of the year, we can estimate his annual teaching income at 486 gulden on 1782 prices. This is, however, no more than a rough approximation. Furthermore, the seasonal nature of the work meant that journeys undertaken during the winter months, such as the two visits to Prague in 1787, entailed serious losses of revenue.

An account of Mozart's teaching practice would be incomplete without mention of the small but significant band who learnt composition under his guidance. It is not clear whether he gained financially from this work, since although some pupils were members of the wealthy aristocracy, others were young boys (Thomas Attwood and Johann Nepomuk Hummel being the most celebrated). The small fee of 200 gulden charged by Leopold Mozart for teaching children of this kind suggests that the profits were meagre.[6]

In 1782, Mozart began a pattern of concert performances that continued for many years, and formed the backbone of his income. Concerts were most popular during the season of Lent, since the theatres did not operate. Mozart appeared at public concerts and privately in the salons of the nobility, playing his own works, or improvizing to the astonishment of the audience. His popularity at private functions cannot unfortunately be gauged with accuracy. These occasions were only periodically noted in letters or diaries, and they certainly occured with a greater frequency than the surviving records would imply. The dividing line between an evening salon at which music was played and an informal concert cannot be firmly drawn. The only period for which Mozart listed his engagements in detail was for the Lenten season of 1784. From the end of February, Mozart appeared on five successsive Thursdays at the residence of the Russian ambassador, Count Galitzin. Every Monday and Friday, he was engaged

---

[5] See H. W. Hamann, 'Mozarts Schülerkreis', *Mozart-Jahrbuch 1962-3*, 115–39. The problems in 1790 were mentioned in a letter Mozart wrote to Michael Puchberg in May.

[6] This is the sum mentioned by Leopold when he was considering accepting Fraulein von Hamm as a resident pupil in 1777–8.

at the Palace of Count Johann Eszterházy, while he also held three subscription concerts of his own on Wednesdays at the Trattnerhof. On 1 April, he hired the Burgtheater to give a concert for his own benefit.

This extraordinary activity reflects the fashion for instrumental music during Lent, and also indicates the level of enthusiasm felt for Mozart's keyboard gifts in the mid-1780s. It is impossible to be sure how much Mozart was paid at private functions. Certainly on some occasions the rewards were high. For instance, when Mozart competed with Clementi at the Hofburg in December 1781, Emperor Joseph gave him 225 gulden. Yet this was an exceptional event; Mozart knew only too well how the aristocracy preferred to reward musicians with snuff-boxes and watches. Even royal patrons were not always generous. Thus although he received 450 gulden for playing to the Court at Dresden in 1789, the Elector of Mainz handed over just 15 Carolins (165 gulden) for the same privilege a year later.

The number of public concerts in which Mozart participated can be estimated with more confidence. He mounted a benefit concert at the Burgtheater during the Lenten season annually from 1782 to 1786, and also appeared at the benefits of other popular musicians (such as Aloisia Lange and Nancy Storace). These occasions provided an excellent opportunity for making money, although the receipts from public concerts during this period were again variable. For example, when *Davidde penitente* (K. 469) was presented by the Tonkünstler-Societät in March 1785, ticket sales totalled 733 gulden; but for the repeat performance two days later the audience paid only 163 gulden *in toto*.[7] According to Leopold Mozart, the oboist Ludwig August Lebrun took 1,100, 900, and 500 gulden in three successive concerts. At the highest extreme, Nancy Storace is said to have made over 4,000 gulden profit from her farewell concert in Vienna.

The record of Mozart's public performances on the keyboard in Vienna is summarized in Figure 1. The total may seem small by modern standards, but publicly promoted orchestral concerts were not yet in vogue.[8] Mozart's five public appearances in 1783 included performances at concerts put on by Aloisia Lange and Therese Teyber. Between these, he gave a Burgtheater concert of his own, at which the Haffner Symphony (K. 385), the early Concerto in D major (K. 175) and the newly composed C major (K. 415) were played. Both Teyber and Lange sang arias at

---

[7] O. E. Deutsch, *Mozart: A Documentary Biography*, trans. E. Blom, P. Branscombe, and J. Noble (London, 1966), p. 240.

[8] Figure 1 includes all concerts promoted by Mozart, plus benefits and charity concerts at which he also appeared. Only occasions to which the public had access, and for which there is reasonably good evidence, are included. The record is extracted mainly from Deutsch, *Mozart*, and O. Biba, Grundzüge des Konzertwesens in Wien zu Mozarts Zeit', *Mozart-Jahrbuch 1978-9*, 132–43. Further details are to be found in E. Hanslick, *Geschichte des Concertwesens in Wien* (Vienna, 1869).

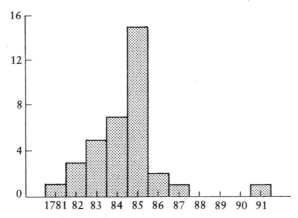

Figure 1.    Mozart's Public Performances as a Soloist in Vienna 1781–1791

Mozart's concert, thereby compensating him for his playing. The concert also included solo improvisations at the keyboard. These were an important part of any Mozart performance, for the boldness of modulation, harmonic adventurousness, and melodic charm astounded both *cognoscenti* and the general public. Contemporary accounts of his improvisatory style are tantalizingly vague, but this endearing description of his performance on the organ at Prague in 1787 gives some idea of Mozart's impact:

He now began a four-part fugue theme, which was the harder to perform in that it and its counter-subject consisted largely of mordents, which are exceptionally hard to perform on an organ with such a heavy action. . . . I concentrated my entire attention on the development of the theme, and would have been able to write it out to the end; but the late Regens Chori, Father Lohelius, then came into the choir. He disturbed me so much with his questions that I lost the entire thread, just at the moment when my attention was most necessary. Mozart had soared up so high from G minor with the pedal and left hand, that he was able to continue in B minor. Lohelius of blessed memory interrupted me at that point, so that I could not tell how he modulated so swiftly into D sharp major. And now he wanted to conclude in this key, and therefore set about making a pedal-point. Holding a B flat in the bass as his dominant, he attacked the two topmost octaves of the keyboard with both hands, . . . All his fingers were so fully employed, partly on account of the mordents, partly on account of the inner parts, that none of them was at rest for an instant, . . . Scarcely had I answered Lohelius's first questions, than a great many more had to be answered. He said, 'My brother'—'What is it?' 'He is sustaining B flat on the pedal.'—'Yes'—'He wants to modulate into D sharp major.'—'Yes, of course'—'But he is playing in B major.'—'Yes, I know'—'How can that harmonize?'—'But it does'. . . .[9]

[9] Quoted in Deutsch, *Mozart*, p. 517.

Mozart reached the peak of popular acclaim as a keyboard virtuoso in 1785. No fewer than fifteen public appearances are documented, including a Burgtheater concert and benefits for the singers Luisa Laschi and Elizabeth Distler. Leopold Mozart was fortunately present in Vienna during the 1785 season, and carefully scrutinized his son's finances. He noted with satisfaction that the Burgtheater benefit brought 559 gulden profit.

Mozart also promoted his own series of subscription concerts in 1784 and in 1785. Patrons paid a fixed sum in advance for each series, whether or not they actually attended. From the 176 subscriptions for the 1784 series proudly listed by Mozart in a letter to his father, a total deposit of 1,056 gulden can be calculated (assuming that none of the places was complimentary). The rent of the Hall was only 38 gulden, but the costs of heating and lighting, transport of instruments, tuning, and copying had also to be covered. No record survives of the amount Mozart was obliged to pay his musicians, but his contemporary Josepha Dušek paid 200 gulden to the orchestra for a single benefit concert, while Heinrich Marchand paid 115 gulden in 1785.[10] Mozart collected a subscription of 2,025 gulden for his six Friday evening Mehlgrube concerts in Lent 1785, and a further unknown sum for the three concerts hastily mounted in the autumn of that year.

The success of these years led to an increasingly expansive way of living. Mozart and Constanze were married in 1782, and for the first eighteen months they lived in a series of lodgings in the inner city. Then in January 1784, they moved to the Trattnerhof in the Graben. This huge building was the centre of Johann Trattner's papermaking business (see Plate 5). The lodging cost 130 gulden a year, but within a few months the couple moved to an even larger apartment on the Schulerstrasse. It consisted of four rooms apart from the domestic services, and the rent was 480 gulden—a little more than Mozart's entire salary in Salzburg. It was kept for more than two years, and marked the apex of Mozart and Constanze's material success. It may have been during this period that Mozart bought his expensive modern fortepiano with pedal (probably worth 900 gulden).[11] Even Leopold was optimistic, as he told his daughter in a letter dated 9th March 1785:

If he has no debts to pay, I think that my son can now lodge two thousand gulden in the bank. Certainly the money is there, and so far as eating and drinking is concerned, the housekeeping is extremely economical.

The composer's good fortune did not last, however, and Count Arco's

---

[10] See C. Bär, 'Er war . . . kein guter Wirth', *Acta Mozartiana*, 25 (1978), 30–53.
[11] Bär, 'Er war', p. 37.

prophecy was soon fulfilled. As Figure 1 indicates, Mozart suffered a catastrophic decline in popularity in 1786. The public lost interest in his skills as a performer. He gave his last Burgtheater concert in Lent, presenting a new concerto in C minor (K. 491). But the only other concert in which he may have performed was the benefit mounted by Josepha Dušek. She was an old acquaintance of Mozart, but lived in Prague, so may therefore have been unaware that his style was no longer fashionable in the capital. Although some of his orchestral works were performed, it is notable that he was not involved as a soloist in any of the benefits given by Viennese singers.[12] Not one single appearance as a soloist is documented between 1788 and 1790. Mozart's attempt to promote a series of concerts in 1789 failed miserably, since only Gottfried van Swieten was willing to subscribe.

Mozart was buffered from the loss of concert revenue by two other developments: the purchase of his compositions by publishers and his entry into the field of Italian Opera. Stanley Sadie has suggested that much of the music written after 1786 may have been planned with a view to publication, and this may account for the high proportion of chamber works.[13] Once again, however, there is little information about fees. The publisher Artaria is known to have paid 100 ducats (450 gulden) for the six 'Haydn' Quartets in 1785, but other records are lacking. Mozart received few known commissions for non-operatic works. The fee from his anonymous patron for the *Requiem* is said to have been 270 gulden, but this may be hearsay. He is reputed to have been paid 100 Friedrichs d'or (700 to 800 gulden) by Kaiser Friedrich Wilhelm for the first (K. 575) of a projected set of string quartets commissioned in 1789, although documentary evidence is again unavailable.

The most substantial fees were undoubtedly paid for operas. Mozart earned 450 gulden each for *Die Entführung* and *Le nozze di Figaro*, and half that sum for *Der Schauspieldirektor*. The combined Prague and Vienna fees for *Don Giovanni* totalled 675 gulden. An exceptional 900 gulden, double the Burgtheater's standard rate, is said to have been paid for *Così fan tutte*. The official Burgtheater records for this period are missing, so authority for this lies in a letter Mozart wrote to Michael Puchberg in 1790; in this letter, the high fee is used by Mozart as an argument for being lent more money. Nevertheless, Paisiello received

[12] The information concerning concerts in Vienna during Mozart's time there has been diligently examined by M. S. Morrow, 'Mozart and Viennese Concert Life', *The Musical Times*, 126 (1985), 453–54. She argues that the lack of positive identifications of performances by Mozart does not imply that he was absent from the concert platform. However, she has failed to uncover any hitherto unknown concerts at which he played as a soloist.

[13] S. Sadie, *The New Grove Mozart*, (London, 1982), 113. Mozart's publishing activities and appearances in contemporary anthologies are documented by A. H. King, in *A Mozart Legacy*, (London, 1984).

1,350 gulden (300 ducats) for his Vienna opera of 1784, so extra fees were not unknown. 450 gulden were again probably paid for *La clemenza di Tito*, while Mozart may have received benefits or a share in the profits of *Die Zauberflöte*.

Opera commissions thus became increasingly important to Mozart's financial well-being, compensating for the loss of earnings as a performer. Yet his change in circumstances could not be completely disguised. The disenchantment of the Viennese audiences forced Mozart and Constanze to leave their Schulerstrasse apartment in the spring of 1787, and move to a garden house in the Landstrasse suburb. The rent here was only 50 gulden, compared with the 460 gulden paid previously. The physical separation of the suburb from the city may not have been large, but it represented a serious social disadvantage (see Plate 6). The couple were now compelled to find cheap lodgings in the suburbs each summer (when there were no pupils to be visited), only returning to the city in the autumn. Nevertheless, a series of events in the later 1780s augmented Mozart's revenue. His father Leopold died in May 1787, triggering not only great grief, but a reappraisal of his attitude to life and adulthood. The estate was divided with his sister Maria Anna, and Mozart's share was 1,000 gulden. Later in the year, the fourth Prague performance of *Don Giovanni* was given over to a benefit for the composer. Benefits of this type could be highly profitable, and Mozart received the proceeds of another opera performance in 1788, when his arrangement of Handel's *Acis and Galatea* was mounted by Gottfried van Swieten and other devotees of classical music. On each occasion, the profit may have amounted to several hundred gulden.

Finally, in 1787, Mozart was awarded the one and only fixed salary of his maturity, when he was appointed Imperial kammermusicus. His annual stipend was 800 gulden. The salary was low in comparison to the 2,000 gulden paid to Gluck as the previous intendant, although Gluck of course had very special status in Vienna at the end of his life. It also compared unfavourably with payments to other leading musicians. Christian Cannabich was earning 1,800 gulden shortly before 1780 as kapellmeister at Mannheim, while Dittersdorf's salary rose to 2,700 gulden over his period of service. On the other hand, Mozart's 800 gulden was considerably more than the typical salary of an ordinary musician. The average stipend of members of the Eszterháza orchestra was less than 400 gulden, although some, such as the violoncellist Kraft and the leader Tomasini, received rather more.[14] Leopold Mozart's salary

---

[14] These musicians were paid 680 gulden, plus a lodging subsidy, candles, wood, and uniforms. The 1790 salaries are detailed in H. C. Robbins Landon, *Haydn, Chronicle and Works*, ii (London, 1978), 70.

was 350 gulden a year, while Mozart himself earned only 450 gulden during his final years in Salzburg. Moreover, Mozart was not expected to live on his salary alone, and the amount of work required did not reflect the demands of a full-time post. The position of kammermusicus seems, in fact, to have been superfluous, being a personal appointment rather than an essential component of the Imperial household. It had few obligations, apart from writing dances for the Court. After Mozart's death, two musicians applied for the post but were rejected, and the title was discontinued. Count Ugarte, the Hof Musik Graf, wrote that Mozart had been employed 'solely out of consideration that so rare a genius in the world of music should not be obliged to seek abroad for recognition and his daily bread'.[15] In the light of the modest duties imposed on the kammermusicus, it was Gluck rather than Mozart who received the exceptional salary.

In any event, neither operas, benefits, nor salary prevented Mozart from attempting more desperate remedies for his artistic and financial situation in Vienna. In April 1789, he set out on a tour of German States in the company of Prince Karl Lichnowsky, son-in-law of his early Viennese patron, the Countess Thun. Mozart's ill-judged and unprofitable visit to the Prussian Court has already been described in Chapter 2, but Leipzig and Dresden were more congenial. Leipzig in particular, with its famous coffee houses and booksellers, was guaranteed to appeal to an enlightenment intellect. Mozart's public concert there took the usual Viennese form, with two concertos, symphonies, vocal scena sung by Josepha Dušek, and solo keyboard pieces. Yet as Mozart told Constanze in a letter dated 16 May 1789, 'From the point of view of applause and glory this concert was absolutely magnificent, but the profits were wretchedly meagre'.

Mozart undertook another journey in 1790, travelling to Frankfurt where Joseph II's successor Leopold was to be crowned Emperor. After his long residence in Tuscany, Leopold had absorbed Italian tastes in music, so the coronation was dominated by the works of Righini and Salieri. Mozart therefore had no official role, but he promoted his own concert in the Theatre. It must have been a gloomy affair; only five or six violins could be mustered for the orchestra, and there were long pauses between the works. It lasted from 11 a.m. until 2 p.m., even without the last symphony. By this time, the small audience was impatient for dinner, so the music was abandoned.[16]

1791 marked a revival in Mozart's fortunes in Vienna, after years of disappointment. For the first time since 1786, he performed a concerto at

---

[15] Quoted in Deutsch, *Mozart*, p. 430.
[16] See Deutsch, *Mozart*, p. 375 for a contemporary account.

a public concert. The work (K. 595) was a success, and was published by Artaria later in the year. Orchestral and vocal compositions were also included at a Tonkünstler-Societät concert in April, while later in the year *La clemenza di Tito* and *Die Zauberflöte* were staged. The latter in particular brought a new public into contact with Mozart's works. Produced at the suburban Theater auf der Wieden (Freihaustheater) instead of the Burgtheater, it received more performances in Vienna during the autumn alone than did any *opera buffa* throughout Mozart's whole lifetime. Segments of the work were quickly published, both in manuscript and engraving. But for his untimely death, the next few years might have been much more prosperous for Mozart[17].

This sketch of Mozart's career and sources of income in Vienna indicates that his position fluctuated widely. Yet he was never quite without resource. The question remains: did his periodic insolvency derive then from some character flaw, his carelessness or fecklessness, or were external circumstances responsible? Over the years, a variety of explanations have been offered.

## Mozart's Lifestyle, Standard of Living, and Debts

Leopold Mozart was financially astute and fastidiously precise about money. He attempted to instil a similar feeling into his son, constantly exhorting him to make material success his prime aim in life, as in this letter dated 15 October 1777:

> You must not lose sight of your main object, which is to make money. All your endeavours should thus be directed to earning money, and you should be very careful to spend as little as possible.

This training evidently had little effect. In Paris, Baron Grimm had ample opportunity to observe the young Mozart, and told Leopold:

> He is too trusting, too inactive, too easy to catch, too little intent on the means that may lead to fortune. To make an impression here one has to be artful, enterprising, daring. To make his fortune I wish he had but half his talent and twice as much shrewdness, and then I should not worry about him.[18]

When Mozart finally abandoned Salzburg for Vienna in 1781, he filled his letters home with suitable resolutions:

---

[17] Mozart was not the only composer who worked for the suburban Singspiel companies. Dittersdorf, Salieri, and Martín y Soler also wrote for German companies, or adapted their Italian works. For a discussion of the vigour and success of this tradition, see E. M. Batley, *A Preface to The Magic Flute* (London, 1969), 70.

[18] Quoted in Deutsch, *Mozart*, p. 177.

Believe me, my sole purpose is to make as much money as possible; for after good health it is the best thing to have.[19]

But Leopold Mozart soon realised that his son lacked determination in the quest for wordly success:

He is far too patient or rather easy-going, too indolent, perhaps even too proud, in short, . . . he has the sum total of all those traits which render a man inactive; on the other hand, he is too impatient, too hasty and will not bide his time. . . . If he is not actually in want, then he is immediately satisfied and becomes indolent and lazy. If he has to bestir himself, then he realizes his worth and wants to make his fortune at once.[20]

Mozart's biographers have reached diverse conclusions about the reasons behind the financial instability that forms such a tortured backdrop to his years in Vienna. Franz Xaver Niemetschek, the early Bohemian commentator, argued that the expenses of living in Vienna, coupled with the slanders of jealous rivals, were responsible for the composer's parlous state:

It is true that he often earned considerable sums, but with an insecure and irregular income, added to the frequent accouchements and lengthy illnesses of his wife in an expensive town like Vienna, Mozart in fact very nearly starved. . . . As it was impossible to belittle his greatness as an artist, ill-natured people tried to defame his moral character.[21]

Alfred Einstein on the other hand laid the blame firmly on Constanze Mozart's fecklessness:

She was not even a good housewife. She never looked ahead, and instead of making her husband's life and work easier by providing him with external comforts she thoughtlessly shared the bohemianism of his way of living.[22]

Rather different inferences have been drawn by Uwe Kraemer.[23] Generalizing from the limited documentary evidence available, Kraemer has argued that far from being poor, Mozart regularly earned large sums throughout his adult life. However, he frittered away the money on billiards and gambling at faro. These vices were later concealed by Constanze through a shrewd suppression of undesirable material, and it was she who cosmetically created Mozart's unblemished posthumous

---

[19] Letter to Leopold Mozart dated 4 Apr. 1781.
[20] Letter to Baroness von Waldstädten dated 23 Aug. 1782.
[21] F. X. Niemetschek, *The Life of Mozart*, trans. by H. Mautner, (London, 1956), 39, 49.
[22] A. Einstein, *Mozart: His Character—his Works*, trans. A. Mendel and N. Broder (London, 1971), 81. The sexism of Einstein's remarks is astounding, but it is shared in the more recent account by W. Hildesheimer, *Mozart*, trans. M. Faber, (London, 1983). Here is Hildesheimer's verdict on Constanze Mozart (p. 253): She yielded to her drives, loved pleasure, was totally impressionable and therefore, of course, very adaptable; she 'went along with everything'.
[23] U. Kraemer, 'Wer hat Mozart verhungern lassen?', *Musica*, 30 (1976), 203–11.

reputation. In partial agreement with this thesis, Rudolph Angermüller suggested that Mozart spent large sums trying to emulate the lifestyle of his aristocratic friends.[24]

The summary of Mozart's resources provided earlier in the chapter allows us to calculate his income with some degree of confidence. If Mozart and Constanze's outgoings are then examined, it ought to be possible to come to reasoned conclusions concerning these alternative explanations. Although the records are incomplete, it is clear that Mozart's earnings were high during his early years in Vienna. Without including payment for private performances, his revenue in 1784 and 1785 must have exceeded 4,000 gulden. Appearances at the concerts and salons organized by the nobility may perhaps have supplemented this income by as much as 40 per cent.[25] In his most prosperous period, Mozart not only lodged in the Schulerstrasse, but could afford to employ a friseur, two serving-women, and a cook. But this state of affairs did not last. The abrupt reduction in concert fees after 1785 was never restored by payments for operas and other works. After 1787, his average income from teaching, composition, salary, and miscellaneous other sources may never have been more than 3,000 gulden; it is probable that revenue from private functions was correspondingly reduced.[26]

Nevertheless, even during the lean periods, Mozart's income was adequate for survival. Mozart's poverty was never desperate, in the sense of imminent starvation or homelessness. Many people lived decently on earnings that were well below his level. Professional people were often miserably paid; teachers in Prussian schools earned 300 to 600 gulden, while the salary of a primary school teacher in Austria was only 100 gulden.

Mozart and Constanze did not, however, move in such circles. The question is not whether they had sufficient money to survive, but whether their income was commensurate with the position they maintained in society. The appropriate comparison is with the standards and lifestyle adopted by friends and colleagues. The actors and singers of the Burgtheater figured prominently among Mozart's acquaintance, as will become clear in Chapter 4. He and Constanze were on friendly terms with the leading players, including Johann Müller, the Stephanie brothers, and Friedrich Schröder (the 'German Garrick'), together with Nancy

---

[24] R. Angermüller, *'Auf Ehre und Credit': Die Finanzen des W. A. Mozart* (Munich, 1983).

[25] Kraemer's estimates for income from performances at private functions are somewhat inflated. They are based on the fees paid at the exceptional occasions in 1781 described earlier, and not on more mundane gatherings.

[26] Bär, 'Er war', has also conducted a detailed examination of Mozart's income, and reaches similar conclusions to those presented here. He estimates that Mozart's total income over the last six years of his life was 12,000 gulden (2,000 annually). Both estimates are well below Kraemer's calculations.

Storace, Michael Kelly, and other members of the Opera company. As in the case of instrumental musicians, stage performers were expected to supplement their salaries by private appearances. But even their fixed stipends exceeded those of all but the wealthiest kapellmeister. For example, Joseph Lange (the husband of Constanze's sister Aloisia) earned 1,400 gulden, while Müller and the elder Stephanie received 1,600.[27] The highest-paid actor was Schröder, who played in Vienna during the early 1780s for 2,500 gulden per annum. If anything, singers were even better off. Aloisia Weber was offered 1,000 gulden on moving to Munich when she was still very young, while Michael Kelly recalled that his salary in Vienna was 2,000 gulden, plus lodging, fuel, and 4 wax candles per day. At the highest extreme, Joseph II instructed the Burgtheater directorate to offer Nancy Storace no less than 1,000 ducats (4,500 gulden) to tempt her back to Vienna following her departure in 1787.[28]

Moreover, the gratuities awarded both to singers and actors were disproportionately high. This was apparent at the Schönbrunn entertainment in 1786 for which Mozart composed *Der Schauspieldirektor*. His Singspiel was interspersed with scenes from plays in the Burgtheater repertoire, and Salieri also wrote a short *opera buffa*. The occasion was considered a special engagement for the actors and singers, although they were already under contract. So all those who took part, including the Stephanie brothers, Joseph and Aloisia Lange, Francesco Benucci, and Nancy Storace were paid 225 gulden—the same amount that Mozart received, not merely for performing but for composing the music.

Incomes among Mozart's acquaintances were therefore quite considerable, for his social network included prominent merchants and professional families as well as artists. Nor was Vienna a cheap place to live. The actor Müller rented an apartment for 700 gulden, while the younger Stephanie (librettist of *Die Entführung*) paid 500 gulden for a smaller lodging near the Michaelerplatz. Clothes were also expensive. Men's silk stockings cost 5 gulden, and 9 pairs were listed among Mozart's effects on his death. A man's suit or coat cost between 30 and 50 gulden, and 100 might easily be paid for a good lady's dress. Shoes, hair, and pomade were all very dear, although the cost of food and servants was modest.[29]

---

[27] See E. Wlassack, *Chronik des K. K. Hof-Burgtheaters* (Vienna, 1976), for details of actors' incomes in Vienna.

[28] Kelly later states that his performance in Paisiello's opera *Il rè Teodoro* so pleased the Emperor that his salary was increased by 100 zecchini (*c.* 500 gulden). The instruction concerning Nancy Storace is contained in a memorandum from Joseph II to Count Rosenberg dated 11 June 1788. Quoted by R. Payer von Thurn, *Joseph II als Theaterdirektor* (Vienna, 1920). Castrati enjoyed even higher salaries. In Salzburg, the castrato Ceccarelli was paid 800 gulden, compared with Mozart's 450 gulden in the late 1770s. When Marchesi was engaged in London for the 1789 season, he was paid £1,500 (the equivalent of 15,000 gulden).

[29] The price of clothes and other items is discussed in W. H. Bruford, *Theatre, Drama and*

Mozart's laſt years were also burdened with extra expenses such as doctors' and apothecaries' bills. Both he and Constanze suffered severe illnesses during these years, and on the composer's death, some 180 gulden were owed to different apothecaries. Carl Bär has estimated that Constanze's Baden cures alone cost 500 gulden.

When these prices are taken into account, Mozart's financial position can be placed in a clearer perspective. He and Constanze lived in comparatively expensive circles, since they consorted with a wealthy section of urban society. Their success in maintaining this status depended both on the popularity of Mozart's art, and upon his health. For with little guaranteed income, continuous hard work was needed to ensure the family's survival. As Leopold Mozart noted so ardently in a letter written on 11 December 1777.

I now close with the hope that God may keep you in good health, for which I pray to Him constantly, and with the earnest reminder that you must take the greatest care of it. For a breakdown would be our most crushing misfortune and would plunge us all into the deepest misery.

The evidence therefore suggests that claims about Mozart's prodigality have been exaggerated. In addition, the tragic impression of poverty gained from the letters to Michael Puchberg is misleading. Armed with estimates of Mozart's income during his maturity, we can begin to appraise his correspondence with Puchberg more critically.

Mozart's dealings with Puchberg may have commenced in 1787, although his first surviving letters date from 1788. Puchberg was a Freemason, and Mozart's early requests stress the bond of mutual aid and comfort:

I have now opened my whole heart to you in a matter which is of the utmost importance to me; that is, I have acted as a true brother. But it is only with a true brother that one can be perfectly frank. And now I look forward eagerly to your reply, which I do hope will be favourable. . . . I take you to be a man who, . . . will like myself certainly assist a friend, if he be a true friend, or his brother, if he be indeed a brother.[30]

Over the next year however, Mozart's tone changed to one of desperation, so that on 12 July 1789 he wrote:

Great God! I would not wish my worst enemy to be in my present position. And if you, most beloved friend and brother, forsake me, we are altogether lost, both my unfortunate and blameless self and my poor sick wife and child.

---

*Audience in Goethe's Germany* (London, 1950). The *Eipeldauerbriefe* suggest that food would cost only 1–2 gulden a day for the whole family. As for wages, a cook could expect between 12 and 30 gulden per annum, plus lodging; under-servants would earn less. Mozart and Constanze paid their servant Liserl Schwemmer 12 gulden per annum year in 1784.

[30] Letter to Puchberg sent before 17 June 1788.

At times, the composer's self-respect deserted him completely, as he begged for pittances, as on 14 August 1790:

In a week or a fortnight I shall be better off—certainly—but at present I am in want! Can you not help me out with a trifle? The smallest sum would be very welcome just now. You would, for the moment at least, bring peace of mind to your friend, servant and brother.

Yet it is easy to be misled by these appeals for assistance. They loom large in our impression of Mozart's last years only because of Puchberg's thoroughness in preserving his correspondence (which may have been used in his accounting system). Puchberg noted the sum of money sent in reply at the bottom of each letter. He sent cash to Mozart intermittently and only on demand, and rarely in amounts larger than 200 gulden. The accumulated loan for 1788 was 300 gulden, 450 gulden for 1789, and 610 gulden in 1790. These are minor sums in comparison even with the most pessimistic computations of the composer's income. In 1788, for example, Mozart's salary, his earnings from *Don Giovanni* and the benefit performance of *Acis and Galatea*, together with income from lessons and publishers, almost certainly totalled more than ten times the total lent by Puchberg. In no year did Puchberg's loans amount to more than 15 or 20 per cent of Mozart's revenue.

Indeed, Puchberg did not permit Mozart's debts to mount substantially, since he refused to lend on a large scale. Mozart proposed that their dealings be raised to a much higher level in June 1788:

If you have sufficient regard and friendship for me to assist me for a year or two with one or two thousand gulden, at a suitable rate of interest, you will help me enormously!

Similarly in May 1790, Mozart almost wistfully mentioned the sum of 600 gulden. Neither appeal was successful, and Puchberg continued with his piecemeal assistance. Puchberg was also shrewd in the timing of his generosity. One of the largest single loans (for 300 gulden) was sent to Mozart at the end of 1789, just at the time that payment for *Così fan tutte* was imminent. Puchberg may have been encouraged by the especially large commission Mozart claimed he was to receive for this opera.

It seems therefore that Mozart looked to Puchberg only under special circumstances. He importuned his brother in the Craft when he was in acute need of small sums, knowing that his requests would be granted with the minimum of formality or security (the question of interest was never raised for these small loans). Most of Mozart's demands were made during the summer months or periods of illness, when other sources of finance were difficult to mobilize. Mozart was fortunate to have such a friend, in view of the chronic shortage of credit in Austria during the 1780s. Interest rates were high, partly because of Emperor Joseph's seizure of capital assets from private funds, and partly because of the repeal of the usury laws in 1787.[31] Additional burdens, such as the special War Tax imposed late in the decade, put further pressure on the borrower.

The financial difficulties Mozart encountered late in his life were almost inevitable for an artist reliant on irregular sources, who was in ill health and, at the same time, somewhat unpopular. It is not necessary to infer that Mozart and Constanze were profligate or extravagant in order to account for their predicament. She in particular has received an excessive degree of blame. Her supposed thriftlessness and caprice are hard to reconcile with her financial shrewdness as a widow. Poverty was an ever-present threat in eighteenth-century Austria, and death of the head of a family frequently brought ruin. Even for those who enjoyed a regular salary, pensions were meagre. When the Salzburg Cathedral organist Anton Kajetan Adlgasser died in 1777, he had been employed for more than fifteen years; yet his family received a pension of only 8 gulden a month for one year.[32] Constanze, however, negotiated tenaciously with publishers and the State in order to ensure the future of her family. She persisted in demands for a State pension, although Mozart had not completed the necessary period of Imperial service, and was eventually granted one-third of her husband's salary by the Exchequer. In addition, she and her advisers secured substantial payments for Mozart's remaining manuscripts over the decade following his death.

Mozart and Constanze certainly endured periods of acute shortage. But it is sobering to remember that affluence was fragile; Michael Puchberg, Paisiello, Boccherini, and Dittersdorf were all wealthy and successful in their maturity, yet ended their lives in poverty. Mozart's unconventional career obliged him to be self-sufficient. His security depended entirely on how hard he worked. It was the price he paid for independence.

## Circumstances and Creativity

Since Mozart evidently relied on his own effort, activity, and skill to survive, it is important to know whether his productivity was affected by the financial straits and domestic concerns that afflicted him. Mozart was a prolific composer, and the sheer weight of his output leaves an impression of facility and fluency. Not only was he highly productive, but he could also write extremely rapidly. For example, during the composition of *Die Entführung* (October 1781), he declared that:

What would at other times require fourteen days to write I could do now in four.

[31] E. Wangermann, *From Joseph II to the Jacobin Trials* (London, 1959), 26.
[32] Details in a letter from Leopold Mozart dated 25 Feb. 1778.

I composed in one day Adamberger's aria in A, Cavalieri's in B♭ and the trio, and copied them out in a day and a half.

It was once thought that Mozart composed *La clemenza di Tito* in less than three weeks. He apparently began working on the score late in August 1791, and the première was on 6 September. Evidence from paper-typing now suggests that several ensembles and at least one aria were written somewhat earlier.[33] Nevertheless, the rate of composition was still remarkable, considering the other ventures he was tackling at the same time.

Yet this facility must be put in perspective. Our present-day attitudes to artistic creativity are conditioned by the tortuous soul-searching of nineteenth-century composers, some of whom would be delighted to produce a single symphony in a year. In Mozart's time, many musicians wrote at great speed, completing works only days before the performance was due. The prolific nature of Haydn's working life is well known. Dittersdorf too managed to compose one Italian and three German operas during his eighteen-month sojourn in Vienna (1785–7). Moreover, although on occasion Mozart wrote rapidly, other compositions were considered for long periods. The six 'Haydn' Quartets occupied him irregularly for three to four years, and were subject to extensive revisions. Indeed, on close examination, large fluctuations in his rate of composition emerge. It becomes clear that Mozart went through periods of comparative creative sterility. Fortunately, with the aid of Köchel's monumental catalogue, Mozart's own record of compositions during his Vienna years, and more recent investigations, it is possible to construct a relatively accurate picture of when pieces were completed.

The pattern of major works completed during Mozart's Vienna period is summarized in Table 3. The total number of compositions is shown for three four-month periods in each year. The first, January to April, covers the major instrumental performing season, through the Carnival and Lent. The second segment includes the summer months, when musical activity was attenuated, while the final third runs through the autumn season from September to December. It is clear from this division that the rate at which Mozart completed large-scale works varied markedly. Despite his creative fertility, he did not sustain a steady level of composition; the number of major pieces written within any four-month period fluctuated between zero and eight.[34]

---

[33] See A. Tyson, '*La clemenza di Tito* and its chronology', *The Musical Times*, 116 (1975), 221–7.

[34] The present discussion is based on L. von Köchel, *Chronologisch-thematisches Verzeichnis sämtlicher Tonwerke Wolfgang Amadé Mozarts*, 6 edn., ed. F. Giegling, A. Weinmann, and G. Sievers (Wiesbaden, 1964). Attention has also been paid to the alterations in chronology implied

Before considering the influence of pressures such as financial exigency, failure with the public, and ill health, a number of other explanations of this pattern may be relevant. The variations in output could perhaps be accounted for by seasonal effects, except that there is no systematic variation with time of year. A second possibility is that the pattern is a product of the size of the works composed at different times. Again, this can be rejected as a general explanation, since the pieces composed in Mozart's more fertile periods were as substantial as those written at other times.[35] There is, however, an important exception to this rule. The largest-scale compositions of all were the operas, and these do seem to have absorbed all Mozart's energies. They have been omitted from Table 3, but their timing is pertinent. *Don Giovanni* was produced in October 1787, *Così fan tutte* in January 1790, and *Die Zauberflöte* in the late summer of 1791. In each case, little else was written during the adjacent months. Mozart's concentration seems to have been focused almost entirely on the opera, to the exclusion of other work.[36]

---

by paper-typing studies detailed in A. Tyson, 'The Mozart fragments in the Mozarteum, Salzburg: A Preliminary Study of their Chronology and Significance', *Journal of the American Musicological Society*, 34 (1981), 471–510. It is of course difficult to give an accurate estimate of work rate, since compositions vary enormously in size and complexity: anything from a single song of 30 bars to an opera might be entered by Mozart as an independent work, and appear separately in Köchel's taxonomy. The method of assessing output that perhaps introduces the least distortion is to limit consideration to large works: only longer pieces, or those in more than one movement, have been included for the present purposes. Inevitably, this excludes some small works of great beauty and importance, such as the *Ave verum corpus* of June 1791. Some further points should be noted about the pattern outlined in Table 3. Firstly, arias written for insertion into the operas of other composers have been excluded, since many of them are relatively slight works. Secondly, the Handel orchestrations have been omitted; they may have absorbed a good deal of time, but scarcely required the mobilization of great creative resources. Thirdly, the abundant sets of dances that Mozart wrote at various times are not considered: the eighteenth-century composer was expected to produce such works without compunction, and Mozart is unlikely to have expended much energy upon them (but see note 35, below). Incidentally, the picture that emerges is quite different from that painted by Leo Schrade in *W. A. Mozart* (Bern, 1964). Dividing Mozart's life into four-year periods, he was able to show a consistent rate of composition, evidently as a result of selecting a long time interval—a great deal can happen in four years. In conclusion, it should be pointed out that the pattern detailed for 1784 may not be accurate. Mozart probably did not begin his catalogue until late 1784, and may have entered the first items retrospectively. See D. Leeson and D. Whitwell, 'Mozart's Thematic Catalogue', *The Musical Times*, 114 (1973), 781–3.

[35] There are perhaps two periods in which the pattern is somewhat distorted by the omission of smaller-scale works. One is the summer and autumn of 1789, when Mozart wrote several arias for insertion into operas being produced at the Burgtheater, so that his output was not quite as low as Table 3 might suggest. The second was the spring of 1791, when some ten sets of dances were composed.

[36] *Le nozze di Figaro* is anomalous in this respect, since it appeared during a comparatively abundant period in the late spring of 1786. However, there is evidence that much of the opera was composed during the autumn of the preceding year—see Introduction and the discussion of this issue in the *Neue Ausgabe sämtliche Werke*, ed. L. Finscher (Kassel, 1973). The hiatus in output evident in 1785 is consistent with this possibility; between May and the end of Aug. only the Fantasia in C minor (K. 475) was completed. This supports the contention that it was the composition of operas, rather than their production, that drained Mozart's creativity.

TABLE 3.  MAJOR COMPOSITIONS COMPLETED BY MOZART BETWEEN 1784 AND 1791

| Year | Period | No. of major works |
|------|--------|--------------------|
| 1784 | Jan. – Apr. | 6 |
|      | May – Aug. | 0 |
|      | Sept. – Dec. | 4 |
| 1785 | Jan. – Apr. | 5 |
|      | May – Aug. | 1 |
|      | Sept. – Dec. | 4 |
| 1786 | Jan. – Apr. | 3 |
|      | May – Aug. | 6 |
|      | Sept. – Dec. | 4 |
| 1787 | Jan. – Apr. | 1 |
|      | May – Aug. | 3 |
|      | Sept. – Dec. | 1 |
| 1788 | Jan. – Apr. | 2 |
|      | May – Aug. | 8 |
|      | Sept. – Dec. | 2 |
| 1789 | Jan. – Apr. | 1 |
|      | May – Aug. | 2 |
|      | Sept. – Dec. | 1 |
| 1790 | Jan. – Apr. | 0 |
|      | May – Aug. | 2 |
|      | Sept. – Dec. | 2 |
| 1791 | Jan. – Apr. | 2 |
|      | May – Aug. | 1 |
|      | Sept. – Dec. | 2 |

These factors cannot account entirely for the fluctuations in output, suggesting that Mozart's personal experiences may have provoked some variations in productivity. On cursory examination, this notion may seem improbable. For example, between 1783 and 1791, the couple had six children, four of whom died in infancy after living less than six months. Yet neither births nor deaths coincided with troughs in musical activity, even though they may have caused great emotional upheaval. From his earliest years, Mozart apparently possessed iron detachment. During the family's travels through Holland in 1765, Mozart's sister developed pneumonia and was near death. Leopold Mozart told a friend:

I prepared her to resign herself to God's will . . . she was often so weak that she could hardly utter what she wanted to say. Whoever could have listened to the conversations, . . . during which we convinced her of the vanity of this world and the happy death of children, would not have heard it without tears. Meanwhile, little Wolfgang in the next room was amusing himself with his music.[37]

There is also a well-known story that Mozart worked on the Quartet in D minor (K. 421) while Constanze gave birth to their first child in a nearby room. Commentators have made much of this, using it as an illustration of Mozart's extraordinary concentration and detachment, the 'callousness of genius' as Eric Blom called it.[38] Yet the incident should be put in perspective. Husbands did not participate in labour or birth-scenes, and Mozart's work is better viewed as a displacement activity than a sign of insensitivity.

A more remarkable case is the summer of 1788, when conditions of exceptional difficulty did not prevent a prolific outpouring of great music. Early in June, Mozart wrote to Michael Puchberg begging for more money, even though he was already in debt:

Your true friendship and brotherly love embolden me to ask a great favour of you. I still owe you eight ducats. Apart from the fact that at the moment I am not in a position to pay you back this sum, my confidence in you is so boundless that I dare to implore you to help me out with a hundred gulden until next week, when my concerts at the Casino are to begin. By that time I shall certainly have received my subscription money.

There is no record that these concerts ever took place. The subscription refers not to the concerts, but to the three string quintets (K. 406, 515, and 516) that Mozart was trying to publish at 4 ducats (18 gulden) a copy. The subscription was a failure, and Mozart was eventually obliged to sell the quintets to Artaria for publication. On 17 June, Mozart and his family moved again from the inner city to the cheaper suburbs, and about this time another letter went to Puchberg:

I beg you to lend me until tomorrow at least a couple of hundred gulden, as my landlord in the Landstrasse has been so importunate that in order to avoid an unpleasant incident I have had to pay him on the spot, and this has made things very awkward for me!

---

[37] Letter from Leopold Mozart dated 5 Nov. 1765.
[38] See E. Blom, *Mozart* (London, 1974).

The Landstrasse landlord's impatience is not surprising, in view of the fact that Mozart had left that lodging the previous autumn. Puchberg sent 200 gulden in reply, but even this was insufficient, since ten days later, Mozart wrote again:

I am very much distressed that your circumstances at the moment prevent you from assisting me as much as I could wish, for my position is so serious that I am unavoidably obliged to raise money somehow. But good God, in whom can I confide? In no one but you, my best friend.[39]

Yet only the day before, Mozart had completed the Symphony in E♭ (K. 543), having already written the Piano Trio in E major (K. 542) earlier in the month.

Two days later, Mozart's daughter Theresia died after six months of life. Although infant mortality was high in this period, few parents were insensitive to such tragedies.[40] Nor were Mozart's troubles purely personal. All Vienna was in turmoil because the bakers were holding back the sale of cheap rye breads in anticipation of the removal of statutory price limits.[41] Thus only expensive white rolls were available. In July, matters came to such a pass that there were riots in the city as hungry crowds looted the bakeries. Mozart's own fortunes declined even more at the beginning of July, as he told Puchberg:

Owing to great difficulties and complications my affairs have become so involved that it is of the utmost importance to raise some money on these two pawnbroker's tickets. In the name of our friendship I implore you to do me this favour; but you must do it immediately.

Despite all these privations, Mozart continued in a mood of unparalleled creative activity, with the Symphony in G minor being completed on 25 July, and the Symphony in C major on 10 August. It is likely that the first two movements of the last piano concerto (K. 595) were also written during the summer, possibly in anticipation of the projected concert series.[42] Other works emerged during these months, including a piano trio, a keyboard sonata, and the set of canons (K. 553–562). Although the latter are minor works, they seem to reflect a mood of high spirits and conviviality that is very distant from the despairing tone of the letters. The texts of the canons were written by Mozart himself, and illustrate his typically scatological humour. The testimony of

[39] Letter to Michael Puchberg dated 27 June 1788.

[40] See L. Stone, *The Family, Sex and Marriage in England 1500–1800* (London, 1977), for descriptions of grief in the eighteenth century. Parents' care and concern for children has been discussed in detail by L. Pollock, *Forgotten Children: Parent-Child Relations from 1500–1800* (Cambridge, 1983).

[41] Wangermann, *From Joseph II*, p. 30.

[42] Tyson, 'La clemenza di Tito and its chronology'. See H. C. Robbins London, *Mozart's Last Year* (London, 1988) for a discussion of whether the concert series actually took place.

a Danish visitor also confirms that Mozart was far from despondent at the time:

Sunday August 24th . . . In the afternoon, Jünger, Lange and Werner came to fetch me to go to Kapellmeister Mozardt's. There I had the happiest hour of music that has ever fallen to my lot. This small man and great master twice extemporised on a pedal pianoforte so wonderfully! so wonderfully! that I quite lost myself. He intertwined the most difficult passages with the most lovely themes. His wife cut quill-pens for the copyist, a pupil composed, a little boy aged four walked about in the garden and sang recitatives–in short, everything that surrounded this splendid man was musical![43]

We might conclude from this example that personal tragedies and acute privations did nothing to stem Mozart's creative vigour. However, this is not to say that Mozart was impervious to circumstance. The output from the summer of 1788 was exceptional even by Mozart's standards, and was juxtaposed with very lean periods. It is apparent from Table 3 that Mozart's rate of composition slowed markedly from 1787 onwards. Only four major non-operatic works were completed during each of the year 1789 and 1790, compared with at least ten annually in the period before 1787.

A factor that may have contributed to this reduction in output was poor health. Mozart contracted a serious illness in 1784, and was treated by Sigmund Barisani. Barisani was a contemporary from Salzburg who rose rapidly in his profession, becoming a senior physician at the Allgemeine Krankenhaus. He died in September 1787 when only 29, but not before stating in Mozart's album that he had twice saved the composer's life. The 1784 illness was evidently a renal complaint, and Peter Davies has suggested that Mozart developed glomerulo-nephritis following a streptococcal throat infection complicated by Schönlein-Henoch syndrome.[44] Certainly the illness coincided with a temporary diminution in his rate of composition.[45] The disorder may have recurred in April 1787 and in the summer of 1790, when Mozart complained of headache, rheumatic pains, and malaise. His death was said at the time to be due to inflammatory rheumatic fever, although a cerebral haemorrhage and broncho-pneumonia superimposed on renal failure seem more probable as immediate causes of death. The many fantastic theories of poisoning or mercury overdose have little foundation in fact.[46]

[43] Joachim Preisler's *Journal*, quoted in Deutsch, *Mozart*, p. 325.

[44] See P. Davies, 'Mozart's Illnesses and Death', *Journal of the Royal Society of Medicine*, 76 (1983), 776–85.

[45] Leeson and Whitwell, in 'Mozart's Thematic Catalogue', suggest that this illness increased Mozart's sense of his own mortality, provoking him into creating the catalogue.

[46] See C. Bär, *Mozart: Krankheit, Tod, Begräbnis* (Salzburg, 1966). The poisoning theories are also discussed in detail by P. Davies, 'Mozart's Illnesses and Death, 2: The Last Year and the Fatal Illness', *The Musical Times*, 125 (1984), 554–60.

Constanze Mozart also suffered a series of illnesses that may have distracted her husband from composition. The nature of her complaints is difficult to identify, although they were evidently associated with her regular but difficult pregnancies. The months surrounding the birth of their daughter Anna Maria in late 1789 were especially distressing. She developed what was probably a varicose ulcer, and the couple contacted Johann Nepomuk Hunczowsky as well as their regular physician. Hunczowsky specialized in gynaecology, and may have recommended that Constanze visit the sulphur baths at Baden. Baden was generally favoured for disorders such as rheumatism and gout, glandular enlargements, and hemorrhoids, while in the nineteenth century, Dr Macpherson considered the waters valuable for functional uterine disorders, and for their laxative properties.[47] Since Mozart sent his wife purgative electuaries in 1789, it is likely that constipation was a serious problem. In August, Mozart sent her a batch of ant's eggs, but eighteenth-century texts considered these effectual mainly against deafness, and the hairiness of the cheeks in children! Even more extraordinarily, Niemetschek mentions another 'cure' that Constanze was supposed to undertake, involving baths made from cooked giblets.

All these illnesses clustered in Mozart's later years, when his creative output reached its lowest ebb. There are indications from the composer's letters that concern for Constanze's health prevented concentration on work. In July 1789, he told Puchberg:

Last night, she slept so well and has felt so much easier all the morning that I am very hopeful; and at last I am beginning to feel inclined for work.

But a few days later, matters had worsened again:

Since the time when you rendered me that great and friendly service, I have been living in such misery, that for very grief not only have I not been able to go out, but I could not even write.

Mozart's waning success in Vienna may also have contributed to his depressed mood and decline in output. He had always written symphonies and concerti for specific occasions, and in the absence of public concerts, this incentive was lost.

It can perhaps be concluded that although specific events may not have influenced Mozart's ability to compose, the combined pressures of the later years did have an impact. The decline in output was associated with increasingly poor health, while his resolution was sapped by failure to retrieve his position in Vienna. In addition, there was another important way in which the composer's experience in life affected his work that has

---

[47] See J. Macpherson, *The Baths and Wells of Europe* (London, 1869).

not yet been discussed: it influenced the nature and content of his compositions. The most obvious examples arose from his encounter with Freemasonry, but there are more subtle connections. Two themes are particularly relevant to Mozart's operatic ventures-the intellectual milieu in which he existed, and his evolving attitude to close relationships and love. As will be seen in the next chapter, the two were tightly interwoven.

# 4

# Mozart and his Personal Circle

Yet who is sufficiently cultivated not to make his superiority
over another sometimes overtly evident? Who is sufficiently
elevated not to have to suffer sometimes under such behaviour?

Goethe[1]

## The Composer's Early Life and Beliefs

Although Mozart's childhood was exceptional in so many ways, he was
raised in an atmosphere of faith in God and trust in hard work typical of
the mid-eighteenth century urban classes. Leopold Mozart was a firm
Catholic, but his creed was tinged with Calvinist restraint. He was not, for
example, above castigating the excesses of Italian worship:

You must not expect me to give you a description of the church services here. I
am far too irritated to do so. They merely consist of music and of church
adornment. Apart from these the most disgusting licentiousness prevails.[2]

Yet his travel diaries are full of pious sentiment, and he never appears
seriously to have questioned the ordering of heaven or earth. Leopold had
taken to heart the contemporary belief that 'a man who is not in service to
the highborn will not enjoy much regard, however honest and able he
may be.'[3] The subordinate position of the musician might be distasteful,
but alternatives were not to be contemplated.

This adherence to traditional beliefs was reflected in the ordering of the
Salzburg household. Life was focused entirely on the men, with the
women receiving only secondary consideration. Leopold Mozart's wife,
Anna Maria, was little more than a superior domestic, her life revolving
round the kitchen and nursery. Even in the nineteenth century, the
subservience of German and Austrian women in the professional classes
astonished foreigners. Few attempts were made to educate women; rather,
they were instilled with the virtues of service to father, brothers, and
husband. Anna Maria Mozart was barely literate, and took little part in
major family decisions. One of the interesting features of the letters

[1] J. W. von Goethe, *Die Wahlverwandtschaften* (*'Elective Affinities'*), trans. R. J. Hollingdale,
(London, 1971), 30.
[2] Letter from Leopold Mozart to Anna Maria Mozart dated 10 Feb. 1770.
[3] Quoted by E. Sagarra, *A Social History of Germany* (London, 1977), 92.

written by Leopold Mozart during the extensive tours undertaken in the 1760s is that his wife is rarely mentioned. Mozart recognized this attitude in his father, and as an adult he tried to play on it to his own advantage. When writing to Leopold about his proposed marriage to Constanze Weber, Mozart described the prospective bride in terms calculated to appeal to the older generation. He accordingly denied Constanze beauty or elegance, but claimed she was parsimonious and an excellent house-keeper, as in this letter dated 15 December 1781:

She is not ugly, but at the same time far from beautiful. Her whole beauty consists in two little black eyes and a pretty figure. She has no wit, but she has enough common sense to enable her to fulfil her duties as a wife and mother. It is a downright lie that she is inclined to be extravagant. . . . Moreover she understands housekeeping and has the kindest heart in the world. I love her and she loves me with all her heart. Tell me whether I could wish myself a better wife?

Wolfgang was of course the major family asset, but Leopold Mozart's devotion outstripped purely material concerns. The double standards of the household are typified in his response to a crisis in 1767. The family had settled temporarily in Vienna, and in November a member of their landlord's establishment contracted smallpox. Immediately, Leopold arranged to move with his son to a friend's house, but left his wife and daughter in the infected lodgings.

Leopold Mozart's beliefs were absorbed by his young son, and the composer's early correspondence is full of opinions that might have come directly from his father. When writing from Paris, the twin virtues of religion and money were firmly proclaimed by the 22 year-old Mozart in this letter dated 1 May 1778:

I pray to God daily to give me grace to hold out with fortitude and to do such honour to myself and to the whole German nation as will redound to His greater honour and glory; and that He will enable me to prosper and make a great deal of money.

Like his father, Mozart did not accept people blindly, and his youthful letters reveal some reservations about piety and religious pretentions.

We have the honour to go about with a certain Dominican, who is regarded as a holy man. For my part I do not believe it, for at breakfast he often takes a cup of chocolate and immediately afterwards a good glass of strong Spanish wine; and I myself have had the honour of lunching with this saint who at table drank a whole decanter and finished up with a full glass of strong wine, two large slices of melon, some peaches, pears, five cups of coffee, a whole plate of cloves, and two full saucers of milk and lemon.[4]

---

[4] Letter to Maria Anna and Marianne Mozart dated 21 Aug. 1770.

Even more remarkable, in view of his later conversion, was Mozart's hostility towards the Enlightenment. This was caused in part by his fear and dislike of Archbishop Colloredo. The Archbishop was a disciple of Voltaire, and challenged the entrenched clerical mores of Salzburg. This may account for Mozart's exclamation of delight at Voltaire's death, relayed from Paris in July 1778:

Now I have a piece of news for you which you may have heard already, namely, that that godless arch-rascal Voltaire has pegged out like a dog, like a beast! That is his reward!

Within a few years, Voltaire's rationalism was admired and emulated by Mozart himself.

Nevertheless, it is clear that despite family influences, Mozart and his father soon parted company as far as their attitudes to life were concerned. Leopold Mozart was confident and calculating in his aims, meeting the world's challenge with a blustering efficiency. His son was sensitive and less certain. The contrast is nowhere more illuminating than during Mozart's sojourn in Paris in 1778. The city was a mecca for men of energy and ambition, but Mozart felt alienated and gloomy.

I am tolerably well, thank God, but I often wonder whether life is worth living—I am neither hot nor cold—and don't find much pleasure in anything.[5]

These complaints received short shift from Leopold, who seemed unable to acknowledge emotional worries:

There is no reason whatever why you should be unhappy. God has bestowed great talents upon you, . . . At least you are in a city where, even though everything is exceptionally dear, a lot of money can be made. But pains and hard work are necessary! Nothing can be achieved without some effort![6]

It was not until he reached Vienna that Mozart encountered a social milieu that liberated his intellect and brought him spiritual comfort and a belief in personal dignity.

## Enlightenment Circles in Vienna

Mozart was taken up by two important patrons in 1781, and they may have been influential in his decision to leave Archbishop Colloredo's service. The Countess Wilhelmine Thun (born 1744) was considered one of the most cultivated ladies of the city. She was mentioned admiringly in the memoirs of the diplomat Nathaniel Wraxall, who noted that 'No

---

[5] Letter to Leopold Mozart dated 29 May 1778.
[6] Letter to Mozart dated 11 June 1778.

capital on earth can bring forth [a person] more distinguished by natural and acquired gifts, wide horizon and free spirit'. She invited the young Mozart to her palace regularly, and introduced him to prominent nobles. By March 1781, Mozart was writing warmly to his father:

I have lunched twice with Countess Thun and go there almost every day. She is the most charming and most lovable lady I have ever met; and I am very high in her favour.

Mozart treated her artistic opinions with respect, and played *Die Entführung* to her during its composition. The Countess's son-in-law was the music-loving Karl Lichnowsky with whom Mozart travelled to Prussia in 1789, and who was later to play such a prominent part in Beethoven's life.

The second noble family with which the young composer rapidly developed close ties was that of the Countess Rumbeck (Rumbeke). The Countess, only a year older than Mozart, was his first pupil in Vienna, and she received the dedication of a set of keyboard variations in the summer of 1781. He gave her a lesson every day, and frequented her house at other times as well:

I have begun a reply to your last letter of January 7th, but I cannot possibly finish it, as a servant of Countess Rumbeck has just come with an invitation to a small musical party at her house. . . .[7]

He became friendly with the Countess's relative Johann Philipp Cobenzl, then Vice-Chancellor of the Empire and a distinguished politician. More than once, Mozart stayed at the Cobenzl country estate on the Reisenberg, near Vienna (see Plate 7). It was here that Mozart came nearest perhaps to stating an opinion on aesthetics and the visual arts, when describing the estate in a letter to his father, dated 13 July 1781:

The little house is nothing much, but the country—the forest—in which my host has built a grotto which looks just as if Nature herself had fashioned it! Indeed, the surroundings are magnificent and very delightful.

These aristocrats were not members of the old nobility, but came from the class of Court officials that had risen through service to the Habsburg dynasty. They had reached their positions by ability, not hereditary tradition, and their sense of public duty was strong. Culturally, they were closer to the wealthy bourgeois than the families of ancient lineage; consequently, they mixed freely with members of the middle classes. Thus when Mozart mounted a concert in 1781 at the house of Josepha Auernhammer, the daughter of a senior civil servant, a number of nobles

---

[7] Letter to Leopold Mozart dated 12 Jan. 1782.

attended.[8] A few years later, when *Idomeneo* was staged by amateurs at the private theatre of the wealthy Prince Auersperg, nobles were prepared to associate with professional musicians and people from Mozart's own circle.

The manner in which Mozart was received in these households was crucial to his self-esteem. He was not treated as a servant or lesser being, but as an independent man of ability. Mozart appears to have survived his awesome childhood surprisingly unscathed. One of the few legacies of those early years was his heightened social sensitivity. He had become accustomed to grand circles as a child, and was fêted by the crowned heads of Europe. Mozart did not realize that this regal condescension was less a response to his merits than to his youth. As a charming and talented boy, he was permitted intimacies with the great, rather as a favoured pet animal might be allowed special privileges. His illusions were soon shattered, and his pride suffered severely in Salzburg. Subsequently, he developed the tendency to interpret even the conventional haughtiness of the aristocrat as a personal slight.

Now at last, Mozart enjoyed the respect owed to his talent rather than his origins. It was clear in Vienna that an individual with ability might rise socially, and could not be held back by arbitrary power. Among Mozart's middle-class acquaintance, there were many examples of self-made success. Johann von Trattner, for example, came from peasant origins to build up the publishing, printing and, papermaking empire centred on the Trattnerhof. Trattner married the daughter of a high government official, but she died young. Later, he married a woman more than forty years his junior, and she became Mozart's pupil. Trattner was godfather to three of Mozart's children, and their friendly association seems to have continued long after the composer and his family moved out of their lodgings in the Trattnerhof in 1784. The career of Michael Puchberg offers another instance of ability coupled with opportunity. He progressed by marrying the widow of his employer in the textile industry. Frau Elisabeth Puchberg did not survive long, and left her husband with a large fortune.

Perhaps the most remarkable cases of advancement, considering the period, were those of the wealthy Jewish bankers. Maria Theresa's antipathy for the Jews was marked, but since the seventeenth century the Habsburg Emperors had employed a Hoffaktor or 'Court Jew', who arranged credit for the Exchequer, and undertook all kinds of supply, from building materials to food and jewellery. The Court Jews also amassed great fortunes and took up positions in the noble hierarchy

---

[8] They included Countess Thun, Count Firmian, and Barons von Swieten and Wetzlar—most of the old aristocracy would never have condescended to such company.

commensurate with their wealth.[9] Mozart was familiar with several scions
of these families. Baron Raimund Wetzlar was one of Mozart's landlords,
and provided the composer with empty rooms in the house for his private
ball in January 1783. Another was Nathan von Arnstein, who was left a
fortune by his father, and married into a distinguished Jewish family
from Berlin. The Arnsteins moved in the highest circles, and their salon
was a meeting-place for aristocrats, scholars, and artists. Mozart must
have known them; for he almost certainly played at their palace in 1784,
in the presence of Prince Kaunitz, Prince Auersperg, Count Lichtenstein,
and others.

It was inevitable that association with such company brought Mozart
into contact with the Enlightenment. One of the first indications of his
changing beliefs was this assertion of personal dignity, made to his father
on June 20 1781:

It is the heart that ennobles a man; and though I am no Count, yet I have
probably more honour in me than many a Count. Whether a man be Count or
valet, the moment he insults me he is a scoundrel.

Such sentiments have much in common with the tenets of Freemasonry,
and became common currency among intellectuals in general. It is difficult now to disentangle Masonic principles about death, truth, love, and
equality from Enlightenment thinking as a whole. Many members of the
society in which Mozart moved were Freemasons. They belonged to rational rather than mystical Lodges, and were concerned with social change as
well as spiritual brotherhood.[10] Undoubtedly, some brothers were also
motivated by material considerations, for as Caroline Pichler observed.

At that time, it was not unadvantageous to belong to this brotherhood, which
had members in every circle and had known how to entice leaders, presidents
and governors into its bosom. For there, one brother helped the other.[11]

Mozart certainly found the social gains attractive, but his dedication went
beyond such motives, particularly in the second half of the 1780s when
the brotherhood came under serious attack.

Mozart appears to have been familiar with the genuine radicals of the
Craft, as well as its conventional members. Their influence was sufficient
to provoke the reaction from the authorities described in Chapter 1, and
ultimately to bring about the Jacobin Conspiracy of 1794. During this
episode of authoritarian hysteria, a number of intellectuals were arrested
and charged with revolutionary intentions. Many of the accused,

---

[9] Sagarra, *A Social History*, p. 158. Samson Wertheimer for example left 2 million gulden in
1724.
[10] See K. Thomson, *The Masonic Thread in Mozart* (London, 1977).
[11] Quoted in H. C.Robbins Landon, *Haydn Chronicle and Works*, ii (London, 1978), 308.

including the Abbé Strattmann and the magistrate Prandstetter, belonged to van Swieten's circle and were probably known to Mozart.[12] The connection may have been even closer, since one of the conspirators was Cajetan Gilowsky von Urazowa; he was condemned to death, but managed to commit suicide in prison. Mozart was friendly with a family of this name both in Salzburg and Vienna, and Franz Gilowsky von Urazowa was a witness at the composer's wedding.

On the other hand, it is simplistic to infer Mozart's attitude to life solely from Masonic principles. It will be seen later that some of his actions and feelings, particularly those related to women, were far from Masonic. Instead, they were founded on more general Rationalist trends. It is important therefore to identify the beliefs and standards of behaviour espoused by Mozart himself.

One helpful approach may be to consider what Mozart read. One of the books found among his effects after his death was *Automathes*, and this provides a useful illustration of the range of Enlightenment tenets. The book was written anonymously in English, and its full title was:

*The capacity and extent of the human understanding; exemplified in the extraordinary case of Automathes; a young nobleman who was accidentally left in his infancy, upon a desolate island, and continued nineteen years in that solitary state, separate from all human society.*

The manuscript, supposedly found by the narrator in a bottle washed up by the sea, describes an ideal State. The country is governed with justice and benevolence. Hospitals, schools, and poor relief are freely provided. The Church is powerful but spiritual, eschewing wealth and worldly politics. Church buildings are fine and imposing, yet without luxuriant or superfluous ornament, while the clergy are devoted to teaching the young. Much attention is paid to education, since humans are only distinguished from brutes by knowledge. Children are encouraged to modesty and patience, unruly passions being subdued by reason. These themes are exemplified in the tale of Automathes, for although he is isolated in infancy, he has fortunately benefited from the best of educations during his first two years. This is sufficient to permit him to develop as a philosopher rather than a savage in his solitude, and to emerge enriched from his ordeal.

Many of these ideas are reflected in Mozart's own thought. The author of *Automathes* dwells eloquently on the transience of the world's favour and material joys, contrasted with the comforts of true religion. This parallels Mozart's well-known homily to his father, written shortly before the latter's death:

---

12 See E. Wangermann, *From Joseph II to the Jacobin Trials* (London, 1959), 134–6.

I have now made a habit of being prepared in all affairs of life for the worst. As death, when we come to consider it closely, is the true goal of our existence, I have formed during the last few years such close relations with this best and truest friend of mankind, that his image is not only no longer terrifying to me, but is indeed very soothing and consoling! And I thank God for graciously granting me the opportunity (you know what I mean) of learning that death is the key which unlocks the door to our true happiness. I never lie down at night without reflecting that—young as I am—I may not live to see another day.[13]

Another major tenet is the belief in forgiveness and reconciliation, the resolution of differences in the light of higher truth. This too was absorbed by Mozart, and expressed in another letter:

For I maintain that kindness cures everything, that magnanimous and forbearing conduct has often reconciled the bitterest enemies.

The composer's faith found expression in many of the later operas (including *Così fan tutte* and the apparently conventional *La clemenza di Tito*), and of course in the music he wrote for Masonic events.[14] It also permeates more intimate work, even such a trivial piece as *Das Bandel* (K. 441), written for performance in the family circle. This trio concerns a minor incident with a ribbon belonging to Constanze; yet the moral of the text has unmistakable overtones: 'What joy, noble sun, to live in true friendship'.

A great deal of Enlightenment criticism was directed at religion, and the organized Church was a prime target for the overtly anticlerical Masonic Lodges. It is interesting to consider how far Rationalism undermined Mozart's attitude to the established Church. His output of religious works certainly ceased when he came into contact with Viennese intellectual circles, and the one Mass begun during these years (C minor, K. 427) was never completed. Yet this change may have been governed as much by practical as ideological factors. The critics of the Church berated the expense of services, considering them to be over-elaborate. Many thought that flamboyant and extended music was inappropriate, turning churches into Opera Houses. Joseph II was in sympathy with these views, and it is apparent from a letter sent by Mozart to his father as early as 1782

---

[13] Letter to Leopold Mozart dated 4 Apr.1787. W. Hildesheimer (*Mozart*, trans. M. Faber (London, 1983), 193) has noted that this letter paraphrases a work called *Phädon* by Moses Mendelssohn. By a curious logic, he therefore assumes that Mozart was not sincere, but was writing conventional platitudes. Of course, the substance of Mozart's letter resembles much Enlightenment thought about death, and the fact that Mozart did not express himself uniquely has no bearing on his sincerity or lack of it.

[14] For details, see Jacques Chailley, *The Magic Flute, Masonic Opera*, trans. H. Weinstock (London, 1972), and J. Morehen, 'Masonic Instrumental Music of the Eighteenth Century: A Survey', *The Music Review*, 42 (1981), 215–24. H. C. Robbins Landon's book *Mozart and the Masons* (London, 1982) provides further interesting speculations about the extent of Mozart's contacts with members of the Craft.

that restrictions on instrumental music had begun in Vienna. Finally, a Decree published in 1786 prohibited loud choral singing, on the specious grounds that it was medically dangerous, and directed that it be replaced by quiet singing or prayer.[15] It is not surprising therefore that Mozart, never a man to produce extended works without a specific purpose, produced no Masses during the Vienna years; even the incomplete Mass in C minor was put to good use by its transformation into *Davidde penitente* (K. 469).

Mozart's conversion to Rationalism had a significant impact on many aspects of his life, and two of these are particularly relevant to the subject of the operas. The first concerns a mystery that has already been mentioned: why Mozart did not leave Vienna in the late 1780s, and travel to regions in which his talent was not stale. It was argued earlier that such a move may well have relieved some of the financial and professional distress with which he was confronted during these years. Mozart was already aware of the Emperor's parsimony in 1782, and expressed frustration at his prospects in Vienna:

The Viennese gentry, and in particular the Emperor, must not imagine that I am on this earth solely for the sake of Vienna. There is no monarch in the world whom I should be more glad to serve than the Emperor, but I refuse to beg for any post. I believe that I am capable of doing credit to any Court. If Germany, my beloved fatherland, . . . will not accept me, then in God's name let France or England become the richer by another talented German, . . . You know well that it is the Germans who have always excelled in almost all the arts. But where did they make their fortune and their reputation? Certainly not in Germany!

This letter was written on 17 August, shortly after the production of *Die Entführung*, and during a period in which Mozart's keyboard performances were increasingly popular. Later in the decade he continued to suffer economic uncertainties and artistic disappointments in Vienna, even though he was aware that greater success might be gained elsewhere:

But I must mention that in spite of my wretched condition I decided to give subscription concerts at home in order to be able to meet at least my present great and frequent expenses, . . . But even this has failed. Unfortunately Fate is so much against me, though only in Vienna, that even when I want to, I cannot make any money.[16]

Niemetschek argued that Mozart was persuaded to remain in Austria by his appointment as Kammermusicus. This is improbable, for as we have seen, the salary was quite insufficient to act as an inducement in the absence of other advantages.[17] Much more important was the sense of

---

[15] E. Wangermann, *The Austrian Achievement 1700-1800* (London, 1973), 102.

[16] Letter to Michael Puchberg dated 12 July 1789.

[17] Hildesheimer (*Mozart*, 305) has produced rather more fanciful explanations, suggesting for

personal dignity that he was accorded in Enlightenment Vienna. Mozart was treated with honour and justice by his patrons, and was not reduced to the status of a domestic servant or valet. When at the Lodge, he was treated as an equal by these same patrons. Allied to this was the informality and accessibility of Emperor Joseph, instances of which have already been recounted in Chapter 1. Mozart may have received from the Emperor that 'condescension' to which he had been accustomed in early life. Such powerful reinforcements of self-respect would have been worth all the disappointments suffered at the hands of public taste.

The second major influence of Rationalism was on Mozart's emotional life and personal conduct. Since these coloured his attitude towards women, friendship, and the family, they are of course important to our understanding of his operas. Mozart did not share his father's stereotyped outlook on private relationships; nor, interestingly enough, did he espouse the misogyny of the Masonic creed. Instead, his own experience was moulded by the new views about love and marriage that were percolating through the middle classes of Vienna.


## The Companionate Marriage and Mozart's Attitude to Love

Love and the frailties of the human heart are major concerns in all Mozart's mature operas. Many commentators have speculated on the links between Mozart's personal experience and portrayals of love in the operas. Such questions are legitimate, although inferences have often extended well beyond the evidence, falling into the biographical fallacy. For example, it has been suggested that *Così fan tutte*, in which Ferrando and Guglielmo each woo first one sister and then another, parallels Mozart's ambivalence about Aloisia and Constanze Weber.[18] Recently, Wolfgang Hildesheimer has emphasized Mozart's latent passion for Aloisia, describing her as the composer's 'great love . . . the *prima donna* in life as on stage'.[19] However, after Mozart's initial outburst of anguish over Aloisia Weber's coolness late in 1778, there is no evidence of a lasting attachment. It is all speculation, supported only by the assertion of the aged Aloisia Lange to Mary Novello in 1829 that Mozart had always loved her.[20] There is much to be said for dismissing this recollection, not least that the composer apparently worked alongside

---

example that the invitation from London reproduced in Chapter 2 was hidden by Constanze or some rival.

[18] B. Brophy, *Mozart the Dramatist* (London, 1964), 121.

[19] Hildesheimer, *Mozart*, pp. 9 and 230.

[20] V. & M. Novello, *A Mozart Pilgrimage*, ed. N. Medici and R. Hughes (London, 1975), 150.

Aloisia for many years in the Opera House without apparent qualms.

Mozart's marriage to Constanze Weber has generated an extraordinary amount of animosity from later writers. It seems clear that he was partly compromised and manoeuvred into the union by Constanze's mother. Joseph Lange, who married Aloisia Weber just eighteen months after the death of his first wife, may have had similar experiences with the family.[21] In addition, however, all manner of derogatory comments have been made about Constanze's poor education, fecklessness, and lack of musicality; the speculations about what 'might have been' without this union are endless.[22] It appears that many writers do not simply wish that Mozart had chosen a more compatible spouse, but resent any person having been the composer's intimate companion, as if no one could be worthy of such a genius. Nevertheless, all the surviving documents and letters that relate to Mozart's personal feelings in his maturity are directed towards Constanze. Their marriage must therefore be considered for the light it may shed upon Mozart's dramatic portrayals of women and their emotional commitments.

At first sight, some interesting parallels do appear to exist between Mozart's marriage and his stage representations of women. It may be no accident that during the stormy period of his engagement in 1782, the composer was simultaneously creating the staunch but tender Constanze of *Die Entführung*. Even more striking were the events of 1789, which coincided with work on *Così fan tutte*. Constanze was then taking the cure at Baden, a fashionable spa that was known more for its social than therapeutic properties. It was not a resort for those 'seriously in quest of health', according to one nineteenth-century physician. Not only did it boast a theatre and saloons for Balls and assemblies, the spa also encouraged the 'undesirable' habit of mixed bathing. In this *risqué* atmosphere, Constanze displayed improprieties that provoked a severe rebuke from Mozart in August 1789:

Dear little wife! I want to talk to you quite frankly. You have no reason whatever to be unhappy. You have a husband who loves you and does all he possibly can for you. As for your foot, you must just be patient and it will surely get well

---

[21] See A. Einstein, *Mozart: His Character — his Works*, trans. A. Mendel and N. Broder (London, 1971), 74. Lange's first wife was Anna Maria Schindler, one of the founding members of the German Opera Company created by Joseph II in 1778.

[22] Hildesheimer is only the most recent of a long line of commentators to take this view: 'It seems improbable that she ever suffered mental torment, and even her physical sufferings seem primarily to be an excuse for her visits to spas. Constanze had a lighthearted, instinctual nature; she granted Mozart (and perhaps not only him) erotic, or at least sexual, satisfaction, but was unable to offer him the happiness a lesser man needs for self-realisation', *Mozart*, p. 243. The condescension of this perspective is staggering. It has been suggested by a number of commentators that Constanze had an affair with Mozart's pupil Franz Süssmayr, and that the latter fathered the child born in July 1791. This liaison is however extemely improbable, as has been shown by J. Eibl in 'Süssmayr and Constanze', *Mozart-Jahrbuch 1976-7*, 277–80.

again. I am glad indeed when you have some fun—of course I am—but I do wish
that you would not sometimes make yourself so cheap. In my opinion you are far
too free and easy with N. N. . . . Now please remember that N. N. are not half
so familiar with other women, whom they perhaps know more intimately, as
they are with you. Why, N. N. who is usually a well-conducted fellow and
particularly respectful to women, must have been misled by your behaviour into
writing the most disgusting and most impertinent sottises which he put into his
letter. A woman must always make herself respected, or else people will begin to
talk about her. My love! Forgive me for being so frank, but my peace of mind
demands it as well as our mutual happiness. Remember that you yourself once
admitted to me that you were inclined to comply too easily. You know the
consequences of that. Remember too the promises you gave to me. Oh, God, do
try, my love!

The names here were later deleted, probably by Constanze. Shortly after
this incident, Mozart started composing *Così fan tutte*, an opera which
dissects the emotional fragility of women, separated from their formal
commitments and besieged by new lovers in a sensuous atmosphere.

The temporal association of these concerns in Mozart's private and
artistic lives is remarkable. But inferences about a direct parallel are
superficial. It is interesting that Constanze mutilated rather than suppressed this letter, so it is unlikely to have referred to any gross infidelities.
Constanze's behaviour in Baden appears mild beside the aristocratic
improprieties described in Chapter 1. This is perhaps the nub of the
problem—it was precisely because Constanze seemed to be engaging in a
flirtatiousness that would be acceptable among the nobility that Mozart
was distressed. For the overt indiscretions of the ruling class were products
of a marriage system in which personal choice played little part, and
where there was no identification of sexual satisfaction with the conjugal
bed. In contrast, the fabric of personal relationships that was developing
in the intellectual middle classes was based on an entirely different
model. This is the form that Mozart espoused, and it has been characterized as the companionate marriage.[23]

The companionate marriage had a number of features that set it apart
both from the *ancien régime* system and the behaviour of the rural
peasantry. The first was the personal choice of partner. Formerly, the
decision had been taken by parents (who were influenced by material and
hereditary arguments), although the child might have a veto. Later these

---

[23] This notion has been developed by Lawrence Stone, *The Family, Sex and Marriage in England
1500–1800* (London, 1977). Stone's methods and interpretations have however been severely criti-
cized by A. Macfarlane, *History and Theory*, 18 (1979), 103–26, and L. Pollock, *Forgotten Children:
Parent—Child Relations from 1500–1800* (Cambridge, 1983). For a discussion of other contemporary marriage forms, see P. Laslett, *Family Life and Illicit Love in Earlier Generations* (Cambridge,
1977).

positions were reversed, so that parents could exert sanctions over unsatisfactory choices by children. But in Mozart's case, parental wishes were of no consequence. The opposition of his father to his desire to marry Constanze Weber is well known. Leopold was horrified with his son's resolution, which he saw as a product of the machinations of Frau Weber. Yet this displeasure had little impact; Mozart carried on regardless.

Allied to this change in the decision-making process was an alteration in the basis of choice. Personal affection became an overriding motive at the expense of economic and social considerations. This was acknowledged quite specifically by Mozart in a letter dated 7 February 1778:

I want to make my wife happy, but not to become rich by her means. . . . We poor humble people can not only choose a wife whom we love and who loves us, but we may, can and do take such a one, because we are neither noble, nor highly born, nor aristocratic, nor rich, but on the contrary, lowly born, humble and poor.

Writers such as Steele, Addison, and Defoe in England had long proclaimed anathema on marriage without affection, and gradually this view became popular, as is evident from this quotation from a periodical late in the century:

Some few grovelling spirits among the ladies may, indeed, form a systematic plan of advancing their interests, or gratifying their ambition, by a matrimonial connection. Some, even, who pass current in the muster-call of virtuous women, may yet be base enough to dispose of their persons, by a species of legal prostitution, to the highest bidder.[24]

Continental Europe lagged behind, and arranged marriages remained the norm in Italy. None the less, the more sophisticated classes came to accept this new outlook by Mozart's time.[25]

There can be little doubt about Mozart's affection for Constanze. Sometimes it was expressed with almost childlike playfulness, as in this letter from the 33 year-old composer dated 13 April 1789:

If I were to tell you all the things I do with your dear portrait, I think that you would often laugh. For instance, when I take it out of its case, I say 'Good day, Stanzerl!—Good day little rascal, pussy-pussy, little turned-up nose, little bagatelle, Schluck and Druck', and when I put it away again, I let it slip in very slowly, saying all the time, 'Nu-Nu-Nu-Nu!' with the peculiar emphasis which

---

[24] From the *Monthly Museum* of 1799, quoted by R. Sennett, *The Fall of Public Man* (Cambridge, 1977), 273.

[25] See P. Schmidtbauer, 'The Changing Household: Austrian Household Structure from the Seventeenth to the Early Twentieth Century', in *Family Forms in Historic Europe*, ed. by R. Wall (Cambridge, 1983).

this word so full of meaning demands, and then just at the last, quickly, 'Good night, little mouse, sleep well'. Well, I suppose that I have been writing something very foolish (to the world at all events); but to us who love each other so dearly, it is not foolish at all.

Yet Mozart's was not a blind romantic love. Along with other late-eighteenth century artists, he ridiculed romantic passion—with its belief in love at first sight, the demand for expression regardless of social constraints, the blindness to blemishes in the object of idolatory—and satirised it mercilessly (most notably in *Così fan tutte*). Mozart's greater need was for domestic companionship and affection. This emerges clearly in the letters written to Constanze during his various journeys and concert tours. For example, when he was in Frankfurt for the coronation of Emperor Leopold in 1790, he wrote:

I am as excited as a child at the thought of seeing you again. If people could see into my heart, I should almost feel ashamed. To me, everything is cold—cold as ice. Perhaps if you were with me I might possibly take more pleasure in the kindness of those I meet here. But, as it is, everything seems so empty, . . .

While I was writing the last page, tear after tear fell on the paper. But I must cheer up—catch!—An astonishing number of kisses are flying about—The deuce!—I see a whole crowd of them! Ha! Ha! . . .[26]

His profound dependency on Constanze was manifest in despondency and indecision, and decided him against moving on from Frankfurt towards potentially more lucrative cities. A year later, Mozart felt lonely and isolated even when Constanze was in Baden, just two posts from Vienna:

You cannot imagine how I have been aching for you all this long while. I can't describe what I have been feeling—a kind of emptiness, which hurts me dreadfully—a kind of longing, which is never satisfied, which never ceases, and which persists, nay rather increases daily. When I think how merry we were together at Baden—like children—and what sad, weary hours I am spending here! Even my work gives me no pleasure, because I am accustomed to stop working now and then and exchange a few words with you. Alas! this pleasure is no longer possible. If I go to the piano and sing something out of my opera, I have to stop at once, for this stirs my emotions too deeply.[27]

Some nineteen letters and notes survive to chart their six week separation in the summer of 1791, and all display an affectionate solicitude and concern. Mozart summed up the qualities he evidently found in this relationship with Constanze as early as 1782, when he signed a letter to his father: 'W. A. Mozart Mann und Weib ist ein Leib'.

---

[26] Letters to Constanze Mozart dated 30 Sept. and 17 Oct. 1790.
[27] Letter to Constanze Mozart dated 7 July 1791.

This emphasis on the affectionate, loyal marriage was scarcely compatible with the tone of promiscuity described in Chapter 1. Among those following the *ancien régime* models, pleasure and physical gratification were sought in the arms of lovers. But in the companionate marriage, sexual attraction became one component of a fulfilled and contented union. Of course, sensuality has never been confined solely to marriage, in Mozart's circle or any other. The miscellaneous pairings of musicians and singers in Vienna and at Haydn's Eszterháza make this quite clear. Nor are the limits of Mozart's fidelity certain; it has been argued that Nancy Storace was the composer's lover at one time, and that she destroyed their love letters, but little documentary evidence has yet come to light.[28] Nevertheless, there is no doubt about the sexuality of Mozart's relations with Constanze:

But the first thing I shall do is to take you by your front curls; for how on earth could you think, or even imagine, that I had forgotten you? How could I possibly do so? For even supposing such a thing, you will get on the very first night a thorough spanking on your dear little kissable arse, and this you may count upon.

On June 1st I intend to sleep in Prague, and on the 4th—with my darling little wife. Arrange your dear sweet nest very daintily, for my little fellow deserves it indeed, he has really behaved himself very well and is only longing to possess your sweetest. . . . Just picture to yourself that rascal; as I write he crawls on to the table and looks at me questioningly. I, however, box his ears properly—but the rogue is simply. . . . and now the knave burns only more fiercely and can hardly be restrained.[29]

Furthermore, Mozart denied trafficking with the then conventional sources of sexual gratification, as he indignantly told his father in a letter dated 15 December 1781:

The voice of nature speaks as loud in me as in others, louder, perhaps, than in many a big strong lout of a fellow. I simply cannot live as most young men do in these days. In the first place, I have too much religion; in the second place, I have too great a love of my neighbour and too high a feeling of honour to seduce an innocent girl; in the third place, I have too much horror and disgust, too much dread and fear of diseases and too much care for my health to fool about with whores. So I can swear that I have never had relations of that sort with any woman. . . . I stake my life on the truth of what I have told you.

Mozart and Constanze's passion found overt expression in her numerous confinements. Between the summers of 1783 and 1791, she gave birth six times. An average of one pregnancy every sixteen months was

---

[28] See R. Fiske, *English Theatre Music in the Eighteenth Century* (London, 1973), 499.
[29] Letters to Constanze Mozart dated 19 and 23 May 1789. The passages indicated by '. . . .' were deleted from the originals.

relatively high in eighteenth-century urban classes, particularly in view of Constanze's poor health.[30] It suggests that contraceptives were not used, even though they were now widely available. In any event, it is interesting to note that although Constanze was only 35 when she first associated with Georg Nissen (the pair married some twelve years later), she had no more children after Mozart's death.

The emotional strength of their relationship had another important, although less attractive, feature: Mozart came to identify his personal honour with Constanze's behaviour. Again, this is in stark contrast to aristocratic models, where the woman's indiscretions did not reflect unduly on the man (and seem on occasion almost to have been encouraged). Mozart's acute sensitivity to social nuance and decorum led to persistent anxieties about Constanze's behaviour. This is illustrated by an episode during the early stages of their attachment. Constanze was staying at that time with the Baroness von Waldstätten, and had taken part in a game of forfeits. As a sanction in the game, Constanze permitted a young man to measure her calves. Mozart was horrified, and wrote his fiancée a letter full of reproach (dated 29 April 1782). He appears distressed less by Constanze's flirtatiousness than by the potential threat to reputation:

No woman who cares for her honour can do such a thing. It is quite a good maxim to do as one's company does. At the same time there are many other factors to be considered—as, for example, whether only intimate friends and acquaintances are present—whether I am a child or a marriageable girl—more particularly, whether I am already betrothed—but, above all, whether only people of my own social standing or my social inferiors—or, what is even more important, my social superiors are in the company?

This seems a suprising response from a man in love. But the difference between his own standards and the behaviour acceptable among the nobility is implicit in Mozart's comments on the Baroness (then separated from her husband):

If it be true that the Baroness herself allowed it to be done to her, the case is still quite different, for she is already past her prime and cannot possibly attract any longer—and besides, she is inclined to be promiscuous in her favours. I hope, dearest friend, that . . . you will never lead a life like hers.

Several years later, Mozart continued to mingle tender solicitude for Constanze with concern for her dignity, as in this letter dating from 16 April 1789:

---

[30] See Laslett, *Family Life*, for estimates of natural pregnancy rates. For the distribution of contraceptives in late eighteenth-century Europe, see A. McLaren, *Birth Control in Nineteenth-Century England* (London, 1978).

Dear little wife, I have a number of requests to make;
  (1) not to be melancholy
  (2) to take care of your health and to beware of the spring breezes
  (3) not to go out walking alone—and preferably not to go out walking at all
  (4) to feel absolutely assured of my love. . . .
  (5) I beg you in your conduct not only to be careful of your honour and mine, but also to consider appearances

This link between female behaviour and male honour or pride is also a significant strand in his *opere buffe*. It was a facet of Mozart's preoccupation with social presentation. His obsession is perhaps not surprising in a man whose status in respectable circles was founded solely on personal qualitites, unsupported by birth or wealth. Nevertheless, it can also be seen that Mozart's attitude to marriage was far from the dismissive superiority fostered by the Masonic creed. The tension between the two views is finally played out in the text of *Die Zauberflöte*, the authorship of which has been hotly disputed. On the one hand, the text is littered with misogynistic, untruthful, and foolish statements about the bad influence of women. Yet on the other hand, Pamina is given equal status with Tamino in the search for truth. Indeed, she leads him through his initiation, guiding him and participating fully in the transformation.[31]

A pattern emerges from Mozart's letters and other sources of a growing tenderness and dependence on family companionship. Unfortunately, little evidence has survived about Mozart's feelings for his children. The two surviving boys are rarely mentioned in existing documents, while few comments were passed on the deaths of the other four babies. It is often assumed that as a result of the high infant and child mortality rates then prevailing, parents did not suffer excessively over the deaths of children. However, evidence from contemporary sources indicates that immense distress was frequently experienced over the untimely death of children by many parents in pre-industrial Europe.[32] The Enlightenment orthodoxy had firm opinions concerning the rearing and education of children, beginning at the earliest stages. Thus in *Automathes* we read:

A mother, be her rank never so high, who should think it beneath her to nurse her own child, would be thought highly unworthy of the name of a mother, and be looked upon as little better than a monster of nature.

---

[31] It has been argued, most recently by Hildesheimer, that Karl Ludwig Giesecke was responsible for parts of the libretto. However, this view has been discounted by P. Branscombe in 'Die Zauberflöte : Some Textual and Interpretative Problems', *Proceedings of the Royal Musical Association*, 92 (1965–6), 45–63. For further discussion of the ambivalence concerning women in *Die Zauberflöte*, see Hildesheimer, *Mozart*, p. 309, and D. Heartz, 'La Clemenza di Sarastro', *The Musical Times*, 124 (1983), 152–7.
[32] Stone, *The Family*, p. 248 and Pollock, *Forgotten Children* provide ample illustrations.

The endorsement of breast-feeding was an attempt to discourage wet-nursing, a practice that promoted high infant mortality in the eighteenth century. This, however, was a matter on which Mozart did not accept advanced thought. After the birth of their first child, Mozart insisted that the infant be weaned on water as he himself had been; he was overruled by his mother-in-law and the midwife. Sadly, when the couple visited Salzburg later in the year, the baby was put into the hands of a wet-nurse, where he died after a few weeks.

The very fact that Mozart took an interest in such matters at all suggests a certain domesticity. It was yet another aspect of his union with Constanze that had little in common with the *ancien régime* stereotype. There is scarcely any parallel with the relationships portrayed in the *opera buffa*. Don Giovanni, the lovers in *Così fan tutte*, Figaro and the Count cannot be traced in Mozart's own life.

## Impressions of Mozart in Vienna

The private circle in which Mozart and Constanze moved seems to have been high-spirited, and this cheerfulness persisted in spite of adverse circumstances. Michael Kelly recalled his first meeting with the composer in his *Reminiscences*:

We sat down to supper, and I had the pleasure to be placed between him and his wife, Madame Constanze Weber, a German lady of whom he was passionately fond, and by whom he had three children. He conversed with me a good deal about Thomas Linley, the first Mrs. Sheridan's brother, with whom he was intimate in Florence, and spoke of him with great affection. . . . After supper the young branches of our host had a dance, and Mozart joined them. Madame Mozart told me, that great as his genius was, he was an enthusiast in dancing, and often said that his taste lay in that art, rather than in music.

He was a remarkably small man, very thin and pale, with a profusion of fine fair hair, of which he was rather vain. He gave me a cordial invitation to his house, of which I availed myself, and passed a great part of my time there. He always received me with kindness and hospitality. He was remarkably fond of punch, of which beverage I have seen him take copious draughts. He was also fond of billiards, and had an excellent billiard table in his house. Many and many a game have I played with him, but always came off second best.[33]

This penchant for dancing led Mozart and Constanze to hold a private ball in their own apartment (or the rooms adjacent to it) in January 1783. Each man paid 2 gulden at the door, and the party lasted from 6 pm until 7 the next morning. Patrons such as the Baroness Waldstätten and Baron

---

[33] Kelly, *Reminiscences*, ed. R. Fiske (London, 1975), 112.

Wetzlar attended, together with actors and musicians, including Gottlieb Stephanie, Joseph Lange, and the tenor Valentin Adamberger. This social mixture typified Mozart's acquaintance through much of his adult life. He was on familiar terms both with minor nobility and upper middle-class households on the one hand, and members of his own profession on the other. Among the former group, the noble families of Thun and Cobenzl who favoured him in the early 1780s were later replaced in his affections by Count August Hatzfeld and the Jacquin household. Nikolaus von Jacquin (1727–1817) was a celebrated botanist, and his children Gottfried and Franziska were both competent musicians. It was to Gottfried that Mozart described his adventures in Prague in 1787. Gottfried von Jacquin was seven years younger than the composer, but outlived him by only one year.

Mozart also shared many leisure hours with the actors of the Burgtheater company. Early in the 1780s, the stage was dominated by Friedrich Schröder, and after him the leading players were Johann Müller, the Stephanie brothers, and Joseph Lange. Lange was described by Michael Kelly as 'the most perfect representative of the lover and gentleman on the German stage', although Baron Riesbeck was less complementary:

Mr Lange is a handsome man and has a very good voice. His fault consists in his being a painter. All his attitudes on the theatre are academical. . . . He has a perversity about him which is a sign of small understanding. . . . By means of friends he often possesses himself of parts to which he has no other pretensions. He is likewise one of the few players who are rich.[34]

Lange was the favoured Hamlet in Vienna, and also played such parts as Prince Hal in Henry IV (see Plate 8). He painted a celebrated incomplete portrait of Mozart, and in 1783 took part in a Masquerade devised by the composer (K. 446). This entertainment, which was performed during a Redoutensaal Ball in Vienna, was accompanied by verses by Müller, and the whole circle seem to have participated: Mozart played Harlequin, Aloisia Lange was Columbine, while Joseph Lange took the part of Pierrot. Mozart's good relationship with this group of actors is endorsed by their response to Leopold Mozart's visit to Vienna in 1785. Leopold's stay was marked by dinners at the houses of Müller, Stephanie, and Lange, all of whom appeared anxious to pay their respects to the composer's father. Later in his life, Mozart became intimate with the less distinguished theatrical circle surrounding Emanuel Schikaneder.[35] This

---

[34] J.C. Riesbeck, *Travels through Germany*, trans. Revd Mr Maty (London, 1987), i. 298. Interesting details of Burgtheater casting are provided by E. Wlassack, *Chronik des K. K. Hofburgtheaters* (Vienna, 1876).

[35] See Hildesheimer, *Mozart*, p. 295.

included members of the cast of *Die Zauberflöte* such as Benedikt Schack (Tamino) and Franz Xaver Gerl (Sarastro). His other brother-in-law by marriage, the violinist Franz Hofer, was involved with this group as well; Hofer's wife Josepha (Constanze's sister) was the first Queen of the Night.

It is inevitable that intimate social ties with actors and actresses would be coupled with interest in the spoken theatre. In this respect, Mozart needed little encouragement, since he had long been devoted to the stage. As early as 4 July 1781, Mozart told his sister that

My sole entertainment is the theatre. How I wish you could see a tragedy acted here in Vienna! Generally speaking, I do not know of any theatre where all kinds of plays are really well performed. But they are here. Every part, even the most unimportant and poorest part, is well cast and understudied.

It is probable that Mozart gained his sophisticated awareness of literary fashions through his familiarity with the theatre. This point should be borne in mind when considering the Viennese operas, and the provenance of the libretti supplied by Da Ponte. Mozart's comments on acting in Vienna are especially interesting in view of the opinions expressed by more cosmopolitan theatregoers such as Baron Riesbeck:

Dying is the principal business of every German actor, and when he knows how to give life to his death, like some great actors I have seen, whose convulsions began in the feet and ran through the whole body, he is sure of the applause of a German pit. . . . It is a fact that the pieces which have the most madmen and murderers in them, meet with the greatest approbation.[36]

It would seem that much of the acting lacked subtlety. Mozart's enjoyment and appreciation confirms the impression left by acquaintances, that outside the musical sphere the composer was not above being facetious and crude. Joseph Lange had ample opportunity to observe Mozart, and was struck by the fact that while the composer was preoccupied with work, he:

Occasionally made jests of a nature which one did not expect of him, indeed he deliberately forgot himself in his behaviour. . . . Either he intentionally concealed his inner tension behind superficial frivolity, for reasons which could not be fathomed, or he took delight in throwing into sharp contrast the divine ideas of his music and these sudden outbursts of vulgar platitudes, and in giving himself pleasure by seeming to make fun of himself.[37]

Caroline Pichler considered the composer to be something of a buffoon:

---

[36] Riesbeck, *Travels*, iii. 52.
[37] O.E. Deutsch, *Mozart: A Documentary Biography*, trans. E. Blom, P. Branscombe, and J. Noble (London, 1966), 503.

[Mozart and Haydn] were persons who displayed in their contact with others absolutely no other extraordinary intellectual capacity and almost no kind of intellectual training, of scientific or higher education. . . . Silly jokes, and in the case of Mozart an irresponsible way of life, were all that they displayed to their fellow men.[38]

It is difficult now to disentangle the truth from exaggeration resulting from the feeling that creative sensibility should be coupled with refinement. Contemporaries may have been jealous, or else shocked and disappointed that Mozart's behaviour deviated from the seemliness they expected from the composer of such delicate music. Certainly Niemetschek believed that Mozart was slandered by jealous and hostile critics in Vienna, and he may have been in a position to know. Rumours of Mozart's unpopularity circulated very soon after his arrival in Vienna. Leopold Mozart heard from independent sources that his son was boastful and critical of other musicians. Mozart denied these stories vigorously in a letter dated 22 December 1781:

I must tell you candidly that I do not think it worth the trouble to reply to all the filth which such a lousy cad and miserable bungler may have said. He only makes himself ridiculous by doing so. . . .

These uncertainties and mysteries about Mozart's behaviour will probably not be resolved until fresh evidence comes to light. The safest conclusion is that Mozart may indeed have acted in a rumbustious, indecorous, and indiscrete manner at times, but that this mood was far from habitual. It is certainly difficult to agree with the portraits of banality, crudeness, and insensitivity offered by some commentators.

[38] Quoted by Robbins Landon, *Haydn*, p. 502.

# 5

# Da Ponte and the *Buffa* Plot

> In poetry there are no contradictions. These exist only in the
> real world, not in the world of literature. What the poet creates
> must be accepted as he created it. His world is as he made it
> and not otherwise.
>
> Goethe[1]

Lorenzo Da Ponte lived his life with much the same adventurous oppor-
tunism that characterizes his *buffa* creations. Talented and ambitious, he
turned his hand to a variety of occupations as circumstances dictated. He
supplanted less ruthless men in favoured positions, not on the basis of
well-tried ability or reputation, but by seizing the chances that presented
themselves. A certain moral flexibility brought him success, yet more
than once guided him to disaster on the rocks of social and political
convention. His early life tells us much about the origins and style of his
libretti for Mozart.

Da Ponte was born into the family of a Jewish leather dealer in Cenada,
now known as Vittorio Veneto, in 1749. When his father married a
Catholic in 1763, the whole family was baptized. The 14 year-old Lorenzo
subsequently entered the local Seminary, where he was educated for the
priesthood. Almost at once, the child showed himself to be a precocious
scholar, mastering Latin, Greek, and Hebrew, while passionately devour-
ing the works of Italian Renaissance poets. Ariosto, Tasso, and Petrarch
become the models for his stylistic imitations, and helped him to develop
a literary facility and speed of composition that were later to prove
invaluable.[2]

A sedate, scholarly life was mapped out for the young man, but Da
Ponte was irresistibly attracted to Venice. The gradual decline of the
Republic as an independent power had continued for many decades, and
Venice itself became celebrated for its decadence and sensual pleasure.
The city lived for the night, and gambling and prostitution were con-
doned. Protected by masks and the darkness, high patrician families
participated in sordid intrigue. The clergy were in the forefront of social

---

[1] J. W. von Goethe, from a conversation with Heinrich Luden. Quoted in *Goethe: Conversations
and Encounters*, ed. and trans. by D. Luke and R. Pick (London, 1966), 62.

[2] For details of Da Ponte's life, see J. L. Russo, *Lorenzo Da Ponte* (New York, 1922), and
S. Hodges, *Lorenzo Da Ponte* (London, 1985).

activities, mixing freely with all ranks, and pursuing love affairs under the cloak of respectability.

Da Ponte flung himself into this turbulent world with gusto. His first stay in Venice during 1773 was disappointingly brief, since he was soon appointed to a teaching post in Treviso. Nevertheless, he managed to form an intimate liaison with a fascinating and unscrupulous patrician, Angela Tiepolo. The affair achieved some notoriety, and Da Ponte later admitted that he had been passionately in love, despite the fact that he did not 'learn anything which I did not know before, or which was worth knowing'. The following two years in Treviso were comparatively sober, as the Abbé da Ponte took the opportunity to deepen his knowledge of Italian literature. He also refined his imitative skills:

I must needs transfer into Latin the noblest passages of our authors, copying and recopying them again and again, criticizing them, expounding them, learning them by heart, trying my hand repeatedly at every style of metre and composition, striving to imitate the most beautiful thoughts, to use the most agreeable phrases.[3]

He wrote poems for public recitation, producing works more notable for their adroitness than profundity. The last piece he composed at the Seminary is typical. It was an attack on the laws of Society in the manner of Rousseau, comprising four Latin and eleven Italian poems of varying metre and type, in each of which the poet showed his talent by fitting his sentiments wittily into the precisely defined forms. However, the inflammatory nature of this work prompted official censure, and resulted in Da Ponte's expulsion from the Seminary together with a ban on his teaching throughout the Venetian Republic. The case become known in the city, and the ambitious Abbé found himself to be something of a celebrity on his return to Venice in 1776. Far from being ruined by his temerity, Da Ponte was taken up by the literary patricians Pietro Zaguri and Gasparo Gozzi. Gasparo was the brother of Carlo Gozzi, then the most formidable writer active in Venice. Da Ponte was later to owe much to Carlo Gozzi's ironic style, and he imitated the whimsical atmosphere of Gozzi's fairy-tales in several libretti.

The mixture of drollery and gravity that characterized this literary circle can be seen in the proceedings of the Accademia Granallesca, described by Carlo Gozzi in his *Memorie Inutile*. The title of the group was intended humorously (granelli = coglioni = testicoli), and they elected a patrician of absurd vanity as 'Prince', ridiculing him unmercifully. Yet at the same time they

drew from our portfolios compositions in prose and verse serious or facetious as

[3] L.Da Ponte, *Memoirs*, trans. E. Abbott (New York, 1967), 37.

the theme might be, but sensible, judicious, elegant in phrase, varied in style, and correct in diction. . . . This Academy had for its object to promote the study of our best authors, the simplicity and harmony of chastened style, and above all the purity of the Italian tongue.[4]

Da Ponte's satirical verse delighted the patricians, and his improvisatory skills were much admired. However, his personal behaviour was outrageous, even for the city where sensual pleasure ruled. He continued his religious duties while initiating an infamous affair with Angioletta Bellaudi, with whom he had more than one child. Da Ponte even lived in a brothel for a period, and was said to be found entertaining the clientele by playing the violin, dressed in his clerical paraphernalia. Yet although the poet's dissipation alienated patrician patrons, his position was secure until he chose to dabble in serious political matters. As every eighteenth-century visitor to Venice was told, all activities were licensed so long as they did not involve politics:

'In this city,' said he, 'you will find innumerable pleasures; your youth and good spirits will lay you open to many temptations; but against one thing, and one thing only, I particularly caution you:—never utter one word against the laws or customs of Venice, . . . You never know to whom you speak; in every corner spies are lurking, numbers of whom are employed at a high price to ensnare the unwary, . . .'[5]

Da Ponte ignored these prohibitions, and joined the clique led  by Giorgio Pisani. He put his satirical pen at Pisani's service, and wrote seditious political verse. His reward was denunciation and banishment from the Republic.

Da Ponte fled to Austria in 1779, and after a period in Gorizia travelled on to Dresden. It was in these cities that he probably first came into contact with the professional theatre. He may have assisted his compatriot Catarino Mazzolà (the future author of *La clemenza di Tito*) in the adaptation and translation of German and French plays, but he did no original work. A combination of ambition and circumstance ultimately brought him to Vienna in 1782. He arrived with no appointment, and few friends or contacts save a recommendation to Antonio Salieri—and yet within a year, he had insinuated himself into the influential position of Poet to the Imperial Theatres. His progress over this period is a tribute to his talent and boldness. He had written no plays, had little literary reputation, and only the slightest experience of the theatre. But he mobilized the support of the Italian party of Salieri and Count Orsini-Rosenberg, and managed to gain access to the Emperor. Here, his confidence and personal charm soon secured him the post.

[4] C.Gozzi,*Useless Memoirs*, trans. J.A.Symonds, (London, 1962), 159.
[5] Advice given to Michael Kelly,in M. Kelly, *Reminiscences*,ed. R. Fiske (London, 1975), 65.

The work that Da Ponte completed in Vienna will be examined later in the Chapter. Although few of his productions were popular successes, he nevertheless retained the Emperor's favour. His life still followed its unconventional course. On one occasion, the price of intrigue was the loss of his teeth. According to his memoirs, a 'wretched Italian' loved a young woman from the family with which Da Ponte lodged. She repulsed the man, claiming to be attached to the poet. The Italian subsequently nursed a hatred for Da Ponte, and this soon bore fruit. He met the Abbé one day in a miserable state, owing to toothache. He persuaded Da Ponte not to have the tumour lanced, but instead to apply an ointment. Da Ponte complied faithfully for several days, until a maid discovered in horror that the 'ointment' presented by the kind compatriot was nitric acid; fortunately, the treatment resulted in the disappearance of only a few teeth.

Da Ponte was not a heartless libertine, for his irregular life was complemented by an intensely sentimental affection for his family. He rarely met his relations, yet became the principal support of three brothers and nine sisters, and he never wrote of them with less than tender devotion. Moreover, Da Ponte became strongly attracted to the soprano Adriana del Bene (known as La Ferrarese after her birthplace). The liaison ultimately contributed to his downfall in Vienna, but not before having a decided effect on his work. Without the poet's infatuation with the singer who created Fiordiligi, the nature and form of *Così fan tutte* may have been very different. It is worth therefore sketching a little of what is known about this soprano.

Although Adriana Ferrarese was named after her native city, she grew into a true daughter of Venetian sensuality.[6] She was educated at the Ospedaletto, one of the four Venetian charitable institutions for young women that were famed for their musical training. The choral and orchestral concerts given by pupils were a great attraction in the eighteenth century. Here, she was fortunate to be trained by Antonio Sacchini, and to acquire experience of the operatic as well as sacred repertoire. This was possible since the serious music of the church concerts was followed by informal gatherings in the parlour. On these occasions, 'They accompanied their voices with the forte-piano, and sang a thousand buffo songs, with all that gay voluptuousness for which their country is famed'.[7] The girls competed in performing feats of technical virtuosity. Charles Burney actually heard Adriana Ferrarese herself, while she was still a pupil at the Ospedaletto. Already as an adolescent she was developing the

---

[6] The singer was born in Ferrara, and her maiden name was Gabrieli; she may have taken the pseudonym of Ferrarese to avoid confusion with the celebrated singer Catarina Gabrieli.

[7] H.L. Piozzi, *Observations and Reflections made in the course of a Journey through France, Italy and Germany* (London 1789),i. 176.

unusually wide vocal range that was to become her trademark, and which Mozart exploited to such effect in *Così fan tutte*:

La Ferrarese sang very well, and had an extraordinary compass of voice, as she was able to reach the highest E of our harpsichords, upon which she could dwell a considerable time, in a fair, natural voice.[8]

The young soprano absorbed the voluptuous spirit of her adopted city, and was not above using her charms to advantage. She was mentioned frequently in the gossiping letters of Zaguri and Casanova, long before she met Lorenzo Da Ponte.[9] In 1783, she eloped with and later married Luigi del Bene, the son of the Roman consul in Venice.

Adriana Ferrarese was 33 when she joined the Italian Opera in Vienna for the 1788 season. She soon became intimate with Da Ponte, apparently with the knowledge of Luigi del Bene. Da Ponte later described their affair with (for him) a rare candour:

There came a singer, who without having great pretensions to beauty, delighted me first of all for her voice; and thereafter, she showing great propensity toward me, I ended by falling in love with her, . . . She had in truth great merit. Her voice was delicious, her method new, and marvellously affecting. She had no striking grace of figure. She was not the best actress conceivable. But with two most beautiful eyes, with very charming lips, few were the performances in which she did not prove infinitely pleasing.[10]

Others were less impressed by her. When her name was proposed for the Vienna company, Joseph II commented as follows:

Autant que je me souviens de La Ferrarese, elle a une voix assés foible de contrealt, sait très bien la musique mais est d'une laide figure.[11]

Count Zinzendorf was also not entirely convinced, although he did approve of the voice itself:

Elle chant à ravir, elle ne joua pas mal, mais elle était mal vetue surtout tant qu'elle portait le manteau, la gaze l'empechait de marcher.[12]

Adriana Ferrarese seems to have used her power over Da Ponte to

---

[8] C. Burney, *The Present State of Music in France and Italy*, 2nd edn. (London, 1773),150.

[9] See 'Lettere Inedite del patrizio Pietro Zaguri a Giacomo Casanova', ed. by P. Molmenti, *Atti del Reale Istituto Veneto di Scienze, Lettere ed Arti*, 70 (1910–11).

[10] Da Ponte, *Memoirs*, p. 184.

[11] Memorandum from Joseph II to Count Rosenberg dated 26 July 1788. See R. Payer von Thurn, *Joseph II als Theaterdirektor* (Vienna, 1920).

[12] This comment was made following a performance of *L'arbore di Diana*. See L. and K. Zinzendorf, *Ihr Selbstbiographien* (Vienna, 1879). His compliments of Adriana Ferrarese's singing were endorsed by the review of this performance in the *Rapport von Wien*, quoted in Hodges, *Lorenzo Da Ponte*, p. 84: 'Connoisseurs of music claim that not within living memory has such a voice been heard within the walls of Vienna.'

maintain a position at the Opera for which her talents were barely adequate. He insisted that she be given leading roles in three operas he had written: Martín y Soler's extremely successful *L'arbore di Diana*, Salieri's *La Cifra* and *Così fan tutte*. The soprano had performed at the Italian Opera in London during the middle years of the decade, and a number of contemporary descriptions of her singing survive. William Parke played in the orchestra during her first season, and later recalled that 'Ferrarese had a sweet voice, and sang with taste, but she was not calculated to shine as a prima donna'.[13] Lord Mount Edgcumbe was a fanatical devotee of the opera, although unfortunately very partisan in his tastes (being a great admirer of Brigida Banti and the *opera seria*). His comments on Adrianna Ferrarese may not therefore be reliable:

Ferrarese del Bene, who had been very much extolled to me, was but a very moderate performer. She was this year [1786] disgraced to *prima buffa* [from the seria], but even in this subordinate line was . . . ineffective.[14]

Mozart's opinion of the singer can be inferred from two of his surviving letters. In the first, penned during the North German tour of 1789, he commented on an opera in Dresden:

But the leading woman singer, Madame Allegranti, is far better than Madame Ferraresi, which, I admit, is not saying very much.[15]

Later that summer, she took the role of Susanna in the successful revival of *Le nozze di Figaro*, and insisted on being given new arias. Mozart obliged by replacing the Act IV aria with 'Al desio di chi t'adora' (K. 577), while La Ferrarese probably sang the short 'Un moto di gioia' (K. 579) in place of Susanna's Act II 'Venite inginocchiatevi':

The little aria, which I composed for Madame Ferrarese, ought, I think, to be a success, provided she is able to sing it in an artless manner, which, however, I very much doubt. She herself liked it very much. I have just lunched at her house.[16]

Rivalry among the singers at the Burgtheater was intense, and Da Ponte alienated many with his support of Adriana Ferrarese. Matters were not helped by the Abbé's own arrogant and conceited manner. Michael Kelly, who once aped the Italian in an opera by Righini, has left a concise portrait. Da Ponte had

a remarkably awkward gait, a habit of throwing himself (as he thought) into a

---

[13] W. Parke, *Musical Memoirs* (London, 1830), i. 49

[14] Mount Edgcumbe, *Musical Reminiscences* (London, 1827), 60. Contemporary newspaper critics in London (as in the *Morning Chronicle*, 24 May 1786) were also unimpressed, describing La Ferrarese as 'not quite perfect in her musical task'.

[15] Letter to Constanze Mozart dated 16 Apr 1789.

[16] Letter to Constanze Mozart, end of Aug 1789.

graceful attitude, by putting his stock behind his back, and leaning on it; he had also a very peculiar, rather dandyish, way of dressing; for in sooth, the Abbé stood mighty fine with himself, and had the character of a consumate coxcomb; he had also a strong lisp and broad Venetian dialect.[17]

Furthermore, Adriana Ferrarese herself was not an engaging character; according to Da Ponte, she 'had an impulsive, violent disposition, rather calculated to irritate the malevolent than to win friendships'.

The discontent within the Italian Opera was becoming increasingly vehement when Da Ponte lost his major patron on the death of Joseph II. Emperor Leopold was not a particular admirer of his, although generally deferring to Salieri on musical matters. Da Ponte was also unfortunate to come under the general suspicion accorded to literary foreigners in the months following the Bastille. The chief of police, Count Pergen, imposed surveillance on French and Italian émigrés, and upon the coffee houses and inns they frequented. The articulate and potentially dangerous Da Ponte was particularly vulnerable, but he was also foolhardy. In a desperate effort to retain his position, he wrote a letter to Leopold in blank verse, and this was soon released by his enemies to the city. In it, he mixed his complaints with egalitarian boldness ('My destiny does not depend on you; with all your power you have no rights over my soul . . .'). His contract was abruptly terminated, and he left Vienna in April 1791.[18]

Da Ponte wrote or adapted fifteen works for the Opera over his years in the Austrian capital. His tally of successes was not outstanding, although this is scarcely surprising with collaborators such as Righini and Piticchio. He acknowledged the three libretti for Mozart as his most significant work only after the blossoming of the composer's posthumous reputation in the early nineteenth century. The later history of Da Ponte's liaison with La Ferrarese is predictable. They left Vienna together, but the soprano abandoned him in Trieste. She travelled on to Venice, where he was still *persona non grata*. Da Ponte wrote bitterly of their separation:

But in spite of terrible sacrifices I had made for her, in spite, in a word, of a thousand promises, a thousand protestations of love and of gratitude, a vain yearning for a wealth longed for but never attained filled her natively romantic head with a thousand dreams of vanity and grandeur, . . . she forgot . . . every sentiment of affection and gratitude.[19]

Other evidence suggests that he was not being candid about the affair. Adriana Ferrarese's father-in-law had recently died, and Luigi del Bene

[17] Kelly, *Reminiscences*, p. 119.
[18] Hodges, *Lorenzo Da Ponte*, p. 110.
[19] Da Ponte, *Memoirs*, p. 213.

was hoping to succeed him as consul in Venice. But in a despicable attempt to ingratiate himself with the Venetian authorities, Da Ponte released private letters incriminating del Bene as disloyal to the State. Even Zaguri and Casanova were horrified by Da Ponte turning informer, and Adriana Ferrarese's break with him is not surprising.

They were, however, to meet once more some years later, when the rehabilitated Da Ponte was travelling through Italy commissioning singers for the Opera in London. La Ferrarese, now rather older although still needing employment, tried to insinuate herself back into his favour. As they were riding in a gondola towards the theatre in Venice, they stopped for an ice. La Ferrarese complemented him,

'Do you know, Da Ponte, you are handsomer than ever?' Delighted by a chance to have my little revenge for the wrongs she had done me, I replied: 'I'm sorry not to be able to say as much of you!' She fell back silent, blushed, and I thought her eyes filled with tears.[20]

## Themes in *Opera Buffa*—Da Ponte's Adaptations

The literati of the eighteenth century were ambivalent about *opera buffa*. On the one hand the form was admired since it represented bourgeois taste and not the refined pomposity of the nobility. Characters were drawn from everyday life, rather than being abstract ideals, and different figures in the plot shared similar thoughts and desires, irrespective of social status. They reflected the underlying natural identity of all people—a sentiment much approved by the Enlightenment.[21] On the other hand, *buffo* was considered to be musically and intellectually inferior to *seria*, so cultivated people were embarrassed at being identified too closely with the form. Even Goldoni felt that he had to excuse himself for writing any *buffa* at all. Instead of taking pride in the refinements he introduced into the form, he denigrated the whole enterprise:

What are the precepts of comic opera? What are its rules? It has none. All is done by routine; I know from experience . . . I never thought of composing any from taste or choice, and I never laboured on them but from motives of complaisance or interest.[22]

Some of Goldoni's misgivings were certainly due to the looseness of form in *opera buffa*. Eighteenth-century Italian writers were anxious to obey the rules of classical drama, and this was difficult within the constraints of the comic text. The Aristotelian concept of the Unities was a

[20] Da Ponte, *Memoirs*, pp. 284–5.
[21] See C. Rosen, *The Classical Style* (London, 1971), for a discussion of this issue.
[22] C. Goldoni, *Memoirs*, trans. by J. Black (London, 1838), ii. 157.

central ideal, and remained a powerful force throughout this period. The
good drama should obey the unities of time (24 hours), place, and theme.
Goldoni was at pains to explain that his comic works respected the
Unities, despite an apparent diffuseness of plot:

The unities requisite for the perfection of theatrical works have at all times been
the subject of discussion among authors and amateurs . . . The action of my
comedies was always confined to the same town; and the characters never
departed from it. It is true they went from one place to another; but all these
places were within the same walls; . . . in this manner the unity of place was
sufficiently observed.[23]

Da Ponte was educated in the same beliefs, and the plots of his libretti are
also confined in time and place. The complaints made about the
improbable speed of the action—the construction of the Commendatore's statue in *Don Giovanni*, or the rapidity of the seductions in
*Così fan tutte*—have little meaning in this context. These elements were
deliberately engineered to comply with contemporary ideals, and are not
consequences of inept plotting or poor characterization.

Another formal convention retained in comedy was the *lieto fine*—the
happy ending, produced either through revelation, clemency, or change
of heart, in which all characters were reconciled and the status quo
restored. This concept underlies the abrupt transposition of affection at
the end of *Così fan tutte*, when the lovers return to their original
pairings (having spent most of the opera escaping from them). Here
again, critics who have failed to take account of eighteenth-century rules
have berated Da Ponte for satisfying the obligations of form.[24] It will be
seen in Chapter 6 that similar dislocations occurred in many works of the
period, and are unlikely to have disturbed contemporary audiences.

Da Ponte turned to *opera buffa* with little prior experience, and no
respect for his predecessors:

Poor Italy, what trash! No plots, no characters, no movement, no grace of
language or style! Written to produce laughter, anyone would have judged that
most were written to produce tears. There was not a line in those miserable
botches that contained a flourish, an oddity, a graceful turn calculated in any
sense to produce a laugh . . . I guessed that it should not be a difficult matter to
compose something better than that![25]

He and Mozart have been credited with bringing the form to maturity,
transforming an enjoyable but trivial entertainment into one celebrating
the richness and diversity of human experience. It has been suggested

[23] Goldoni, *Memoirs*, i. 262.

[24] For further discussion of this point, see A. Steptoe, 'The sources of *Così fan tutte*: A
Reappraisal', *Music and Letters*, 62 (1981), 281–94.

[25] Da Ponte, *Memoirs*, p. 131.

that these advances were made possible by the fusion of serious elements with the comic, and the introduction of socially significant themes into a medium that was formerly designed merely to please. While there is prima-facie evidence for this view in the fact that few earlier *buffo* operas have enjoyed any sustained reputation, it is worth pausing to consider whether Da Ponte himself developed the form, or if he was simply a talented, flexible adaptor fortunate enough to collaborate with a composer of genius.

As the music of the mid-eighteenth century becomes more familiar through the efforts of academic researchers and performers, it is clear that many of the 'advances' formerly ascribed to Mozart and Da Ponte had important precedents. Thus Da Ponte was not the first to combine serious and comic features in *opera buffa*. The *partie serie* were well established in earlier compositions, although they tended to be sharply distinguished from *buffo* types.[26] These serious characters aped the formalities of *opera seria* with refined speech and a general aloofness from the proceedings. The potential for parody in such parts was recognized by Goldoni:

Comedy, which is an imitation of nature, ought not to reject virtuous and pathetic sentiment, if the essential object be observed of enlivening it with those comic and prominent traits which constitute the very foundations of its existence.[27]

Yet *buffo* authors understood that sentiment could be touching as well as amusing, and exploited these elements even while satirizing them. *Opera buffa* did not reject the serious, but shunned solemnity. It is true that Mozart's works are difficult to classify, owing to the profundity with which apparently light themes are developed; yet little responsibility for this can be attributed to the librettist.[28]

The majority of Da Ponte's works for the stage are adaptations, and his original pieces are rare. *Don Giovanni, Una cosa rara*, and *Le nozze di Figaro* are all reworkings, as are most of the less well-known pieces: *Il burbero di buon cuore, La Cifra, Axur* and *Il pastor fido*. The Abbé not only searched out earlier opera libretti for revision, but also found old plays that were quite suitable. Along with his contemporaries, he was attracted to seventeenth-century Spanish works, and based *Una cosa rara* on Guevara (or Calderon as he thought). Similarly, Carlo Gozzi derived his notorious *Le droghe d'amore* from a play by Tirso, while Johann

---

[26] For a discussion of this and other precedents for Da Ponte's approach, see M. F. Robinson, *Opera before Mozart* (London, 1978). The Singspiel tradition also incorporated satires on the effusive melodrama of *opera seria*; see E. M. Batley, *A Preface to The Magic Flute* (London 1969), 22.

[27] Goldoni, *Memoirs*, i. 264.

[28] Mixed-genre works were written by many authors, and titles such as *dramma giocoso* and *dramma eroicomico* abounded. See M. Hunter, 'The Fusion and Juxtaposition of Genres in *Opera Buffa* 1770–1800: Anelli and Piccinni's *Griselda*', *Music and Letters*, 67 (1986), 363–80.

Gottlieb Stephanie culled a work of Calderon for *Der Oberamtman und die Soldaten*. Da Ponte acknowledged only one completely original libretto: *L'arbore di Diana*, a piece in Gozzi's fairytale style written for Adriana Ferrarese and set by Martín y Soler. *Così fan tutte* may also have some claim to originality, although it will be seen in Chapter 6 that the story has a long ancestry. Moreover, despite his avowed contempt for other *buffo* librettists, Da Ponte was not above absorbing some of their ideas into his own work. It is well established that he based the text of *Don Giovanni* on Giovanni Bertati's *Don Giovanni Tenorio*, and it appears that he even borrowed from his arch-rival Giambattista Casti.[29] Casti was the author of *Il rè Teodoro*, the opera by Paisiello that was so hugely successful in Vienna in 1784. Alberto Ghislanzoni has pointed out that the Catalogue Aria from *Don Giovanni* is closely modelled on the list of accusations read by the chief of police to the disgraced Teodoro.[30] Similarly, Cherubino's Act II aria 'Voi che sapete' is derived from Lisetta's song 'O giovinette innamorate' from Act I of Casti's piece.

Da Ponte was a realist with a shrewd sense of stagecraft, and he did not regard his work as sacrosanct. Accordingly, he was prepared to tailor his verse to immediate requirements:

I realised that it was not sufficient to be a great poet to write a good play; that no end of tricks had to be learned—the actors, for instance, had to be studied individually, that their parts might fit; that one had to watch actual performances on the stage to note the mistakes of others and one's own, and then, after two or three thousand booings, find some way to correct them.[31]

Mozart also considered flexibility to be a major asset in a librettist:

Why, an opera is sure of success when the plot is well worked out, with words written solely for the music and not shoved in here and there to suit some miserable rhyme (which, God knows, never enhances the value of any theatrical performance, be it what it may, but rather detracts from it)—I mean, words or even entire verses which ruin the composer's whole idea. Verses are indeed the most indispensible element for music—but rhymes—solely for the sake of rhyming—the most detrimental. Those high and mighty people who set to work in this pedantic fashion will always come to grief, both they and their music. The best thing of all is when a good composer, who understands the stage and is talented enough to make sound suggestions, meets an able poet, that true phoenix; . . .[32]

---

[29] See Introduction, fn 7 for references to the origins of *Don Giovanni*. It has been suggested that the first opera on the theme was *La privatà castigata* by Eustachio Bambini, written in 1734 and produced in Brno. In this version, the role of Don Giovanni was sung by a woman. See C. Russell, 'The First Don Giovanni Opera: *La privatà castigata* by Eustachio Bambini', *Mozart-Jahrbuch 1980-83*, 385–92.

[30] See A. Ghislanzoni, *Giovanni Paisiello* (Rome, 1969).

[31] Da Ponte, *Memoirs*, p. 136.

[32] Letter to Leopold Mozart dated 13 Oct. 1781. Instances of Mozart's own theatrical pragmatism are discussed in Chapter 7.

This suggests that Mozart was not reticent in his demands on his poets, nor Da Ponte reluctant to comply. Unfortunately, the full extent of Mozart's influence on the Abbé's verse is difficult to assess. Some propagandists have ascribed the delights of the operas entirely to Mozart, achieved despite rather than with Da Ponte's help. Yet the argument is two-edged. If Mozart is to be credited with the glories of these works, he must also take responsibility for the less effective and dramatically weaker sections. The issue is not to be settled by belief or faith however, but through evaluation of the evidence.

One way of identifying the composer's influence is to distinguish features that are common to all the poet's libretti from those that are prominent only in the Mozart works. The elements characteristic of the partnership can then be separated from those attributes of the poet's style that are found in his other work. Mozart's contribution may thus be delineated by comparing *Le nozze di Figaro*, *Don Giovanni*, and *Così fan tutte* with Da Ponte's remaining works. Limitations of space preclude a detailed analysis. However, one of the most striking features to emerge from such a comparison is the high proportion of ensembles included in the Mozart works. Arias consistently make up a smaller portion of the whole in the Mozart operas compared with libretti written for other composers. In *Le nozze di Figaro* and *Don Giovanni*, arias comprise some 50 per cent of the musical numbers (14 out of 28 and 13 out of 24 respectively, in the original versions). When the size of the ensemble finales (counted here as single numbers) is taken into account, an even larger proportion of the music is given over to interaction and exchange between characters. In contrast, the highly successful *Una cosa rara* contains 19 arias in 30 numbers (63 per cent), while *L'arbore de Diana* has 19 in 32, so solo contributions predominate in these works. The emphasis on ensemble was developed even further in *Così fan tutte*, where only 12 pieces out of 31 (39 per cent) are solo pieces. The composer's will must be in evidence here, since Da Ponte clearly had no personal predilection for ensemble. These differences indicate that Mozart must have felt himself 'talented enough to make sound suggestions'.

## The Compression of *Le nozze di Figaro*

Da Ponte's first two major works for Mozart both reflect the exigencies of adaptation. The problem in *Le nozze di Figaro* was to prune a large and complex plot, while in the case of *Don Giovanni* it was necessary massively to expand the source material. The omissions that Da Ponte chose to make in *Le nozze di Figaro* are enlightening. Beaumarchais's five-Act play is rich but discursive, and Da Ponte was compelled either to simplify or remove several strands of plot. The first step was to reduce the cast of characters playing a full dramatic role to a manageable number. The prime victims of this process were the music master Bazile, Marceline, and Bartholo. In Beaumarchais's play, Bazile nurses some affection for Marceline, and causes a number of complications in Acts II and IV. These were excised from the libretto, leaving Don Basilio as a mere factotum of Count Almaviva, with no desires of his own. Marcellina suffers a similar fate, albeit retaining some personal force. Beaumarchais's matronly figure shows a desire for Figaro that is ridiculous but not incomprehensible, and she displays much insight into masculine expectations of female behaviour (notably in Act III, Scene xvi). Most of this material is lost in the opera, and the character is only partly compensated by the rarely performed Act IV aria, 'Il capro e la capretta'.

Other abbreviations were forced upon Da Ponte by the requirements of the *buffo* form. This is clearly seen in the finales, which according to tradition were completed by fast tutti sections. Beaumarchais was under no such constraint, so was able to complete Acts quietly and without emphasis. For example, the Act II Finale of the opera is closely based on the play until the entry of Marcellina, Bartolo, and Basilio, and the statement of their case against Figaro. At this point, Beaumarchais dispersed his characters, and ended the Act delicately with the Countess and Susanna plotting their next move. Da Ponte however was obliged to close with material suitable for 'tutti allegro' and 'prestissimo' sections. It is possible that this juncture caused Mozart and Da Ponte some difficulties, for when Mozart came to set the Finale, he composed the music up to the entry of Marcellina and her associates. He then stopped and turned his attention to the unfinished segments of Act I.[33] It is probable that Mozart insisted on a rumbustious closing section for the Finale, and that the verse was not written until a later stage.

Similarly, in Act IV, Da Ponte was constrained to remove some of the subtler irony from the disguise scenes in order to maintain the momentum of the Finale. In Beaumarchais's original, the Count has a long interview with his wife, under the impression that she is Susanna (Act V, Scene vii). The passages in which the Count admires 'Susanna's' skin and hands, comparing them favourably with the Countess, are retained in the opera. But in the play, the Count is then induced to explain his dissatisfaction with married love; his telling condemnation of mundane legitimised unions, with their lack of sparkle and adventure, does much to deepen the characterization. Unfortunately, such an exposition might have inhibited the forward thrust of the musical finale, so was omitted from the libretto.

[33] For a detailed account of the order in which the score was completed, see W. Mann, *The Operas of Mozart* (London, 1977), 371. See also A. Tyson, '*Le nozze di Figaro*, Lessons From the Autograph Score', *Musical Times*, 122 (1981), 456–61.

Such modifications were doubtless required in order to fit the complex plot into a suitably operatic form. However, Da Ponte also introduced more radical alterations, with the distinct (albeit related) purpose of allowing the characters to operate unambiguously in the comedy of intrigue. Beaumarchais's play concerned multidimensional people with mixed, sometimes inconsistent, motives. Da Ponte stripped the central protagonists of their complexities, so that they could articulate the plot almost as familiar stereotypes—rapacious nobleman, neglected wife, wily servant, and so on.

The results of Da Ponte's simplifications are therefore most evident in his treatment of the major figures in the story. Beaumarchais's Countess is an enigmatic creation, whose ambivalent feelings for the Count and Chérubin are not disguised. In her first scenes (Act II, scenes i and iii), she becomes inattentive and absent-minded as she muses on Chérubin, even before meeting him on stage. Her feelings expand in the closing stages of the Act, when it is revealed that Chérubin has been wearing a ribbon of hers that he purloined illicitly. In scene xxv she takes up the ribbon as a talisman, and by doing so acknowledges her feelings for the boy, while covertly reproaching the Count. For the Count's jealous actions have not only distressed and humiliated her, but have at the same time precipitated deeper sentiments about Chérubin than she has formerly cared to admit. The Countess's commitment becomes firmer (although still unexpressed) in Act IV, Scene iii, when the ribbon tumbles from its hiding-place in her bosom shortly before the Page enters dressed as a girl. By contrast, Da Ponte's Countess is rather less elusive. She is introduced expressing the conventional emotion of regret for lost connubial love in 'Porgi amor', and rarely departs from this level throughout the text. Da Ponte permits her to feel flattered and even flustered by Cherubino's attentions, but prevents such sensations from introducing any equivocal passions, or from casting doubt on her desire for her husband's reform.

The Count is also realized at a shallower level in the operatic text. The man portrayed in the libretto is little more than a bullying philanderer, with pride and lust his chief motives, except when occasionally overcome by guilt. Beaumarchais's Count has added dimensions of dignity appropriate to a Spanish aristocrat, while also displaying considerable insight into his own mentality. The principal confrontation between the Count and Figaro (Act II, Scene v), during which the two test each other's metal across a range of comic and serious subjects, is also unfortunately lost; and it is a mark of the librettist's approach that the operatic Count cannot begin to match Figaro for insight or quickness of thought in awkward situations. These alterations in the presentation of the Count were deliberate, and not merely by-products of abbreviating the plot, since a number of Da Ponte's additions coarsen the character still further. For example, the Count's threats to Cherubino (whom he supposes to be in the Countess's closet) in the Act II Finale ('Mora, mora, e più non sia . . .' 'He shall die, die, and I'll be rid of the source of all my torment') are far in excess of the brisk anger portrayed by Beaumarchais. Similarly, the text of the Count's aria 'Vedrò mentr'io sospiro' indicates that he is arrogantly concerned with loss of dignity ('Must I see a serf of mine made happy while I am left to sigh'), rather than distressed at slighted affection. Both these instances are interpolations by Da Ponte.

The Figaro of the play is a portrait in the mould of Beaumarchais himself, fit to have undertaken many of his creator's own exploits. Beaumarchais frequently displayed a cynical, somewhat distasteful moral pragmatism in his behaviour. For example, when he travelled to Spain in 1764–5, he was engaged in a series of dubious projects. His sister had formed a liaison with the poet Clavijo that needed to be disentangled, and he was involved in speculative plans to modernize Madrid. His brief was covertly diplomatic as well, since he was secretly acting as an envoy of the French Court. In Madrid, he rapidly acquired as mistress the Marquise de la Croix, a beautiful and popular lady in Court circles. Yet with a ruthlessness and eye to advancement that Figaro would have admired, Beaumarchais not only discharged his business, but contrived to transfer his mistress to the Spanish King before returning to France.[34]

This wide sweep is omitted from Da Ponte's adaptation. The operatic Figaro is more at home baiting his master over trivia. His disreputable side is also subdued, and he is presented as an endearing and fundamentally honest individual. It is clear in Beaumarchais's play, for example, that Figaro fathered the younger son of the judge, Don Guzman Brid'oison (himself a caricature of Councillor Goezman, Beaumarchais's opponent in a notorious lawsuit). No such aspersions are cast in the libretto. The transformation of Figaro from a grand satirical observer to *buffo* schemer is nowhere more apparent than in his Act IV aria, 'Aprite un po'quegli occhi'. Instead of the far-reaching critique of social injustice penned by Beaumarchais, Da Ponte's barber produces the typical comic opera diatribe of the cuckolded male against all women. Da Ponte's Figaro cannot with any justification declare like his original that he has 'seen everything, done everything, used up everything' (Act V, Scene iv).[35]

[34] See C. Cox, *The Real Figaro* (London, 1962), 29.

[35] Siegmund Levarie, among others, has argued that the aria 'Non più andrai farfallone' reflects Figaro's resentment of the aristocratic Cherubino, and is evidence of Mozart's subtle revolutionary intentions in this opera: see *Mozart's Le nozze di Figaro: A Critical Analysis* (Chicago, 1952). This view has however been discredited by W. J. Allanbrook, *Rhythmic Gesture in Mozart* (Chicago 1983), 95, who marshals numerous arguments to support the notion that Figaro feels affectionately towards Cherubino, and indeed wishes to enlist him in the schemes against the Count.

All these alterations had the purpose of rendering the characters in the opera less equivocal in their motives and behaviour. They could therefore be mobilized in a swiftly moving plot where the action left little room for reflection. The same aim may have governed Da Ponte's other changes from the original. The Abbé has often been accused of blunting the political edge of the play, smoothing away the controversial elements so as to serve up an acceptable product to his *ancien régime* patrons. Indeed, in his *Memoirs*, Da Ponte relates how he persuaded Joseph II to permit an operatic adaptation of the banned play by assuring him that all political references had been excised. Yet this is only half the truth. Da Ponte not only emasculated the original politically, but also removed almost all material peripheral to the central intrigue. Thus themes that were generally accepted as legitimate targets for satire, even by the ruling classes, were also taken out of the text.

This point is supported by a glance at the wealth of comment on social and political matters contained in Beaumarchais's play. Figaro's great speech of Act V (Scene iii) was considered highly inflammatory, with its denunciations of hereditary power ('Nobility, wealth, a station, emoluments: all that makes one so proud! What have you done to earn so many honours? You took the trouble to be born, that's all . . .') and censorship ('Provided I do not write about the government, or about religion, or politics, or ethics, or people in power or with influence, or the Opera, or other theatres, or about anybody connected with something, I can print whatever I chose under the supervision of two or three censors . . .').[36] Da Ponte cut out this outburst, as one might expect, but at the same time also eliminated Beaumarchais's attacks on quite uncontroversial topics. Thus the satire on legal absurdities found in the Act III Court Scene disappeared from the libretto. Similarly, a whole series of polemics on intrigue (Act III, Scene v), injustices to women (Act III, Scene vi) and gambling (Act V, Scene iii) have no place in Da Ponte's fast-moving plot. Yet these were acceptable subjects for stage satire, and were permitted in other plays produced during the 1780s in Vienna. One is drawn to the conclusion that Da Ponte's motive was not political timidity but theatrical pragmatism; all these speeches, from the most to the least contentious, were removed primarily because they were tangential to the central comedy.

The portrait of the aristocracy drawn in Mozart's opera does not break new ground in realism or audacity, but parallels contemporary trends on the stage. The nobility had long been presented in *opera buffa*, not only in *partie serie*, but as absurd caricatures. Ridiculous figures such as the Marquis de Rippafratta (in Haydn's *L'infideltà delusa* of 1773) were

---

[36] Quotations from the translation of *Le nozze di Figaro* by Vincent Luciani (New York, 1964).

created for the exquisite Court at Eszterháza. In the 1780, however, the nobility emerged in a more threatening guise, as the abuse of power and privilege became a popular theme on the stage. A fashion emerged for stories in which virtuous middle-class heroines were attacked or seduced by irresponsible social superiors, and works like *Das Fräulein von Sternheim* by Sophie de la Roche enjoyed a vogue.[37] A few months before the appearance of *Le nozze di Figaro*, the Italian Opera in Vienna had witnessed even more open denunciations of aristocratic caprice in Bianchi's *La Vilanella rapita* (text by Bertati). It is probable that much of the social and class tension of Mozart and Da Ponte's opera was defused by its conformity with current fashions.

The modifications made to *Le nozze di Figaro* were largely consequences of the problems presented by the original play. Beaumarchais's text was too long, involved, and discursive for the *opera buffa* format. Da Ponte resolved these difficulties by shearing away subplots, aspects of character, and topical allusions that were not essential to the basic imbroglio of love and jealousy. In doing this, he was able both to streamline the drama, and to evade the censor; the features which tightened his libretto as operatic material simultaneously softened the political force of the play. Paradoxically, these changes may in part account for the lukewarm reception accorded the opera on its first appearance, as will be seen in Chapter 8.[38]

*Don Giovanni* presented Da Ponte with other difficulties, since he was obliged to expand rather than compress his source. Before we consider the way in which he went about this task, a more fundamental issue must be addressed: why did Mozart and Da Ponte decide to set the story of *Don Giovanni* at all? It is astonishing that two cosmopolitan and sophisticated artists chose a plot for which the intelligentsia showed such blatant contempt. An explanation of this paradox may lie in the nature of the audience for which *Don Giovanni* was written, and in the special position of Prague during the late eighteenth century.

---

[37] See N. Elias, *The Civilising Process*, trans. E. Jephcott, (Oxford, 1978), 23.

[38] In a recent extensive discussion of the opera, Wye Allanbrook dismisses the view that Da Ponte and Mozart produced a blander version of Beaumarchais's play, arguing instead that they transformed the political satire into a 'radiant romantic comedy', centring on the friendship between Susanna and the Countess: *Rhythmic Gesture*, p. 77. In my view, this does not accord with the emphases either of the libretto or of the score. Allanbrook also suggests that Marcellina retains a more important place in the opera than is implied here: see 'Pro Marcellina: The Shape of "Figaro", Act IV', *Music and Letters*, 63 (1982), 69–84. Certainly Beaumarchais considered Marcellina a significant and interesting figure, embodying the desperate fate of many contemporary women. In the introduction to the play, he describes her as 'a woman of wit, with lively instincts, but whose mistakes and experience have reformed her character'. Little of this sympathetic presentation remains in Da Ponte's libretto, and Marcellina's abrupt transformation from opponent to supporter of Susanna in Act IV is not made plausible. For a recent detailed discussion of the relationship between Da Ponte's libretto and Beaumarchais's play, see T. Carter, *W.A. Mozart: Le nozze di Figaro* (Cambridge, 1987), 32–48.

## Opera in Context: Vienna, Prague, and *Don Giovanni*

Mozart and Da Ponte's reworking of the Don Juan legend appeared more than 150 years after Tirso de Molina wrote the story *El Burlador de Sevilla*. During the intervening period, the tale had enjoyed mixed fortunes in a series of revisions and adaptations. These debased the story to such an extent that by the middle of the eighteenth century, Don Juan had fallen very low in the esteem of intellectual and cultured people. It had been reduced to a clown's piece in the German-speaking world; a pantomime on the theme was performed annually in Vienna on All Soul's Day until 1772. There were several versions for puppets, with gruesome titles such as *Don Juan or the Quadruple Murderer*, while a Don Juan folk play was regularly given under Marinelli's direction at the Theater in der Leopoldstadt.[39]

None of these versions was likely to appeal to elevated tastes, and cultivated people viewed the story with contempt. Although Gluck's ballet *Don Juan* was received favourably in the 1760s, its success was primarily a result of the popularity of Noverre's production. In 1764, it was considered that

The Incidents are so cramm'd together in it, without any consideration of Time or Place, as to make it highly unnatural. The Villainy of Don Juan's character is worked up to such an Height, as to exceed even the Limits of Possibility.[40]

A later Italian critic was even more dismissive of the tale, and was in no doubt about the intended audience:

The common people still flock to see *Il Convitato di Pietra*, which is a Spanish comedy full of machines and devils, no longer acted in Spain. And it is no excuse that educated persons are well aware of the improprieties of such comedies, which please only the ignorant lower classes; for in the theatre the taste of the common people upheld by the educated classes is the national taste.[41]

Eighteenth-century Rationalists found the magical and unrealistic aspects of the story particularly distasteful, and regarded them as childish. Even Goldoni, who wrote a version for the stage, was anxious to disclaim responsibility for the absurdities of the plot:

Everyone knows that wretched Spanish tragicomedy which the Italians call *Il Convitato di Pietra* and the French *Le Festin de Pierre*. I have always regarded it with horror in Italy, and I could never understand why this farce should have

---

[39] See H. Abert, *Mozart's Don Giovanni*, trans. P. Gellhorn (London, 1976), 30. See also J. Austen, *The Story of Don Juan: A Study of the Legend and the Hero* (London, 1939), and O. Mandel, *The Theatre of Don Juan: A Collection of Plays and Views 1630–1963* (Lincoln, Nebr. 1963).

[40] Quoted by E.J. Dent, *Mozart's Operas* (London, 1960), 123.

[41] Quoted by Dent, *Mozart's Operas*, p. 129.

maintained itself so long, attracting crowds of spectators and being regarded as the delight of a cultivated nation. Italian actors held the same opinion, and either in jest or in ignorance, some said that the author had made a bargain with the Devil to have it kept on the stage.[42]

Giovanni Bertati, upon whose work Da Ponte based his libretto, also seems to have felt somewhat embarrassed about using the story. His *Don Giovanni Tenorio* is preceded by a prologue, in which a touring opera troupe is desperately searching for a piece that will be popular and stave off financial ruin. Don Juan is suggested as a last resort. The piece is described as 'una bella e stupenda porcheria', whose noise and bustle might appeal to the German provinces. Several of the cast promptly develop sore throats, and have to be cajoled into staging the work. Such a prologue is unlikely to have inspired the audience with reverence for the plot.

Why then was this work selected by Mozart and Da Ponte? Neither was an unworldly artist; indeed, both were unusually sensitive to the pulse of musical and dramatic taste. Yet they followed *Le nozze di Figaro*, an opera based on the most contemporary risqué material, with an old pantomime story of hellfire and seduction.

Several factors may have influenced the decision. In the first place, the pantomime elements so disparaged by the literati probably appealed to Mozart's own taste. The comments of Mozart's contemporaries outlined in Chapter 4 indicate that his humour was not elevated, and the demonry of *Don Giovanni* undoubtedly excited his imagination. More important, however, was the startling popularity of the tale. Apart from the operatic version by Bertati and Gazzaniga which appeared in January 1787, four other operas on the theme were produced in the decade before Mozart's masterpiece. Righini's *Il convitato di pietra* was given in Vienna in 1777, while others appeared in Venice and Naples. Don Juan was so popular in Rome that Goethe found that an opera of this name

was played every night for four weeks, which excited the city so much that the lowliest grocer's families were to be found in the stalls and boxes with their children and other relations, and no one could bear to live without having fried Don Juan in Hell, or seen the Commendatore, as a blessed spirit, ascend to Heaven.[43]

Even this would not have been sufficient to justify an attempt at the Don Juan story for Vienna. But Prague was a different matter. The prosperity of the city had declined since its hey-day as an Imperial Court in the seventeenth century. In Mozart's time, Prague was little more than a provincial backwater, as John Moore observed:

[42] Quoted by Dent, *Mozart's Operas*, p. 124.
[43] Quoted by Abert, *Don Giovanni*, p. 33.

It is a very large town, retaining some marks of former splendour, but many more evident symptoms of present decay—. . . for the Bohemian nobility, who are in circumstances to bear such an expense, live at Vienna.[44]

Hester Lynch Piozzi summed up the position succinctly when she concluded that 'everything seems at least five centuries behind'. The audience for the Opera was very different from the sophisticated public of Vienna:

The ladies looked more like masquerading figures than anything else, as they sat in their boxes at the opera, with rich embroidered caps, or bright pink and blue satin head-dresses . . . which gives a girlish look, and reminded me of a fashion our lower tradesmen in London had about fifteen or eighteen years ago . . .[45]

This was a city that might respond to an opera on a pantomime theme. Although some of the cultivated Bohemian nobility who lived in Vienna visited Prague and attended the theatre, the majority of the audience was drawn from a provincial public with unsophisticated tastes. Mozart and Da Ponte wrote their opera specifically for these musically appreciative, but intellectually unpretentious, listeners. The comparative failure of *Don Giovanni* in Vienna is not surprising, given the wide gulf between Prague and the capital in the late eighteenth century. Mozart's letters from Prague to Gottfried von Jacquin suggest that he did not really expect the work to appear in Vienna at all. The lack of enthusiasm that greeted *Don Giovanni* in the capital resulted principally from the unsuitability of the subject matter. It led some commentators to conclude that 'Mozart was a great genius; however, he actually had little culture and little or no informed taste'.[46]

The distinction between Prague and audiences in Vienna may also account for another interesting facet of Da Ponte's adaptation: his failure to rationalize the story. When Goldoni wrote his play, he tried to reclaim the tale for the eighteenth century by removing the magical and unrealistic components. The 'childish' talking statue was omitted, while the Don was struck by lightening, instead of being dragged down to hell. Similarly, Bertati placed the story in a context that acknowledged its absurdity. Such modifications made the plot more reasonable, at the expense of much of its dramatic power. Da Ponte on the other hand retained the supernatural elements and made few concessions to Rationalism. The response of contemporaries is interesting. Johann Friedrich

---

[44] J. Moore, *A View of Society and Manners in France, Switzerland and Germany* (London 1779), ii. 290–1.

[45] Piozzi, *Observations*, ii. 318.

[46] Quoted by Abert, *Don Giovanni*, p. 33. Audiences in Prague had in fact responded positively to earlier Don Juan works, including Righini's Opera, see J. Kristek, *Mozart's Don Giovanni in Prague* (Prague, 1987).

Schink was an admirer of Mozart, but even he emphasised how the whimsicality of the story prevented proper appreciation of the music:

According to the operatic ideal which the Italian poets have given us in their musical works, . . . a more fit and proper subject for a Singspiel could hardly have been found than this originally Spanish absurdity . . . Don Juan combines all the nonsensical, extravagant, contradictory and unnatural features that ever qualified a poetic absurdity of a human being for the role of an operatic hero. He is the stupidest, most senseless creature imaginable, the misbegotten product of a crazed Spanish imagination. The most dissolute, base and profligate fellow, whose life is an uninterrupted series of infamies, seductions of the innocent and murders. . . . At any spoken play, such a caricature would be chased off the stage with oranges and nutshells and hissed into the wings; but in an opera he is found uncommonly entertaining.[47]

As in the case of *Le nozze di Figaro*, Da Ponte relied heavily on another poet's work in building his libretto. However, his adaptation of Bertati's *Don Giovanni Tenorio* was not straightforward, since this was an opera in a single Act, and involved too many characters for the Prague company. Thus although most of Bertati's material was retained, it was elaborated extensively, and new plot developments had to be invented. The manner in which Da Ponte completed the work reflects the rapid maturation of his stagecraft, while at the same time exposing the limits of his creative imagination.

Bertati's play revolves almost exclusively around Don Giovanni. Although most of the other characters have arias, they possess little dramatic existence independently of the eponymous hero. In lengthening the work, Da Ponte was compelled to broaden the plot, and lighten the weight on Don Giovanni. He could have achieved this simply by embellishing other characters, but instead he chose a more flexible, interesting strategy. He brought forward two pairs of lovers: Anna–Ottavio and Zerlina–Masetto, and accorded them an autonomous life. In Bertati's version, Maturina (Zerlina) plays a substantial role, while her bridegroom is rapidly dismissed from the stage. Similarly, Anna disappears after the opening scenes. By enlarging these roles, Da Ponte was able to pace each pair of lovers evenly through the work, and their counterpoint provides a dramatic contrast to Don Giovanni's adventures. This can be illustrated graphically by outlining the progression of musical numbers, as in Figure 2. They are evidently grouped together rather than ordered in a haphazard fashion. The Anna–Ottavio and Zerlina–Masetto axes alternate

---

[47] Quoted in O. E. Deutsch, *Mozart: A Documentary Biography*, trans. E. Blom, P. Branscombe, and J. Noble (London, 1966), 353–4. Da Ponte mounted a production of *Don Giovanni* in 1794 at the King's Theatre in London. Instead of using Mozart's score, the work was set to music by Gazzaniga, Sarti, and others. However, according to *The Times* report of 10 Mar. 'So determined an opposition to this kind of entertainment we have never witnessed'.

# Notes to Plates

## PLATE 1

A general view of Vienna, engraved by P. F. Tardieu and published in Paris in 1785. The view shows the old city enclosed by its bastion, surrounded by the open glacis which is crossed by numerous roads and tracks. The suburbs form a ring outside the glacis, at some distance from the inner city. The Prater is to the east across the branch of the Danube that separates the old city from the newer Leopoldstadt, while the Augartan is the more formal garden lying to the north. The Landstrasse suburb lies to the south-east on this view, and the Wieden suburb is due south. The Wieden was the site of the Freihaus Theater, where *Die Zauberflöte* received its first production in 1791.

## PLATE 2

A view of the inner city of Vienna published by Artaria in 1796. It details the tightly crowded houses and mansions enclosed within the ramparts. The Imperial Palace lies to the south of the city on this view, occupying the area near the Burg Thor. The Michaelerplatz (Michaelsplatz) adjoins the palace complex, and was the site of the Burgtheater. Immediately to the east of this is the Kärntner Thor, near which the second theatre of the city was located. Access to the Landstrasse suburb was via the gates due east on this view. In the centre of the inner city, the Graben can be seen. This led to the west into the Kohlmarkt, and to the east into the Cathedral square (Stephansplatz). Mozart lived in a number of lodgings in this area over the years of his maturity.

## PLATE 3

The Michaelerplatz, from the *Collection de Vues de la Ville de Vienne*, published by Artaria in 1798. This view was engraved by Karl Schütz in 1783. The Burgtheater is seen on the right, dwarfed by the massive structure of the K. K. Reitschule (Imperial Riding School), designed by Fischer von Erlach. On the left is the Michaelskirche. The archway in the centre leads into the Josefsplatz. The leading horses of a troop of the Polish guard is depicted passing in front of the Burgtheater.

## PLATE 4

An early groundplan of the Burgtheater is shown in the left panel. The stage was situated at the end of the building adjoining the Michaelerplatz. To the left, the arena of the Reitschule can be seen. The right panel shows details of the seating arrangements for a contemporary performance, allocated according to the social status and sex of members of the audience. The relatively small number of seats is apparent. From Wlassack, *Chronik*.

## PLATE 5

The Graben, engraved by Karl Schütz in 1781, from the *Collection de Vues de la Ville de Vienne*. This view of one of the main squares of the inner city is taken from the east, looking towards the Kohlmarkt. On the right is the Trattnerhof, five stories high and decorated with collosal figures. This building contained the lodgings of some 200 families, together with the workshops of Johann Trattner's printing, publishing, and papermaking business. Mozart and Constanze lived there (on the second staircase, third floor) from January 1784 for several months.

## PLATE 6

The river (Wien Fluss) to the east of the city, crossed by the bridge and road to the Landstrasse, engraved by Johann Ziegler in 1792, and published in the *Collection de Vues de la Ville de Vienne*. This perspective from the inner city indicates the distance of the suburb from the centre of commercial and artistic activity. Mozart lived in the Landstrasse on more than one occasion in his later years, when forced by poverty to seek inexpensive lodgings. The large building to the left of the road is the Invalidenhaus, converted in 1783 by Joseph II into a hospital for wounded soldiers and veterans. In front of it, the cattle pen called the Ochsenstand can be seen. The Landstrasse was the main thoroughfare for traffic from Hungary and the east, and cattle driven through the suburb from the country were kept in the Ochsenstand until required by the butchers of the city.

## PLATE 7

A view of the gardens of the Reisenberg with a group of unidentified ladies and gentlemen admiring the view, engraved by Johann Ziegler and published in the *Collection de Vues de la Ville de Vienne*. The Reisenberg was the summer residence of Count Johann Philipp Cobenzl, and was situated on the eastern spur of the Kahlengebirge in the Wienerwald. It overlooked Vienna, and was celebrated for its gardens and grotto. Cobenzl was an early patron of Mozart in Vienna, and the composer spent several weeks at the Reisenberg in 1781. He praised the park in the letter to Leopold Mozart described in Chapter 4.

## PLATE 8

Joseph Lange in a typically heroic pose. The actor is shown playing the role of

Count Albrecht in Count J. A. von Torring's *Agnes Bernauerinn,* engraved by Carl Pfeiffer in 1793. Lange specialized in romantic leading roles at the Burgtheater (see Chapter 4).

## PLATE 9

An engraving of Nancy Storace by Bettelini, published in 1788. Nancy Storace was a soprano of mixed English and Italian descent, and was a member of the Italian Opera in Vienna from 1783 to 1787. She created the role of Susanna in *Le nozze di Figaro*, and was a close friend of Mozart (see Chapter 7).

## PLATE 10

An engraving of the Italian singer Francesco Benucci. Benucci was the foremost *buffo* in Europe during the 1780s, and appeared for several seasons at the Italian Opera in Vienna. He was the first Figaro, the first Leporello in Vienna, and created the role of Guglielmo in *Così fan tutte* (see Chapter 7).

## PLATE 11

An engraving of the stage of the Burgtheater, after a picture by Canaletto. The view shows the stage during the performance of a ballet pantomime entitled *Le Turc Genereux* in April 1758. Although dating from several years before Mozart's maturity, the arrangement of the orchestra that persisted through the 1780s is clearly depicted. The picture is also interesting as an early example of the presentation of Turks in a favourable light on the stage.

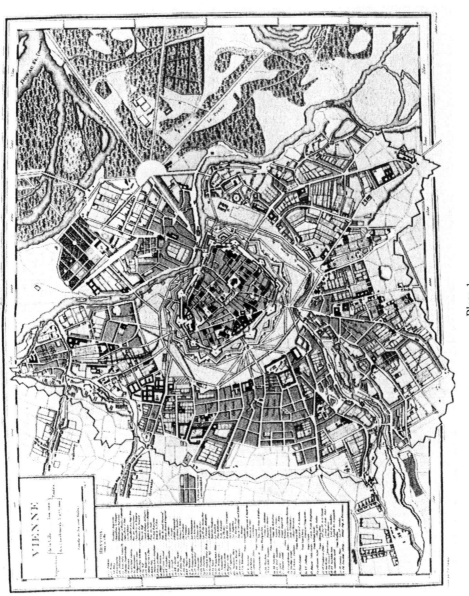

Plate 1

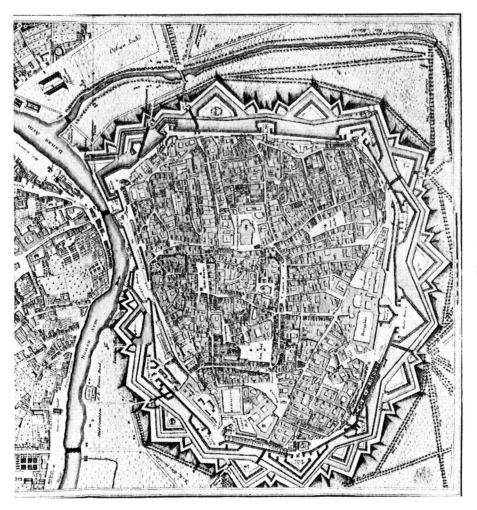

Plate 2

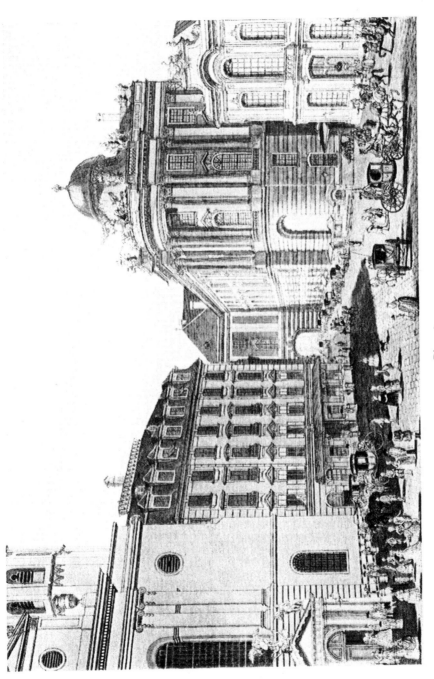

Plate 3

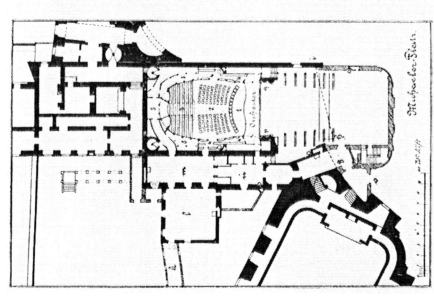

Das Burgtheater 1748, 1759 und ff.

Plate 4

Plate 5

Plate 6

Plate 7

Plate 8

Plate 9

Plate 10

Plate 11

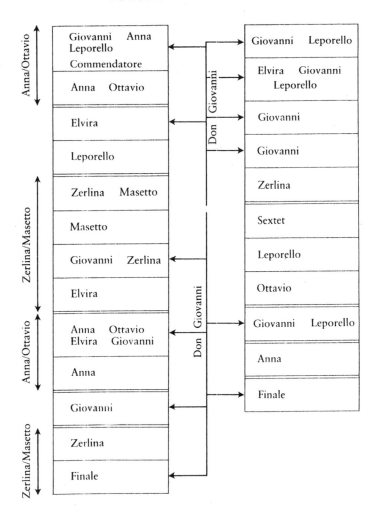

Figure 2.   Overall Plan of *Don Giovanni*. The figure shows the sequence of musical numbers in *Don Giovanni*. The column on the left represents Act I and that on the right, Act II. The arrows on the left of the figure illustrate the alternation of Anna/Ottavio and Zerlina/Masetto in the action of Act I. The arrows emerging from the central line indicate the involvement of Don Giovanni himself in the musical numbers. The double horizontal lines represent major scene changes.

throughout the first Act, each appearing twice before the Finale. Don Giovanni himself is usually involved at some point, but always disappears to allow the couples to pursue their own relationships as well. By expanding the dramatic importance of these pairs of lovers, Da Ponte decentralized the whole structure, so that it did not flag when the hero was absent.

This pattern breaks down in Act II. As Julian Rushton has noted, many commentators have lamented Da Ponte's lack of inspiration in the second Act.[48] The pedestrian aspects of Act II stem from the fact that Da Ponte was lengthening (perhaps at haste) rather than creating. Apart from the cemetery scene and the denouement, most of Bertati's material was exhausted in Act I. Da Ponte unfortunately failed to introduce any powerful new motifs in Act II, but fell back on the stock *buffo* device of disguise. Thus Don Giovanni and Leporello exchange roles with amusing consequences. The master in the guise of his servant gulls and beats Masetto, while Leporello's concealment as Don Giovanni leads to universal uproar and recrimination in the Sextet.[49] The dramatic form was further diluted by the necessity of providing arias for Ottavio and Anna. Yet at the end, Da Ponte greatly strengthened the Finale by focusing Bertati's scenario more sharply. In *Don Giovanni Tenorio*, the supper scene is complex and relatively extended. Elvira's entry and plea for Don Giovanni's repentance is followed by an aria in which she determines to retire to a convent. Thereupon, the servant Pasquarello is given an aria in order to toast the city in which the opera is being performed (originally Venice); only then does the statue arrive. Da Ponte's distillation unifies the Finale, by generating the momentum and contrast that he achieved so successfully in *Le nozze di Figaro*.

Since Da Ponte relied heavily on earlier models for *Le nozze di Figaro* and *Don Giovanni*, these libretti reveal little of the man himself. *Così fan tutte* is more illuminating of the poet's own predilections. The absence of a close contemporary model on which to base the text gave Da Ponte and Mozart an opportunity to explore current fashions of thought and sentiment with greater flexibility. However, the questions of authorship and originality present special problems in *Così fan tutte*, as will be seen in the next chapter.

---

[48] J. Rushton, *W. A. Mozart, Don Giovanni* (Cambridge, 1981), 46.

[49] The autograph score of the opera suggests that the work was originally planned in four Acts, and that the Sextet was to be the Finale of Act III.

# 6

## *Così fan tutte* and Contemporary Morality

Why do we live in such an age, and among such men, that one
may, and indeed must, consider it a merit to be not merely
tender, but human with women

Restif de la Bretonne[1]

The sources for the text of *Così fan tutte* are mysterious. The ingenious,
symmetrical plot derives from themes with a long history in European
literature; nevertheless, the opera bears a marked contemporary gloss.
Features such as the Moorish disguises and the Mesmeric episode in the
Finale of Act I indicate that Da Ponte was writing in full knowledge of the
most recent theatrical fashions. Yet even the basic question of whether
Da Ponte followed his usual practice of adapting an earlier play, or
produced an original libretto, remains unresolved. Very little information survives about the composition of the opera, or its first performance.
Moreover, until recently, arguments concerning the libretto have been
tinged by the opprobrium in which the story has been held. Commentators have tried to absolve Mozart of responsibility for setting this 'immoral'
work. It has been suggested that Mozart was commanded to write the
music by Joseph II, and could not refuse because of his straightened
circumstances in 1789. Joseph was said to have proposed the story after he
had heard about a true incident in contemporary Vienna. Niemetschek,
in his early biography, clearly found it impossible that his idol could have
set *Così fan tutte* except under duress:

Everyone was astonished that this man could have demeaned himself to waste
his heavenly melodies on such a worthless libretto. It did not, however, lie in his
power to refuse the commission, and the libretto was specially provided. [2]

However, there is no tangible evidence for these theories. The notion of a
true origin for the plot was first propagated in 1837, no less than forty-
eight years after the première, by Friedrich Heinse in his *Reise und
Lebens-Skizzen*. Joseph II was in fact extremely ill throughout the period
in which the opera was being planned, and his energies were entirely
devoted to the management of the Turkish Wars and the civil unrest in

---

[1] Restif de la Bretonne, *Monsieur Nicolas*, trans. and ed. R. Baldick (London, 1966), 457.
[2] F. X. Niemetschek, *The Life of Mozart*, trans H. Mautner (London, 1956), 38.

the Empire.[3] There is no mention of *Così fan tutte* in Joseph's extensive memoranda to Count Rosenberg, nor indeed proof that the Emperor knew of the work's existence.

Da Ponte himself was reticent about his contribution. Not that he was generally reluctant to take responsibility for any work that involved Mozart; his memoirs are punctuated with passages of self-congratulation:

> I can never remember without exultation and complacency that it was to my perseverance and firmness alone that Europe and the world in great part owe the exquisite compositions of that admirable genius.[4]

Yet *Così fan tutte* receives only a passing reference as one of the pieces written for his mistress, the soprano Adriana Ferrarese. He neither claims the libretto as original nor specifies a source for an adaptation; rather, he preferred to keep the whole matter of authorship quiet. It should be borne in mind, however, that he wrote his memoirs during the early nineteenth century in New York, when the moral climate was far stricter than that pervading in his youth.

If Da Ponte did invent the libretto unaided, it was a departure from his usual practice. As was noted in Chapter 5, almost all his texts were derived from earlier stage works.[5] The only piece for which Da Ponte claimed complete originality was *L'arbore di Diana*, written for Martín y Soler in 1787. It is a classical fantasy in the style of Carlo Gozzi. The story concerns a magic tree in the garden of the chaste Goddess Diana. Whenever a pure nymph walks beneath the tree, beautiful music is heard and the apples shine; but if the lady is guilty in thought or deed, the fruit blackens and falls. This state of affairs is anathema to Cupid, who enters the garden in disguise and undermines the virtue of the nymphs. Subsequently he introduces Endymion, and it is the turn of Diana herself to become enamoured. The Goddess and her companions are eventually put to the test by the priest of the cult, and all are convicted by the tree. Diana orders the tree to be cut down, and the garden is transformed into a palace of love.

---

[3] See Chapter 1. For a day-to-day account of the Emperor's health, and the repeated fears for his life in 1789, see the reports from George Hammond, British Chargé d'affaires in Vienna, Public Records Office, Foreign Office 7, Vol. 17, etc.

[4] L. Da Ponte, *Memoirs*, trans. E. Abbott (New York, 1967), 148.

[5] In 1965, Ann Livermore suggested that the origins of *Così fan tutte* could be found in *La celosa de si misma* and *El amor medico*, two plays by Tirso de Molina (see A. Livermore, '*Così fan tutte*: A Well-kept Secret', *Music and Letters*, 46 (1965), 316–21). Tirso was of course the author of the Don Juan story adapted by Mozart and Da Ponte in 1787, and there was considerable interest in his plays during the eighteenth century (See A. H. Bushee, *Three Centuries of Tirso De Molina* (Philadelphia, 1939)). None the less, some years ago this attractive suggestion was effectively discounted by Kurt Kramer (see 'Da Ponte's *Così fan tutte*', *Nachrichten der Akademie der Wissenschaften in Göttingen*, (Phil.-Hist. Klasse, 1973), No. 1). He showed that the textual similarities identified by Livermore are largely Metastasian conceits rather than direct quotations from the Spanish, and that the other parallels between the works are slight.

This story is apparently far removed from the contemporary tone of *Così fan tutte*, yet the contrast may be largely superficial. Apart from overt differences of period and style, there is much in common between the works. Both create highly artificial worlds in which the temptation and fall of women is displayed in clinical detail. *L'arbore di Diana* proclaims that all struggle against Cupid's will is futile, while *Così fan tutte* documents a more cynical route to the same conclusion. *L'arbore di Diana* actually had topical implications as a satire on monastic practices. Furthermore, both operas are strongly indebted to Gozzi, who invented not only fairytale stories such as *Il re cervo* and *L'amore delle tre melerance*, but also jaundiced satires and comedies of passion like *Le droghe d'amore* and *Il segreto publico*. Thus it is not surprising that two such disparate pieces should have come from Da Ponte's pen.[6]

The question of Da Ponte's originality is impossible to resolve on the evidence currently available. Whatever the truth, the germs of the story of *Così fan tutte* are not his personal invention. The plot can be seen as the fusion of two traditional stories, developed by Da Ponte in the light of contemporary theatrical fashions.

## The sources of *Così fan tutte*

The story of *Così fan tutte* is compounded of two threads, each of which had been employed frequently by earlier writers. The 'wager theme' concerns a man who publicly declares his confidence in his wife's fidelity, and wagers that she cannot be seduced by a supposed admirer. He thereby sanctions a trial of her affections, giving the seducer permission to approach her, usually with disastrous results. The wager theme can be traced back to the thirteenth century, and may have even earlier origins. Its most famous versions were written by Boccaccio and Shakespeare; however, the plot also appeared in French, German, and Scandinavian literature of the sixteenth century.[7] The social status of the characters varied in each presentation, as did the moral purposes of the authors.

The basic wager story is related in the ninth novella of the second day of Boccaccio's *Decameron* (1348–53). It concerns a group of wealthy Italian merchants visiting Paris. They agree among themselves that their wives are probably unfaithful when left alone during such journeys. The merchants are not censorious, since they admit that they too indulge in illicit affairs if given the opportunity. The merchant Bernabo, however, maintains that his wife is virtuous: despite the behaviour of the others, she is

---

[6] There are also important musical parallels between the two operas, as will be seen in Chapter 10.

[7] For a discussion of these versions, see W. W. Lawrence, *Shakespeare's Problem Comedies* (New York, 1931; repr. 1969).

chaste and would remain true to him whatever the circumstances. This boast is greeted with incredulity by Ambrogiuolo, who attacks Bernabo in terms reminiscent of Don Alfonso in *Così fan tutte*:

> Thou dost not deny that thy wife is a woman, a creature of flesh and blood like the rest; and if so, she must have the same cravings, the same natural propensities, as they, and no more force to withstand them; wherefore 'tis at least possible that, however honest she be, she will do as others do.[8]

Bernabo himself proposes the wager that Ambrogiuolo will be unable to seduce the lady. Ambrogiuolo accepts and travels back to Italy. There he fails in his assault, but manages to enter the wife's bedroom, steal tokens, and convince Bernabo of her guilt. The furious husband orders his wife's execution, and the story continues with further adventures. In this version, the husband's confidence is presented as a virtue, set against the sophisticated sinfulness of the other merchants. The moral of the tale is that 'the deceived has the better of the deceiver', since Bernabo and his wife are later reunited, while Ambrogiuolo is bound to the stake, covered with honey, and eaten by insects. Nevertheless, a more cynical interpretation is made by the next storyteller in the cycle; Dioneo considers Bernabo foolish to have deluded himself about his wife's constancy under such circumstances.

The wager theme was adapted for different moral purposes by Shakespeare in *Cymbeline* (1609–10). Here, the wager is made in an atmosphere of medieval chivalry; the characters are of the highest rank, the woman in question being no less than the daughter of the King of England. It is emphasized that her husband, Posthumus Leonatus, is honourable and virtuous:

> a creature such
> As, to seek through the regions of the earth
> For one his like, there would be something failing
> In him that should compare, I do not think
> So fair an outward and such stuff within
> Endows a man but he.
>
> (Act I, Scene i)

Posthumus maintains that Imogen is fair and chaste above all others. He is challenged by Iachimo, who is angry that Imogen is held in higher esteem than his Italian compatriots, and that Posthumus considers that Italy holds no one sufficiently accomplished to win her. The dispute becomes heated, and Iachimo offers the wager. Posthumus has no choice but to accept—it is the only chivalrous option—and a refusal would

---

[8] Giovanni Boccaccio, *The Decameron*, trans. J. M. Rigg (London, 1963), 133.

impugn Imogen's honour, and imply lack of trust. The apparently distasteful operation of gambling on a spouse's virtue is transformed into an honourable act by setting it within the rarefied atmosphere of chivalry. *Cymbeline* was written during a period of revived interest in courtly romance, and the wager would have been received in like spirit by the audience.

The opening scene of *Così fan tutte* is a clear derivation from the wager theme. Ferrando and Guglielmo believe that their mistresses are above temptation, but Don Alfonso is doubtful. They become angry, and the wager is struck. However, the later stages of the opera plot—the feigned departure of the men, their return in disguise, and most importantly the success of the seduction by the pretend lovers—are foreign to the wager theme. These elements probably have a completely different source in the myth of Cephalus and Procris.

Sir Ernst Gombrich was the first to explore the connection between *Così fan tutte* and the myth of Procris.[9] According to Ovid, Cephalus has recently married the beautiful Procris, when his suspicions about her faithfulness are aroused by Aurora, and he is incited to test her virtue. He pretends to leave on a journey, but returns incognito as a supposed admirer and tempts Procris with presents. She does not reject him outright but hesitates, whereupon he reveals his true identity. Much abashed, Procris flees to join Diana's nymphs. Eventually the pair are reconciled, and she gives her husband two gifts from Diana—a hound, and a spear which returns to the thrower. They live contentedly until she in turn becomes suspicious that he is secretly meeting a nymph while out hunting. One day she hides herself in the undergrowth to spy, but is unfortunately mistaken by Cephalus for game, and is killed with the spear.

The basic story of a suspicious husband disguising himself, and testing his wife's virtue by attempting to woo her as a stranger was transformed many times, and continued in circulation throughout the medieval period. In *De claribus mulieribus*, Boccaccio castigates Procris for having succumbed first to avarice and then to jealousy. The story re-emerged in the early Renaissance as a play which received a sumptuous production at the d'Este court of Ferrara (1487), and it also attracted a number of artists, from Piero di Cosimo to Poussin.[10] Da Ponte's extensive classical reading would have made him familiar with Ovid's story in its original form. In addition, the theme resurfaced prominently in the works of one of Da Ponte's favourite poets, Ludovico Ariosto. In cantos 42 and 43 of *Orlando*

---

[9] E. H. Gombrich, '*Così fan tutte* (Procris included)', *Journal of the Warburg and Courtauld Institutes*, 17 (1954), 372–4.

[10] I. Lavin, 'Cephalus and Procris: Transformations of an Ovidian Myth', *Journal of the Warburg and Courtauld Institutes*, 17 (1954), 260–87.

*furioso*, Rinaldo meets a Mantuan knight, who recounts his sad history. The knight had been married to a tender, beautiful, and loving wife, with whom he lived in peace and prosperity. Unfortunately, a sorceress named Melissa fell in love with him, and tried to win him by sowing seeds of doubt in his mind:

> But how know you (saith she) your wife is true,
> That of her faith as yet no proof have made,
> You never let her go scant from your view,
> When none can come to vice her to persuade,
> Nor none can see her, none to her can sew,
> Tis easy to resist where none invade.[11]

The knight was convinced by this logic, and pretended to leave on a long journey. He returned in the guise of a young admirer from Ferrara, and offered his wife riches and jewels in return for her favours:

> At first she blushed, and looked with low'ring chear,
> And would not harken, but still did retire,
> But th'Orient pearls, and stones that shone so clear
> Did mollify her heart to my desire.
> Softly she saith, but so as I might hear,
> That for the thing, which I so oft require,
> She grant it would, and would on me bestow it,
> So she were sure that none beside might know it.

The horrified husband took off his disguise at once. The wife in return was mortified, but her mood quickly changed to indignation:

> Much was the shame, but much more the disdain,
> That of my foolish usage tane she hath,
> Within due bonds she could not it contain,
> But that it break to spite, to hate, to wrath:
> Resolved with me no longer to remain.

She promptly left him to go and live with the very man that her husband had counterfeited, abandoning the knight to bewail his folly.

Da Ponte was a passionate admirer of Ariosto, as was noted in Chapter 5. His debt to Ariosto in the construction of *Così fan tutte* is supported by the names of the characters in the opera, as Kurt Kramer has pointed out. In *Orlando furioso*, Fiordiligi is the faithful wife of Brandimart, Doralice is an inconstant lover, while yet another character is called

---

[11] Quotations are taken from the translation of *Orlando Furioso* by Sir John Harington (1591; facsimile ed. Amsterdam, 1970).

Fiordespina. It is also interesting that the duped wife in *Orlando furioso* is not overcome with penitence and remorse; rather she is angered, and recognizes the extreme folly of her husband.

A number of aspects of *Così fan tutte* were donated by the Procris myth rather than the wager theme. They include the pretend departure and subsequent return of the male lovers in disguise, and the successful assault on the women's constancy. There appear to be no major precursors of this particular fusion of the stories. Cervantes's *La novela del curioso impertinente*, however, involves a different blending of the themes, and has considerable significance for Mozart and Da Ponte's opera, as will be seen later in the chapter. The story, interpolated into *Don Quixote* (1605–1615), concerns two Florentine gentlemen who are inseparable friends. Anselmo marries the beautiful Camila but soon begins to doubt her virtue; since she has never had the opportunity to stray, he cannot be certain of her fidelity. He therefore asks his friend Lotario to lay siege and test her. Lotario is reluctant and puts forward many arguments against such a foolish venture. Nevertheless, Anselmo is adamant, so his friend eventually agrees to the conspiracy. At first, Lotario deceives Anselmo by reporting fictitious encounters with Camila and her outraged repulsion of his advances. But the trick is discovered, and Anselmo is so incensed by the betrayal of friendship that Lotario swears to carry on the attack in earnest. Camila resists stoutly but is astonished by her husband's lack of support. She is therefore won over by Lotario's admiration and ardour, and the two lovers succeed in deluding the foolish husband.

Elements of both stories are apparent here, since the motive behind the test is typical of the Procris myth (the husband's uncertainty about his wife's fidelity), while the means of the test derive from the wager plot (a man tempting a woman's virtue with her husband's permission and complicity). The seduction of the wife is carried out through love and praise, as in the wager theme, rather than the presents and jewels generally employed in the Procris myth. Yet the husband is shown up as foolish, and his behaviour alienates his wife: both these features belong to the Procris myth. Cervantes's story thus pairs the motives of the Procris myth with the methods of the wager theme. In *Così fan tutte*, the two stories are integrated differently. The impetus derives from the wager, while the methods are reminiscent of Procris. By having two pairs of lovers instead of one, Da Ponte was able to explore a much broader range of human response. The manner in which these two threads of story intertwine are redolent of the eighteenth-century theatre, both in form and content.

## Così fan tutte and the Eighteenth-Century Gloss

*Così fan tutte* begins with the traditional exposition of the wager theme, as the male lovers proclaim the steadfastness of their ladies, while acknowledging the fickleness of women in general. In contrast to earlier versions, there is little evidence that these assertions are based on a long acquaintance with the women, nor on accurate knowledge of their sobriety and chastity. It is improbable that the men would even find such virtues particularly attractive. The couples are not married, so this reason for expecting faithfulness is absent. Instead, the soldiers' belief in their lovers is founded upon personal pride. Any doubts are taken by Ferrando and Guglielmo as slights to their honour and attractiveness. Thus the motive for the wager stems not from an honest defence of virtue, but from masculine complacency.

The wager is suggested by Don Alfonso, and accepted by the soldiers as a suitable method of defending their honour against a non-combatant civilian. There is no hint of moral impropriety in gambling on a woman's affections in this fashion, and this parallels other wager stories. If anything, the test proposed in Da Ponte's libretto is rather less stringent than those devised by Boccaccio and Shakespeare, since the couples are not married. One can imagine that the horror of nineteenth-century commentators would have been multiplied tenfold if the opera had remained faithful to its origins in this respect.

The emphasis shifts to the Procris plot after the opening scenes, as Ferrrando and Guglielmo feign a journey, only to return in disguise. The testing of Fiordiligi and Dorabella is of course performed by the transposed lovers. This unique feature of the libretto is a product of fusing the two plots. The device induces a satisfying symmetry and permits a deeper penetration of the characters' motives and experience than the traditional form. For if the men seduced their own betrothed, it could be argued that the women did not succumb but unconsciously detected the fundamental qualities of their admirers.[12] The men's conceit would thus be bolstered, as they could be seen both as conquerors and as objects of lasting affection. Their humiliation and enlightenment could only follow the loss of their idols to another party. It is appropriate for the age of sentiment that the ladies are assaulted with pity (Act I Finale) and ardour (Act II) after the initial offers of exotic wealth and glamour have been repulsed.

Fiordiligi and Dorabella fail the test and are won over by their new admirers. This turn in the plot, so repellant to early critics, is not a reflection of Da Ponte's ruthless cynicism, for it is a feature common to all

---

[12] An argument used with devastating effect in the version of the story written by the Hungarian playwright Ferencz Molnar (*The Guardsman*, 1910). An analagous piece of reasoning is deployed by Falstaff in Act II of *1 Henry IV*.

manifestations of the Procris myth. *Così fan tutte* is not exceptional but follows the conventional form. Da Ponte did, however, depart from earlier models in the subsequent action. Previous versions show the lady not only ashamed but indignant and furious at her husband's foolish deception. It is the man who falls in estimation and ultimately suffers. Yet Da Ponte was constrained by the *lieto fine* to re-establish the status quo by the end of the work. Fiordiligi and Dorabella's recriminatory responses are thus curtailed in favour of a guilty misery, which can be relieved by propitiation and forgiveness. The reversal of emotions and the ending are extremely abrupt, and Da Ponte has been condemned for this betrayal. Joseph Kerman, for example, was particularly harsh in his influential *Opera as Drama*:

Fiordiligi's experience goes up in smoke as she turns blankly back to Guglielmo, whose insufficiency has been made only too clear by the action. The volte face . . . is improbable and immoral. . . . The lovers are back in their original anonymity, without any explanation of the abrupt lowering of the imaginative level. [13]

But criticisms of this type reflect the concerns of realism, rather than appreciation of *opera buffa* convention. The form demanded, and the audience expected, a reconciliation and a strengthening of the accustomed order, even if this was improbable in terms of the characters' earlier behaviour.

Da Ponte was not the only artist obliged by theatrical law to manufacture an abrupt and not wholly satisfying reconciliation. There are several examples in Shakespeare, from Bertram's churlish acknowledgement of Helena in *All's Well that Ends Well*, to the improbable pairing of Isabella and the Duke in *Measure for Measure*. Eighteenth-century writers were no more free, and even the sophisticated Marivaux suffered from having to engineer joyous conclusions (in *L'Heureux Stratagème*, for example). Both Marivaux and Da Ponte were much more concerned with the journey—the development and expression of feelings—than with the goal. Moreover, the alternative pairings in *Così fan tutte* could not persist, any more than Procris could remain with the disguised Cephalus. Such a conclusion is logically impossible for any rendering of the Procris myth, since it would imply permanent diguise for the husband. It is not viable in Da Ponte's operatic version either, for it is misleading to suppose that Fiordiligi comes to love Ferrando (or Dorabella to love Guglielmo); rather the women are overcome by the disguised forms of these men. For Fiordiligi to remain with Ferrando, and Dorabella with Guglielmo, knowing who they really were, would be psychologically improbable and emotionally without foundation.

[13] J. Kerman, *Opera as Drama* (New York, 1956), 116.

Da Ponte's transformation of the wager and Procris themes departs from the traditional models in several interesting ways. His libretto suggests an acute awareness of fashionable trends in contemporary literature and drama. It is permeated with a cynical, anti-sentimental spirit. This is seen not only in the dispassionate development of the entire plot, but in the satirical treatment of romantic sentiment. Dorabella's 'Smanie implacabili' is a parody of exaggerated passion as well as of *opera seria* grandiloquence. Similarly, as Otto Jahn has pointed out, Ferrando's vapid sentiment was intended to inspire ridicule rather than sympathy.[14] This mood was compatible with the rationalist view of emotions and human relationships, although it stemmed from a more specifically theatrical reaction against sentiment. The sentimental comedy and novel were immensely popular in the mid-eighteenth century, and were accompanied by a peculiarly cloying sensibility that irritated more robust individuals.[15] In Germany, the sentimental movement was permeated by 'Wertherism', as Goethe's novel enjoyed spectacular popularity. Goethe himself was one of the first to react against the cult, since he soon recognized its dangers. In 1778, a young lady-in-waiting, crossed in love, was found drowned in the river near Weimar with a copy of *Werther* in her pocket[16]; later in the same month, Goethe unleashed his antagonism in the little-known play, *Der Triumph der Empfindsamkeit* (The Triumph of Sensibility).

The hero of this extravaganza is a sentimental prince who adores Nature. However, he is attracted only by the charming and delightful aspects. Rocks are picturesque but seem uncomfortable in the wind and cold, while the sunrise tends to be rather damp. He solves these problems by constructing an imitation of nature—a mechanical system which produces a sunset or melancholy grotto without inconvenience. Similarly, the prince is charmed by his mistress, but her moods and caprice are irritating. He therefore prefers to spend his hours of rapture with a doll that has none of these tiresome habits. After a great deal more ridicule in the same vein, the doll is ripped open to reveal a heap of fashionable sentimental books, including *Werther*. These are held up to severe condemnation.[17]

The Italian reaction to sentiment may have had less serious aims, but it was equally ruthless. In *Le femmine puntigliose* of 1750, Goldoni berates men for their idolatry of women:

[14] O. Jahn, *The Life of Mozart*, trans. P. Townsend (London, 1882), iii. 255.

[15] One such was Fanny Burney, who in her diary *The Diary of Fanny Burney*, ed. L. Gibbs (London, 1940) noted with disgust the complaint of one gentleman that he 'Could not bear to have himself the picture of anyone he loved, as in case of their death or absence, he should go distracted by looking at it.'

[16] W. H. Bruford, *Theatre, Drama and Audience in Goethe's Germany* (London, 1950), 290.

[17] For more details, see G. H. Lewes, *The Life of Goethe* (London, 1864), 243.

There are things which make one die of laughter, in a society where there are ladies with their *cavalieri serventi*. The ladies, stiff as statues, allow themselves to be adored. And the men!—one sighs here, another kneels there; one offers a cup, another picks up a hand-kerchief from the floor . . . men reduce themselves to the condition of slaves, idolators of beauty, profaners of their self-respect, and a scandal to youth.

*Così fan tutte* belongs firmly in this ironic tradition. Ferrando and Guglielmo begin by showing all the blind worship ridiculed by Goldoni, while the ladies release a torrent of extravagant protestations at every opportunity. These delusions and façades are shattered by subsequent events, which bring enlightenment as well as despair.

Most of the plot documents the temptation and seduction of the women by their disguised lovers. The process is presented with such orderly detachment and clarity that the subtitle *La scuola degli amanti* is perfectly justified. The libretto demonstrates a number of strategies for ensnaring the heart. The brusque attempt to take the sisters by storm fails, so an effort is made to elicit their pity through mock suicide. The successful seduction only follows a division of forces, with each man tailoring his approach to his own prey. Dorabella rapidly acquiesces after a show of conventional histrionics, while Fiordiligi is overcome by a display of extreme, and apparently sincere, passion.

The sense of clinical objectivity pervading this emotional experiment has led many writers to view the four lovers as marionettes, whose stiff conventional feelings are manipulated by Don Alfonso.[18] However, these aspects of characterization are best understood within the context of psychological rationalism, a genre that reached its apogee in Choderlos de Laclos's *Les Liaisons dangereuses* (1782). In this influential book, the protagonists Valmont and the Marquise de Merteuil ruthlessly exploit the passions of others for their own purposes, while the seduction of the virtuous is presented quite dispassionately:

I forgetting my plans, risked losing by a premature triumph the charm of long struggles and the details of a painful defeat. . . . Let her yield herself, but let her struggle! Let her have the strength to resist without having enough to conquer; let her fully taste the feeling of weakness and be forced to admit her defeat. Let the obscure poacher kill the deer he has surprised from a hiding place; the real sportsman must hunt it down.

They are not concerned with adding names to their lists of lovers, but with power and the defeat of self-righteousness. As in *Così fan tutte*, several lines of attack are opened up, while the campaign is organized with military precision:

18 See, e.g. E. J. Dent's description, *Mozart's Operas* (London, 1960), 192.

I forced the enemy to fight when she wished only to refuse battle; by clever manoeuvres I obtained the choice of battlefield and of dispositions; I inspired the enemy with confidence, to overtake her more easily in her retreat. . . . I left nothing to chance.[19]

There are other interesting parallels between the opera and this novel. Both works end somewhat disconcertingly with an abrupt volte-face. Choderlos's villains, having achieved all their aims in seducing and destroying their victims, are themselves unconvincingly brought low and punished. In addition, in neither *Così fan tutte* nor *Les Liaisons dangereuses* can it be assumed that the authors' views coincide with those of their characters. Choderlos's intentions were heavily ironic, and the emotional nihilism of the protagonists was not a reflection of his own *modus vivendi*. Likewise, Mozart and Da Ponte's attitudes to love cannot be inferred from developments in the opera.

These contemporary influences on the style and content of *Così fan tutte* are matched by equally powerful factors that affected its form. Da Ponte's plot is remarkable for its symmetry, in which no character stands alone. Each has a sympathetic opposite, and all the combinations are explored in perfect balance. This pattern of relationships is illustrated schematically in Figure 3. The two sisters Fiordiligi and Dorabella are set against the brother officers Ferrando and Guglielmo. The pairings at the start of Fiordiligi with Guglielmo and Dorabella with Ferrando counterpoint the affinities revealed in the disguise sequence, for Dorabella and Guglielmo share an amorous though superficial disposition, while Fiordiligi and Ferrando manifest deeper sensibilities. Alfonso and Despina are opposites in the social scale, yet are joined through their cynical, pragmatic views of love and sexual feelings. They stand as mirror images in their associations with the lovers, each advising and receiving the confidences of their own sex, while abetting the pair of the opposite gender.

This pattern satisfied the demand for order and balance, while exploiting the variety of interaction made possible by the permutation of the lovers. It is typical of an eighteenth-century design that was perfected by Marivaux.[20] In these French models, the balanced sets of lovers tend to be master and mistress and their respective servants, while the action is frequently supervised by an omniscient elder. Social divisions of course prevent any spontaneous variation in the pairing, so many of the plots are launched by the same device as used in *Così fan tutte*—disguise.[21] One

---

[19] Choderlos de Laclos, *Les Liaisons dangereuses*, trans. R. Aldington (London, 1946), 292.

[20] The influence of Marivaux on Da Ponte's style has previously been noted by C. Rosen, *The Classical Style* (London, 1971), 314.

[21] e.g. *Le Triomphe de l'amour* (1732), *L'Epreuve* (1740), and *La Dispute* (1744). The use of disguise to forward the plots of contemporary English plays is too frequent to catalogue.

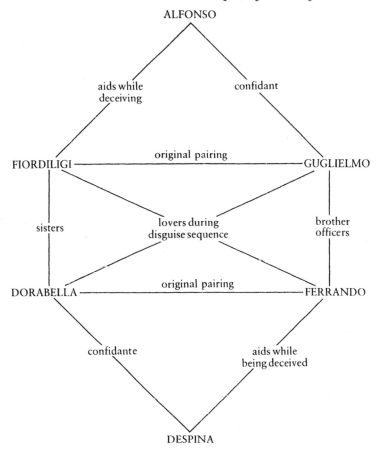

Figure 3. Outline of *Così fan tutte*

of Marivaux's most successful plays, *Le Jeu de l'amour et du hasard* (1730), has a structure that closely parallels that of *Così fan tutte* (see Figure 4). Silvia and her servant Lisette are set opposite Dorante and his valet Arlequin. Silvia and Dorante are betrothed without having ever met. Silvia wishes to discover Dorante's true character by examining him incognito, and so she exchanges roles with her maid. Dorante has a similar concern, and also disguises himself. During the subsequent trial period, Silvia is horrified by the supposed 'master', while being instinctively drawn towards her supposed social inferior. The two servants, both disguised as employers, also sense a natural affinity. The comedy is controlled and directed by Orgon, who knows of both disguises and encourages the experiment.

The dramatic possibilities of the symmetrical plot certainly appealed to

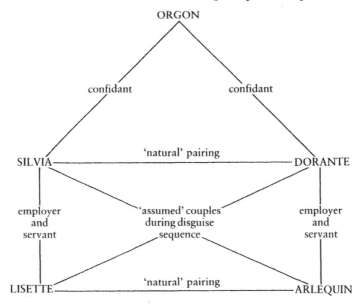

Figure 4.   Outline of *Le Jeu de l'amour et du hasard*

Mozart as well as to Da Ponte. In 1783, Mozart began to convert another balanced, symmetrical work, Goldoni's *Il servitore di due padrone*, into an opera, but it was later abandoned. It too concerns two brace of lovers, Beatrice with Florindo, and Silvio with Clarice. Beatrice's disguise ensures that the different pairings possible will emerge in due course. The plot is dominated by the servant Truffaldino, who is employed both by Florindo and Beatrice, and causes great confusion by passing money, letters, and challenges to the wrong parties. The complicated plot is of refined proportions, although little opportunity is left for characterization outside the action. This problem may ultimately have deterred Mozart from following his plan through.

## Così fan tutte and Vienna

The influences on form and content described in the last section reflect the theatrical fashions that pervaded all Europe during the 1780s. However, more specifically Viennese precedents for *Così fan tutte* can also be identified. The work followed a whole crop of 'Scuola' pieces given in Vienna during the decade, in each of which the characters are given a sentimental education. They included Salieri's *La Scola de' gelosi* (a title that might have suited *Così fan tutte* in some respects), and translations of English plays such as *School for Scandal* (Sheridan), *School for Wives* (Hugh Kelly), and *School for Lovers* (Whitehead).

Mozart and Da Ponte were possibly alerted to the potential of the Procris and wager themes by Anfossi's opera *Il curioso indiscreto*. This work was based on that other fusion of the themes, Cervantes's *La novela del curioso impertinente* (described earlier in the chapter). It was certainly very familiar to Mozart. He first encountered it in Paris, when it shared the bill with *Les petits riens* (K. 299b) at the Grand Opera in 1778. Later, he was commissioned to reset three numbers for the Vienna production of 1783. These insertions (K. 418–420) were intended for Aloisia Lange and the tenor Valentin Adamberger, and were designed to show off their vocal abilities to the full. Mozart had cause to remember the occasion with some bitterness, owing to events outlined in this letter to his father:

I should like you to know that my friends were malicious enough to spread the report beforehand that 'Mozart wanted to improve on Anfossi's opera'. I heard of this and sent a message to Count Rosenberg that I would not hand over my arias unless the following statement were printed in the copies of the libretto, both in German and in Italian,

'The two arias on p. 36 and p. 102 have been set to music by Signor Maestro Mozart to suit Madame Lange, as the arias of Signor Maestro Anfossi were not written for her voice, but for another singer. It is necessary that this should be pointed out so that honour may be given to whom it is due and so that the reputation and the name of the most famous Neapolitan may not suffer in any way whatsoever.'

And now for a trick of Salieri's, which has injured poor Adamberger more than me. . . . During a short rehearsal, before the rondo had been copied, Salieri took Adamberger aside and told him that Count Rosenberg would not be pleased if he put in an aria and that he advised him as a good friend not to do so. Adamberger, provoked . . . and not knowing how to retaliate, was stupid enough to say, with ill-timed pride, 'Alright. But to prove that Adamberger has already made his reputation in Vienna and does not need to make a name for himself by singing music expressly written for him, he will only sing what is in the opera, and will never again, as long as he lives, introduce any aria.' What was the result? Why, that he was a complete failure, as was only to be expected! [22]

The advantages of having two rather than one pair of lovers may ironically enough have become apparent to Mozart and Da Ponte through their study of an opera by their arch-rivals, Salieri and Giambattista Casti. This was *La grotta di Trofonio*, presented at the Burgtheater in 1785. It proved to be one of Salieri's more popular *opere*

---

[22] Letter to Leopold Mozart dated 2 July 1783. The Procris myth itself stimulated a number of operas, including *Céphale et Procris* written by Grétry in 1775 to a libretto by Marmontel, and a Singspiel *Cephalus und Prokris* by Karl Wilhelm Ramler (1778).

*buffe* and was given twenty-six times up to 1788. The plot again concerns two sisters, Daphne and Phaedra, who are respectively of serious and frivolous dispositions. Their lovers Amintas and Dorilas are similarly contrasted, but each is attached to his opposite in temperament. This set of misallied protagonists resembles Da Ponte's characters for *Così fan tutte*. The device which permits the pairs to reverse is Trofonio's grotto, which has the property of transforming the character of any who enter it. The sisters enter first, and at a later stage Amintas and Dorilas are also transformed. Numerous whimsical incidents follow, and the whole affair is supervised by the magician Trofonio, who eventually sets all to rights.

Casti's libretto for *La grotta di Trofonio* is brilliantly ironic, although the overall effect of the opera is compromised by Salieri's somewhat pedestrian setting. Despite his jealousy of Casti, Da Ponte was not above borrowing successful theatrical devices from him, as was illustrated in Chapter 5. But when the analytic tone of *Così fan tutte* is considered, a more important model can be identified in the works of Da Ponte's Venetian mentor, Carlo Gozzi. Gozzi was much admired in German-speaking countries, and during the 1780s no fewer than five of his works were produced in Vienna. One critic, writing in the *Berliner Litteratur und Theater Zeitung*, waxed quite lyrical over Gozzi's talent:

We are full of admiration for the powerful mind of this man, which he uses to collect, arrange and execute his trivial subjects . . . how truthfully, how powerfully this poet permits the creations of his fancy to speak . . . We cannot help but wish, however, that many of our dramatic writers would read Gozzi immediately after Shakespeare.[23]

The trend in Gozzi's work that culminated in *Le droghe d'amore* is particularly pertinent. This piece, based on a work in Spanish by Tirso da Molina, had a stormy reception in Venice, and this fact may have appealed to Da Ponte as he searched for an appropriate sequel to *Le nozze di Figaro*.[24] The basic framework of the plot parallels many others described in this chapter. There are two pairs of lovers: Federico and the Countess Leonora (who out of pride and reticence will not declare their love), and Donna Ardemia who is loved by the jealous Alessandro. The vain Don Adorno is the caricature who caused the scandal on publication of the play in Venice, but the whole structure is dominated by the detached, philosphical Carlo. He is the confidant of Federico, and has a powerful mistrust of women. The drug of the title is jealousy, a weapon

[23] See H. H. Rusack, *Gozzi in Germany* (New York, 1930); the quotation is from p. 27.

[24] The notoriety of the play stemmed from the characterization of a vain fool in the plot. This was taken as a satire of Signor Gratarol, with whom Gozzi was engaged in a well-publicized legal and literary dispute. Gozzi was at such pains to justify himself that he appended the entire play to the 1797 edition of his *Memorie Inutile*. This remains the most accessible source of the play, and I am indebted to Professor Ludovico Zorzi from Florence for drawing it to my attention.

that is used in turn by most of the lovers in order to incite their beloved. Leonoro pretends to be attracted to Adorno, at which the frantic Federico simulates love for Ardemia. This leaves Leonora in despair, while Alessandro is transported with jealousy. Later the complications increase, as Leonora and Alessandro announce their engagement, to the anguish of Federico and Ardemia. Only after this imposture are true feelings revealed, and the rightful partnerships restored.

The similarities with *Così fan tutte* are numerous. The individual lovers are carefully contrasted, so that the hot-tempered Leonora is mirrored by the phlegmatic Ardemia. Each uses the eponymous drug in turn, but instead becomes its victim, just as the test in *Così fan tutte* recoils on Ferrando and Guglielmo. Even more striking is the resemblance between the misogynist philosopher Don Carlo and Don Alfonso. Early on in the play, Carlo makes his opinions of women quite clear:

What frail devices! What inconstant minds! How many deceits! Vanity, lechery and sordid avarice are the motives behind women's sighs, declarations, excitations and expressions of love. I have sworn to desire love no more, and none do I desire.

(Act I, scene ii)

He spends much of the remainder of the play trying to keep Federico's passion within bounds, constantly undermining his faith:

O Duke, do not seek for rational love . . . from their sex. Ephemeral thoughts, flightiness, pettiness are the ruling spirits of these little machines, . . . Do not hope for mature thought in womankind.

(Act II, scene iii)

Another intriguing parallel lies in the ambivalence between real and simulated passion. Just as in *Così fan tutte*, where the true extent of Ferrando's feeling for Fiordiligi remains tantalizingly uncertain, so Federico's pretended love for Ardemia steps beyond the bounds of artifice. The strict division between sincerity and falsehood is blurred, adding an enigmatic quality to the play, as it does to Mozart and Da Ponte's opera.

These stage models for *Così fan tutte* were spiced with modish theatrical devices, designed to appeal to the sophisticated taste of Vienna. This is especially apparent in the satire on Mesmerism that brings Act I to a close. Until five or six years before the opera's composition, Mesmerism had been no laughing matter but a cult with considerable popular support, and much of fashionable European Society had been devoted to the technique. Then in 1784 the bubble burst. Professional resentment, fuelled by the increasing popularity of the method, led to the establishment of a French Royal Commission to investigate the cult. This distinguished group of scientists, including Lavoisier, Guillotin, Bailly, and

Benjamin Franklin, concluded that Mesmer's 'magnetic fluid' was a fiction, although the cures themselves were not denied. This result, together with a number of other setbacks and treatment failures, led to the appearance of satirical attacks and ridiculous cartoons. Playwrights joined the fray, with the prolific Jean-Baptiste Radet producing *Les docteurs modernes* in 1784, to be closely followed by *Le baquet de santé*. Da Ponte was thus following a very recent trend in guying the magnetic approach to health, and was one of the first in Vienna to satirize Mesmer on the stage.[25]

I have discussed the libretto of *Così fan tutte* in greater depth than those of *Le nozze di Figaro* and *Don Giovanni*, since the impetus for its creation stemmed from Da Ponte and Mozart, instead of being a reworking of earlier material. The plot can be seen as a restatement of old themes tempered by popular theatrical forms and fashions.[26] The author and composer were making a special effort to please the Viennese Court audience. Both men were in desperate need of success in 1789 and 1790. Mozart hoped to escape from immediate financial stringencies, Da Ponte to re-establish his position in Vienna, which had been seriously eroded by his arrogant behaviour and ruthless support of Adriana Ferrarese. The dubious but tantalizing subject-matter was selected to engage the interest of the Court. It was evidently successful in this respect if the reaction of Count Zinzendorf is anything to go by ('the music by Mozart is charming and the subject rather amusing').[27] It is ironic that the opera emerged at

---

[25] I have discussed the relationship between Mozart and Mesmer in more detail in 'Mozart, Mesmer and *Così fan tutte*', *Music and Letters*, 67 (1986), 248–55.

[26] A paper containing these theories about the origins of *Così fan tutte* was published in *Music and Letters*, 62 (1981), 281–294. When this was shown to Sir Ernst Gombrich, he made the following comments in a letter dated 14 Mar. 1983:

> I should like to thank you very much indeed for showing me your excellent and convincing paper on Così. I am sure you have successfully unravelled the tangled skein. I still feel, though, that the moral 'message' may have been meant more seriously than you imply. 'Let us be guided by reason'.

> The trouble is that one man's rationalism is the other's cynicism, but by putting his characters into the traditional test tube of passions Da Ponte might still have wanted to plead for tolerance and reasonableness against the remnants of feudal concepts of honour and vengeance. The secular process by which these pillars of social cohesion were undermined until they are barely intelligible to our age is after all a fascinating one. Maybe Così among other things, belongs also to this story. It may be a reinterpretation of those traditional motifs you so convincingly identified.

[27] O. E. Deutsch, *Mozart: A Documentary Biography*, trans. E. Blom, P. Branscombe, and J. Noble (London, 1966), 362. The theme of inconstancy in women was well established in *opera buffa*, with works such as Anfossi's *La donna istabile* and Guglielmi's *La donna amante di tutti e fedele a nessuno*. For these and other precedents for *Così fan tutte*, see C. Kritsch and H. Zeman, 'Das Rätsel eines genialen Opernentwurfs—Da Pontes Libretto zu *Così fan tutte* und das literarische Umfeld des 18. Jahrhunderts', in *Die Österreichische Literatur: Ihr Profil an der Wende vom 18. zum 19. Jahrhundert (1750–1830)*, ed. H. Zeman, i (Graz, 1979).

the moment when the world for which it was designed began to crumble. The shock waves of popular discontent from Paris undermined the complacency of the Court, while the death of Joseph II dealt the opera a further blow. He died less than a month after the first performance, by which time the opera had been given only five times.

*Così fan tutte* represents one of Mozart's last attempts to please Viennese Court circles. The lukewarm response, following the failure of his Prussian tour, drove the composer further towards bourgeois culture and the suburban theatres. There seems to be an enormous gulf between the pragmatic *Così fan tutte* and the idealism of later works such as *Die Zauberflöte*. Yet many of Mozart's later preoccupations are prefigured in *Così fan tutte*. As in *Die Zauberflöte*, the protagonists undergo trials in order to acquire knowledge. Human relationships are strained to the utmost, so that they may gain additional strength. The main difference lies in the fact that the knowledge in *Così fan tutte* is worldly while the insights of *Die Zauberflöte* are spiritual; perhaps this change of emphasis reflects Mozart's own progress.

*Così fan tutte* is generally regarded as Lorenzo Da Ponte's finest text, well structured and paced, with a timely variation of sentiment and humour. Yet these virtues are perhaps little more than efficient stage-craft. Few aspects of the libretti discussed thus far mark out Da Ponte's work as exceptional. The features that characterize the creative genius of the collaboration between Mozart and Da Ponte are only to be found with a finer-grained analysis. It will be seen in later chapters that Da Ponte tailored his verse on a minute scale to integrate with Mozart's style. His most impressive achievements lie in the manner in which each number is paced, giving Mozart the opportunity to exploit all the dramatic possibilities of classical musical forms.

# 7

## Mozart and *Opera Buffa*

Mozart had developed firm ideas about opera long before his collaboration with Lorenzo Da Ponte. The perennial controversy resurfaced during the second half of the eighteenth century between those who asserted the primacy of music in opera, and traditionalists who valued the poetry of the libretto most highly. After decades during which a composer's highest ambition was to set one of Metastasio's sanctified texts, musicians were beginning to recognize the possibility of a more flexible operatic art. Mozart identified with this reforming force, and was in no doubt that the music came first:

I should say that in an opera the poetry must be altogether the obedient daughter of the music. Why do Italian comic operas please everywhere—in spite of their miserable libretti—even in Paris, where I myself witnessed their success? Just because there the music reigns supreme and when one listens to it all else is forgotten. [1]

This opinion was shared by so many composers of the period that the controversy even became the subject of opera itself. The title of Salieri's work of 1785, *Prima la musica, poi le parole*, is self-explanatory. [2]

This emphasis on the music could only be sustained if the librettist was compliant, and Mozart was frequently discontented with the inflexibility of his collaborators. In letters to his father, he voiced his pent-up complaints about Gottlieb Stephanie during the composition of *Die Entführung*. He had similar reservations about Gianbattista Varesco, the librettist of *Idomeneo*. When he and Varesco were considering a new project in 1783, Mozart spoke out to his father in no uncertain terms:

Of one thing he may be sure and that is, that his libretto will certainly not go down if the music is no good. For in opera the chief thing is the music. If then the opera is to be a success and Varesco hopes to be rewarded, he must alter and recast the libretto as much and as often as I wish and he must not follow his own inclinations, for he has not the slightest knowledge or experience of the theatre. [3]

Unfortunately, Leopold did not survive beyond the first of the collaborations with Da Ponte, so Mozart was unable to express his feelings in the

---

[1] Letter to Leopold Mozart dated 13 Oct. 1781.
[2] This was the piece that shared the bill with *Der Schauspieldirektor* at the Schönbrunn reception held in Feb. 1786. The libretto was by Giambattista Casti.
[3] Letter to Leopold Mozart dated 21 June 1783.

old manner. But it is unlikely that Mozart would ever have been completely satisfied with his librettist's attitude, however self-effacing; and Da Ponte was not known for his modesty. On the other hand, Mozart's complaints were silenced during the composition of *Le nozze di Figaro*, so perhaps his partnership with Da Ponte was more felicitous.

When it came to selecting a suitable opera for Vienna, Mozart was in no doubt about the central ingredient: 'The chief thing must be the comic element, for I know the taste of the Viennese.'[4] Mozart's stress on the comic was no quirk of personal taste, but a shrewd assessment of the local situation. Vienna had a strong preference for *opera buffa*, although works of a sentimental character (such as *Una cosa rara*) vied with the genuinely comic in the operatic repertoire.[5] Mozart could also point to the success of comedy on the spoken stage. The repertoire of the Burgtheater was dominated during this period by translations of English, French, and Italian comedies, despite the recent introduction of Shakespearean tragedy by Friedrich Schröder. As has already been mentioned in Chapter 6, Carlo Gozzi was played as much as Goldoni in the 1780s. The British contributions included pieces by Sheridan, Cumberland and Whitehead, while Marivaux and Molière were to be found among the French. Michael Kelly later recalled having seen excellent productions of *The School for Scandal*, in which Schröder played Sir Peter Teazle, and Cumberland's immensely popular *The West Indian*, in which Schröder appeared as the eccentric Irishman, Major O'Flaherty, opposite the Belcour of Joseph Lange.

Mozart's long theatrical apprenticeship, commencing properly with *Ascanio in Alba* when he was only fifteen years old, helped him to develop a skilful sense of theatrical effect and stagecraft. He was not idealistic about dramatic effects, but quite explicit on the need for careful engineering. This is nowhere better illustrated than in the interesting letter to his father, written during the composition of *Die Entführung* (26 September 1781). As usual, Mozart asserted the primacy of the music:

I have explained to Stephanie the words I require for this aria—indeed, I had finished composing most of the music for it before Stephanie knew anything whatever about it.

His description of the way in which theatrical effects are achieved must seem almost cynical to those taking a more inspirational view of composition. For example, the end of an Act needs careful planning,

Then the major key begins at once pianissimo—it must go very quickly—and

---

[4] Letter to Leopold Mozart dated 21 May 1783.

[5] The ratio between *buffa* and *seria* was higher in Vienna than in almost any other major city during this period. See M. Hunter, *The Fusion and Juxtaposition of Genres in Opera Buffa 1770–1800: Anelli and Piccinni's Griselda'*, *Music and Letters*, 67 (1986), 363–80.

wind up with a great deal of noise, which is always appropriate at the end of an Act. The more noise the better, and the shorter the better, so that the audience may not have time to cool down with their applause.

An even more striking aspect of Mozart's stagecraft was his concern to suit the music to the preference and capacity of the performer. This factor pervades all Mozart's work for the stage, yet is seldom given sufficient consideration by commentators.[6] The omission is all the more surprising in that it is clear that in many instances the development of a character depended in part on the performer selected. Mozart's universality was paradoxically linked to an especial concern with the minutiae of production.

## The Composer and his Interpreters

Composers of all eras have been obliged to tailor their music to the forces available, and to the particular individuals involved in performances. There are two reasons why this tendency was unusually marked in the eighteenth century. In the first place, the prestige of singers was higher than ever before. Just as in the spoken theatre, the celebrity of the performer far outweighed the dramatic vehicle. When the public flocked to the Opera House, they wanted to hear their favoured singers displayed to best advantage, showing off the vocal characteristics for which they were famous; the music itself was of secondary importance.[7] Secondly, the resources at the disposal of the composer varied widely between locations. Music could not therefore be written for a standard combination of voices or instruments, in the expectation that it could be reproduced throughout Europe. Indeed, it is probable that a major reason for the delay in presentation of Mozart's operas in London was a lack of personnel. Nancy Storace (the first Susanna) rapidly transferred her other Viennese successes, such as Paisiello's *Il barbiere di Siviglia* and *Il rè Teodoro in Venezia*, and would doubtless have pressed for *Le nozze di Figaro* as well. But London was not equipped with sufficient leading baritones, preferring to award principal contracts to tenors.[8]

The identification of music with its home theatre was sometimes extreme, as in the case of Haydn's operas. In 1787, Haydn refused the request of an impresario in Prague to release one of his Eszterháza works, on the grounds that his operas were not suitable for any other setting:

---

[6] Edward Dent was an honourable exception.

[7] The emphasis has shifted slightly in the present day. Although many singers have an international following, the desire of most listeners is to hear a particular artist interpret a famous role (Otello, Isolde, etc.), rather than to hear the voice displaying all its tricks at any cost.

[8] R. Fiske, *English Theatre Music in the Eighteenth Century* (London, 1973), 498.

You wish me to write an opera buffa for you. Most willingly, if you are inclined to have a vocal composition of mine for yourself alone, but not with a view to produce it on the stage at Prague. I cannot in that case comply with your wish, all my operas being too closely associated with our personal circle, so they could never produce the proper effect, which I calculated in accordance with the locality.[9]

There is abundant evidence that Mozart too was highly sensitive to the requirements of his performers. This fact was recognized by Edward Dent as crucial to our understanding of the composer's output:

In considering Mozart we are confronted all along by merely external consider-ations—the exigencies of patrons, the peculiarities of individual executants, as well as the direct influence of other composer's works. What the musician of today can learn best from Mozart . . . is that pride in craftmanship which enabled him to adapt himself to the conditions of the moment, to rewrite and rewrite again to suit the convenience of a singer or the necessity of the stage, and in every case to preserve and even to intensify his own individuality.[10]

At one extreme, Mozart sometimes replaced entire movements of his compositions. This might happen at the behest of the performer, as when the Salzburg konzertmeister Brunetti dismissed the slow movement of the Violin Concerto in A major (K. 219) as 'too studied', and was pro-vided with a fresh one (K. 261). On other occasions, Mozart himself felt that the music would not suit the taste of the audience, and introduced more appropriate material. Thus when he revived the early Keyboard Concerto K. 175 for the Vienna season of 1782, he inserted a new rondo (K. 382); the original finale, composed in 1773 for Salzburg, was not in the effervescent style that pleased the Capital.

Drastic modifications were often required in vocal music as well, lead-ing to the practice of inserting new arias into operas that had been written with other performers in mind. The necessity for displaying vocal tech-nique to advantage took precedence over the integrity of a composer's work. Indeed, if the composer was not available to make the necessary revision, this job was carried out by local musicians. Mozart was fre-quently commissioned to write arias for singers in the Burgtheater com-pany, displacing pieces by Martín y Soler (K. 582 and 583), Bianchi (K. 479 and 480), Anfossi (K. 418–420), and even his own original music for *Le nozze di Figaro* (K. 577 and 579) and *Don Giovanni* (K. 540 *a,b,* and *c*). These interpolated arias are interesting, since they give some clues to the special skills of the singers for which they were intended. But in addition to these large-scale alterations, changes of a less dramatic nature were constantly required in vocal writing. Such modifications were again

[9] Quoted in Lady Wallace, *Letters of Distinguished Musicians* (London, 1867) 107.
[10] E. J. Dent, *Mozart's Operas* (London, 1960), 18.

instigated by the singers, who in general showed little deference to the composer's intentions. For much of the time, Mozart seemed content with this arrangement. Indeed, he showed a tendency to speak of music as so much cloth, to be cut about and trimmed neatly to the customer's desires:

I asked him [the tenor Raaff] to tell me candidly if he did not like it or if it did not suit his voice, adding that I would alter it if he wished or even compose another [aria]. 'God forbid', he said, 'the aria must remain just as it is, for nothing could be finer. But please shorten it a little, for I am no longer able to sustain my notes.' 'Most gladly', I replied, 'as much as you like. I made it a little long on purpose, for it is always easy to cut down, but not so easy to lengthen. . . .'.[11]

Only when the singers' whims conflicted with dramatic cohesion did the composer balk at change. When Mozart was composing *Idomeneo*, the tenor Anton Raaff proved an exacting associate, constantly seeking small changes in the vocal score. Mozart complied as far as arias were concerned (as can be seen from the previous quotation), but when Raaff requested the removal of the entire Act III quartet in favour of another aria, Mozart refused.

His concern to suit music to individuals was further documented during the composition of *Die Entführung*. Each role was precisely matched to the singer, as Mozart admitted when describing Belmonte's aria 'O wie ängstlich':

This is the favourite aria of all those who have heard it, and it is mine also. I wrote it expressly for Adamberger's voice.[12]

Ludwig Fischer, who played Osmin, was also provided with music appropriate to his range and style:

As we have given the part of Osmin to Herr Fischer, who certainly has an excellent bass voice . . . we must take advantage of it, particularly as he has the whole Viennese public on his side. . . . In working out the aria I have allowed Fischer's beautiful deep notes to glow.

Mozart conceded still more to Catarina Cavalieri in the role of Constanze. Here, he came close to admitting that the singer's satisfaction was achieved at the expense of musical quality:

I have sacrificed Constanze's aria a little to the flexible throat of Mlle Cavalieri, 'Trennung war mein banges Los und nun schwimmt mein Aug' in Tränen'. I have tried to express her feelings, as far as an Italian bravura aria will allow it.

---

[11] Letter to Leopold Mozart dated 28 Feb. 1778.
[12] Letter to Leopold Mozart dated 26 Sept. 1781. The two ensuing quotations are also taken from this letter.

The score of *Die Entführung* gives a vivid impression of what Mozart meant by her 'flexible throat'. The Act II aria 'Martern aller Arten' covers a wide vocal range (*b* to *d'''*), and includes passages of abrupt change in register, as can be seen in Example 1.

Example 1.  *Die Entführung*, no. 11, bars 221–33

It is interesting to compare this with another part written expressly for Caterina Cavalieri, in which vocal display was the foremost requirement. This was the role of Madame Silberklang in *Der Schauspieldirektor*, the 'entertainment' designed for the Schönbrunn Palace audience of 1786. In her part as the volatile prima donna Madame Silberklang, Caterina Cavalieri tries to convince the impresario of her merits by rounding off a pathetic lament with a show of bravura. The writing is contrasted with that for the other soprano in *Der Schauspieldirektor*, Madame Herz. This part was taken by Aloisia Lange, and her style was of course very familiar to Mozart. Her voice was if anything higher than Caterina Cavalieri's, and she too possessed a coloratura of spectacular virtuosity. The subtle variation between the music of the two characters reveals some of the ways in which Mozart approached the problem of vocal display. He did not simply produce elaborately decorated parts for each singer, but differentiated carefully between the skills they offered. The individuals who created roles in Mozart's operas thus exerted important influences on musical characterization.

## The Singers of the Burgtheater Company

Perhaps the most striking fact about singers of Mozart's time is their extreme youth. The ages at which they were accepted as mature members of the operatic community seem incredible by present-day standards.

Nancy Storace arrived in Vienna as a prima donna when only 18, having already toured Italy for more than two years. Anna Gottlieb was 12 years old when she appeared as Barbarina in the première of *Le nozze di Figaro*, while Marianne Hellmuth was 17 when she played Constanze during Mozart's visit to Berlin in 1789. The situation was similar in other countries. Mrs Crouch sang in *Artaxerxes* at 18, and Catherine Barnett was a principal singer in the 1786 Vauxhall concert series in London at the age of 9.[13] Madame Mara and Brigitta Banti first made impressions on the public in their early twenties. The same was true of male singers. Luigi Bassi created the role of Don Giovanni in Prague when only 22. Anton Forti, who was a favourite at the Eszterházy theatre in Kismarton during the first decade of the nineteenth-century, sang Don Giovanni when he was eighteen years old.

Public taste rather than biological precocity are likely to determine the age at which singers enter their professional careers. It cannot be argued that standards were simply lower in the eighteenth century, since this implies that judgements of absolute quality are possible. Singing styles do not flourish in isolation, but depend on the circumstances and settings in which they are nurtured. One explanation may lie in the size of the theatre. Although some of the auditoria approached present-day dimensions, many, like the Burgtheater, were small Court buildings attached to Palaces.[14] It is often apparent that young singers have an artistry and technique developed well in advance of physical capacity and resonance, making their voices appropriate for smaller theatres. Readers who have heard opera sung in one of the remaining eighteenth-century theatres, such as Drottningholm or the Cuvilliés in Munich, may recall how unpleasant the fully developed voices of mature present-day singers can sound in confined surroundings, swamping the noise of small orchestras and producing an ugly reverberation.

Nevertheless, the early exposure accorded to eighteenth-century singers could be a mixed blessing, as some suffered through forcing their vocal resources. The soprano Corona Schröter is an instance. Born in 1751, the sister of pianist Johann Schröter, she concentrated her activities around Leipzig and Weimar. Goethe wrote admiringly of her expressive performances as early as 1767, when she was just 16. But premature forcing damaged her upper register and she soon became husky. Fortunately, she was able to establish a successful acting career in the 1770s, becoming in addition a composer of some renown.[15]

---

[13] See P. McGairl, 'The Vauxhall Jubilee, 1786', *The Musical Times*, 127 (1986), 611–15.

[14] Not all contemporary auditoria were small. The theatres in London, for example, were extremely large. The King's Theatre held some 3,000. It is interesting however that many contemporary connoisseurs considered such auditoria too large for the proper appreciation of music and acting. See D. Nalbach, *The King's Theatre 1704–1867* (London, 1972).

[15] See M. J. Citron, 'Corona Schröter; Singer, Composer, Actress', *Music and Letters*, 61 (1980), 15–27.

Nancy Storace avoided a similar fate, and pursued an operatic career for some thirty years. She is especially intriguing to us now, since Mozart valued her highly (see Plate 9). Nancy Storace was born in 1765, the daughter of a Neapolitan bass player and an English mother, and was taken by her father to Italy when her musical precocity became apparent. By the age of 17 she had appeared successfully in Naples, Florence, and Livorno, emulating even the great castrato Luigi Marchesi in prodigious vocal feats. She joined the Burgtheater company when she was 18, remaining in Vienna until 1787. She rapidly became very popular—witness the high salary offered by the Emperor in an effort to tempt her back in 1788 (see Chapter 3). Count Zinzendorf was full of admiration for her opening performance in Vienna (in Salieri's *La scola de' gelosi*):

Mlle Storace, l'inglesina, jolie figure voluptueuse, belle gorge, bien en bohémienne . . . L'inglesina chanta comme un ange.[16]

Soon after her arrival in Vienna, she contracted an unfortunate marriage with an English musician, John Abraham Fisher (1744–1806). The marriage was disastrous, and Fisher was ordered by the Emperor to leave Vienna.[17] Mozart not only wrote the part of Susanna for her, but also the exquisite concert scena 'Ch'io mi scordi di te' (K. 505), described as 'a declaration of love in music' by Einstein. Another work dedicated to her is now lost; this was the cantata *Per la ricuperata salute di Ofelia* written by Da Ponte and set by Mozart in collaboration with Salieri and Cornetti. It was devised to mark Nancy Storace's recovery from a debilitating illness, during which she lost her voice. Mozart was also very fond of her brother Stephen, who came to Vienna as a composition pupil. After some successes on the operatic stage, Stephen Storace died tragically in 1796 when only 34 years old.

It is interesting that despite these signs of success and Mozart's favour, Nancy Storace did not reach the standards of vocal perfection demanded by contemporary connoisseurs. Even the impartial Charles Burney regretted that,

though a lively performer and intelligent actress, and an excellent performer in comic operas, her voice, in spite of all her care, does not favour her ambition to appear as a serious singer. There is a certain crack and roughness which, though it fortifies the humourous effects of a comic song, in scenes where laughing, scolding, crying or quarreling is necessary: yet in airs of tenderness, sorrow or supplication, there is always reason to lament the deficiency of natural sweetness, where art and pains are not wanting.[18]

---

[16] Quoted in D. Heartz, 'Setting the Stage for Figaro', *The Musical Times*, 127 (1986), 256–60.

[17] It has been suggested that Nancy Storace was the Emperor's mistress, and that this provoked Fisher's expulsion. Nancy Storace's name has also been linked with Mozart and Francesco Benucci. However, no adequate proof for these speculations has yet come to light.

[18] C. Burney, *A General History of Music*, ii (London, repr. 1935), 900.

Indeed, when Nancy Storace returned to England after her four years in Vienna, she was only intermittently employed by the Italian Opera at the King's Theatre. Instead, she established herself in the Drury Lane company, which specialized in more popular genres such as ballad opera. Later, she became the long-standing lover of John Braham (1774–1856), one of the leading tenors of his generation. They toured and performed together for some twenty years, and had an illegitimate child called Spencer (marriage was impossible, since her husband Fisher was still living). Sadly, Nancy Storace was abandoned in 1816 in a bitter separation when Braham (moving in increasingly distinguished circles) enhanced his respectability by marrying Frances Elizabeth Bolton. Heart-broken, Nancy Storace died a year later at Herne Hill.

The key to Mozart's approval of Nancy Storace may lie in her engaging style and commitment to the drama. Mozart seems to have prefered vitality to vocal perfection. Nancy Storace's comic abilities were renowned, and in Vienna she was famous for her skilful imitations of other singers and their vocal idiosyncracies; the tenor Adamberger was ruthlessly guyed, to the delight of *cognoscenti*. Her duplication of Marchesi's virtuoso tricks led to her dismissal from the Teatro Pergola in Florence, since the castrato refused to remain in the same company as her. Nancy Storace was able to get her revenge in Vienna when Salieri's opera *Prima la musica, poi le parole* was presented at Schönbrunn in 1786. Storace took the part of the haughty prima donna Elenora. In order to display her talents to the composer and poet, Elenora sings extracts from Sarti's *Giulio Sabino*, including the arias with which Marchesi had dazzled Vienna only a year before. Nancy Storace's perfect imitation of the castrato was highly appreciated by the Court audience.[19]

All this stood in marked contrast to the conventional detachment of the Italians, in whom vocal beauties were achieved at the expense of dramatic involvement. The Italian attitude was a product of the favour accorded to vocal display *per se*. The emphasis on moderation, orderliness, and a 'pleasing' impression encouraged singers to develop beauty and elegance of execution above all other skills. Vocal style and quality were judged on the extent to which they appeared to be 'natural', no matter how dry and flat the outcome. In the 1780s, however, some of the more sapient critics were beginning to reject this neutral, stultifying approach:

That which is called expression in song and penetration into the spirit and

---

[19] Emperor Joseph's delight in Nancy Storace's Adamberger imitation is expressed in a memorandum to Count Rosenberg dated 14 Aug. 1783 (R. Payer von Thurn, *Joseph II als Theaterdirektor* (Vienna, 1920), 35). Her Marchesi imitation was described by Michael Kelly, and was also noted by Count Zinzendorf on the occasion of the Schöbrunn performance. See L. Salter, 'Footnotes to a Satire: Salieri's *Prima la musica, poi le parole*', *The Musical Times*, 126 (1985), 21–4.

personality of the characters, as represented by the composer, is extremely rare in all our opera houses. Nearly everywhere singers make such a wintry approach towards song as though they had been brought up at Spitzbergen and had had their hearts chilled and their feelings turned to a rigid January frost.[20]

Joachim Preisler, a Danish actor, visited the Burgtheater in 1788, and was horrified by the casual stage behaviour of singers who assumed that the beauty of their singing was all that mattered:

These artists permitted themselves liberties on the stage for which the Emperor should have them put in the stocks. The tenor, for instance, quite familiarly greeted a good friend in the stalls—it was a wonder he did not offer him a pinch of snuff!—and the bass, who squatted under a table so as not to be seen by his partners, made faces at them.[21]

Nevertheless, vocal display continued to be in vogue with the public, and led to complete domination of the Burgtheater company by Italians. Nancy Storace was perhaps accepted as she was half-Italian, but Aloisia Lange, Mozart's early love and later his sister-in-law, suffered particularly from discrimination. She was brought to Vienna in 1779 at the age of 19 as part of the ill-fated attempt to establish a German Opera. After the demise of this venture she was never fully accepted into the Italian company. She was rarely involved in Burgtheater premières, rather in less prestigious revived productions. It was clear to Preisler that she was excluded through prejudice rather than lack of talent:

Her high range and her delicacy, her execution, taste and theoretical knowledge cannot fail to be admired by any impartial critic. Nevertheless, hers will be the same fate as that for which so many good subjects of foreign nations are destined.—Whatever is outlandish must be admired, be it extraordinarily good or extra-ordinarily bad. She receives scarcely half the salary given to the Italians, and yet she is made to and can sing the longest and most difficult parts incomparably better than the songstresses who are here pampered by the Viennese nobility.[22]

Mozart certainly valued her highly, and composed much music especially for her, including the two elaborate arias (K 418 & 419) prepared for the Burgtheater production of Anfossi's *Il curioso indiscreto*. Even he could not however insist on her inclusion in his works. Thus apart from the Vienna production of *Don Giovanni*, in which she played Donna Anna, Aloisia Lange did not appear in Mozart's Italian operas at all.

One of the few Austrian sopranos to establish herself was Dorotea Sardi

[20] Quoted in O. E. Deutsch, *Mozart: A Documentary Biography*, trans. E. Blom, P. Branscombe, and J. Noble (London, 1966), 356.
[21] Quoted in Deutsch, *Mozart*, p. 324. Deutsch suggests that the bass in question was Francesco Albertarelli.
[22] Quoted in Deutsch, *Mozart*, pp. 323–4. It should be noted, however, that Preisler made these comments soon after visiting the Lange family at home, so his opinion is not impartial.

(born 1763). She was the daughter of a professor at the military academy in Vienna, and made her debut in Vienna as Cherubino when only 23. She rapidly gained popularity with her lively delivery and trim figure. In 1786, she married the bass Francesco Bussani, who was several years her senior, but seems to have maintained her freedom. Instead of gravitating towards more substantial roles, she specialized in the soubrette repertoire. Thus when she made her English debut more than twenty years later, she continued to woo the audience with her pert charms:

Madame Bussani, the new prima buffa, is an admirable comedian, but she appears to be above forty years of age. She was warmly applauded in a song of action in the second Act, in which she displayed great vivacity and playful expression.[23]

Dorotea Bussani was the obvious choice for Despina in *Così fan tutte*, and the part was written with her in mind. She later created the role of Fidalma in Cimarosa's *Il matrimonio segreto*. Da Ponte held her in very low esteem:

An Italian diva who, though a ridiculous person of little merit, had by dint of facial contortions, clown's tricks, and perhaps by means more theatrical still, built up a great following among cooks, barbers, lackeys.[24]

Nevertheless, as a librettist he was shrewd enough to bring out those very characteristics in Despina that especially attracted the public to Dorotea Bussani. She seems in fact to have conformed naturally to Carlo Gozzi's description of contemporary actresses:

Let no man deceive himself by supposing that it is possible to converse with actresses without love-making. You must make it, or pretend to make it . . . Love moulds and kneads them in flesh, bones and marrow. Love begins to be their guiding star at the age of five or six, . . . Among actresses, the term friendship is something fabulous and visionary. They immediately substitute the word love, and do not attend to distinctions. Their idea of friendship only serves as the means of mutual deception between women, accompanied by deluges of endearing phrases and Judas kisses.[25]

The manner in which the other soprano roles in Mozart's operas were distributed among the Vienna and Prague companies provides us with further insight into contemporary practices. Sopranos tend to specialize in the present day, so that a singer with the Countess in her repertoire will probably play Donna Anna or Elvira in *Don Giovanni*, while a Susanna might well select the part of Despina in *Così fan tutte*. But in Mozart's

[23] Review in the *Morning Chronicle* dated 18 May 1809 of Dorotea Bussani's performance in Guglielmi's *La serva raggatrice*.

[24] L. Da Ponte, *Memoirs*, trans. E. Abbott (New York, 1967), 185.

[25] C. Gozzi, *Useless Memoirs*, trans. J. A. Symonds (London, 1962), 194.

time, roles were allocated on a hierarchical basis, with the prima donna taking the major part whether it was suitable or not. When this pattern is considered, it appears that Zerlina was probably regarded as the prime role in *Don Giovanni*, while Susanna had a decided edge over the Countess in *Le nozze di Figaro*. When *Le nozze di Figaro* was first produced, Nancy Storace was the leading soprano and played Susanna, and the Italian Luisa Laschi was the Countess. Soon afterwards Nancy Storace left Vienna, and Laschi became prima donna and the most highly paid member of the cast.[26] Yet when *Don Giovanni* was transferred to Vienna in 1788, she played Zerlina rather than either of the heavier female roles. The pattern was similar in Prague. Catarina Bondini, the wife of the impresario, sang Susanna in 1786, provoking the composition of ecstatic verses from the gallery:

> Bondini sings
> And pleasure brings
> To th'melancholy heart;
> Sorrows at least depart
> The while Bondini sings,
> The while her roguish art
> Its vocal changes rings.[27]

She too chose Zerlina above all the female roles in the première of *Don Giovanni*.[28] This emphasis on the casting of Zerlina in Mozart's time is most significant for understanding the form of *Don Giovanni*; as will be seen in Chapter 9, it may account in part for the less than satisfying structure of Act II. By contrast, Elvira was played in Prague by a somewhat indifferent performer (Catarina Micelli) who later specialized in soubrette roles.

The soprano contingent in Vienna fluctuated constantly over the decade of Mozart's maturity, with no single individual retaining her position for many seasons. The pattern among *primi buffi* was very different, since the period was dominated by Francesco Benucci (Plate 10). Kelly called

[26] Luisa Laschi married the tenor Mombelli while in Vienna. Emperor Joseph was inspired by *Le nozze di Figaro* when he gave his consent in a memorandum to Count Rosenberg dated 29 Sept. 1786 (quoted in R. Payer von Thurn, *Joseph II als Theaterdirektor*, p. 70): 'The marriage of Mombelli with La Laschi can be performed without waiting for my return, and I cede to you *Le droit de Seigneur*.' However, Luisa Laschi and her husband fell out with the management of the company soon after the Vienna production of *Don Giovanni*, and they were dismissed later in 1788.

[27] Quoted in Deutsch, *Mozart*, p. 281. It has been suggested that there was uncertainty until some way into the composition of *Le nozze di Figaro* about which soprano role was to take precedent. See A. Tyson, 'Some problems in the text of *Le nozze di Figaro*: did Mozart have a hand in them?' *Journal of the Royal Musical Association*, 112 (1987), 99–131.

[28] Julian Rushton has suggested that Luisa Laschi was given the role of Zerlina in Vienna only because she was pregnant, and would not be able to continue for the entire sequence of performances (J. Rushton, *W. A. Mozart, Don Giovanni* (Cambridge, 1981), 67). This does not however account for Catarina Bondini's choice. Luisa Laschi in fact sang until the day before her confinement, and was on stage again within a month.

him the 'best comic singer in Europe', and he was much admired by Joseph II. The Emperor was in Rome during the 1783/4 season, when Benucci enjoyed remarkable success. Later he instructed Count Rosenberg, the director of the Imperial theatres, to engage the Italian whatever the cost. Indeed, the very survival of the Italian company after the first season at the Burgtheater seems to have been contingent on Benucci's availability. Joseph declared that Benucci was worth two Nancy Storaces, but ruefully admitted that three such *buffi* cost as much as one hundred grenadiers.[29]

Benucci was 40 years old when *Le nozze di Figaro* was written, and was the obvious choice for the title role. He was one of the few singers to elicit a favourable comment from Mozart in his private letters to Leopold:

The Italian *opera buffa* has started again here and is very popular. The buffo is particularly good—his name is Benucci.[30]

His great strength was comedy, and this is reflected in the roles that Mozart wrote for him. It is to his singing of Figaro that we owe Michael Kelly's vivid reminiscence of Mozart, quoted in the Introduction. When *Don Giovanni* was presented in Vienna, the part of Leporello was expanded to give further opportunites for Benucci to display his talent. The duet 'Per queste tue manine' (K. 540*b*) and the ensuing recitative (during which Leporello makes his escape), are clearly designed for comic effect. Benucci's roster of Mozartean parts was completed in 1790 when he created the role of Guglielmo in *Così fan tutte*.

Benucci was also responsible for introducing London audiences to Mozart. He was engaged by the King's Theatre in 1789, and together with Nancy Storace inserted the duet 'Crudel perche finora' from *Le nozze di Figaro* into *La vendemmia* (by Gazzaniga). However, he was not a great success in England, probably because of the prevailing bias against comic opera; for as Mount Edgcumbe observed, 'Notwithstanding his fine voice and excellent acting, he was not so much admired as his talents deserved'.[31] Nonetheless, Benucci was party to an interesting spectacle while in London. A most extraordinary feature of the King's Theatre was the subscribers' right of free access to the stage. This practice had died out in most European theatres. But in London, members of the audience, and in particular the young bloods of the aristocracy, were able to saunter about the stage during performances, conversing or ogling the dancers. They frequently interrupted performances, sometimes completely preventing the opera from continuing. When, for example, the castrato Rubinelli appeared in 1786, there were so many people on stage that the

[29] Payer von Thurn, *Joseph II als Theaterdirektor*, pp. 32 and 34.

[30] Letter to Leopold Mozart dated 7 May 1783. Benucci's influence on the nature of the roles written for him by Mozart has been emphasised by D. Heartz, 'Constructing *Le nozze di Figaro*', *Journal of the Royal Musical Association*, 112 (1987), 77–98.

[31] Mount Edgcumbe, *Musical Reminiscences* (London, 1827), 66.

performance could not start, and was eventually abandoned.[32] But for one of the performances of *La vendemmia* sung by Benucci and attended by Queen Charlotte, the unusual step was taken of posting sentinels round the stage to prevent incursions from the audience. The *Morning Post* took strong exception, and the resulting disturbance was probably not favourable to relaxed enjoyment of the opera:

This unusual prohibition very highly disgusted John Bull, who seemed to think that he was conveyed into France, and murmured very strongly against this military intrusion.[33]

Benucci was supported in Vienna by a second *buffo*, the Italian, Francesco Bussani. Bussani (born 1743) had first sung on the stage in 1763, beginning his career as a tenor. There was never any doubt about the hierarchy, since Bussani played the secondary bass parts in *Le nozze di Figaro* (Antonio and Bartolo) and *Don Giovanni* (the Commendatore and Masetto), and finally Don Alfonso. The allocation for *Così fan tutte* is significant, since in the present day the part of the manipulating cynic Alfonso is often given a special emphasis over the lovers. In Mozart's time, there was no doubt of Guglielmo's precedence, since the status, acting, and singing of the performer were in every way superior. Moreover, Guglielmo was very definitely a bass role. It was not intended for the baritone voice, but for the *primo buffo*; the Figaro rather than the Count.

The dearth of leading tenors in Mozart's comic operas may be related to a change in singing styles that gradually took place over the last decades of the eighteenth century. There had been a tendency for both tenors and baritones to use falsetto over large parts of their range. Tenors commonly switched to falsetto at *d* or *e* above middle *c*—notes that are now comfortably within the compass of male voices. Falsetto was not considered reprehensible, but an acceptable facet of vocal style. The flautist J. J. Quantz wrote approvingly of the manner in which Giovanni Paita combined head and chest voices. Roger Fiske quotes a description of another leading tenor of the day, Charles Incledon:

He had a voice of uncommon power, both in the natural and the falsetto. The former was from A to g, a compass of about fourteen notes; the latter could be

[32] C. B. Hogan, *The London Stage 1776–1800. A Critical Introduction* (Carbondale, Ill., 1968), p. cciv. Apparently the audience were kept well entertained by the confusion on the stage, since the majority remained for more than two hours without complaint. The presence of audience on stage had been widespread in Europe in the mid-eighteenth century, and was condemned by Diderot in his *Discours sur la poésie dramatique* of 1757. For a description of the difficulties incurred at the King's Theatre by allowing the audience on stage, see Nalbach, *The King's Theatre*, 65.

[33] Quoted in W. C. Smith, *The Italian Opera and Contemporary Ballet in London, 1789–1820* (London, 1955), 8.

used from d to ee or ff, or about ten notes, . . . His falsetto was rich, sweet and brilliant, but totally unlike the other (his natural voice). He took it without preparation, according to circumstances, either about d, e or f, or ascending an octave, which was his most frequent custom.[34]

The use of falsetto was dying out by the end of the century, as tastes changed. Michael Kelly astonished London audiences with his full-throated high notes in Storace's *The Haunted Tower* (1789). The custom nevertheless took many years to disappear, so even the leading tenor at the turn of the century, John Braham, sometimes raised his voice 'to an unpleasant falsetto'. It is possible, however, that Mozart was reluctant to use this uneven voice in his Italian works, and only wrote extended parts when a strong tenor was available. Two Italians, Vincenzio Calvesi and Antonio Baglioni, seem to have been especially favoured. Calvesi entered the Burgtheater company in 1785, when he appeared in Bianchi's *La villanella rapita*, and as Antipholus in Stephen Storace's setting of *The Comedy of Errors*. He participated in the concerted pieces Mozart inter-polated into Bianchi's work (K. 479 and 480), and later had the part of Ferrando written for him. Joseph II considered Calvesi to be 'un homme zélé pour le bien du téatre', and his career continued in Central Europe long after Mozart's death. Antonio Baglioni on the other hand was attached to the Prague company, having already gained some success in Italy before moving to Bohemia. The part of Don Ottavio was taken by him in Prague, and he remained in that city long enough to play Tito in the 1791 première of Mozart's last opera.[35]

It is evident from this brief summary that definite constraints were placed on the composer by the availability of singers and their relative strengths. Mozart was exceptional in the trouble he took to match his compositions to individuals. When working with singers he did not know, he never wrote their arias before hearing them in person. Some-times this shortened the time remaining for composition to an alarming extent.[36] Nevertheless, his practice should alert us to study other aspects of the original productions of these operas, for the light they too may shed on the works.

[34] R. Fiske, *English Theatre Music*, 271.

[35] The opinion about Braham's singing was from Mount Edgcumbe. Interestingly, Antonio Baglioni also created the role of Ottavio in Gazzaniga's Don Juan opera. Francesco Morella, the first Ottavio in Vienna, had taken the part of Don Giovanni himself in the opera *Nuovo convitato di pietra* by Francesco Guardi, produced in Venice in 1787. See N. Pirrotta, 'The Tradition of Don Juan Plays and Comic Operas', *Proceedings of the Royal Musical Association*, 107 (1980–81), 60–70.

[36] Perhaps the most remarkable occasion was during the preparation of *Lucio Silla* for Milan in 1772. The first performance was due on 20. Dec., but by 14 Nov. no arias had been written since the singers had not arrived. The primo uomo and prima donna were in Milan by 5 Dec., but the tenor was not available until 17 Dec. Thus the major part of this long work was completed within 3 weeks.

## Opera Production in Mozart's Time

Much of the stiffness of formal opera had disappeared from productions by Mozart's time. Vienna was comparatively advanced in this respect, and a flexible technique of action and response in ensemble was developed there.[37] It was subsequently introduced to England by Michael Kelly and Nancy Storace on their return in 1787, replacing older conventions (such as singers standing in a line facing the audience). However, with the honourable exceptions mentioned in the last section, the acting of most singers left a great deal to be desired. There was no real director or producer, so these responsibilities usually devolved in a casual way on the prompter. Naturalism was hampered by the formality of costumes, with fashionable outdoor clothing complete with wigs and cocked hats being seen even in domestic scenes. Poor people were rarely depicted as such, but were smartened up to reflect the aristocratic view of rustic life. Costumes were chosen with care, and public taste could on occasion be moulded by the stage. This happened in Vienna late in 1786, when the success of Martín y Soler's *Una cosa rara* led to a craze for Spanish 'pastoral' styles.

Scenery was confined to rolling backcloths and decorated canvas flats fixed on wooden frames with wheeling undercarriages. These were set through slits in the stage, and rolled on rails underneath.[38] The system had been mechanized by the designer Torelli in the seventeenth century, so that scene changes could be very rapid. A number of lighting arrangements competed during this period, all making away with the need for chandeliers on stage. Frequently, candles were fixed behind battens in the wings, and some dimming could be achieved by lowering footlights (oil lamps floating in a trough of water) through the stage.

Musical aspects of the opera were under dual command, since the kapellmeister directed the performance, while the konzertmeister took responsibility for the orchestra (see Plate 11). In common with most composers, Mozart acted as kapellmeister for the première and early performances of each opera, and was later replaced by a pupil or the resident keyboard player. Orchestras varied considerably in size in different cities, and were sometimes expanded for particular occasions. So when *Mitridate, Rè di Ponto* was given in Milan in 1770, twenty-eight violins, six basses, and two violoncellos were assembled. The King of Prussia maintained a large band with twenty violins. However, in 1781 to 1783, the Burgtheater mustered just a dozen violins, four violas, three

---

[37] The explanation of this development in Vienna may lie in the taste of Viennese audiences for comic works.

[38] See M. Baur-Heinhold, *Baroque Theatre* (London, 1967). Systems of this type survive at Česk ý Krumlov (Krumau) and Drottningholm.

'cellos and three basses, with double woodwind and horns.[39] The famous
Mannheim orchestra was of a similar size to that in Vienna, while the
Prague theatre boasted only six violins and two violas in the year of *Don
Giovanni*. Skill did not necessarily compensate for these small forces, and
Mozart's orchestration of *Don Giovanni* may have been affected by the
limitations in local resources.

The style of orchestral playing is perhaps to be inferred more accurately
from contemporary compositions than from any written description.
Nevertheless, an interesting comparison between the Berlin and Vienna
Court orchestras of the era was unearthed by Adam Carse, and suggests
some important differences in playing technique. The Viennese specialized in light bowing, producing a flexible, springy line. When the music
required short, forcible bowing, the Viennese 'played such passages with
a unanimity and precision such as is not yet practiced by the Berlin
players, nor probably in any large orchestra'.[40] The Berliners on the other
hand had the advantage in long, sustained phrases, since the lighter
Viennese style was less suitable in these circumstances.

As far as the woodwind are concerned, the pattern is more complex.
Mozart used the woodwind in three distinct fashions in his later *opera
buffa*. Firstly, they could be solo instruments, either alone or more commonly in combination, sustaining the principal melodic material of a
piece. The combination of oboe and bassoon, for example, figures prominently in *Le nozze di Figaro*, playing a major part in the duets 'Se a caso
madama' and 'Che soave zefiretto', and in 'Dove sono'. Secondly, the
woodwind combined in wind concertantes, as in the serenade 'Secondate,
aurette amiche' from *Così fan tutte*, and the opening scene of the Act II
Finale of *Don Giovanni*. The third role of the woodwind was to bolster
tutti sections, acting strictly as accompaniment. Mozart's use of the
woodwind in these different modes varied in the three Da Ponte operas,
and the patterns provide important clues to the availability and quality of
players in the orchestras of the Burgtheater and Prague opera. Thus the
oboe and bassoon combination heard in *Le nozze di Figaro* was used
only sparingly in *Don Giovanni*. It pervades the texture of Anna's aria
'Or sai chi l'onore', particularly in the short, rhythmically tight phrases of
the opening, but elsewhere it gives way to the unusual pairing of flute
and bassoon. This striking orchestral colour makes an early entrance at the
start of the Molto allegro of the Overture, where it sustains the woodwind
responses to the violin theme (bars 41–2). It later becomes prominently
attached to the 'peasant' segments of the score, including Masetto's aria
'Ho capito, signor, sì', and Don Giovanni's seduction of Zerlina, 'Là ci

---

[39] See A. Carse, *The Orchestra in the Eighteenth Century* (New York, 1969), 26–7.
[40] Quoted in Carse, *The Orchestra*, p. 65.

darem la mano'. Mozart clearly favoured the combination of flute and bassoon, since it reappears on several occasions in *Così fan tutte*, notably in Guglielmo's aria 'Non siate ritrosi', Despina's 'Una donna a quindici anni' and the Act II Quartet.

The instrument to show the greatest development in use over the three collaborations with Da Ponte was the clarinet. Although clarinets are included in several sections of *Le nozze di Figaro*, they are rarely given any prominence. The main exception is in the Countess' Act II cavatina, 'Porgi amor', where the clarinets assume a role that was later to figure extensively in *Così fan tutte*: etching a sinuous line in thirds, coupled with the bassoon.[41] The score of *Don Giovanni* displays a curious imbalance between the two Acts in the way the woodwind are used, with a major expansion in the use of the clarinet in Act II, largely at the expense of the oboe. Thus the clarinet appears only three times in Act I (and on one of these occasions, Don Giovanni's aria 'Fin ch'han dal vino', it adds little independent colour). By contrast, the clarinet steals much of the limelight in Act II, from the trio in which Elvira is seduced ('Ah, taci, ingiusto core'), to the prominent obbligati in Zerlina's and Donna Anna's arias. The contribution of the oboe to Act II is correspondingly modest; even on the occasions in which it does participate, its place is in the general woodwind sound mass rather than as an independent solo instrument.

Mozart's use of the clarinet in Donna Anna's 'Non mi dir, bell'idol mio' prefigures the instrumental colouring of *Così fan tutte*, with sensuous semiquaver motifs played in thirds. *Così fan tutte* itself reveals the clarinets in their full glory in many parts of the score.[42] Much of the credit for this development must lie with Anton Stadler, the clarinet virtuoso for whom Mozart wrote the Quintet (K. 581) and the Concerto (K. 622). Stadler (1753–1812) and his brother Johann arrived in Vienna in 1780, but did not join the Imperial orchestra at once, since clarinets were only just achieving respectability, having hitherto been considered suitable only for outdoor occasions or wind bands. There is some uncertainty about when they entered the Imperial orchestra. Weston states this did not happen until 1787 although they are listed in the *Theater Almanach* of 1782.[43] The later date would account for Mozart's modest use of

[41] It is difficult to decide whether the exclusion of the clarinet from a more prominent role in *Le nozze di Figaro* was for reasons of taste or necessity. Certainly there are a number of occasions in the score, such as 'Dove sono' and 'Sull' aria', where similar material would have called for clarinets in later operas.

[42] Notably in the sisters' first duet, 'Come scoglio', the Act II Serenade, Ferrando's cavatina 'Tradito, schernito', and several parts of the two Finales. This use of the clarinet is prefigured in the two arias 'Chi sa qual sia' and 'Vado, ma dove?' (K. 582 and 583), that Mozart wrote in Nov. 1789 for inclusion in a revival of Martín y Soler's *Il burbero di buon cuore*.

[43] P. Weston, *Clarinet Virtuosi of the Past* (London, 1971). See also M. Kingston Ward, 'Mozart's Clarinettist', *Monthly Musical Record*, 85 (1955), 8–14.

the clarinets in his earlier operas and in *Le nozze di Figaro*, compared with *Così fan tutte*. On the other hand, the clarinet is included in *Die Entführung*, and a memorandum from Joseph II dated 8 February 1782 decreed that:

The two brothers Stadler, who play the clarinet, are to be admitted to the orchestra, as they are needed so frequently, and also because they might otherwise enter service elsewhere, or go travelling.[44]

Stadler was certainly in the service of the Emperor in 1784. He became a Freemason in 1785, played in a number of Mozart's Masonic works, and became intimate with the composer. The Serenade for Thirteen Instruments (K. 361) was performed during Stadler's benefit concert at the Burgtheater in the Lenten season of 1784. None the less, Stadler's reputation amongst biographers of Mozart is low. This is chiefly the result of an incident concerning a pawn ticket related by Constanze Mozart to Nissen. Mozart had pawned a number of possessions in 1790 in order to raise money to travel to Frankfurt for the coronation of Emperor Leopold. On his return he wished to redeem some of Constanze's jewellery, and to renew the pawn on his plate. He entrusted these commissions to Stadler, who apparently purloined the renewal ticket. The truth of this story is not certain. What is known, however, is that 500 gulden were lent by Mozart to Stadler in the mid-1780s. They had not been repaid by the composer's death, and were written off as a bad debt.

Stadler may have been a virtuoso, but the same cannot be said for many of the musicians playing in the orchestras of Mozart's time. According to Charles Burney, even the celebrated Mannheim orchestra showed poor intonation in the wind section.[45] It is evident from contemporary comments that Mozart's instrumental writing was beyond many bands, and severely limited the appeal of his works. Here, for example, is a comment on a presentation of *Die Entführung* at Lübeck early in 1789:

Die Entführung . . . is an opera which in any case is difficult, . . . on account of the considerable demands it imposes on all sorts of wind instruments, and the concertante arias and passages which it contains. Now when this task is approached by an orchestra that has not worked together, and indeed mediocre and often less than mediocre wind players, then there is bound now and again to be a lamentable howling, enough to make one grind one's teeth.[46]

---

[44] Payer von Thurn, *Joseph II als Theaterdirektor*, p. 30.

[45] 'I found, however, an imperfection in this band, common all others that I have ever yet heard . . . the defect, I mean, is the want of truth in the wind instruments. . . . This was too plainly the case tonight, with the bassoons and hautbois, which were rather too sharp, at the beginning, and continued growing sharper to the end of the opera.' Quoted in G. Pestelli, *The Age of Mozart and Beethoven*, trans. E. Cross (Cambridge, 1984), 267.

[46] Quoted in Deutsch, *Mozart*, p. 333.

Such complaints appeared repeatedly in the journals and periodicals of the time, indicating that appreciation of Mozart's operas was almost certainly compromised for audiences. Neither the orchestras nor the casts were generally given sufficient rehearsal time to master unfamiliar idioms and styles. Moreover, the whole enterprise seems to have been accompanied by an inordinate number of political difficulties and intrigues. Many of these may have stemmed from the looseness of organization, and the absence of a professional director or controller of productions. Performers were therefore left with considerable independence, and friction arose in the competition for roles or contracts. Lobbying of influential officials and courtiers was frequently valuable to the artist, but success was invariably accompanied by slander. Italian performers were notoriously unscrupulous, as Carlo Gozzi knew to his cost:

Educated in deception from the cradle, they learn the art of making falsehoods with an air of candour so completely, that it requires great gifts of penetration to arrive at their true heart and character. . . . the chief idol of all actors is their venal interest. . . . The merest scent of coming profit makes them disregard and blindly sacrifice the persons who have done them good; the reputation of the whole world is nothing to them then; they take no thought of the damage they may have to suffer in the future, . . . The present moment is all that actors think about.[47]

It is difficult to know whether Vienna bred more than the usual amount of intrigue, but Mozart was apparently the object of several conspiracies, ranging from the machinations surrounding the première of *Le nozze di Figaro* (mentioned in the Introduction), to the débâcle of his insertions into Anfossi's *Il curioso indiscreto* (see Chapter 6). Nor was he alone in these difficulties. Da Ponte recalled in his *Memoirs* how the production of Martín y Soler's *Una cosa rara* was 'subject to great opposition from the singers until the Emperor over-ruled them'. The theatre company that shared the stage with the opera was likewise rent with discord:

The cabals and intrigues which exist . . . you can have no conception of: every new part makes a quarrel in which the courtiers take part . . . as things are now, the authors are greatly injured.

The domination of the Italian camp may have led to difficulties for almost all other nationals. Yet the obstacles placed in Mozart's way (on his own doorstep) may have heightened his already acute social sensitivity. He must have been all the more determined to excel in the design and imaginative power of his operas.

---

[47] Gozzi, *Useless Memoirs*, p. 188. By the time Gozzi wrote his memoires, he was thoroughly disillusioned with the theatre.

# 8

## Drama and Musical Form in *Le nozze di Figaro*

> . . . the light touch, the light touch! The last and highest
> effect of art is charm . . . The depths must laugh! Profundity
> must smile, glide gently in, and smiling yield itself to the
> initiate alone . . . For the people, gay pictures; for the
> cognoscenti, the mystery behind.
>
> Mann[1]

### Classical Musical Forms in Mozart's Work

The integration of musical style with dramatic meaning in Mozart's *opera buffa* is based on the concept of 'form'. The fundamental element underlying form in the classical style is tonality, since the tension and dynamism of the music derives in large part from harmonic contrasts. An outline of tonal or key structures in Mozart's music is therefore a necessary preliminary, although this treatment is far from exhaustive. Perhaps the most illuminating recent descriptions of Mozart's style are to be found in Charles Rosen's *The Classical Style* (1971) and *Sonata Forms* (1980), and the present summary is heavily indebted to these works.

It has often been pointed out that Mozart's style is ideally suited to dramatic representations. The dramatic qualities of his music are based on tonal or harmonic contrasts, rather than on searing melodic flights, fierce rhythms, or the other paraphernalia of nineteenth-century romanticism. To quote Rosen, 'The expressive force of sonata forms was concentrated as much in their structure, the large-scale modulations, and the transformations of the themes as in the character of the themes themselves'.[2]

These tonal contrasts follow an ordered pattern of relationships that is ultimately based on natural harmonics. The basic and most important relationship is between the tonic or home key of the piece and its dominant (the triad at the fifth, derived harmonically from the powerful overtone at the twelfth). This tonic (I) – dominant (V) contrast over-shadows all other associations between keys in late eighteenth-century

---

[1] Words attributed to Goethe by Thomas Mann, *Lotte in Weimar*, trans. by H. T. Lowe-Porter, (London, 1968), 229.
[2] C. Rosen, *Sonata Forms* (New York, 1980), 11.

music, creating an underlying polarity. However, the tonic–dominant axis is not static, since the tonic is itself the dominant of another key. Thus all keys are related through a hierarchical circle of fifths, illustrated in Figure 5. Successive dominants are shown in the clockwise direction.

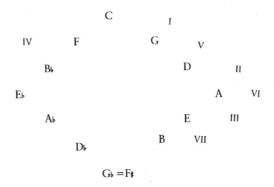

Figure 5.   Circle of Fifths

The importance of this pattern lies in the fact that modulations between related keys sustain the changes of tension in Mozart's music. A move in the dominant or clockwise direction generally increases the tension and dramatic momentum, while release and stability follow the 'descent' from dominant to tonic. Other modulations derive their energy from the positions reached on the circle of fifths (in relation to the tonic). The subdominant (IV) weakens the tonic, and moves towards the subdominant tend to reduce tension in the music—so much so that F major came to be seen as a 'natural' low-tension key, and was favoured for pastoral moods.[3] On the other hand, the mediant (III) and submediant (VI) are closer to the dominant, and modulations towards these keys increase the sense of disturbance and imbalance.

The systematic progression from tonic to dominant and more remote keys is not simply a dry product of formal analysis, but articulates the whole structure of Mozart's music. Although the basic elements interlock differently for the various types of instrumental or vocal piece (the patterns subsumed under the title 'sonata form' are very diverse), certain features are universal.[4] Each movement or number in an opera begins in the tonic key, and the major event in the first part (exposition) is the move to the dominant. This is often prepared for by an excursion into II (the dominant of the dominant), since the stability of a key is enhanced if it is

[3] See W. J. Allanbrook, *Rhythmic Gesture in Mozart* (Chicago, 1983), for details of the pastorale in eighteenth-century music.

[4] See C. Rosen, *The Classical Style* (London, 1971), 99, and *Sonata Forms*, for details of the different styles popular in the classical period.

approached through a perfect (V–I) cadence. The length of the opening tonic section might vary enormously, from a few bars in an opera to many minutes in larger instrumental works.

The dominant section of the exposition is generally marked by a new theme or melodic group in Mozart's compositions.[5] In operatic numbers, the modulation to the dominant is marked in other ways as well, with contrasts of instrumentation, dynamic, and rhythm. These result in the emergence of a new sound mass rather than a simple change in key. Joseph Kerman notes in his book *Opera as Drama* that 'Successive keys were interpreted with new force as areas of contrast rather than as formal adjuncts to the opening tonic'.[6]

The dominant section raises the level of tension in the music, leaving it in a state of some stability which is nevertheless unresolved. It is followed by a section in which even more adventurous tonal excursions can be tolerated. This harmonically bold phase might blossom into a full 'development' section in large-scale works. It is characterized by conflict and occasional dissonance. The thematic material and texture of the earlier exposition is transformed and exploited in violently juxtaposed keys, while rhythmic and dynamic elements are likewise dissected and reconstituted. Unlike many composers of the period, Mozart frequently introduced new melodies into this section as well. On the other hand, some pieces (particularly those based on slow-movement form) have very limited developments, and move directly to the closing section (the recapitulation) which balances the exposition.[7]

The event that heralds the recapitulation is equal in importance to the tonic–dominant modulation of the first section: it is the return of the tonic. If the intervening development has been intense, this resolution is prepared for by a gradual harmonic relaxation. A favourite device of Mozart's was the descending sequence sustained by a dominant pedal, which helped to restabilize the tonality before the tonic.[8] The second significant feature of the recapitulation is the repetition of material from the exposition. Although music originally presented in the tonic may be shortened or even omitted from the recapitulation, this is seldom true of the dominant group. The tension associated with the dominant group has to be resolved in order to balance the piece as a whole, for 'All the material played in the dominant is . . . conceived as dissonant, i.e.

---

[5] This is called the second subject in traditional analysis, but the name is confusing, since the tonic exposition may itself have more than one theme.

[6] J. Kerman, *Opera as Drama* (New York, 1956), 75.

[7] Similarly, many of Mozart's arias were based on extensions of the *da capo* form, in which the section sung between the exposition and recapitulation was an elaboration of the old trio section, rather than a formal development.

[8] For details of this aspect of form, see B. Shamgar, 'On Locating the Retransition in Classic Sonata Form', *Music Review*, 42 (1981), 130–43.

requiring resolution by a later transposition to the tonic'.[9] Dominant music is therefore systematically transposed into the tonic during recapitulation. The process was sometimes assisted by modulations to the subdominant, further to contrast with the dominant of the exposition. While such transposition appears to be a straightforward exercise in instrumental works, it will be seen later that this requirement of classical form placed major constraints on Mozart's operatic compositions.

The harmonic forays and retreats in Mozart's style are therefore underpinned by a framework of profound equilibrium and symmetry. Moreover, as Rosen so aptly puts it,

The large-scale symmetry is mirrored in the rich symmetry of details, so that the music seems to achieve a state of constant balance, untroubled by the expressive violence that nevertheless so frequently characterizes Mozart's work. The symmetry is a condition of grace.[10]

Radical tonal excursions are tolerated within the framework through their relationships with the home keys. The melodic aspects of Mozart's style are also intergrated within this general structure. Composers earlier in the eighteenth century had favoured long, flexible, and complex melodic strands. Such linear melodic continuities were less suitable for the interplay of contrasted sound masses characteristic of the classical period. In Mozart's music, the themes are short, often consisting of basic-four bar phrases of a supreme simplicity that Alfred Einstein called 'second naïveté'. These segments are designed for symmetrical handling, so that even within themes, one phrase is answered and balanced by another.

The overall unity of tonality, rhythm, and melody in Mozart's compositions is undisputed. Nevertheless, the full classical sonata form is seldom exploited to its limits in the operas. In some ways, the musical form is too rich and inherently too dramatic to be dedicated to the comparatively modest emotional requirements of the *buffo* text. This is particularly true of development sections, which have been described as expressing 'struggle, hazardous exploration, terror, uncertainty, dramatic clarification or trial'.[11] It is no accident that these are all descriptions of moods or events that might be depicted on the stage, particularly in tragedy. Such intensity is rarely appropriate in the operas composed by Mozart. Consequently, extended development sections are infrequent, and the tonal excursions are correspondingly restricted. Despite this, arias and ensembles are always subject to the classical principles of dynamic construction that apply in instrumental works.

The theatrical potential of the style derives from its basic elements.

9 Rosen, *Sonata Forms*, p. 25.
10 Rosen, *The Classical Style*, p. 187.
11 Kerman, *Opera as Drama*, p. 78.

The tension developed between tonalities has a parallel in dramatic incident. The charged contrast between keys during exposition and development is the natural vehicle for conflict on the stage, while recapitulation brings harmony and reconciliation. Mozart's treatment of tonalities as sound masses rather than simple harmonic components of a line also had advantages in stage works. It allowed him to incorporate contradictory and opposing forces without disrupting the overall form. Musically telling points and unexpected modulations could be made within quite short sequences, promoting the concentration of incident which is essential to the vitality of *buffo*. In addition, the short, broken phrases of classical themes are well suited to fast-moving drama, particularly during ensembles. The static beauty of mid-century *bel canto* was superseded in Mozart by a melodic line that could be divided, fragmented, or compressed, providing a fluid substratum for interchange between characters. The themes themselves are flexible, yet confined within a restricted *tessitura*; it is remarkable how the melodies found in Mozart's instrumental works can be translated into song without difficulty, in contrast to the wide-ranging angular themes of the baroque.

The relevance of classical musical forms to our understanding of Mozart's purposes in *Le nozze di Figaro* will be discussed below. Yet one fundamental caveat must first be considered. It is conceivable that the harmonic patterns uncovered in analysis are serendipitous, theoretical artefacts with no meaning in eighteenth-century consciousness. Just because a musical description can be based upon tonal relationships does not mean that composers of the period were aware of such forces, or that they explicitly used them for dramatic purposes. Few composers have left written descriptions of the processes governing their choice of material, so arguments about the validity of musical analyses are based on other sources: precedent, the observations of contemporary theorists, and the identification of similarities between unrelated pieces. Fortunately, Mozart is exceptional, since his few surviving comments (not intended for publication) indicate that he was conscious of harmonic mechanisms, and exploited them quite deliberately for dramatic effect. The most important source is the letter to Leopold written on 26 September 1781 during the composition of *Die Entführung*. The passage below describes Osmin's aria 'Solche hergelaufne Laffen', and in particular the final Allegro assai:

but as Osmin's rage gradually increases, there comes . . . the *allegro assai*, which is in a totally different tempo and in a different key; this is bound to be very effective. For just as a man in such a towering rage oversteps all the bounds of order, moderation and propriety and completely forgets himself, so must the music too forget itself. But since passions, whether violent or not, must never be expressed to the point of exciting disgust, and as music, even in the most terrible situations, must never offend the ear, but must please the listener, or in other words must never cease to be *music*, so I have not chosen a key remote from F (in which the aria is written), but one related to it—not the nearest, D minor, but the more remote A minor.

Here the tonal organization is clearly recognized. Mozart wished to engineer an unexpected dramatic coup within the constraints of harmonic convention. He was not therefore prepared to modulate into a completely unrelated key, since this would flout the tonal order. The relative minor was not sufficiently startling, while the dominant (C major) had already played a major part in the aria. Instead he selected the minor form of the mediant, thus reconciling the need for order with histrionic requirements.[12] In his maturity, structural thinking of this type was second nature to Mozart.

## The Classical Style in *Le nozze di Figaro*

The tonal relationships, melodic contrasts, and variations of colouring outlined in the last section underpin the dramatic developments of each number in *Le nozze di Figaro*. No single piece can be taken as the archetype, however, since all have unique characteristics.[13] The richness of style is perhaps best seen in ensemble. Rosen has provided an illuminating analysis of the Act III Sextet, selecting it as the 'least complex and most perfect' example in the opera.[14] But the first major ensemble, the trio 'Cosa sento! tosto andate' between Susanna, Count Almaviva, and Basilio, can also be used to demonstrate Mozart's treatment of classical forms, even though it has some unusual features.

The ensemble accommodates a series of minor dramatic incidents, including the Count's sudden appearance during Basilio's conversation with Susanna, Susanna's fainting and recovery, during the build-up towards the major climax. This is the discovery of Cherubino in most suspicious circumstances. Three musically distinct personalities are involved, and the relationships between them alter in the course of the piece. The Count's initial fury at Basilio's gossip is transformed to lascivious sympathy for Susanna during her collapse, embarrassment on her wakening, to end with ironic aspersions concerning her honesty. Susanna on the other hand moves from confusion at the beginning to the attack in the central section (taking advantage of the men's doubtful behaviour

---

[12] These remote but ordered tonal relationships are of great significance in *Don Giovanni*, as will be seen in Chapter 9.

[13] For an exhaustive analysis see S. Levarie, *Mozart's Le nozze di Figaro: A Critical Analysis* (Chicago, 1952).

[14] Rosen, *The Classical Style*, pp. 290–5.

during her 'faint'), only to retire in disarray after Cherubino's discovery. Mozart incorporates this wide range of action and mood within a short span of consummate unity.

All three actors are introduced within the tonic section of the exposition, yet they are clearly delineated. The ensemble begins with a cadence from the dominant to the tonic B♭. This device was used by Mozart when he wished to emphasize continuity with the preceding text, in this case the Count's precipitate emergence from hiding. The Count's opening phrases barely constitute a theme, although the outline is sustained by a rising string motif (Example 2). His statement closes with a tutti fortissimo cadence on the tonic. Basilio's response (bars 16–23) balances the rapid, ascending contour of Example 2 with longer, falling phrases (Example 3), again accompanied by the strings alone. The entrance of Susanna introduces a third distinctive colouring, since her agitation (bars 23–27) is reflected in chromatic melody (Example 4), block woodwind chords, and continuous quaver oscillations from the second violins. The three singers are thus immediately characterized on their entry into the ensemble. The Count's brusque interrogatives, with clipped phrases and abrupt changes in dynamic, are contrasted with Basilio's insinuating slyness and insincerity. Finally, Susanna's nervousness is expressively outlined. The three are distinguished not only in melody, but in rhythm, dynamic, and orchestral texture.

Example 2.   *Figaro*, no. 7, bars 4–7

Example 3.   *Figaro*, no. 7, bars 16–19

Example 4.  *Figaro*, no. 7, bars 23–6

Example 5.  *Figaro*, no. 7, bars 43–6

Example 6.  *Figaro*, no. 7, bars 51–7

**Example 6.** (*cont'd*)

**Example 7.** *Figaro*, no. 7, bars 101–3

Susanna's entry is followed by the first concerted passage (bars 27–36), which prepares for the dominant F major by way of its dominant, C major. The modulation into the dominant proper occurs as Susanna resumes her interrupted solo line ('me meschina! son' oppressa dal terror'), with the texture thickened by a sustained plaintive viola countersubject (bars 37–43).[15] Mozart uses typical *buffo* word-painting as Susanna faints, with disjointed, gasping phrases colouring her collapse. The dominant section (bars 43–57) of the exposition continues with a new theme (Example 5) sung by Basilio and the Count in canon. The melody is embellished by subdued fanfare motifs from the clarinet and bassoon, while the quaver violin line established at Susanna's entry is continued. But the most important component of the dominant section is the ensemble passage that closes the exposition (Example 6), elaborating the chromaticism first introduced by Susanna with Example 4.

The exposition ends in bar 57, and the next sequence (equivalent to the development) is harmonically more adventurous.[16] A variant of Example 4 is heard from the first violins (bars 57–59) as Susanna recovers from her fit of the vapours. Her indignation on becoming aware of the prurient attentions of the men is mirrored by a cadence on the dominant of G minor (bar 69). This too is promptly replaced by a repetition of the dominant exposition (bars 43–57) in the subdominant E♭ (bars 70–84). Harmonic stability begins to be re-established as Basilio repeats Example 3 (bars 85–92), closing on the dominant. It is further strengthened in the next eight bars by an increase in tempo and volume supported by a dominant pedal from the horns and basses. The brief but telling shift in dramatic ascendancy as Susanna takes advantage of events is thus accommodated by the development without disturbance of the musical line, principally through the juxtaposition of contrasting harmonies.

The tonic returns (bar 101) with a variant (Example 7) of Example 2. Here, the advantage of using a slight, nondescript theme is heard. Example 2 is transformed from the inquisitorial cutting-edge of the opening to the very different tone of 'Parta, parta il damerino' without modifying its basic contour. However, the repetition of the exposition is not permitted to continue without interruption, since an unexpected pause on the dominant occurs after a further twenty bars. This hiatus is used to prepare for the dramatic highlight of the Trio: the discovery of Cherubino. The Count falls into narrative mode, and although his recitative phrases are unrelated to the thematic material of the Trio, they are nevertheless not musically arbitrary; for each is echoed by brief figures reminiscent of the bustling quavers of the Overture. Moreover, as Count Almaviva

---

[15] For other examples of this use of the viola in Mozart's mature works, see Chapter 10.

[16] This trio does not contain a true development, since most of the section repeats material from the exposition, albeit transposed to remote keys. Nevertheless, the structural role of the section remains clear.

approaches the concealed Cherubino, he adopts Basilio's descending motif, Example 3 (at bars 129–38). The discovery is thus made with the greatest possible delicacy. No loud expostulation, but quiet astonishment, brings the music round to another pause on the dominant (bar 146).

The recapitulation recommences (bar 147) with a further variant on Example 2 and Example 7. Now the Count has gained the upper hand, and addresses Susanna with quiet irony ('Onestissima signora'). The music remains in the tonic, and material previously heard in the dominant is transposed into the stable home key. Thus the section first heard as Example 6 returns in bars 168–75 and again in bars 191–200. The texture of the score becomes denser during this section, as the characters express their own preoccupations. It is interesting that in Basilio's case, his rueful observation on the fickleness of women uses phrases (Example 8) of prophetic appropriateness, since they are reproduced precisely in *Così fan tutte*. The Trio ends with a coda (bars 200–21), in which the quaver figures introduced earlier as accompaniment come into prominence. They now evolve into unison flowing phrases that recall the contour of the main theme in the Overture. The vocal lines are subsidiary, and the sound is enriched by sustained chords from the woodwind.

Example 8.   *Figaro*, no. 7, bars 160–3

The Trio is typical of Mozart's mature use of the classical style, in the way that form matches the dramatic action. The melodic germs are comparatively trivial, but this is an asset in opera, since they can be freely adapted to suit a range of text. Both Example 2 and Example 3 are utilized to convey quite different sentiments in the exposition and recapitulation, whereas stronger themes might have been less flexible. The contrasts within the musical structure are based on solid tonal progressions, but yet are also pointed by variations in orchestration, rhythm, and dynamic. Tonality forms the skeleton on which the other elements are exploited.

Mozart's style is clearly suited to ensemble pieces of this type, where the strands of complex plotting can be drawn into a concise format. However, many *buffo* numbers are of a different nature, and do not lend themselves to such integrated structuring. In particular, the conventional aria places severe constraints on dramatic movement, since the emotions expressed are typically static. Instead of using the architectural facets of the style to articulate developments in stage action, the composer was obliged to describe a single sentiment, resolve, or state of mind.[17] Mozart was evidently aware of this problem, and seems for this reason to have avoided reflective arias. As was noted in Chapter 5, his operas contain a relatively low proportion of arias, and of those that were included, a large number involve some kind of 'business'. In *Le nozze di Figaro*, there are fourteen solo numbers. Only five of these are in conventional mode, with an individual expressing his or her emotional preoccupations in soliloquy. Three of the four principals were conceded one full *recitativo accompagnato* and aria in soliloquy, while Marcellina and Bartolo were given exit arias. The other solo numbers are integrated dynamically into the action of the story. Susanna's major scena 'Giunse al fin il momento. . . . Deh vieni non tardar' is sung to the unsuspecting Figaro, and gains its dramatic point from his presence. Susanna and Figaro both have other arias involving stage action: 'Venite, inginocchiatevi' accompanies the disguising of Cherubino, while Figaro's 'Non più andrai' acts as the finale to Act I, with full mock-military accoutrements. Cherubino's two pieces are presented as songs within the text, thus legitimizing their static nature. Basilio's aria 'In quegli anni' is sung as a moral tale to Bartolo, and fills out the character of the sycophantic music teacher. None of these are soliloquies, since they are directed at (and sometimes involve) other characters on the stage. Figaro's brief cavatina might have been clothed in the full paraphernalia of the exit aria by contemporary composers. Mozart, however, produced an ironic dance that lightened the form while losing none of the venom. The other solo pieces belong to the Countess and Barbarina. Both numbers have formal roles, setting the stage for Acts II and IV respectively. 'Porgi amor' also plays a crucial part in the dramatic action, since it rapidly sketches in an important character whose entrance has been delayed for a dangerously long interval. Its languid beauty immediately establishes an understanding in the audience about the Countess and her behaviour, so that she can assume her place in the intrigue without further introduction.

Mozart therefore found several ways of avoiding an accumulation of static arias. Such pieces were uncongenial both to his temperament and style. This pattern could not have been produced without the connivance of the librettist, and Da Ponte was instrumental in restricting conventional soliloquy emotions to a minimum. But there was another serious problem that confronted Mozart in his application of classical musical forms to *opera buffa*: how to deal with the extended musical sequences that constitute the *buffo* finale. Fortunately for posterity, Mozart's solution to this difficulty brought him to the pinnacle of his art.

---

[17] The Metastasian aria admittedly consisted of verses that were contrasted in poetic imagery, but this seldom provoked dramatic conflict.

## Extended Musical Spans: The Finale of Act II

It was suggested in the last section that the musical forms developed by Mozart were able to accommodate aria less well than ensemble. However, the application of the style to extended, interlinked plot sequences was ultimately more problematic. Despite their inherently dramatic nature, the musical forms cultivated by Mozart were closed and symmetrical in organization, with the adventurous harmonic excursions in the first part of a movement being balanced by the recapitulation. Since the return of the tonic implies resolution and a reduction of tension, there is an inevitable relaxation at the emotional level as well. Moreover, the thematic material of the exposition is typically repeated in the later stages. These symmetrical requirements meant that the style was not suited to a text that demanded a gradual but inexorable rise in tension across linked sections.

The strategies by which Mozart turned this constraint to his advantage can best be illustrated with the music of the finales. The finale offered composers of the eighteenth century an opportunity to display their skills in binding extended material into a coherent unit, while at the same time illuminating a plethora of stage incident. Da Ponte's description of the *buffo* finale amusingly ennumerates these demands:

This finale, which has to be closely connected with the rest of the opera, is a sort of little comedy in itself and requires a fresh plot and a special interest of its own. This is the great occasion for showing off the genius of the composer, the ability of the singers, and the most effective 'situation' of the drama. Recitative is excluded from it; everything is sung, and every style of singing must find a place in it—adagio, allegro, andante, amabile, armonioso, strepitoso, arcistrepitoso, strepitosissimo, and with this the said finale generally ends. . . . In this finale it is a dogma of theatrical theology that all the singers should appear on the stage, even if there were three hundred of them, by ones, by twos, by threes, by sixes, by tens, by sixties, to sing solos, duets, trios, sextets, sessantets; and if the plot of the play does not allow of it, the poet must find some way of making the plot allow of it, in defiance of his judgement, of his reason, or of all the Aristotles on earth; and if he then finds his play going badly, so much the worse for him![18]

Da Ponte's outline is perhaps a little misleading, since it implies a progressive increase in dramatic pitch through the sections. In fact, the heightening of pace and bustle occurs only at the close of the finale in Mozart's operas. Yet the librettist vividly emphasizes the way in which

---

[18] Quoted in E. J. Dent, *Mozart's Operas* (London, 1960), 104. It has however been noted that by Mozart's time, both composers and librettists found the writing of *buffo* finales burdensome, and critics complained that long finales were tedious. Jommelli grumbled that a finale was as much work as eight arias. See D. Heartz, 'The Creation of the *Buffo Finale* in Italian Opera', *Proceedings of the Royal Musical Association*, 104 (1977–8), 67–78.

the finale comprises a series of interlocking sections (really separate numbers), each with its own internal form. Excitement is sustained by the
harmonic and textural relations between these segments, rather than
through an unrelenting drive towards the climax. Da Ponte's libretto had
therefore to provide a series of dramatic steps, interspersed with brief
plateaux of repose or resolution, in order to satisfy the interior musical
architecture of the sections.

TABLE 4.   OUTLINE OF ACT II FINALE

| Section | Key | Tempo and time signature | | Bars | Action |
| --- | --- | --- | --- | --- | --- |
| A | E♭ | 'allegro' | 4/4 | 1–125 | The Countess admits to her husband that Cherubino is in the closet. He is furious, condemns her, and vows vengeance. |
| B | B♭ | 'andante' | 3/8 | 126–66 | Susanna appears from the closet. The Count and Countess are stupefied. |
| C | B♭ | 'allegro' | 4/4 | 167–327 | The Count pleads for forgiveness. The Countess prevaricates, but eventually relents. |
| D | G | 'allegro' | 3/8 | 328–97 | Figaro enters, eagerly preparing for his wedding. He is soon put on his guard by the Count's behaviour. |
| E | C | 'andante' | 2/4 | 398–466 | Figaro is confronted with the letter written to the Count. He refuses to admit responsibility, despite pressure from the Countess and Susanna. Figaro, Susanna, and the Countess beg the Count to allow the wedding to proceed. |

TABLE 4.   OUTLINE OF ACT II FINALE (cont.)

| Section | Key | Tempo and time signature | Bars | Action |
|---------|-----|--------------------------|------|--------|
| F | F | 'allegro molto'  4/4 | 467–604 | Antonio enters, complaining about someone jumping from the Countess's window. Confusion as the Count tries to hear him out, while the others attempt to suppress the story. Figaro then claims it was he who jumped. |
| G | B♭ | 'andante'  6/8 | 605–96 | Antonio gives the dropped document to the Count. Figaro is foiled until, with the aid of Susanna and the Countess, he discovers it is Cherubino's commission. A tutti section follows. |
| H | E♭ | 'allegro assai'  4/4 'più allegro' 'prestissimo' | 697–782 783–907 908–40 | Marcellina, Basilio and Bartolo enter to stake Marcellina's claim over Figaro. General confusion reigns as the curtain falls. |

Table 4 summarizes the main divisions of the mighty Act II Finale of *Le nozze di Figaro*, together with the stage action sustained in each section. It is immediately apparent how systematically the sections are contrasted in time signature and tempo, so that brisk episodes are punctuated by more sedate interludes. Only in the final section *H* does the music build up into the torrent of noise described by Da Ponte. The sections all contribute to an organized key structure based on the tonic E♭ major. The modulations between sections take the form of an harmonic arch, reaching a peak at the centre: E♭–B♭–G–C–F–B♭–E♭. After the G major section *D*, each succeeding key is a step down the circle of fifths (detailed in Figure 5), and heralds greater relaxation and reduction in tension. Conversely, the ascent to the apex in section *D* is approached by modulations in the dominant direction.

It is evident therefore that section $D$ is in an axial position harmonically, since it is here that the structural tension is greatest. It is entered via
a bold modulation from B♭, but more importantly, it is midway between
the tonic (E♭) and the dominant (B♭) of the whole Finale. The keys of
sections $A$–$D$ pick out the E♭ major tonic triad, reinforcing the home key
while generating tension from it. Interestingly however, section $D$ does
not contain the most dramatic confrontation or thorniest intrigue of the
Finale. Instead it introduces a central character (Figaro) to the mêlée,
and provides a watershed to the action. The *sequelae* of the Count's rage
and stupefaction about the intruder in the closet are played out in sections $A$, $B$, and $C$, while in the subsequent sections Figaro finds himself
enmeshed in a series of complex falsehoods. Section $D$ injects a sudden
change of mood between these episodes, emphasized by the use of a
rustic 3/8 dance rhythm and bright orchestral timbre. The key is appropriate for peasant music of this type, and is used by Mozart for bucolic
choruses on other occasions (including Act I, 'Giovani lieti'; and *Don
Giovanni*, Act I, 'Giovinette che fate all'amore'). Furthermore, this G
major section can be seen as a prolonged preparation for section $E$ in C
major, illustrating the technique noted earlier of entering a new key
through preparation on its dominant. The resolution into C major at the
start of the 'andante' in bar 398 brings a new sense of stability, upon
which the internal structure of section $E$ is founded.

The sections outlined in Table 4 are also distinguished from each
other by the weight and colour of the orchestration. The full tutti of
sections $A$, $D$, $F$, and $H$ are interspersed with lighter segments where
different instrumental groups predominate. For example, the stately 3/8
minuet of section $B$ (Example 9) is played by the strings, with the woodwind only entering later to support the vocal line. The metre emphasizes
the fact that Susanna is carrying out Figaro's Act I threat, in teaching the
Count to 'dance'. The following B♭ 'allegro' is scored with alternating
tutti and quieter passages, in which individual wind instruments (flute,
oboe, and bassoon) have prominent solo roles. The colouring of the later
B♭ 'andante' interlude (section $G$) is again different, with delicate quaver
motifs on the strings, supported by woodwind pedals. The distribution of
melodic interest among the different instrumental groups is another
element that contrasts the sections of the Finale. In some sections the
voices carry the melody, while in others the singers take a subsidiary role,
merely commenting on the instrumental themes. Not only does this add
another colour to the musical palette, it also has dramatic implications
that are fundamental to the dynamism of Mozart's art. For the technique
allows exchanges between characters to be sung without melodic append-
ages. The intensity of conversation and repartee is thus compressed so that
the pace of the action can outstrip thematic development.

Example 9.  *Figaro*, Act II Finale, bars 126–33

An example of this type of writing is found at the start of section *B* (see Example 9). The strings have the melody, and Susanna's comments are musically superfluous. The unexpectedness of her entry, and the astonishment of the Count and Countess, are thus reinforced by the disjointed vocal phrases. No sung theme would portray Susanna's control of the confrontation so economically, while at the same time underlining the bewilderment of the onlookers. Similarly, the opening of section *E* (Example 10) might be played without any major losses as a purely orchestral piece. The theme pursues its elegant course in an uninterrupted fashion, while the vocal line passes back and forth between the four protagonists. Their style is conversational and the phrasing appropriate to the context, with challenges from the Count and hints from the Countess and Susanna eliciting monosyllabic rebuttals from Figaro.

Example 10.   *Figaro*, Act II Finale, bars 398–401

The general organization of the Finale into a harmonically balanced sequence is duplicated in the internal structure of sections. Each dramatic confrontation is encapsulated within a section, rather than overflowing from one to another. However, the burden of the plot is not evenly distributed between sections. Consequently, some are more fully developed than others, and complete sonata-like forms are not employed when the dramatic requirements are modest. Thus there are two· shorter bridging sections in the Finale, and these provide musical contrast while connecting more important developments in the plot. Sections *B* and *D* are both concerned with a static dramatic point, and do not present problems that call for solution. Section *B* sees Susanna emerging from the closet, and exulting over her employers' mystification. It is so short and closely related to the ensuing 'allegro' that the composer did not even consider a key change was necessary. Its internal structure is simple, with the theme (Example 9) in the tonic, moving to the dominant at bar 155, and returning to the tonic within a few bars.

A simple tonic–dominant structure is also sufficient for section *D*. Figaro's ebullient entry is confounded by the Count's cautious response, and the remainder of the section is taken up with ruminations about the forthcoming interrogation. But section *D* shows how even this most basic harmonic relationship can be used for subtle dramatic purposes. Figaro's robust 3/8 fanfare music has a conventional form, reaching the dominant (D major) at the midpoint and closing in the tonic. Figaro might be expected to initiate the move to the dominant, but is thwarted by the Count; for instead of moving directly to D major, the Count repeats and extends the cadence (bars 356–9), musically pointing the hesitation in the words 'Pian, piano, men fretta' ('One moment, not so fast'). The quaver figures in the strings are also interrupted by sustained chords. Figaro tries to prepare the modulation with his phrase 'La turba m'aspetta' ('The crowd is waiting'), reinforced by the tutti instrumentation of the opening, but Count Almaviva again pauses, and thereby gains the musical initiative. Thus by the time the modulation is properly completed and the music is allowed to continue in the dominant (bar 369), the balance of power has shifted in favour of the Count, who now gains ascendancy over the situation.

The other sections of the Finale have greater dramatic importance than *B* or *D*, and their musical structures are correspondingly expanded. Instead of a simple tonic–dominant focus, the music is harmonically adventurous, in some cases flowering into complete developments (as in sections *C* and *F*). Sections *E* and *G* utilize more compressed sonata forms, with their tonal excursions confined to the exposition and recapitulation. None the less, in all these sections the musical form places distinct requirements on the plot: for moments of dramatic tension or uncertainty are inevitably followed by brief periods of harmony and reconciliation in the musical recapitulation. Mozart's use of a series of independent, self-contained musical structures required a libretto that could be similarly compartmentalized. Each section needed its own internal plot resolution, in order to suit the growth and dissipation of dramatic force inherent in the musical forms.

This creation of a stepped, discontinuous plot sequence out of the smooth interwoven fabric of the play is perhaps Da Ponte's most masterly achievement. Most of these extended sections of the Act II Finale involve a specific problem or incident that challenges the characters. In section *C*, it is the Count's pleas for forgiveness, and his wife's initial rejection. The resolution comes when the Countess relents, and harmony reigns for a short span in the recapitulation. Section *F* sees new intrigues sparked off by the gardener Antonio's entry, and the revival of the Count's suspicions about Cherubino. When Figaro admits it was he who jumped through the window, the dramatic tension is briefly relaxed. But it is renewed almost immediately, for section *G* brings a fresh dilemma. The bone of contention here is the document given by Antonio to the Count, and resolution only prevails with Figaro's triumphant revelation that it is the unsealed commission of the Page. In all these cases, the dramatic stimulus is presented in the exposition, worked through the central development, and resolved for the recapitulation.

Section *G* is a perfect example of the pattern. As in so many parts of the Finale, the thematic material is of minor importance compared with the tensions generated by the harmony. Hence the material of the B♭ major opening is continued with little variation into the dominant (bar 641) as the Count intensifies his interrogation of Figaro. Figaro's contortions are reflected in modulations to remoter keys such as G minor (bar 651) and E♭ major (bar 659). While these keys hold sway, it seems possible that Count Almaviva will be victorious, and that Figaro's deception will be unmasked. But the atmosphere clears when the Countess and Susanna recognize the unsealed commission. Armed with this information, Figaro resolves with smug relief onto the dominant (bar 671), bringing back the tonic for the final segment (see Example 11).

Mozart's art demanded a coherent internal structure to each section of the Finale, with movements in the plot to parallel musical forms. Da Ponte generally fulfilled this requirement successfully, except perhaps for the text contained in the C major section E. This is in slow-movement sonata form, with a full exposition but no proper development. The recapitulation therefore follows immediately after the exposition, with the themes of the dominant exposition reappearing in the tonic. This attenuated form sustains the somewhat modest dramatic contents of the section, for this is one of the few moments when the plot becomes disjointed. The Count confronts Figaro with the anonymous scurrilous letter, while Susanna and the Countess urge him to admit authorship. Figaro steadfastly refuses. But instead of the impasse being resolved with any cunning or bold presumption on Figaro's part, it is simply dropped. The recapitulation of section E does not therefore present a further triumph of the wily barber over his employer, but introduces the completely irrelevant, tame pleading for permission to marry.

The untidiness of plotting in section E is not the fault of Da Ponte, since in Beaumarchais's play this confrontation also ends ambivalently. The passage in Act II, Scene xx runs as follows:

COUNT: So you admit the note?

FIGARO: Since madam wants it so , Suzanne wants it so, and you yourself want it so, I must certainly want it so too. But if I were you, my Lord, truly, I wouldn't belive a word of anything we are telling you.

COUNT: You're always telling lies in the face of the evidence! In short, it's getting on my nerves!

COUNTESS: [laughing]: The poor fellow! Why do you expect him, sir, to tell the truth even once?[19]

The moment has no flavour of the dramatic coup accompanying Figaro's vindication over the unsealed commission, or Susanna's unexpected appearance from the locked closet. The Count is more concerned with Figaro's lying than with his breathtaking impudence in planting the libellous note. Faced with an inadequate challenge in the plot, Mozart

---

[19] This and other quotations are from the translation of *Le nozze di Figaro* by Vincent Luciani (New York, 1964).

could do little but compress the musical form of section *E* as far as possible.

The first and last sections of the Finale also diverge from the general pattern. It was important for the tonal stability of the finale as a whole to establish the home key firmly at the beginning. Section *A* is thus elaborated with full exposition and development. However, the plot does not progress to any kind of resolution within the span of this passage. Indeed, in many ways a dramatically rounded opening section would weaken the forward thrust of the interlinked structure. The closing section of the Finale, from the entry of Marcellina and her supporters to the curtain, contrasts with the intervening sections in a different fashion. Having regained the home key of Eb major at the 'allegro assai' (bar 697), Mozart does not deviate from it again. The whole section is an insistent affirmation of the tonic Eb, underlined by repeated tonic–dominant cadences. Its length stabilizes the tonality by balancing the harmonic excursions of the earlier sections. Since the key is constant, all the energy and vitality of section *H* has to come from pace, rhythm, and melody. Consequently, there is a continual variation in rhythm, with melisma, syncopation, and alternation between material based on 2/4 and 4/4 pulse. The themes are closely related to each other, while also recalling earlier sections. In addition, the whole sequence shows a gradual acceleration, from 'allegro assai' through 'più allegro' (bars 783–907) to 'prestissimo' (bars 908–40). This is contrived so subtly that faster singing is not required, since the dynamism of the music does not derive simply from rapid notes. It is in this section that Da Ponte's description of 'strepitoso, archistrepitoso, strepitosissimo' is finally vindicated.

Detailed consideration of extended operatic forms refines our understanding not only of Mozart's but of Da Ponte's art. The librettist's skill lay not so much in the overall adaptation and modification of Beaumarchais's play, as in the minutiae of the task. Although many exchanges were lifted wholesale from the play, Da Ponte was obliged to alter the pacing of each confrontation to suit Mozart's style. Beaumarchais relied on a constant build-up of intrigue and confusion, in which one complication follows another with unflagging energy. Mozart required a more relaxed ordering, giving room for reflection between each imbroglio. This is evident at the end of section *G* of the Act II Finale, where the Count's enquiries about the unsealed commission are foiled. Beaumarchais handles the moment brusquely, and Figaro's victory is acknowledged only briefly in the action:

FIGARO: The fact is . . . little is missing. He says that it is the custom . . .
COUNT: The custom, the custom! What's the custom?
FIGARO: To affix the seal showing your coat of arms. Maybe it wasn't worth the trouble . . .

COUNT: [reopens the paper and crumples it angrily]: Confound it! My fate
decrees that I shall know nothing. [Aside] It's Figaro who is the master mind,
and I shall not avenge myself?

(Act II, Scene xxi)

The libretto on the other hand dilates both on the revelation and the
response. The resolution of the quandary is delayed tantalizingly by
Figaro, even after the ladies have provided him with the solution (Example 11). Subsequently, all the characters comment on the situation in
asides. The Count's frustrations are graphically portrayed, while Figaro
exults in his ascendancy. Mozart needed a static moment of reflection to
couple with the musical recapitulation, and this was seized by Da Ponte
for an imaginative comment on the relationships between the protagonists.

It is moments such as this that illuminate the librettist's skill far more
than the broad outline of the adaptation. The pacing of the drama,
knowing when to expand and when to be brief, could only emerge from a

Example 11.    *Figaro*, Act II Finale, bars 660–71 (woodwind omitted)

Example 11.   (cont'd)

thorough understanding of the composer's style. It is unlikely that such
knowledge could develop without collaboration of the closest order, and
a pragmatic attitude that did not set art on a pedestal—just the qualities
Mozart demanded in the 'true phoenix' of a librettist that he sought in
his earlier years.

The fact that *Le nozze di Figaro* did not realize its authors' hopes,
despite its beauty and careful construction, has never been satisfactorily

explained. The audience at the Burgtheater was culturally sophisticated and attracted by novelty. *Le nozze di Figaro* was ideal fare for this public, since it was based on a work that enjoyed a highly scandalous reputation. The play had taken Paris by storm only two years earlier. According to Baron Grimm,

> never did a piece attract such a concourse at the Théatre Francais. All Paris wished to see this famous *Marriage* . . . scarcely half of those who had been besieging the theatre since 8 o'clock in the morning were able to get seats . . . More than one Duchess thought herself lucky that day to find a wretched little stool in the balconies where well-bred women would scarcely sit.[20]

Beaumarchais was obliged to wait six years for his play to be produced, and to submit the piece to no fewer than six censors, each of whom demanded modifications. Public performances in the Austrian Empire had been banned outright by Joseph II, even though twelve German translations were circulating by 1785. Schikaneder hoped to produce a spoken translation at the Kärntnerthortheater in early 1785, but was refused by the Emperor and Count Pergen.[21] Da Ponte's boast about the manner in which he persuaded the Emperor to sanction the opera (see Introduction) cannot be accepted at face value. Nevertheless, he was certainly instrumental in convincing the authorities that most of the overt political references had been exised from his *buffo* libretto.

Mozart's opera was thus eagerly anticipated, less for its musical qualities that for its *risqué* content. Since the play was proscribed, the opera was the first public glimpse of the piece in the Empire. The Viennese viewed it against a background of notoriety—for them it was a *succès du scandale*.

Perhaps this was the root of the problem. Like many other sensational events, it created more excitement in anticipation than execution. The public must have been disappointed that the opera was not more inflammatory. Many later commentators have argued that the musical complexity of the score baffled the audience, but this seems an insufficient explanation of the opera's fate.[22] Nor does it account for the greater appreciation given to the work on its revival in 1788—had taste and discrimination advanced so far in two years? Rather, it seems likely that the lack of sustained interest during the first Viennese season resulted from the audience's failure to look beyond the subject-matter. It was only after the glitter of the original attractions had faded that the music and humour of the work were more fully appreciated, and *Le nozze di Figaro* was judged on its own merits.

[20] Quoted in C. Cox, *The Real Figaro* (London, 1962), 114.
[21] See Heartz, *Setting the Stage for Figaro*, p. 260.
[22] These arguments are summarized in G. Pestelli, *The Age of Mozart and Beethoven*, trans. E. Cross (Cambridge, 1984), 146.

# 9

# *Don Giovanni*: Musical Form and Dramatic Cohesion

> And has not form two aspects? Is it not moral and immoral at
> once; moral insofar as it is the expression and result of disci-
> pline, immoral . . . in that of its very essence it is indifferent to
> good and evil, and deliberately concerned to make the moral
> world stoop beneath its proud and undivided sceptre?
>
> Mann[1]

*Don Giovanni* has a less satisfying dramatic structure than *Le nozze di
Figaro*. It lacks the poise of the earlier work, and Act II possesses a
looseness of form that can lead to disturbing *longeurs* in an uninspired
performance. Yet these imperfections are more than compensated for by
a musical and emotional thrust of overwhelming energy. The dynamic
cohesion of the score raises the composer's art to more electrifying peaks
(if not to a higher plane) than *Le nozze di Figaro*.

A central factor in this development of Mozart's operatic technique was
the manner in which he welded individual scenes and episodes of the
story into the broader sweep of the opera. Instead of a genial sequence of
memorable but distinct musical experiences, the work is characterized by
a powerful unity of purpose.[2] This is of course appropriate for a story in
which the majority of events are mere preludes to the shattering confrontation between the hero and the forces of retribution. Yet it also reflects
Mozart's consciousness of the profound dramatic potential of his musical
style, moving beyond even the coherent large-scale structures of *Le nozze
di Figaro*.

Several procedures were used by Mozart to sustain the dramatic unity of
*Don Giovanni*. The first and most striking technique involved the elimination of musical numbers which impeded the flow of the story. Despite
the efforts described in Chapter 8 that Mozart made to reduce the number of traditional monologues in *Le nozze di Figaro*, the opera is not free
from such irrelevancies. The first occurs in Act I, immediately after the

---

[1] Thomas Mann, *Death in Venice*, trans. by H. T. Lowe-Porter, (London, 1955), 18.

[2] The problem of how to achieve dramatic unity in opera was reiterated frequently in the eighteenth century. The reforms instituted by Calzabigi and Gluck in the 1760s attempted to increase
dramatic coherence by reducing the action to a few central scenes, in place of the short disconnected
episodes then common in *seria*.

plot has got underway in the opening scene involving Figaro and Susanna. Bartolo enters, and after a short exchange with Marcellina embarks on his aria 'La Vendetta' (no. 4). Although magnificently conceived, the aria is entirely peripheral to the main business of the opera. It is sung by a minor character, and transmits no information of importance to the audience or other participants. Instead it elaborates Bartolo's own feelings, which are tangential and play little part in the subsequent action. As befits a stock piece of this type, Bartolo leaves the stage on its completion.

Almost at once, therefore, the unfolding of the plot of *Le nozze di Figaro* is diverted into a charming cul-de-sac. This is no great disadvantage, since the entire story is episodic in nature. It would however have been disastrous for a monothematic drama like *Don Giovanni*. Mozart and Da Ponte avoided this problem by reducing the number of reflective and 'exit' arias to a minimum, and by confining them largely to Act II. The whole of Act I has no obstacles placed in the way of the forward impetus.[3] There are, of course, several arias in Act I, but all have a definite purpose. Each one is sung to other characters on the stage, and expresses public feelings. These numbers tell the audience something about the drama, and contribute to the progress of the plot. A good example is Leporello's aria 'Madamina, il catalogo è questo'. Significantly, this bass aria holds precisely the same position (no. 4) in *Don Giovanni* as Bartolo's monologue in *Le nozze di Figaro*. Yet the effect is quite different. Leporello enlightens both Donna Elvira and the audience in this aria, colouring in his own character while expanding our knowledge of Don Giovanni. The aria is integral to the drama.

A second stratagem employed by Mozart to unify the drama involves the grouping of successive musical numbers into broader harmonic units. Numbers retain their internal structure and identity, yet are embedded within a larger arch by means of harmonic context and thematic reminiscence. The method is an extension of the technique of finale writing developed in *Le nozze di Figaro*, where individual sections are again incorporated into a grander form. Mozart's integration of separate numbers in *Don Giovanni* is looser, but the result is similar: a concentration of dramatic action, and strengthening of the underlying tonality.

The most clear-cut grouping of numbers in *Don Giovanni* occurs at the beginning, where the Overture is closely linked with the opening scena (*Introduzione* (no. 1) and Duet (no. 2)). The numbers are separate, but together comprise a massive block of D minor tonality, preparing the

---

[3] The aria for Don Ottavio, 'Dalla sua pace', is not an original feature, but an insertion for the Vienna production. It is unfortunately rather typical of contemporary *buffo*, since it merely expresses the static feelings of a character. Although very beautiful, it does not contain character or plot developments.

stage harmonically as well as dramatically for the entire opera. Following the D minor/major Overture, the *Introduzione* is not set in an unrelated key, but in F major. F major is the relative major of the central D minor, and asserts this tonality through contrast. The duet between Donna Anna and Don Ottavio sees a return of D minor, so the whole group is closed rather than open-ended. The power of this arrangement can be gauged by contrast with *Le nozze di Figaro*. Here the D major Overture is followed by a grouping of G major with the subdominant keys of B♭ major and F major. Together these keys form a relaxed open group that is appropriate for the modest substance of the conversation between Susanna and Figaro.

The tonal plan is paralleled by the stage action in *Don Giovanni*. Within the opening group, the *Introduzione* holds the place of the development in sonata form. Its key is thus doubly appropriate, as are the extensive modulations that convey the heightened tension in the plot. It is no accident that the most dramatic incidents of the opening group (the assault on Donna Anna and the death of her father) are portrayed within the *Introduzione*. The continuity between numbers in the opening group is further emphasized by the interrogative endings of the Overture and *Introduzione*; neither finishes with a formal tonic cadence, so that in each case the succeeding material presses on without disruption. The return of D minor in the Duet signals the re-establishment of a more stable emotional atmosphere, with the fierce emphasis on vengeance being sustained by a firm restatement of the home key.

The grouping at the beginning of *Don Giovanni* serves both musical and dramatic purposes. The statements of D minor/major and the related keys of F major and B♭ major summarize the harmonic arguments of the opera as a whole. Thematic ideas are introduced that act as germ cells for the developments later in the work. The entire gamut of musical style is experienced, from the supernatural mystery of the Overture's 'andante', through the *seria* fury of the Duet, to the melancholy anguish of the Commendatore's death and Leporello's *buffo* impatience in the *Introduzione*. Dramatically, the group acts as a prologue to the ensuing drama, since much of the later action springs directly from the experiences of the characters during these few minutes. Both the *Introduzione* and the Duet are fine examples of Mozart's art of matching vocal line to dramatic context. There is little opportunity for *bel canto* and sustained singing, as the characters are either in sharp conflict, or else so distracted that they cannot collect their thoughts. Yet emotion is not portrayed at the expense of musicality, for orchestral phrases elaborate the singers' disjointed utterances. The sequence is assembled into a coherent musical unity through the interweaving of vocal and instrumental lines.

No other grouping of separate numbers in *Don Giovanni* has the

compelling tightness of this opening set. Nevertheless, continuity is maintained at other points through thematic reminiscence between suc-
,cessive numbers.[4] For example, there is a close thematic link between the mighty Act II Sextet and Leporello's following Aria (no. 20); indeed, the Aria opens with an offbeat phrase that derives directly from material elaborated towards the end of the Sextet (bar 185 et seq). Other thematic allusions span broader segments of the plot, since melody is used throughout the score to bind disparate sections together. These remi- niscences sometimes underline dramatic parallels between different epi- sodes in the story. The most striking instance is the reappearance of the opening D minor 'andante' in the final confrontation between Don Giovanni and the Stone Guest. The quotation in the Overture of the opera's climax argues more strongly than any words for Mozart's concern with unity in this work. An appendix to this grand symmetry is the reminder of Anna and Ottavio's early Duet (no. 2) in the Act II Finale. The unison close of the Duet, with its semiquaver rhythm (bars 221–2) is repeated as Don Giovanni is engulfed by the forces of darkness in the Finale (bars 600–2). His demise thus sets the seal on the vows of vengeance taken in Act I.

These deliberate associations may be contrasted with occasions when melodic affinities do not make direct dramatic points, but highlight similarities in the emotional situation. Mozart frequently employed this technique ironically. Take the descending chromatic dotted motif that plays such an important role in the Sextet (Example 12(*a*) ). It is identified with Elvira's pleas for her supposed 'marito', Don Giovanni. An identi- cal melodic contour appears very much earlier, during Donna Anna's tussle with Don Giovanni in the *Introduzione* (Example 12(*b*) ). In this case, Anna is pleading for reinforcements in the struggle over her virtue. Mediating between these two, the motif is repeated by Don Giovanni himself in the Act I Quartet (Example 12(*c*) ). His use of the figure deviously counterpoints the other two, since he is in the process of trying to persuade Anna that Elvira is mad.

A less elaborate set of associations is set up with a later fragment of Elvira's music in the Sextet. The falling diminished fifth accompanying her supplicatory cries of 'pietà' in the Sextet (bars 90–3) reappears near the climax of the Act II Finale. A dramatically obvious point might have been made by giving the phrase to Don Giovanni in his anguish. But Mozart as ever had more subtle intentions. Leporello sings the motif, using it to underline his fears for his own safety (Finale, bars 449–50);

---

[4] The thematic allusions in *Don Giovanni* have been enumerated in detail by F. Noske, in *The Signifier and the Signified* (The Hague, 1977). His researches are a sophisticated extension of those made by Jean Chantavoine (*Mozart dans Mozart* (Paris, 1948)). The warnings about thematic inter- pretation detailed in the Introduction should not be overlooked when evaluating these patterns.

Example 12.
(*a*). *Don Giovanni*, Act II Sextet, bars 76–7

(*b*). Act I *Introduzione*, bars 90–2

Donna Anna

Gen – te!  Ser – vi!al tra – di – to – re!

(*c*). Act I Quartet, bars 19–21

Don Giovanni

La po – ve-ra  ra – gaz- za   è paz- za, a-mi – ci  mie- i,

the inference is that Elvira too is more concerned, in the Sextet, with her own peace of mind, than with the physical safety of Don Giovanni.

Still other thematic reminiscences have little dramatic significance of an·overt or satirical type, but serve to emphasize the musical cohesion of the opera. They include the stabbing upward semiquaver or faster-moving figures that punctuate the score. These dominate Donna Anna's Act I Aria (bars 1–3), but also appear in the Trio that introduces Elvira (bars 22–4), the fight between Don Giovanni and the Commendatore in the *Introduzione* (bars 167–74), and the entrance of the Statue in the Act II Finale (bars 406–07). Since all these occasions are associated with the demand for vengeance or its gratification, it might be assumed that the motif reflects this emotion. Yet the same musical device recurs at many other points: the opening of the *Introduzione* (bars 2, 4, 6, etc.), Leporello's Act I Aria (bars 94–5), and the Act I Finale (bars 76, 80, 532–4, etc.), to name but a few. Moreover, similar rapid ascending phrases abound in other works composed during the years of Mozart's maturity (including the Symphony in C major, K. 551 and the Overture of *La clemenza di Tito*). It is improbable therefore that this motif was assigned by the composer to any specific dramatic situation. It was simply part of Mozart's common currency, introduced at various points for purely musical purposes.

The integration of separate numbers into the overall design of *Don Giovanni* is achieved through an amalgam of techniques. However, *Don*

*Giovanni* also bears signs of another important development in Mozart's art: the unification of the score through character. Each major personage, with the significant exception of the hero, operates within a limited tonal range, and is associated with particular musical inflections, rhythms, and melodic forms. Mozart may have felt that there was a danger of losing dramatic cohesion in a work covering such an immense dramatic range, and therefore turned to the musical associations of character as a unifying element. This contrasts with *Le nozze di Figaro*, where the abundance of plot determined the musical structure. The shift in emphasis is also apparent in the harmonic organization of the score, in which concerns not only for symmetry but also for integrity of character preserve the dynamic balance.

## Tonality, Symmetry, and Character

The developments in Mozart's handling of musical structures in *Don Giovanni* can best be understood by reference to the plan established in *Le nozze di Figaro*. The equilibrium of *Le nozze di Figaro* is achieved through an ordered progression of keys, accommodating emotions ranging from anguish to high comedy within a delicate formal balance. The dramatic tensions that arise during the unfolding of the story are paralleled in the key sequence of successive numbers. Consider for instance the progression in Act II, which begins and ends in Eb major. This is remote from the opera's home key of D major, being several steps in the subdominant direction around the cycle of keys. It is however appropriate for the languid cavatina that introduces the Countess for the first time. The entrance of Cherubino raises the dramatic temperature a few degrees, and heralds a move (via Figaro's F major interjection, 'la, la, la') to the dominant key of Bb major (*canzona*, 'Voi, che sapete'). Then follow three numbers in which the pitch is heightened still further by the business involving Cherubino's disguise and the Count's subsequent fury. The trio 'Susanna or via sortite' in C major is framed by two numbers, Susanna's aria 'Venite, inginocchiatevi' and the duet for Susanna and Cherubino, 'Aprite presto, aprite', both in G major. The symmetrical structure is rounded off with the massive Eb major Finale. Thus the complete Act consists of Eb–Bb / G–C–G / Eb. Moreover, in a masterly stroke of classical poise, Mozart repeats the entire structure in the Finale itself. For as can be seen in Table 4 the Finale progresses as follows: Eb–Bb–G–C–F–Bb–Eb.

Key sequences are exploited in a different manner during Act IV of *Le nozze di Figaro*. Musically, the composer was obliged to journey back to the home key of D major, and re-emphasize this pivotal key after the bold explorations of earlier Acts. But since resolution from dominant to tonic implies a relaxation of tension, Act IV was in danger of becoming a musical anticlimax. Mozart circumvented this problem by avoiding dominant keys during the early parts of the Act. There is a progression through the subdominant side, from the F minor of Barbarina's cavatina through the G major and B♭ major of the rarely heard arias for Marcellina and Basilio, to Figaro's E♭ aria 'Aprite un pò que gl'occhi'. 'Deh vieni non tardar' in F major represents the last moment of repose before the busy Finale.[5] The Finale itself is a further manifestation of the drive for symmetry, since the sequence of keys again picks out a musical arch D–G–E♭–B♭–G–D. The grand symmetry of the opera as a whole is underlined when it is seen that the opening sequence of Act I traces out this pattern in reverse, with the Overture (D major) leading to the two Duets in G major and B♭ major (nos. 1 and 2).

The plan of *Le nozze di Figaro* is founded on considerations of tonal balance and order. In the more volatile story of *Don Giovanni*, the dramatic thrust frequently threatens the classical equilibrium. Nevertheless, the constraints of form are still powerful, as is the concern for symmetry. Numerous features in the second half of *Don Giovanni* carefully mirror developments in Act I. The grandest symmetry is between the opening and closing music. The D minor theme of the Overture is extended in the Act II Finale, while the fanfare phrases from the Overture's *allegro* (bars 38–39) reappear at the start of the Finale (bars 3–4).[6] Within this framework, several other features are matched. The major ensemble of Act I (Quartet, no. 9) is balanced by the Sextet in Act II; both Finales have on-stage bands; Zerlina's two arias (one in each Act) are close to each other in style, rhythm, and key; Anna and Ottavio have a duet near the beginning (no. 2), and again near the end of the Act II Finale (bars 712–740);[7] the two trios in which Elvira takes the lead ('Ah chi mi dice mai' and 'Ah taci, ingiusto core') occur at similar points in the two Acts; Donna Anna's arias also hold identical positions in the two Acts (each being the tenth number). These manifold symmetries document Mozart's intentions most forcefully.

However, *Don Giovanni* inevitably diverges from *Le nozze di Figaro* in its concentration on a single theme. In comparison with *Don Giovanni*'s powerful focus, the plot of *Le nozze di Figaro* appears anecdotal, despite being carefully structured.[8] The difference is sustained in the tonal plan

---

[5] Interestingly, modulation to the subdominant is also characteristic of the recapitulation in sonata form (see Chapter 8). This suggests that one might almost view the entire work as a massive sonata-like structure.

[6] These parallels have been described in detail by J. Rushton, *W. A. Mozart: Don Giovanni* (Cambridge, 1981) 109–10.

[7] This may be one reason why such a large portion of the Act II Finale post-mortem is devoted to Anna and Ottavio.

[8] This is not an aspersion on the merit of *Le nozze di Figaro*, but a product of the storyline.

of the two works. *Le nozze di Figaro*'s home key of D major may appear at
the beginning and end of the piece, but it does not play a substantial role
in the drama itself. Large portions of the opera, including Act II and the
second half of Act III, do not touch on D major at all. In *Don Giovanni*,
however, the axial tonality is never far away. All segments of the score are
permeated by its atmosphere. Rosen has argued that this is 'The result of
a total conception of the opera in which everything is related to a central
tonality, which itself has, not only a symbolic reference, but an individual
sonority that it seems to evoke'.[9] The central focus is therefore on D, both
in its major and minor forms. After the Overture, D major reappears
systematically, in the arias for Leporello ('Madamina, il catalogo'), Elvira
('Ah fuggi il traditor'), and Donna Anna ('Or sai chi l'onore'). It is
significant that each of these numbers concludes an expository scene, in
which the protagonists and salient themes of the opera are introduced.
This is illustrated in Figure 6. Leporello (no. 4) rounds off the presentation of the Elvira subplot, Elvira herself (no. 8) concludes the peasant
scenes, while Anna (no. 10) signals the unmasking of Don Giovanni.
Each facet of the story is thus related musically to the central theme. This
key structure matches precisely the libretto's ordered presentation of
characters outlined in Figure 2.

Yet Act I also witnesses the emergence of another key that operates as a
substitute and region of contrast to the central D major. D major itself
presented certain problems to Mozart in the operatic context, since it is a
'sharp' key. If the tensions of *Don Giovanni*'s plot were matched in
modulations to the dominant in the usual way, Mozart would be forced
into remote sharp keys such as E major and B major. But these tonalities
were uncongenial to the composer; he rarely ventured beyond D major's
dominant A major in the circle of fifths.[10] Fortunately, the presence of D
minor expanded the harmonic scope of *Don Giovanni*, and provided a
solution to this dilemma. One of Mozart's favorite techniques for generating tonal contrast and a 'dominant' in minor works was to use the
flat submediant. In the case of D minor, this is B♭ major. Mozart
employed this minor–major link in a number of important instrumental
pieces—the slow movement of the Concerto in D minor (K. 466) is set in
B♭ major, that of the String Quintet in G minor (K. 516) is in E♭ major,
while the Andante of the Piano Sonata in A minor (K. 310) is in F major.
Furthermore, Mozart was acutely aware of the dramatic potential of this
relationship; in reverse, this is precisely the basis of the modulation at the
heart of Osmin's aria 'Solche hergelaufne Laffen', described by the
composer with such relish in the letter quoted in Chapter 8.[11]

[9]  C. Rosen, *The Classical Style* (London, 1971), 299.
[10] Mozart's E major operatic numbers are rare and emotionally highly charged.
[11] Interestingly, the D–B♭ axis is central to Beethoven's Ninth Symphony as well.

| | | |
|---|---|---|
| | Overture | D minor/major |
| 1 | *Introduzione* | F major |
| 2 | Anna    Ottavio  <br> *Duet* | D minor |
| 3 | Elvira <br> *Trio* | E♭ major |
| 4 | Leporello <br> *Aria* | D major |
| 5 | Zerlina    Masetto <br> *Chorus* | G major |
| 6 | Masetto <br> *Aria* | F major |
| 7 | Giovanni    Zerlina <br> *Duet* | A major |
| 8 | Elvira <br> *Aria* | D major |
| 9 | *Quartet* | B♭ major |
| 10 | Anna <br> *Aria* | D major |
| 11 | Giovanni <br> *Aria* | B♭ major |
| 12 | Zerlina <br> *Aria* | F major |
| 13 | *Finale* | C major |

Figure 6.    Key Structure of Act I of *Don Giovanni*

The key of B♭ major is therefore employed as a contrast to D minor/ major throughout *Don Giovanni*. The whole score is characterized by abrupt shifts from flat keys (B♭, E♭, and F major) to keys nearer the home key (A and G major). By using B♭ major in this fashion, Mozart was able to increase tension through tonic–dominant patterns without invading the remoter harmonic reaches. For instance, the closing stages of Act I present a continuous rise in harmonic tension, from the B♭ major of Don Giovanni's aria ('Fin ch'han dal vino'), through Zerlina's F major aria, to the Finale in C major. B♭ major is also a key in which a baritone can be heard to advantage. Since $d'$ itself is close to the upper limit of the baritone's range, the tonic tends to be the highpoint of D major numbers. But B♭ major has the note $d$ as its third or mediant; the home key of the opera is thus brightly emphasized even in B♭ major pieces. Don

Giovanni himself frequently sings in B♭ major, and arpeggio phrases based on the tonic triad (with the third at the peak) abound in his music.[12]

Act II also shows abrupt shifts between the constellations of keys surrounding D and B♭ major. The group at the start, concerning the deceptive seduction of Elvira and Don Giovanni's serenade, proceeds through the sequence G major–A major–D major (nos. 14, 15, and 16), only to be subverted without warning by the F major of Don Giovanni's disguise aria, 'Metà di voi qua vadano'. Later the B♭ major and F major of Ottavio and Anna's arias (nos. 21 and 23) set the E major of the graveyard scene in high relief. It is interesting that even in the Vienna revision, when Ottavio's Act II aria was removed, Mozart ensured a similar tonal contrast by setting Elvira's scena ('In quali eccessi' . . . Mi tradì') in a 'flat' key (E♭ major).

*Don Giovanni* has another pervasive musical characteristic that reinforces the polarity of D and B♭ major. Throughout the opera, there is an emphasis on subdominant relationships. It begins in the Overture (where Hermann Abert has noted the predilection for subdominant modulations) and continues through the first group.[13] Even in moments of dramatic tension, the dominant (C major) of the *Introduzione* is largely avoided. Thus the conflict accompanying the entry of Anna and Don Giovanni is played out in the subdominant (B♭ major). Similarly, the Act I Finale progresses essentially through subdominant sequences. Instead of shifts from the tonic C major to dominant keys such as G and D major, the successive sections of the Finale are ordered as follows: C major–F major–D minor–F major–B♭ major–E♭ major–C major. Crucially, however, the important action of the dance sequence takes place in the dominant section (G major) of the final C major span.

The range of associations between harmony and drama is clearly expanded in *Don Giovanni* beyond the conventional expectations of sonata form. There is no simple relationship between the tension of the stage action and modulations towards the dominant. This may result from the overall shape of the story, which stands in stark contrast to *Le nozze di Figaro*. The musical and dramatic climax of the earlier opera occurs at the halfway point, in the Act II Finale. The imbroglios of the last Act are more conventional in nature, being founded on disguise, a stock *buffo* element. This arch matches the classical form of modulation to the dominant, followed by resolution and recovery of stablity in the final tonic episode. But in *Don Giovanni*, the dramatic climax occurs near the end, when the hero confronts the higher moral power of the Stone Guest.

[12] The joyful and heroic connotations of the interval at the third have been detailed by Cooke in *The Language of Music* (Oxford, 1959), 51–64.

[13] See Abert, *Don Giovanni*, 58.

Mozart was obliged to match this with a musical climax of comparable force. However, he could not afford to emphasize the dominant at such a perilously late point, since insufficient space remained to balance the dominant sound mass with an equally powerful tonic resolution. The tonal pattern would be unbalanced. Mozart therefore adopted a different plan. Because of the emphasis on B♭ major and the subdominant keys, the home D major/minor itself acquired the attributes of a high tension, dramatic key. Hence D became both the centre of the work and its apex. The late musical and dramatic climax could be tolerated without destroying the harmonic balance and classical structure.

The dramatic uses of key in *Don Giovanni* are not confined to these broad outlines, powerful though they may be. Together with rhythm and melody, key helps to define the musical identity of individual characters. With the significant exception of Don Giovanni himself, each of the players operates within a restricted thematic and harmonic milieu. The pattern is most clear for Don Giovanni's three female antagonists and victims. Donna Anna, for example, is closely identified with the phrase outlined in Example 13.[14] It appears in the 'allegro' of the Anna–Ottavio Duet (Example 13(*a*) ), and later announces her entry into the Act II Sextet (Example 13(*b*) ). Between these two, the phrase is employed more energetically by Elvira (Example 13(*c*) ) during the nervous approach of

Example 13.
(*a*). *Don Giovanni*, Act I, Duet (no. 2), bars 63–7

(*b*). Act II Sextet, bars 45–7

(*c*). Act I Finale, bars 173–7

14 Also recognized by H. Abert, *Mozart's Don Giovanni*, trans. P. Gellhorn (London, 1976), 107.

Anna, Ottavio, and Elvira to the Ball scene in the Act I Finale. Additionally, Anna's important musical numbers traverse a limited tonal spectrum. Her entrance in the *Introduzione* is in B♭ major, while her Scena aria 'Non mi dir' is in F major, and between these episodes her music is strongly associated with the central keys of the opera. Thus in Act I, the D minor Duet is followed by an appearance in the B♭ Quartet. This is succeeded immediately by the dramatic aria 'Or sai chi l'onore', located in the axial D major.

Zerlina inhabits a physical world far removed from Donna Anna, and this is reflected in her musical range. Her arias are in the pastoral key of F major and its close neighbour, C major. At no point does she appropriate the opera's more dramatic keys of D and B♭ major. Even the paltry Act II duet between Zerlina and Leporello ('Restati qua', inserted into the score in Vienna), follows this plan, since it is set in C major. The only occasion on which she leaves these tranquil tonal regions is during her seduction ('Là ci darem la mano'), where the tantalizing prospects held out by Don Giovanni are emphasized by the heightened setting in A major. Thematic features also bind Zerlina's music into a recognizable mould, with her two arias sharing a characteristic sonority. Each is set in light rhythms (2/4, 6/8, 3/8), and begins with a long *cantabile* melody far removed from the anguish of Anna or Elvira. 'Batti, batti' is in two parts, while 'Vedrai, carino' has a comparable pause at the midpoint (bar 52). The second sections are both developed with sinuous semiquaver instrumental lines. The distinct triple rhythms in the closing sections of these arias recall Zerlina's first appearance in the vigorous chorus 'Giovinette che fate all'amore'.

Elvira mediates between the realms occupied by Anna and Zerlina. She appears with both parties on different occasions. The numbers in which she sings therefore span a wide range of keys, from the E♭ major of 'Ah chi mi dice mai' to the A major trio 'Ah taci, ingiusto core'. Nevertheless, her music is vividly distinguished from that of the other women, as many commentators have noted.[15] Her line is characterized by irregular, nervous contours, with unusual intervals of pitch and abrupt changes in dynamic. These are apparent in her first entry, where the abundance of descending sevenths and ninths gives an impression of abandon. Similarly, the archaic dotted rhythm of the Act I aria 'Ah fuggi il traditor' accentuates the angularity of the line. In ensemble, too, her phrases stand out idiosyncratically. Her violent interjections during the agitated confrontation with Don Giovanni in the Act I Quartet (Example 14(*a*) ) are transformed into the quasi-devotional lament for her betrayal in the Trio of the masked guests (Act I Finale, Example 14*b*). These resemblances are

---

[15] See particularly Chantavoine, *Mozart dans Mozart*, and Rushton, *Don Giovanni*.

Example 14.

(*a*). *Don Giovanni*, Act I Quartet, bars 37–8

Donna Elvira

sde - gno, rab - bia, di - spet - to, tor - men - to

(*b*). Act I Finale, bars 258–9

Donna Elvira

cie - lo    il mio tra - di - to a-mor,    il mio tra - [dito]

(*c*). Act I Quartet, bars 28–29

Donna Elvira

Ah  non      cre - de - te al per - fi - do!

(*d*). Act II Trio, bars 45–7

Donna Elvira

No, non ti cre- do, o bar-ba-ro!   no, non ti cre- do, o bar - ba-ro!

(*e*). Act II Trio, bars 62–4

Don Giovanni

Più fer- ti - le ta- len-to,    del mio, no, non si  da,

later used with ironic force when Elvira is seduced at the beginning of Act II; her impassioned attempts to warn Anna and Ottavio about Giovanni in the Quartet (Example 14(*c*) ) reappear when she tries to ward off the hero's fresh assault (Example 14(*d*) ). It is as if Elvira recalls the truth about her seducer, but is still unable to repulse him.

Mozart's exploitation of harmony and melodic style to articulate character in *Don Giovanni* represents a development beyond his practice in *Le nozze di Figaro*. In the earlier opera, keys tend to reflect formal musical relationships and dramatic complexities. Mozart introduced further refinements into *Così fan tutte*, where tonal  arguments illuminate not only character and stage action, but the motives or feelings behind the action (see Chapter 10). Moreover, it is clear even from the few examples given here that the element of contrast is central to characterization in *Don Giovanni*. It sustains the fundamental dichotomy between the dark, *seria* face of the score and its lighter *buffo* aspects. The integration of these perspectives is one of the most intriguing features of the opera, and is central to a deeper understanding of the work as a whole. It is therefore worth discussing in more detail.

## Contrasts: Light and Dark in *Don Giovanni*

Mozart frequently worked simultaneously on pieces of quite different character.[16] The composition of contrasted yet complementary works in the same form seems to have satisfied his multifaceted creative faculty. Instances can be cited from all stages of his career. The contrasted compositions from his mature period include the turbulent Concerto in D minor (K. 466) and the serene Concerto in C major (K. 467) completed in February and March 1785, and the String Quintets in C major (K. 515) and G minor (K. 516) from the spring of 1787. Among other complementary works are the Concertos in A major (K. 488) and C minor (K. 491), both of which entered Mozart's catalogue in March 1786, and the last two Symphonies (G minor, K. 550 and C major, K. 551), completed within a short interval of each other in the summer of 1788. In each case, Mozart produced two pieces in the same form that differed radically in style and atmosphere. No simple division can of course be made into romantic and classical, or demonic and sublime; rather, Mozart's creative energy stimulated him to embrace quite distinct realms of expression at the same time.

The operas present a different pattern, since they were not produced in pairs. Moreover, as was noted in chapter 3 the operas are generally isolated in the catalogue, and are not coupled with major instrumental works. The explanation may be that external contrasts were unnecessary, since expressive diversity was provided within the operas themselves. The range of sonority and musical character that Mozart spread over different instrumental works could be incorporated into the single capacious form of an opera.

The internal contrasts within the operas have always presented difficulties of categorization. The *buffo* and tragic elements vie for prominence in *Don Giovanni*, while the sublime shares the stage with farcical

[16] See A. H. King, *Mozart in Retrospect* (London, 1955), for several instances.

pantomime in *Die Zauberflöte*. Some writers have seized on the title *dramma giocoso* in the libretto of *Don Giovanni*, as if this reflected the composer's own ambivalence about his creation. However, this quibble over title is specious; Mozart did not call *Don Giovanni* a *dramma giocoso* in his thematic catalogue, but an *opera buffa*. The description *dramma giocoso* is Da Ponte's, and had no tragic connotations. It was simply one of several terms used by Italian poets to describe their works. The same title was conferred on libretti with no pretensions to tragedy at all, such as *Il barbiere di Siviglia* and *Una cosa rara*.[17]

The arbitrary distinctions set up by taxonomical commentators are not helpful in understanding this opera. Mozart treated the *buffo* format as an amalgam of diverse strands, and strove for stylistic variation rather than uniformity. In deciding how the varied elements of the plot of *Don Giovanni* should be portrayed in music, Mozart adopted a simple strategy: he set most numbers in the libretto in a style appropriate to their surface character. Thus when the scene is tragic the music reflects this dramatic atmosphere, while comic numbers are presented in a lighter mode. When irony was intended, Mozart set the verse to inappropriate *seria* music. The overall constraints of style did not therefore force the composer into a Procrustean mould, although the need for symmetry and balance demanded that these different strands were integrated within the total structure.

The interchange between comic and serious or sentimental scenes is carefully paced in Act I of *Don Giovanni*. The ordered alternation between Anna and Ottavio on the one hand, and Zerlina and Leporello on the other, has already been detailed. Dissatisfaction with Act II as a whole derives from the breakdown of this equilibrium, and the artificial engineering of a series of comic incidents from the disguise of Don Giovanni as Leporello and vice versa. All the other characters become butts for this modest joke to a greater or lesser extent, so the bias inevitably shifts towards the comic element in the early part of Act II. The *seria* personages are inserted into this slight structure in an arbitrary manner. Thus Anna appears only once before her aria 'Non mi dir', while Ottavio is dismissed in equally cavalier fashion. Compare this with Act I, where Ottavio is established as an effective character even without the luxury of an aria. He enters at three crucial junctures—after the murder, at the unmasking of Don Giovanni, and before the final denouement—and becomes thoroughly involved in the action, conveying a credible image through his interjections in ensemble.

[17] See Chapter 5, n. 28. For a discussion of the mixture between serious and comic elements in Viennese theatre earlier in the century, see E. Badura-Skoda, 'The Influence of the Viennese Popular Comedy on Haydn and Mozart', *Proceedings of the Royal Musical Association*, 100 (1973-4), 185-99.

The light tone of the opening of Act II is confirmed by the succession of triple rhythms: 3/4, 6/8, and 3/8 in four of the first five numbers. Mozart also compensated for the lack of dramatic weight by a systematic variation in instrumentation and orchestral colouring. The clarinet is employed extensively (in numbers 15, 18, and 21) as a substitute for the oboe (nos. 14 and 17), while the mandolin is introduced for Don Giovanni's Serenade. However, none of these devices can disguise the shift in equilibrium and loss of momentum. In the present day, the problem is exacerbated by the practice of including both Ottavio's aria 'Il mio tesoro' and Elvira's scena 'In qual eccessi . . . Mi tradì'. Both are reflective pieces which do little to further the action, while their related keys (B♭ and E♭ major) can give a sensation of sameness, further weakening the dramatic structure.[18] Nevertheless, neither the Vienna nor the Prague versions of Act II are entirely satisfactory on their own. In the original score, Elvira disappears after the Sextet, and only returns briefly in the Finale; it is as if Anna replaces Elvira as the female interest halfway through the Act. Elvira's Vienna *scena* balances her appearances, and mediates emotionally between her earlier humiliation and the later desperate pleas to Don Giovanni in the Finale. On the other hand, the Vienna revision reduces Ottavio to a cipher. Without his Act II aria, Ottavio is diminished to a dramatic stature little higher than Masetto.

The weaknesses of Act II stem from Da Ponte's failure of invention. He may have been pressed for time, so unable to devise any more compelling dramatic motifs for expanding the plot before the graveyard scene. However, one crucial factor that is easily overlooked makes the developments in Act II more comprehensible. As I argued in Chapter 7, the principal female role in *Don Giovanni* was probably not intended to be Donna Anna or even Elvira, but Zerlina. Zerlina and Leporello are the main beneficiaries of the incidental form of Act II, and the disjointed presentation of the *seria* characters. Zerlina's importance was further enhanced in the revision for Vienna, where she and Leporello were given the comic scena and *buffo* duet 'Per queste tue manine', now seldom performed.[19] Other parts of the score yield traces of Zerlina's pre-eminence, notably her arias which are in an accessible 'simple' style with immediate appeal. She is also placed in the forefront of ensemble on many occasions. For instance, when all the characters converge on Don Giovanni in the Act I Finale ('Tutto, tutto già si sà . . .', bar 518), Zerlina leads the ensemble while the other characters counterpoint her phrases. Similarly in the

---

[18] Ironically, the singer who took the part of Elvira in the first Vienna production (Catarina Cavalieri) caused further harmonic damage by transposing her E♭ major aria to D major. This detracted from the pattern of harmonic contrasts outlined in this chapter.

[19] The opportunities for Benucci to exhibit his comic abilities are also greatly expanded by this scene, particularly in the Recitative following the Duet, when he extricates himself from his bonds.

closing fugue of the Act II Finale ('Questo è il fin . . .'), Zerlina is the only character to sing the theme as a solo; all the other singers double for the purpose.

The emphasis on the lighter characters during Act II probably reflects the status quo among the performers rather than the characters. The *seria* gravity of Anna and Ottavio is further undermined by the ironic gloss on their characterization. Ottavio can be seen as the mirror image of Don Giovanni, displaying features that are direct reversals of the hero's attributes. He is absorbed in love with a single woman, is indecisive, honest, and honourable; Don Giovanni on the other hand is decisive, dishonest, and profligate. Ottavio attaches importance to external appearances and personal dignity, lives rationally rather than sensually, and is sincere but not passionate. His weakness balances Don Giovanni's strength.

The enigmatic Elvira occupies the ambivalent middle ground in temperament, just as she does in purely musical terms. But when she adopts the graver tones of Anna and Ottavio, the ironic intention is again clear, as in the aria 'Ah fuggi il traditor'. Here is a woman who has already succumbed to temptation (and a promise of marriage from Don Giovanni), denying the same pleasure to another, and she does so with formal archaic severity. The words show an exaggerated, histrionic hostility, quite inappropriate for the simple task of cautioning a peasant maid. The tone of the outburst is a product of Elvira's passion and not the circumstances in which she finds Zerlina. Indeed, the unwavering nature of her passion turns Elvira into a butt for the comic business of the opera. Leporello is able to bait her with impunity in the Catalogue Aria, and much of Act II stems from her absurd folly in mistaking Leporello for Don Giovanni. Yet paradoxically, it is the very intensity and sincerity of her passion in the Act I Quartet that raises doubts about Don Giovanni's honesty in the minds of Anna and Ottavio. Ultimately, Elvira is a passive vehicle in the plot, since all her energies are focused on a single object; she does not initiate developments in the opera, but responds predictably to each of Don Giovanni's actions.

It is the characterization of Don Giovanni himself that has remained most fascinating and elusive. He ranges from transcendent demonic hero to trivial philanderer, and critical opinion has been equally divided. Lascivious computations of his daily tally of seductions are countered by claims that he is completely unsuccessful during the opera. Much of the argument is irrelevant, for as Abert has sensibly concluded, 'The main point of Don Giovanni's nature is not his ability to seduce this or that woman who happens to cross his path ... but ... in the elemental, sensual urge to live and love which he has the uncontrolled energy to satisfy'.[20] One of the most remarkable facets of Mozart and Da Ponte's

---

[20] Abert, *Don Giovanni*, p. 49.

presentation is the chameleon-like quality of the hero. He achieves each
of his purposes by adopting an appropriate image: Ottavio in the
*Introduzione*, the disguise as a servant when seducing a maid in Act II.
This quicksilver nature must have been enhanced by the interpretation of
the role by its creator, Luigi Bassi. Contemporaries noted that

Bassi is also a very skilful actor, who handles tragedy without being absurd, and
comedy without lapses of taste. When he is in a mischievous mood he will, for
instance, parody the faults of the other singers so exquisitely that only the
audience, not the singers, are aware of it . . . He never spoils a part.[21]

Don Giovanni's adaptability is clearly apparent in ensemble, and in
Mozart's construction of his vocal line. The hero's music inevitably blends
with his antagonist's style rather than asserting a separate identity. This is
clear from the very beginning, with Don Giovanni matching Donna
Anna's phrases of protest (*Introduzione*, bars 74–8 and 79–83, etc.),
almost in canon. This might be regarded merely as an apt musical
reflection of Don Giovanni's effort to disguise his identity, but when the
Commendatore arrives on the scene, the music slows to a dignified pace.
Don Giovanni too shifts abruptly from the breathless struggle to a vein of
equal solemnity. Later in the *Introduzione*, Giovanni's commentary
over his dying adversary utilizes phrases first heard from Anna (bars
101–6 and 177–81), thus recalling her style while recapitulating material
originally presented in the dominant section of the exposition.

The *Introduzione* as a whole stands in marked contrast to the musical
basis of Don Giovanni's assault on Zerlina. The peasant girl's identification with triple rhythms is already established in the chorus before Don
Giovanni's entrance. He, however, is not so brusque as to adopt this tone
at once. Instead he selects the middle ground between the common time
of the aristocratic world and peasant triple rhythm for the duet 'Là ci
darem la mano'.[22] Only when Zerlina's agreement is assured does the
duet break into 6/8 ('Andiam, andiam, mio bene'). Don Giovanni thus
glides into the patois in sly fashion, and the pastoral rhythm wryly colours
his 'innocente amor'.[23]

---

[21] Quoted in Abert, *Don Giovanni*, p. 15.

[22] A similar 2/4 tempo re-emerges as Don Giovanni and Zerlina dance in the Act I Finale. On this
occasion, the rhythm lies midway between the stately 'minuetto' and the 3/8 jig. W. J. Allanbrook,
in *Rhythmic Gesture in Mozart* (Chicago, 1983), has discussed at some length the significance of
rhythms in relation to the social world.

[23] On later occasions when Don Giovanni has dealings with the rustics, he again falls into the
appropriate style. An instance occurs in the Act I Finale, when Don Giovanni and Leporello animate
the peasants in their incongruous surroundings (bar 273 et seq.). They are aided by a 6/8 rhythm,
and even adopt the peasants' turn of phrase (e.g. no. 5, bars 17–20 and Finale, bars 287–9). A
similar identification of 6/8 rhythm and G major with the rural proletariat occurs in *Le nozze di
Figaro* (Chorus of Act I). Interestingly, Gazzaniga used the same rhythm, plus G major, for the
villagers' chorus in his Don Giovanni opera.

Don Giovanni's musical character is transformed again in the presence of Elvira. The arpeggio phrases typical of her part are taken up by the hero himself during the proxy seduction in the Act II Trio (Example 14(*e*) ). Don Giovanni's exultation over his amatory talent is thus portrayed, appropriately enough, in a demonstration of his musical facility. Even in solo arias, Giovanni does not necessarily reveal himself musically. The aria 'Metà di voi quà vadano' finds the hero disguised as Leporello, baffling and ultimately disbanding the belligerent peasants; it is no accident that F major, the key of Masetto and Zerlina's Act I arias, is adopted for this purpose.

Don Giovanni's musical character may be adaptable, but it is by no means negative. When he is not deliberately presenting a false appearance to others, his music instinctively reverts to the central keys of the opera: D and B♭ major. His two independent arias ('Fin ch'han dal vino' and 'Deh vieni alla finestra') are set in B♭ and D major respectively. It is remarkable how the first of these is coloured by a bright timbre not normally associated with B♭ major. This is achieved through the preponderance of fanfare-like phrases which have the third *d* as their highest note, and which thereby recall the link with D major. More importantly, the key of D major lies at the heart of Don Giovanni's most profound confrontations with the forces that oppose him. This is evident in the *Introduzione*, when Don Giovanni is struggling with the Commendatore. Earlier, I described how the hero maintains a secondary role through most of this section, concealing his musical identity by matching his opponent's style. But the point comes at which this disguise can no longer be maintained, and with the words 'misero, attendi' (Example 15), he emerges in all his power. The phrase encapsulates the central musical axis of the opera, by asserting D with an octave leap, and ending on B♭. To add further emphasis, the phrase is accompanied by the orchestra in unison.

Example 15.   *Don Giovanni*, Act I *Introduzione*, bars 160–6

The climax of the opera comes in Don Giovanni's struggle with the Stone Guest, and here, again, D is used dramatically to express the waxing and waning of the hero's power. Before the entrance of the statue, Don Giovanni's exuberance blossoms at Elvira's hopeless appeals, echoed in triumphant B♭ fanfares (Act II Finale, bars 303–10). All changes with

Example 16.   *Don Giovanni*, Act II Finale, bars 513–16

the Stone Guest, whose identification with D minor undermines Don Giovanni's tonal base. The statue outlines his message through a shifting series of modulations which gradually weaken Giovanni's bright assertion of Bb and D major. Not to be outdone, Don Giovanni's response to the challenge of the reciprocal dinner invitation ('Hò fermo il core in petto', bars 513–6) reaffirms the note *d* (Example 16). He grasps the out-stretched hand with a careless phrase, and at once the D is flattened as his power begins to ebb (bars 520–1). Yet even now Don Giovanni is not subdued; he batters unrepentantly against the encircling gloom, constantly striving to re-establish D major against the might of the minor key. Finally defeated, his dying phrase ('Che terror!', bars 591–2) falls from D to Bb. The hero proclaims his tonal emblem even at this ultimate moment.

The dramatic pinnacle of the opera is reached in this scene, where the titanic battle between opposing moral powers takes on an almost epic quality. Bernard Williams has described Don Giovanni's defiance as 'a splendidly attractive and grand refusal to be intimidated', and Mozart uses the most sophisticated musical gestures to confirm this status.[24] It appears that the *seria* element has finally gained ascendancy, and that the opera will end on a tragic note. Yet Mozart's conception transcends this natural conclusion, and aims at a higher humanity in equilibrium—the duality of serious and comic is re-created in the closing ensemble. Mozart's confident belief in the beneficence of existence is perfectly expressed in the last twenty bars of the opera. As the singers of the moralistic canon depart about their business, the trilled violin accompaniment of the 'presto' theme is miraculously transformed to suggest the bustle of everyday life and the return of normality (Example 17). With this poignant understatement, Mozart reminds the audience of the loss of Don Giovanni's animal vitality and the re-emergence of the humdrum world. The hero's death robs the other characters of their *raison d'être*, but Mozart does not seize the opportunity for cynical reflection on their banality. Rather, he acknowledges life's variety with an Olympian detachment.

---

[24] B. Williams, '*Don Giovanni* As An Idea', in Rushton, *Don Giovanni*, p. 88.

Example 17.   *Don Giovanni*, Act II Finale, bars 860–71

Example 17.   (*cont'd*)

There is always a danger of overinterpreting *Don Giovanni*, and endeavouring to construct profound analyses of the deeper meanings of the piece. The hero has been seen as symbol, the embodiment of sensuousness, the life force, or repressed, inverted sexual drive. However, the pragmatic approach of Mozart and Da Ponte to opera undermines such grandiose ideas. Hermann Abert wisely rejected the temptation of making subtle inferences from the libretto, arguing that motives in *opera buffa* are invariably transparent, so that any important relationship or emotion will be clear textually rather than covert:

to derive complex problems from the psychology of sex is absolutely alien to its nature. It presents unadorned natural instincts, and never considers the moral consequences of satisfying them.[25]

Another reminder not to inflate the authors' intentions comes from Irvin Singer:

Moving freely through the words and music, [Don Giovanni] embodies the principle of freedom without enunciating it at any length. With nothing to sustain them but their special talent for constructing an 'exotick and irrational entertainment' (as Dr Johnson called Italian Opera in general), no great and new ideas in the areas of religion or morality that pertain to the myth [of Don Juan], Mozart and Da Ponte avail themselves of whatever comes to hand.[26]

At the same time, one of the fundamental underlying themes—the attitude towards women embodied in the work—should not be ignored. It reflects the real ruthlessness prevalent, if not in Vienna, at any rate in Da Ponte's Venice. This was after all the Society that countenanced, and even encouraged, Casanova's masculine arrogance:

The man who loves and knows that he is loved rates the pleasure he is sure he will give the loved object more highly than the pleasure which that object can give him in fruition. Hence he is eager to satisfy her. Woman, whose great preoccupation is her own interest, cannot but rate the pleasure she will herself feel more highly than the pleasure she will give; hence she procrastinates as long as she can because she fears that in giving herself she will loose what concerns her most—her own pleasure.[27]

The ambivalence in Mozart and Da Ponte's treatment of relations between men and women culminates not in *Don Giovanni* but in *Così fan tutte*. This theme is closely linked with another preoccupation of the authors, namely the distinction (and intermingling) of truth and artifice. In *Don Giovanni*, the whole range of veracity is explored; some characters express feelings and sentiments of apparent sincerity, others are more equivocal, while Don Giovanni himself is consistently deceptive. These grades of truth are indistinguishable on the musical level. There is rarely any hint in melody, orchestration, or rhythm to indicate that a particular passage is not to be believed. The music is morally neutral. The enigma of sincerity and falsehood in musical expression seems to have fascinated Mozart in his later years, and it is no accident that *Die Zauberflöte* and *La clemenza di Tito* both explore the theme. But perhaps it is once again *Così fan tutte* that contains Mozart's ultimate statement of musical ambiguity. The entire opera is built around the confusion of truth and deception, until these conflicting feelings almost fuse together.

[25] Abert, *Don Giovanni*, p. 65.
[26] I. Singer, *Mozart and Beethoven: The Concept of Love in their Operas* (Baltimore, 1977), 39.
[27] Giacomo Casanova, *The History of my Life*, v, trans. by W. R. Trask. (London, 1967), 71.

# 10

## *Così fan tutte*

To destroy without hatred, to abandon with a smile . . . imitation, yet a jesting mockery. To reproduce the admired, the
beloved, old and sacred pattern, on a plane and with a content
that sets the stamp of parody.

Mann[1]

### Changing Patterns in Mozart's Style

A series of drastic changes overtook Mozart during the period between
*Don Giovanni* (1787) and the production of *Così fan tutte* in 1790. As
the public's interest in his keyboard virtuosity faded away, Mozart's
personal health and financial security deteriorated (see Chapter 3). His
despondency was further exacerbated by the failure of the tour through
northern Germany in 1789. Perhaps the most disturbing trend of all was
the loss in creative confidence that took place over this period. The
catalogue of works from 1789 and 1790 is unusually thin (see Table 3),
and Mozart had difficulty in completing many pieces. For example, the
first movement of the Clarinet Concerto dates from the end of 1789,
when it was evidently intended for a basset horn soloist (K. 584*b*). The
whole concerto was not however finally completed for another two years.[2]
These years are also scattered with the fragments of unfinished compositions. They include portions of chamber works for wind and strings
(K. 580*a*, 580*c*, 581*a*) and at least four attempts at sonatas for keyboard
(K. 588*b*, 590*a,b* and *c*). It is of course difficult to assess the significance
of such fragments, since they must represent a tiny fraction of the sketches
Mozart produced over his lifetime. Nevertheless, their importance is
heightened by the knowledge that Mozart was probably commissioned to
produce a set of easy piano sonatas by the King of Prussia during his visit
to Potsdam in 1789. Payment for these works would have eased the
composer's financial straits considerably. Mozart apparently tried to fulfil

---

[1] Words attributed to Goethe by Thomas Mann, *Lotte in Weimar*, trans. H. T. Lowe-Porter
(London, 1968), 263.
[2] Similarly, it is probable that the first two movements of the keyboard Concerto in B♭ (K. 595)
date from 1788, even though the work was not completed until 1791. See A. Tyson, 'The Mozart
Fragments in the Mozarteum, Salzburg; A Preliminary Study of their Chronology and Significance',
*Journal of the American Musicological Association*, 34 (1981), 471–510.

the order, for among the unfinished drafts are no less than three F major keyboard movements. Yet he failed with these pieces, and produced only the Sonata in D major (K. 576) in July.

Mozart's creative difficulties are further highlighted by his struggles with the set of string quartets also commissioned by Kaiser Friedrich Wilhelm in 1789. It was once thought that Mozart was forced to draw on material written in the 1770s in the desperate effort to fulfil this obligation.[3] However, paper analyses suggest a different history.[4] The Quartet in D major (K. 575) and the first two movements of K. 589 in B♭ major were written on an unusual ten-stave manuscript paper, probably bought in Dresden on Mozart's return from Potsdam. These movements may therefore have been written during the journey back to Vienna in May 1789, and finished before the supply of more convenient twelve-stave paper was reached at home. The composer's inspiration seems then to have foundered, for it was not until a year later that the final two movements of K. 589 were completed.[5]

The completion of only three or four major works within a year represented a disastrous loss of creative vitality for a musician as fertile as Mozart. Così fan tutte was therefore located at a pivotal moment, and must have been seized upon by the composer both as an artistic challenge and a golden opportunity to recoup financially. There is good reason to suppose that Mozart recognized these wider implications, since he prepared himself carefully for his operatic task. An exceptionally large number of arias survive from the second half of 1789, many of them written for the singers selected to appear in Così fan tutte.[6] Mozart seems to have been testing his facility and exploring the talents of his cast, before embarking on the major project.[7]

Così fan tutte itself shows few signs of artistic sterility or technical difficulty. The only feature that may point to such problems is the number of thematic allusions to earlier compositions. These borrowings suggest some constraints on Mozart's melodic inspiration. They include direct quotations, as when the Kyrie theme of the Mass, K. 317, appears in the 'allegro' of 'Come scoglio' (bar 15), or when the March from La finta giardiniera is repeated in the Act I Chorus. Other reworkings are

[3] See A. H. King, Mozart in Retrospect (London, 1955), 161.

[4] A. Tyson, 'A New Light on Mozart's Prussian Quartets', The Musical Times, 116 (1975), 126–30.

[5] It is also likely that the quartet fragments originally ascribed by Köchel to the mid-1780s belong to this period, and testify to the difficulties Mozart had with K. 589.

[6] They include K. 577 and 579 written for Adriana Ferrarese, 582 and 583 for Louise Villeneuve, and 584 for Francesco Benucci.

[7] It is interesting that the ensembles of Act I were almost all written before Mozart began the arias, suggesting that he wished to consult the individuals involved before producing their solo numbers. See A. Tyson, 'Notes on the composition of Così fan tutte', Journal of the American Musicological Association, 37 (1984), 356–401.

more fleeting, such as the appearance of the Allegretto of the Concerto in C major (K. 503) in the Act II Finale ('ed a guisa di galline . . .' bar 77). Yet it is unwise to infer too much from these parallels. Così fan tutte is not unusual in containing a number of thematic quotations; an even more extreme example is Die Zauberflöte, which emerges from King's analysis as something of a pot-pourri of earlier music.[8] Furthermore, many phrases in Così fan tutte are commonplaces of classical style or variations on stock material, and cannot reasonably be considered as borrowings at all.

The decline in Mozart's productivity over 1789 and 1790 may not have arisen solely from personal or financial setbacks, since there was a positive aspect. During this period, Mozart initiated a series of developments in his compositional method that culminated in a substantial revision of his musical style. Once of the most obvious changes was a growing interest in counterpoint and polyphony. Saint-Foix and others have suggested that this derived from Mozart's appreciation of the Northern masters, both through his reorchestrations of Messiah and Acis and Galatea, and through contacts with the Bach tradition in Leipzig.[9] The first Prussian Quartet K. 575, shows the results of this progression, as does the Sonata in D major, K. 576. In these compositions, counterpoint figures most prominently in the Finales. Mozart's recasting of earlier forms was thus paralleled by a shift in the distribution of expressive weight across movements. The opening movement of instrumental works lost its exalted position as the sole vehicle for intellectual argument, in favour of a more even allocation. In the String Quintet in G Minor of 1787, for instance, the slow movement is placed after the Minuet, while the Finale is introduced by an intense 'adagio'. The 'allegro' of the Finale itself is fiercely dramatic, belying all conventional lightness. Perhaps the most striking case of emancipation in instrumental works occurs in the Symphony in C major, K. 551, with its exuberantly inventive Finale.

Discussion of instrumental works is germane to the background of Così fan tutte, since the opera displays an unusually wide range of orchestral colours. The viola and clarinet come into greater prominence than hitherto, and it is interesting to note that in both cases Mozart was responding to circumstances and available resources. The advent of the clarinet-playing Stadler brothers has already been detailed in Chapter 7, but the elevation of the viola took place for different reasons. Mozart's love of the tonal quality of this instrument was apparent from the beginning of his career, notably in the early Symphonies, and he frequently played the viola himself in chamber works. However, he was frustrated

---

[8] See King, Mozart in Retrospect, ch. 9.
[9] See G. de Saint-Foix, W. A. Mozart: Sa vie musicale et son œuvre, v (Paris, 1946), 21.

from providing very prominent orchestral parts by the generally low standard of performance, for there was a tradition of poor musicianship among violists. The instrument was deliberately disregarded by many composers. Adam Carse has remarked that 'All the harmonic drudgery of the orchestra went to the viola, and if some scrap of melodic movement did chance to come its way, the part was always doubled by some other instrument'.[10] This is confirmed by the doubling of viola melodic lines in Mozart's early Viennese works. Fortunately, it would appear that the violas of the Burgtheater were stronger by the mid-1780s, and Mozart prepared a special place for the instrument in the orchestral palette of his opera scores. He provided it with sustained, slow-moving counter-melodies, often elaborated chromatically and contrasted with fast upper-string figures and detached bass notes. In this guise, the viola typically accompanies pleading, sorrow, or uncertainty, sometimes dividing to enhance the melancholy atmosphere. This colouring pervades two whole numbers of Le nozze di Figaro (the aria 'Non sò più' and Barbarina's Act IV Cavatina, while on other occasions the effect is transient, as in the Act I trio 'Cosa sento! tosto andate!', at the point of Susanna's swoon (bars 38–43).

The situation worsened again when Mozart wrote Don Giovanni for Prague, since the orchestra boasted only two violas in 1787.[11] The viola sustains an independent line of plaintive quality only rarely in this work.[12] The instrument's role was extended once more in Così fan tutte. Its unique sonority pervades some numbers very forcefully (Alfonso's brief Act I aria 'Vorrei dir', the second Quartet, and the trio 'Soave sia il vento' are examples), while its fleeting sadness is adumbrated at many other points. Thus when Fiordiligi and Dorabella extravagantly demand to be slaughtered on the spot in the quintet 'Sento, o Dio, che questo piede' (bars 26–9), and when Ferrando curses Dorabella's 'perfido cor' in his cavatina 'Tradito, schernito' (bars 3–7, etc.), the viola subtly intensifies the passing mood.

The other instrument brought into the foreground during Così fan tutte is the trumpet. Normally confined to choruses and martial themes, the trumpet is employed here as an orchestral sonority in its own right, particularly in 'Come scoglio', Ferrando's aria 'Ah lo veggio quell'anima bella', and the Act II Quartet. On these occasions, the trumpet takes the role that might otherwise have been assumed by the French horn, and there is nothing exceptionally martial about the music. This use of the trumpet is indicative of Mozart's desire to achieve precise sound qualities,

---

[10] A. Carse, The Orchestra in the Eighteenth Century , p. 144.
[11] See Carse, The Orchestra, p. 26.
[12] e.g. in the Sextet (bars 76–86), and in the Cemetery Duet (bars 14–17).

and to experiment even with the basic 'filling' of the orchestral texture.

One final, but even more profound development in Mozart's last style was his move towards simplicity, and the elimination of specious flamboyance. He shunned unnecessary complexities in favour of a tolerant serenity. Although *Così fan tutte* can in many ways be considered one of Mozart's last offerings to the aristocratic world of the Court, it nevertheless offers a calm distillation of his craft. Instead of grand palaces and exotic locations, and a plot stuffed with characters and intrigue, Mozart selected a story that involes modest gardens and houses and the minimum of spectacle. *Così fan tutte* uses a bare quorum of middle-class protagonists in modern dress, and the action is concentrated in a fashion reminiscent of chamber music. Moreover, the thematic unity and harmonic equilibrium of the score is without rival among Mozart's stage works.

## Unity in Ensemble

*Così fan tutte* is known as an ensemble opera. The tightly knit cast and symmetry of plotting are coupled with an exceptionally integrated score, in which even display arias are incorporated into the fabric. Musically, this unity was achieved by extending the methods used in *Le nozze di Figaro* and *Don Giovanni*. Two unifying devices developed in these earlier works—the linking of separate numbers by tonal progression and the technique of thematic reminiscence—were brought to a further level of refinement in *Così fan tutte*.

*Così fan tutte* begins in the same manner as *Don Giovanni*, with a linked group of numbers that introduce the story while establishing the central key structure. The Overture in C major is followed by an expository Trio in the dominant G major. The second Trio moves to the relatively remote key of E major, thus serving as a development section within the larger structure of the group. The note *e* is also the third of the C major triad, so with the return of C major in the last Trio ('Una bella serenata'), a firm diatonic base for the opera is marked out: C–G–E–C. The close relationship between these trios is further underlined by the uniform tempo and time signature. Each inhabits a modest harmonic range and is economic in its use of melody. The effect of the whole is therefore greater than the sum of its parts, and the resulting product is more coherent because less elaborate than *Don Giovanni*.

Later in Act I, the absence of conventional soliloquy arias is remarkable. Indeed, the one piece to develop along standard lines is 'Come scoglio', and this is inserted for ironic purposes; for after displaying the complete panoply of the exit aria, Fiordiligi is not allowed to leave the

stage. Instead, her set piece is deflated by the *buffo* response from
Guglielmo in 'Non siate ritrosi', and her righteous indignation is held up
to ridicule. It is not until Ferrando's 'Un'aura amorosa' (no. 17) that the
composer and librettist permit a conventional reflective aria that does
nothing to forward the plot. But since this is the penultimate number of
Act I, it provides a welcome moment of repose before the excitement of
the Finale.

Thematic reminiscences help to unify the score of *Così fan tutte* in the
same way as in *Don Giovanni*. But their subsidiary purpose of emphasizing
ironic connections assumes added importance here, for they serve as wry
comments on the changes of faith that characterize the story. The technique is used frequently in Alfonso's music, as he sardonically observes
the folly of the lovers. Thus, when his suspicions are aroused by the fierce
protestations of Fiordiligi and Dorabella during their first encounter with
the 'Albanians' (Example 18(*a*) ), Alfonso voices his disbelief in a direct
repeat of the second trio, with the lines doubting the existence of the
'phoenix' of woman's faithfulness (Example 18(*b*) ). Reminiscence is also
used to point the lovers' progress. Take the phrase outlined in Example
19, which documents the history of Fiordiligi and Dorabella's passions. It
first appears in the quintet 'Sento, o Dio, che questo piede', as the sisters
deperately beg their lovers not to leave for war (Example 19(*a*) ). Next, it
is taken up by Ferrando and Guglielmo as part of their mock poisoning,
thereby marking the stage at which the conquest begins to bear fruit
(Example 19(*b*) ). A more poignant version signals Fiordiligi's ultimate
surrender in the duet 'Fra gli amplessi', when she at last succumbs to
Ferrando's passion and her own inclinations (Example 19(*c*) ). Finally,
the phrase comes full circle to underpin Fiordiligi and Dorabella's impre-
cations in the Act II Finale against the part played by Despina in their
deception (Example 19(*d*) ).

Example 18.
(*a*). *Così fan tutte*, no. 13, bars 141–5

Don Alfonso

mi  da un  po - co   di   so - spet- to  quel- la   rab-bia e  quel  fu - ror, —

(*b*). No. 2, bars 5–7

Don Alfonso

che   vi   sia  cia - scun  lo    di - ce....

Example 19.
(*a*). *Così fan tutte*, no. 6, bars 36–8

(*b*).  Act I Finale, bars 434–5

(*c*)  No. 29, bars 101–2

(*d*).  Act II Finale, bars 426–7

Thematic allusion has other functions in this score as well. For on occasion, Mozart's invocations of earlier sentiments are tender rather than ironic, reflecting his refusal to ascribe blame to any party. One subtle connection of this type illuminates Fiordiligi's progression from security to fragile uncertainty. In the Recitative preceding 'Come scoglio', she boldly declares the inviolability of her faith (Example 20(*a*), 'L' intatta fede che per noi già si diede ai cari amanti'—'We will be true unto death to the faith we pledged our dear lovers'). Precisely the same melodic con-

Example 20.

(*a*). *Così fan tutte*, Act I, Scene xi, Recitative, bars 55–8

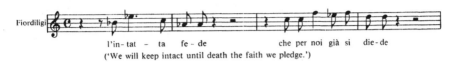

('We will keep intact until death the faith we pledge.')

(*b*). Act II, Scene vi, Recitative, bars 14–16

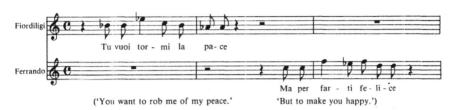

('You want to rob me of my peace.'        'But to make you happy.')

(*c*). Act I, Scene ix, Recitative, bars 35–6

tour re-emerges in her pleading with Ferrando not to tempt her, shortly before her submission in Act II (Example 20(*b*), 'Tu vuoi tormi la pace . . . ma per farti felice'—'You want to rob me of my peace . . . But only to make you happy'). In recalling the phrase, Fiordiligi acknowledges the folly of her earlier confidence. Yet the ramifications do not end there, for the same figure appears even earlier, in Dorabella's mock-tragic Act I Recitative that introduces 'Smanie implacabili' (Example 20(*c*) ). Dorabella's prescient challenge ('Chi schernisce il mio duol'—'Who mocks my grief?') is thereby embedded within a rich network of reminiscence, posing its question to the audience itself.

The unity of *Così fan tutte* is fostered by the methods used in Mozart's earlier operas, but the integrated texture of the score stems above all from the ensemble writing. Through a sequence of vocal chamber pieces, Mozart extends the potential of sonata form as a concise vehicle for characterization and complex expression. This is illustrated in the series of duets for Fiordiligi and Dorabella that annotate the opera.[13] They have

[13] The notion that the singers of these two parts (Adriana Ferrarese and Louise Villeneuve) were sisters in real life is without foundation.

three lengthy duets: the early 'Ah guarda sorella', which finds them secure in the contemplation of their lovers' portraits; the Act I Finale 'andante', 'Ah che tutta in un momento', with its depiction of exhilarated though covert emotional distress; and the frivolous division of spoils in Act II ('Prenderò quel brunettino'). All are 'andante' and bear a striking resemblance to Mozart's instrumental duets, including the Adagios of the Double Concerto, K. 365, and the Sonata for Two Pianos, K. 448. Yet, at the same time, Mozart spares no opportunity for subtly differentiating between the two women. Their first duet prepares the audience for two distinct responses to later events, and the contrast is founded on formal musical patterns.

Each sister is given one subject in the exposition of 'Ah guarda sorella'. Fiordiligi takes the tonic theme (Example 21(a) ) accompanied by gently undulating violin semiquaver figures. The melody is sinuous and sentimental, although a touch of petulance is heard in the repeated demands for her sister's attention ('guarda, guarda,' bars 20–2). Dorabella's entry in the dominant is much more lively. The rhythms in the orchestra quicken, with demisemiquaver violin figures, semiquaver bass passages, and syncopation, while the singer's phrases are broken and abrupt, veering towards the histrionic (Example 21(b); the similarity with Elvira's music is remarkable). They continue to exchange phrases in separate styles throughout the 'andante', only joining when their sentiments finally converge ('Felice son io . . .').

Example 21.
(a). *Così fan tutte*, no. 4, bars 14–18

(b). No. 4, bars 36–9

The distinctions presented in this duet are developed further in the Act I arias for the two sopranos. Dorabella's 'Smanie implacabili' is a supreme parody of distraught operatic passion, while Fiordiligi's 'Come scoglio' is the epitome of *seria* fortitude in adversity. However, by the time we arrive at the Act I Finale, their positions have altered significantly. Both are now troubled emotionally, and enter the Finale with a sense of unanimity. Their feelings in the opening 'andante' of the Finale are articulated by Da

Ponte in Arcadian verse, with the 8–8–8–7 syllabic structure favoured by Metastasio. The metaphor from nature ('Ah, Che un mar pien di tormento È la vita omai per me'—'Ah, a sea filled with tumult / Is life for me now') emphasizes the pathetic sentiment. But Mozart spices the gentle 'andante' with a touch of frivolity, interposing playful woodwind motifs (an effect prefigured in the 'Adagio' of the Double Concerto, K. 365). The third duet sees continued progress in the plot, and confirmation of the characterization of the two sisters. Despite the 'andante' pace, the mood and tempo of 'Prenderò quel brunettino' is light, reflecting the superficial enjoyment planned by the sisters. None the less, their distinct styles continue to shine through. Dorabella's capriciousness is expressed in flamboyant roulades, and counterpoints Fiordiligi's sentimentality, as can be seen in the extract shown in Example 22.[14]

Example 22.  *Così fan tutte*, no. 20, bars 8–17

The flexibility and dramatic adaptability of sonata form is exploited even more fully in the larger ensembles. A fine example is the first quintet, 'Sento, o Dio, che questo piede', considered by Otto Jahn to be one of Mozart's highest achievements. The opening, sung by the men in mock sorrow, is a blend of the martial and of nervous hesitation. Fanfare wind phrases intersperse the broken vocal line, which is restricted almost entirely to the tonic triad (Example 23(*a*) ). This foursquare start contrasts

[14] Fiordiligi's sighing motif is almost identical to that sung by Belmonte in his first Act 1 Aria (no. 4 of *Die Entführung*), as he tries to quell his palpitating heart ('Klopft mein liebevolles Herz', bar 9, etc.).

with the ostentatious display from Fiordiligi and Dorabella, sung as the dominant group (bars 18–30). The pulse doubles from crotchet to quaver, while the troubled emotions elicit surprising harmonic excursions. Fiordiligi and Dorabella's most extravagant expressions ('a entrambe in seno immergeteci l'acciar'—'plunge your swords into our hearts') touch the dominant minor, and are enriched by the poignant divided viola colouring.

The exposition material is elaborated in the next episode, beginning with a repeat of the tonic subject in the dominant (bars 30–6). The sisters' response becomes more agitated, with harmonic forays, semiquaver strings, and 'sforzando' woodwind chords. But *sotto voce* asides from the men (bars 40–6), sung over a dominant pedal, soon bring the music back to the tonic. Instead of returning to the themes of the exposition at this point for the recapitulation, Mozart introduces a new melody. It is related to the first subject (see Example 23(*b*) ), but is more decorated

Example 23.
(*a*). *Così fan tutte*, no. 6, bars 8–14

Example 23a.   (cont'd)

and harmonically compressed. It captures the new mood of resignation in
Fiordiligi and Dorabella, for which the martial Example 23(*a*) would be
quite inappropriate. Mozart thus fulfils structural demands of the
musical form without impairing dramatic credibility. Interestingly, the
theme is closely modelled on the subject of the early trio 'Una bella
serenata' (Example 23(*c*)), originally sung by Ferrando. It can be no
accident that Ferrando imitates the women's sustained phrases in this
section of the Quintet, instead of joining the basses with their jocund
*buffo* interjections. He thereby shows the first signs of that passionate,
sympathetic nature which later colours much of the action. Finally at bar
54, the protagonists join in concerted ensemble for the first time. Significantly, the verse here contains perhaps the only sentiment which all the
characters can express without duplicity ('Ah chi mai fra tanti mali,
chi mai può la vita amar?'—'Ah, among so many misfortunes, who can

Example 23.

(*b*). No. 6, bars 47–50

(*c*). No. 3, bars 3–6

ever love life?'); yet, ironically, it is a moral no one believes, and one that subsequent plotting disproves.

A pause on bar 64 leads into a repeat of the second portion of the ensemble (bars 36–63) in its entirety. It is concluded by a cadential section that re-establishes the tonic after the earlier modulations. There is nevertheless still room for one last subtle reminiscence: a repetition at bars 100–6 of musical phrases from the sisters' first duet (no. 4, bars 75–9). These act as sardonic reminders of Fiordiligi and Dorabella's vows of sincerity:

> Se questo mio core mai cangia desio,
> Amore mi faccia vivendo penar.
>
> If this heart of mine ever changes its desire,
> May Love make me suffer while I live.[15]

This ensemble is just one of many in *Così fan tutte* to compress rich dramatic purpose and subtle characterization into a brief span. One prominent feature is the extravagant emotional expression of the two ladies. These displays are fundamental to our understanding of the opera, since they are prime exemplars of parody, which is one of the central elements in the work.

## Parody: The Mozartean Method

The sense of parody is so pervasive in *Così fan tutte* that it tends to be accepted without question. A little thought however suggests that the matter is not at all simple. How do we know which music is parodic and which sincere? Can we be certain that Fiordiligi's Act I aria 'Come scoglio' is intended as a parody,' while the Act II rondo 'Per pietà, ben mio' is genuine? What is Mozart caricaturing when he makes a parodic effect?

One view is that Mozart was making fun of the original singers when he wrote this music. It has already been noted that Adriana Ferrarese was unpopular in Vienna, and William Mann has suggested that the wide intervals and extreme range typical of Fiordiligi's music was designed to show up the soprano in a ridiculous manner:

Mozart did not care for her and . . . made her expose her gear-change from head- to chest-register, and back, as violently as possible. It is also said that Mozart was playing on Ferrarese's technique of ducking her head for low notes and throwing it back for her top register, so that in these bars she would look as well as sound undignified.[16]

---

[15] This and some of the other quotations from *Così fan tutte* are from the translation by W. Weaver (London, 1963).

[16] W. Mann, *The Operas of Mozart* (London, 1977), 542. He gives no authority for this suggestion.

At the other extreme, Singer has argued that the contour of Fiordiligi's
line was composed less for parodic display than as a reflection of the
character's psychic conflicts:

Mozart demands a soprano with a large variability of register, capable of ranging
from very high notes to very low notes. Moreover, the two extremes seem to exist
independently of one another, as if Fiordiligi contained two female voices
within her. And in a sense she does, for she is a divided woman both psychologically and musically. The highs and the lows do not always mean the same, but
they always signify a split between the two aspects of Fiordiligi's personality . . .
Though the psychiatric terminology may not be very helpful, one can detect in
her musical self-presentation a tendency to schizophrenia.[17]

However, the idea that Mozart was amusing himself at the expense of
particular singers is unlikely, and is not borne out by the music. The
composer would scarcely risk damaging the long-term prospects of his
opera by mounting a personal vendetta. If Mozart disliked Adriana
Ferrarese, his antagonism would be expected to manifest itself not only in
this work, but in other music written for her. But this is not the case. The
highly successful aria 'Al desio di chi t'adora' (K. 577), written for
Ferrarese in July 1789, contains none of the displays of vocal agility found
in Fiordiligi's music.[18] In fact, the aria that most resembles the haughty
style of 'Come scoglio' is 'Vado, ma dove?' (K. 583), composed during
the autumn of 1789 not for the Fiordiligi but for the Dorabella of the first
production, Louise Villeneuve. The beginning in particular, with its brief
declamatory phrases separated by orchestral flourishes, closely prefigures
'Come scoglio'. The similarity suggests that the singer in question was
much less important than the characterization. 'Vado, ma dove?' is sung
by Lucilla in *Il burbero di buon cuore*, and she is another self-pitying
soprano with grandiose aspirations.

The wide vocal range displayed by Fiordiligi is also misleading. An
extensive compass is typical of many *seria* parodies by Mozart and others,
and is not confined to Fiordiligi's music. For example, Madame Herz in
*Der Schauspieldirektor* covers more than two octaves from $d'$ to $f'''$, and
has to navigate exceptionally angular intervals. This is equivalent to the
range of $a$ to $c'''$ written for Ferrarese in 'Come scoglio'. Another instance
occurs in the music written for the pompous Eugenia (a part intended for
Nancy Storace) in the unfinished *Lo sposo deluso* (K. 430), where wide
intervals again abound. Awkward passages are frequent in Elvira's music,
and appear indeed to have been common in many *buffo* parodies of *seria*
style during this period.[19]

[17] I. Singer, *Mozart and Beethoven: The Concept of Love in their Operas* (Baltimore, 1977), 97.
[18] This Rondo was published in Vienna within a month of its presentation on the Burgtheater
stage.
[19] For examples that predate Mozart (including extracts from works by Piccinni and Traetta), see

Travesties of *seria* conventions and passion were popular features of *buffo* operas, and several works were composed expressly for the purpose (such as Gassmann's *L'opera seria*, 1769; Jommelli's *La critica*, 1766; Salieri's *Prima la musica, poi le parole*, 1786). Not only were the conceits of the exit aria burlesqued, but the *recitativo accompagnato* was also brought into the game. Early *buffo* operas had largely eliminated *accompagnato* in favour of the faster-moving *secco*.[20] *Recitativo accompagnato* was therefore confined to moments of intense drama—or imitations of these. A prime example from *Così fan tutte* is the little *accompagnato* section (bars 28–42) interjected into the Recitative of Scene iii (between nos. 13 and 14). Here, the 'Albanians' declare their love for Fiordiligi and Dorabella against a background of sustained strings redolent of seventeenth-century opera. The parodic intent is underlined by the exaggerated metaphoric language ('Vista appena la luce di vostre fulgidissime pupille . . .'), all the more histrionic since it is patently false. Musically, the episode is characterized by stark changes in harmony (from G minor to D major to C minor, via a diminished seventh chord to D major, and so on). It closes with an extravagant syncopated outburst from the orchestra (Example 24). The authors' purposes are confirmed in the last phrase: 'in flebil metro!' ('in plaintive measure!').

There is little doubt about Da Ponte's attempt to ape the Metastasian style in the aria 'Come scoglio'. It is written in the Arcadian verse typical of the genre, expressing a single emotion by means of metaphor. It has the common eight-line form, syllabically organized into Metastasian 8–8–8–7 metre:[21]

> Come scoglio immoto resta
> Contro i venti e la tempesta,
> Così ognor quest'alma forte
> Nella fede e nell'amor.
>
> As the rock remains unmoved
> Against the winds and the storm,
> So this spirit is still strong
> In its faith and in its love.

'Come scoglio' is designed as a parody of the archetypal exit aria. Interestingly however, Mozart's setting is not entirely caricatured. Instead he composed *seria* parodies only for the verses declaring high-flown emotions. Thus the first two lines are given preposterous music, with highly

---

H. Abert, *Mozart's Don Giovanni*, trans. P. Gellhorn (London, 1976), 71, and G. Pestelli, *The Age of Mozart and Beethoven*, trans. E. Cross (Cambridge, 1984), 43.

[20] See A. A. Abert, 'Italian Opera', In *The New Oxford History of Music*, vii: *The Age of Enlightenment 1745–1790*, ed. E. Wellesz and F. Sternfeld, (London, 1973), 52.

[21] See P. J. Smith, *The Tenth Muse* (London, 1971).

Example 24.    *Così fan tutte*, Act I, Scene xi, Recitative, bars 37–42

dramatic orchestral punctuations of the text, in dotted rhythms suggestive of the early eighteenth century (Example 25(*a*) ). But the next two lines with their expressions of faith are treated sympathetically. The texture of clarinets and bassoons that accompanies the theme for these lines in sixths and thirds resembles the 'allegro' of Fiordiligi and Dorabella's first duet, and thereby recalls their early promises of faithfulness (Example 25(*b*) ). The 'allegro' theme itself is derived from the Kyrie of the Coronation Mass, K. 317, of 1779. But in another of the extraordinary allusions that seem to embrace the gamut of emotional expression in this opera, it reappears once more in the 'allegro molto' of the Act II Finale (Example 25(*c*) ), bringing Fiordiligi's faith into harmony with the closing assertion of humanity and tolerance ('Fortunato l'uom che prende ogui cosa pel buon verso, e tra i casi e le vicende da ragion guidar si fa' - 'Fortunate is the man who takes everything for the best, and in all events and trials allows himself to be guided by reason').

The histrionic nature of Fiordiligi's declaration soon reasserts itself in this aria, as she insists on her steadfastness unto death (bars 35–41). The music here reflects her bombast with grandiose vocal flourishes and wide intervals. Such sections come close to the fierceness of Donna Anna's aria 'Or sai chi l'onore', and the parallel is endorsed by the orchestral arpeggio phrases in canon, each with the triplet semiquaver upbeat so prevalent in *Don Giovanni*. 'Come scoglio' is completed by a *più allegro* section that offers ample opportunity for vocal display, with rapid passage-work over a wide compass. The piece thus accommodates a breadth of feeling that extends well beyond the simple burlesque of the ranting prima donna suggested by Da Ponte; in Mozart's music, the sincerity and vulnerability at the core of Fiordiligi's plea are not completely disguised by the satire.

The other aria to guy the tragic passions of *opera seria* is Dorabella's 'Smanie implacabili'. Again, the scale of despair expressed by the singer is quite inappropriate for the situation in which she finds herself. Dorabella goes so far as to invoke the furies, spicing the text with a frenzied rhetoric:

> Esempio misero d'amor funesto,
> Darò all'Eumenidi se viva resto
> Col suono orribile de' miei sospir.
>
> If I remain alive, I'll give the Furies
> A wretched example of doomed love
> With the horrible sound of my sighs.

Example 25.
(a). *Così fan tutte*, no. 14, bars 1–6

Example 25a.   (*cont'd*)

(*b*).  No. 14, bars 15–19

(*c*).  Act II Finale, bars 584–7

Example 26.   *Così fan tutte*, no. 11, bars 1–5

Dorabella's hysteria is marked in the word painting of the agitated vocal line, with its gasps for breath and broken delivery (Example 26). The composer was reworking a double triplet figure of venerable ancestry when devising the accompaniment to this text. It derives from the gentle rippling string lines introduced by Gluck into Orfeo's famous aria 'Che puro ciel'. Curiously, Haydn also borrowed the figure to evoke a pastoral atmosphere for Celia's aria 'Placidi ruscelletti' in Act I of *La fedeltà premiata*. In both these cases, the peace of nature is contrasted with the protagonist's emotional torments. Mozart's technical *tour de force* transforms the motif into a mirror for Dorabella's 'smania' or frenzy. The turbulence of her state is further emphasized by the bold dynamic variations, with stabbing forte wind chords.

These arias ape *seria* conventions by the use of grandiose vehicles for fragile, transient feelings. In this manner, they act as wry counterpoints to the emotional odyssey of the four lovers. The underlying purpose of the entire plot is to disprove the romantic, idealistic convention that lovers are made for each other, and that passion is immutable. Mozart works towards this end by undermining the currency of sentimental motifs as expressions of true feeling. Hence the heavy irony of ensembles such as 'Sento, o Dio, che questo piede', and the Act I Sextet, where violent declarations are deflated by Alfonso's cynical interjections. So too the parallel between the vocal phrases used by the lovers in their original pairings, and in their later transformed liaisons. One such instance is found in the closing bars of Fiordiligi and Dorabella's first duet, when the sisters express their passion in 'sighing' phrases (Example 27(*a*) ). Similar material later re-emerges in the very different atmosphere of their Act II duet, where the sentiments are altogether more frivolous (Example 27(*b*) ).

Example 27.
(*a*). *Così fan tutte*, no. 4, bars 139–43

(*b*). No. 20, bars 62–6

Sardonic reminiscences of this kind are as important to *Così fan tutte* as the more straightforward caricatures of *opera seria*, and they bring us to the kernel of the problem of parody in this work. The ironic emphasis is often so heavy that the normal signs of musical sincerity are quite debased. Yet there is little doubt that Mozart deepened Da Ponte's cynical gloss on the story, so that some characters at least develop feelings of genuine intensity. The struggle that Fiordiligi and Ferrando have with their conflicting passions is altogether on a different plane from the superficial fickleness shown by Dorabella and Guglielmo. But how can we be certain of sincerity in *Così fan tutte*, when feigned emotion frequently takes such 'sincere' forms? Fortunately, some insight into this paradox can be gained by considering the deeper musical structure of the piece.

## Sincerity and Harmony

Deception and insincerity are persistent themes in Mozart's mature dramatic works. Having set many libretti that utilized disguise to heighten dramatic confusion in the conventional *buffo* fashion, Mozart experimented with the deliberate projection of pretended emotion in music. *Le nozze di Figaro* has many such moments, as when Susanna dissembles for the Count in Act III, or Figaro and Susanna antagonize each other briefly in Act IV. Deception also pervades *Don Giovanni*, not only in the hero's diverse role-playing, but more painfully in the transmutation of Leporello into Giovanni at the beginning of Act II. The composer's exploration of false expression is deepened and extended in *Così fan tutte*. In this opera, the mixture of real and feigned emotion is completed at a musical as well as dramatic level; truth and deception are confounded and seemingly inseparable. This ambivalence increases the strain on the characters, while pointing beyond *Così fan tutte* itself to the fundamental moral neutrality of music.

The enigma of musical expression is thus presented in an acute and palpable form in this opera. The puzzle can be illustrated with two ensembles that appear to fall on either side of the thin line dividing sincerity from deception: the F major Quintet, 'Di scrivermi ogni giorno', and the following Trio, 'Soave sia il vento'. The Quintet depicts the 'parting' of the lovers, and is therefore a moment of sorrow for the ladies and barely suppressed laughter for Ferrando and Guglielmo. Yet the two men are utterly caught up in the mood of resigned sadness and pathos, coloured vividly by the sombre viola line. Only Alfonso's *buffo* interjections remind the audience that this is a mock separation and not a moment of genuine melancholy. Moreover, Mozart deliberately ignores many of the cues for histrionics or irony inserted into the libretto by Da

Ponte. Hence Fiordiligi and Dorabella's demands for faithfulness from their lovers ('Sii costante a me sol . . . Serbati fido!' - 'Be true to me alone . . . keep faithful!', bars 7–9) are not exploited for comic effect. Even the word-painting at the start, where the lovers sob out their farewells, is more tragic than absurd. For this enigmatic piece is set in Mozart's most authentic expressive style—several of the motifs reappear in the *Ave verum corpus* (K. 618) of 1791, as Edward Dent recognized.[22]

There is however no doubt that the underlying intention of the Quintet was humorous. Neither Ferrando nor Guglielmo believe for a moment in the genuine parting, so they are feigning their emotions. But what of the subsequent Trio, the celebrated 'Soave sia il vento'? Here the situation seems even more ridiculous, with the cynical Alfonso wishing *bon voyage* to a pair of soldiers he knows will be landing as soon as they are out of sight. Nevertheless, Alfonso participates in the gentle mood of Mozart's inspired setting without any hint of insincerity. He apparently steps out of character completely during this Trio. Two possible explanations for this lapse suggest themselves. Mozart may have deemed Alfonso to be truly moved by the ladies' plight, joining them in the Trio in pity rather than sorrow. Alternatively, his inclusion may have a musical rather than dramatic reason; by involving the bass, Mozart was able to contrast the voices with a wind concertante trio of clarinets and bassoon. Certainly, Alfonso makes up for his behaviour at once with the ensuing Recitative, cynically disavowing all sympathy with the sisters:

Quante smorfie . . . quante buffonerie! . . . questa razza di gente è la più presta a cangiarsi d'umore . . .

All those grimaces . . . all those clowning tricks! . . . This kind of person is the quickest to change mood . . .

Audiences have no difficulty in distinguishing the sincere Trio from the dissembling Quintet, although the contrast may rely more on dramatic context than the quality or style of musical expression. But the ambiguities become more perplexing later in the opera, as the relationship between Fiordiligi and Ferrando deepens. Interpretation is further complicated by the divergence between Mozart's and Da Ponte's aims, for the poet probably intended an even fiercer satire on the conventions of love than was supplied by the composer. For instance, the text of Fiordiligi's Act II rondo 'Per pietà' is another parody of *opera seria*, both in its metre and in the metaphor with gloomy forest shadows. It is preceded by an extravagant *recitativo accompagnato*, in which Fiordiligi not only perceives a catalogue of horrors ('Ho visto un'aspide, un'idra, un basilisco!' - 'I've seen an asp, a hydra, a basilisk!'), but describes her state

---

[22] Igor Stravinsky paid tribute to this ensemble in the Prostitute's Chorus of *The Rake's Progress*.

in a taxonomy of histrionic inflations ('Smania, affano, rimorso, pentimento, leggerezza, perfida e tradimento!' - 'Rage, suffering, remorse, repentance, fickleness, perfidy and betrayal!'). Yet Mozart's setting shows no such exaggeration. In fact, the simplicity of the Rondo's opening sounds an authentic note of fragile honesty. It is no accident that Beethoven paid tribute to this piece in Leonora's mighty prayer 'Komm Hoffnung, lass den letzten Stern'.

It is fortunate that some insight into the enigmatic pattern of sincerity and falsehood may be gained through a quite different avenue from textual analysis: the study of tonal structure. The harmonic framework of *Così fan tutte* is not orientated around dramatic incident like that of *Le nozze di Figaro*, or around character and atmosphere as in *Don Giovanni*. Instead, the key structure penetrates beneath the text and surface plot to delineate the meaning behind actions, and the motivations of the protagonists.

The central key, and the axis around which the work revolves, is C major. Alfred Einstein has pointed out the essentially neutral quality of C major in Mozart's work. It has none of the precise associations of keys such as F major and A major. It therefore acts as an admirable pivot for the ambivalent plot of *Così fan tutte*. Its dramatic importance is emphasized immediately as the curtain rises on the massive C major group (Overture, nos. 1–3) described earlier. Following this, the keys selected for the remaining numbers of Act I fall into a consistent pattern, depending on the nature of the mood behind the action being portrayed. This is illustrated in Table 5, where three categories are distinguished. The pieces depicting palpable insincerity are grouped on the subdominant side of the home key. They include not only the deceits of Alfonso and the other men, but Fiordiligi and Dorabella's two parodies of emotion. The extreme dominant or sharp keys are more rare, and are reserved for portrayals of genuine feeling or unfeigned expression. Notable among these are Ferrando's 'Un aura amorosa' and the trio 'Soave sia il vento'. Between these two categories lies a miscellaneous group, comprising large ensembles (in which motives are inextricably mixed), conventional *buffo* numbers (such as Despina and Guglielmo's arias), and pieces in which pragmatic realism seems to be the predominant feeling.

This summary suggests a comparatively systematic ordering of keys in Act I, based on the motives behind the action. 'Flat' keys are used to depict false or shallow feelings, while authentic emotion is presented in dominant 'sharp' keys. Such a scheme is a logical extension of the application of classical sonata forms to the dramatic medium. Of course, the pattern identified here might be fortuitous, and some of the allocations

TABLE 5. THE KEY STRUCTURE OF ACT I

**False**

| F minor | 'Vorrei dir' (5): Alfonso |
|---------|---------------------------|
| Eb major | 'Sento, o Dio, che questo piede' (6): Quintet |
| Eb major | 'Al fato dan legge quegli occhi' (7): Duet |
| F major | 'Di scrivermi ogni giorno' (9): Quintet |
| Eb major | 'Smanie implacabili' (11): Dorabella |
| Bb major | 'Come scoglio immoto resta' (14): Fiordiligi |

**Neutral–*Buffo*–Realism**

| D major | 'Bella vita militar' (8): Chorus |
|---------|-----------------------------------|
| F major | 'In uomini, in soldati' (12): Despina |
| C major | 'Alla bella Despinetta' (13): Sextet |
| G major | 'Non siate ritrosi' (15): Guglielmo |
| G major | 'E voi ridete' (16): Trio |

**Sincere**

| A major | 'Ah, guarda sorella' (4): Duet |
|---------|---------------------------------|
| E major | 'Soave sia il vento' (10): Trio |
| A major | 'Un'aura amorosa' (17): Ferrando |

in Table 5 might appear questionable. However, Act II gives us an opportunity to test the scheme; if it is reliable, the same relationships between key and sincerity should apply in the second half of the opera as well. Indeed, Act II offers an especially rigorous trial, since the action becomes much more complicated, with one couple (Fiordiligi and Ferrando) exploring far greater depths of feeling than the other pair.

The numbers of Act II are listed in Table 6, along with their keys. The Act begins with another chapter of cynical advice from Despina, and this is again set in a neutral key as befits its *buffo* nature. Despina is fixed in the 'servetta' tradition, epitomized by Pergolesi's Serpina, which evolved in the nineteenth century into the character of the soubrette. Despina derives from the Columbine of *commedia dell'arte*, and remains firmly in the *buffo* style throughout. Her arias are both set in light rhythms reminiscent of Zerlina, and they share identical structures—a brief, slow introduction leading into 6/8 'allegretto'. They exploit the *buffo* convention of multiple repetitions of slight, threadbare motifs over a drone bass. Their popular style was calculated for instant appeal.

Other aspects of the characterization reinforce the implication that Mozart and Da Ponte were capitalizing on Dorotea Bussani's comic

TABLE 6.    THE KEY STRUCTURE OF ACT II

**False**

| Bb major | 'Prenderò quel brunettino' (20): Duet |
|---|---|
| Eb major | 'Secondate aurette amiche' (21): Chorus and Duet |
| F major | 'Il core vi dono' (23): Duet |
| Bb major | 'Ah lo veggio quell'anima bella' (24): Ferrando |
| Bb major | 'E amore un ladroncello' (28): Dorabella |

**Neutral–*Buffo*–Realism**

| G major | 'Una donna a quindici anni' (19): Despina |
|---|---|
| D major | 'La mano a me date' (22): Quartet |
| G major | 'Donne mie la fate a tanti' (26): Guglielmo |
| C minor/ major | 'Tradito, schernito' (27): Ferrando |

**Sincere**

| E major | 'Per pietà, bel mio' (25): Fiordiligi |
|---|---|
| A major | 'Fra gli amplessi' (29): Duet |

pertness. She is given two major disguise sequences (as Mesmerist and notary), and ample opportunity for caricature (as when she imitates the ladies' grandiloquence in the Act II Quartet). The *double entendre* of Despina's philosophy would not have been lost on the audience, if anything Da Ponte had to say about Dorotea Bussani has foundation (see Chapter 7). Despina's pragmatic sensualism was perhaps designed to appeal to the unsophisticated following that the singer was said to cultivate:

E legge di natura e non prudenza sola; amore così? Piacer, comode, gusto, gioja, divertimento, paseatempo, allegria: non è più amore se incomodo diventa . . .

It's not just sensible, it's a law of nature. What's love? Pleasure, convenience, taste, delight, amusement, pastime, enjoyment: it's no longer love when it becomes inconvenient.

(Scene xiii)

Despina's Aria is followed by Fiordiligi and Dorabella's flirtatious duet, placed strategically close to the beginning of the Act in order to balance their declarations in Act I (in 'Ah guarda sorella'). Its lack of sincerity is reflected in the subdominant key (Bb major). Likewise, the seductive Serenade by Ferrando and Guglielmo is set in Eb major. The focus of the plot now shifts on to the individual responses of Fiordiligi and Dorabella to their new admirers. The contrast between the sisters is underlined by the tonal structure. Dorabella is won over gracefully but rapidly, and Guglielmo's advances meet little opposition. The task occupies just one recitative scene and a duet, 'Il core vi dono' (set of course in a subdominant key). Dorabella's capitulation may be prosaic in comparison with Fiordiligi's, but her subsequent commitment is probably slighter. She is true to the spirit of the duet 'Prenderò quel brunettino', and treats her new admirer as an amusing diversion to whom certain concessions are necessary. Her acquiescence throws Fiordiligi's quandary into high relief.

Dorabella's Duet with Guglielmo therefore had the light (3/8), pastoral flavour that immediately appealed to the Viennese public. It was in fact the only number from the opera to be printed in Mozart's lifetime. It incorporates that favoured *buffo* device, the heart-beat motif, and boasts a short-phrased theme well suited to the verse dialogue. Its simple form apparently expresses a natural affection, prefiguring in style and atmosphere the evocation of true love in Pamina and Papageno's duet 'Bei Männern, welche Liebe fühlen'. The irony lies in the fact that neither party means one word.

This duet is juxtaposed against the drama of Fiordiligi's resistance to Ferrando. Their confrontation is again consistent with the key plan of Act I, since Ferrando's conventional and fraudulent declarations in 'Ah lo veggio quell'anima bella' are sung in B♭ major, while Fiordiligi's rondo 'Per pietà' is located in E major. E major is rare in Mozart's vocal compositions, and lies at the farthest extremity of the dominant side of the harmonic axis reached in the opera. The key emphasizes the truth behind this despairing soliloquy, all the more sincere for its acknowledgement of vulnerability. The choice of key also underlines Mozart's lack of parodic intent.

The atmosphere changes abruptly with Guglielmo's aria 'Donne mie la fate a tanti', addressed to the ladies of the audience with wry gallantry. Guglielmo remains in the *buffo* style through most of the opera, and both his arias bear the hallmarks: G major, light rhythms, and slight, repeated motifs. Monotony is prevented by subtle colouring and nuance rather than harmonic or melodic tensions. Guglielmo's arias have much in common with 'Non più andrai', and allow him to emerge genially and without caricature. The parallel is scarcely surprising, since, as has been noted, the part was written for the singer who created Figaro, Francesco Benucci. Since Benucci's strength lay in *buffo*, Guglielmo is given many opportunities for comic business. Instances in Act II include his exaggerated love play with Dorabella (replete with asides to the audience), his fury at Fiordiligi's betrayal ('La Penelope, L'Artemisia del Secolo!

Briccona! Assassina! Furfanta! Ladra! Cagna . . .' - 'The Penelope, the Artemisa of the century! Minx! Murderess! Wretch! Thief! Bitch . . .'), and his double-take on finding the marriage contract (Act II Finale, bars 436–40, 'Un contratto nuziale', etc.). Guglielmo's complacency also provides a source of amusement. When Dorabella has succumbed to temptation while Fiordiligi stands firm, Guglielmo ascribes this to his own qualities, rather than to her fortitude. He infers that he is the better man, not that Fiordiligi is the more faithful woman ('Caro amico, bisogna far delle differenze in ogni cosa. Ti pare che una sposa mancar possa un Guglielmo . . .', Act II, Scene ix).

Ferrando's impassioned recitative and aria 'Tradito, schernito' follows immediately after Guglielmo's *buffo* interlude. This section of the work shows marks of confusion, since Ferrando's fury at Dorabella's betrayal is duplicated in two Recitatives (before nos. 26 and 27). Mozart's preliminary plan was to end the Recitative preceding 'Donne mie la fate a tanti' in C minor, in which case it is possible that Ferrando's Scena was to have followed at once.[23] As it is, Ferrando is moved to anger and despair on first hearing of Dorabella's behaviour, subsides to listen to Guglielmo's frivolity, then promptly revives for the Scena. The Aria itself is in tragic, sentimental vein, and contrasts two warring emotions: horror at betrayal and abiding love. The ambivalence of his feelings is matched by a tonal structure that reflects a growing awareness of reality and loss of illusions. When Ferrando first dwells on his surviving passion ('Io sento che ancora . . .', bar 12, etc.), he adopts the subdominant mode associated with shallow emotions. But for the repeat of these words, the music modulates into C major (bar 41). This effect, coupled with the entry of Alfonso in the background, suggests that Ferrando is maturing from idolatry towards acceptance of the imperfect nature of human affection.

The numbers that succeed Ferrando's outburst, Dorabella's frivolous 'allegretto' (in B♭ major), and the brief Trio of rueful acceptance of the opera's motto by the men (in C major), fit the key structure developed in Act I without difficulty. The subdominant key portrays dissembling flippancy, while C major is Don Alfonso's key of realism. They bring us to the central problem and the emotional climax of the opera: Fiordiligi's surrender to Ferrando in 'Fra gli amplessi'. Here the intensity of Ferrando's assault transcends duplicity, creating an episode of profound ambivalence. The Duet taxes the link between meaning and key to its limits, paradoxically confirming the importance of tonality while undermining its force.[24]

[23] See Tyson, *Notes on the Composition.*
[24] For a detailed analysis of the tonal construction of 'Fra gli amplessi', see L. Fischer, 'Mozarts "Musikalische Regie"—eine musikdramaturgische Analyse', in *Così fan tutte: Beiträge zur Wirkungsgeschichte von Mozarts Oper*, ed. S. Vill, (Bayreuth, 1978), 9–23.

'Fra gli amplessi' begins as a stately 'adagio' in A major, befitting
Fiordiligi's sincere but somewhat high-flown sentiments. Orchestral
phrases separate the fragments of vocal melody, recalling the opening of
'Come scoglio'. This tonic section (bars 1–11) apparently leads into a
bridging passage to the dominant, and as is typical at such points, Mozart
increases the pace with pulsing quavers from the string section. But as the
dominant (E major) materializes at bar 15, the music is suddenly diverted
by Ferrando's entry. The $g$ is flattened, so that the harmony touches the
dominant minor on its way to the substitute dominant (C major), reached
at bar 24 (Example 28($a$) ). This unexpected modulation is an extraordinary coup, instantly raising the emotional pitch by its harmonic boldness.
Charles Rosen has noted that in choosing the flattened mediant as a
substitute dominant, Mozart selected 'a chord sufficiently akin to the
dominant to be reasonably set against the tonic, and yet remote enough
to give a dramatically expressive, large scale dissonance to the structure'.[25]
The substitution is also crucial to the drama. Had Mozart permitted
Ferrando to attempt Fiordiligi's seduction in the extreme sharp key of
E major, the entire network of harmonic meanings would have been
destroyed. Instead, Ferrando sings in C major, the key of cynicism and
realism.

The struggle between Fiordiligi's faith and Ferrando's duplicity is thus
set on neutral ground. The 'allegro' is rich with retrospective thematic
allusions that augment its dramatic importance. Fiordiligi's first phrase
(Example 28($b$) ) begging Ferrando to leave recalls the point in the
Quintet 'Sento, o Dio, che questo piede' at which the lovers contemplated
their sad destiny (Example 23($b$); this was also, of course, the moment at
which Ferrando's musical sympathies were first revealed). Soon afterwards, Ferrando presses his case with a flourish (Example 28($c$) ) derived
from his earlier confident assertions of success in the wager with Alfonso,
made during the trio 'Una bella serenata' (Example 28($d$) ).

Ferrando's pleas become more intense before Fiordiligi's cry of 'taci,
ahime' silences the woodwind and syncopated strings. She introduces a
reflective section (bars 40–75) in which her resistance weakens as the
music moves towards the tonic once more. However, another dramatic
point has yet to be made by the harmony, for it is Ferrando who brings
back the tonic A major. He sings the gentle 'larghetto' theme (Example
29($a$) ), and in doing so finally breaks the tonal code. Having failed to win
Fiordiligi by deceit, he moves to the key which has been identified
throughout the opera with truth and sincerity. He disobeys the 'rule' by

25 C. Rosen, *The Classical Style* (London, 1971), 316. A similar modulation is heard in the
opening Allegretto of the late quartet in D major K. 499, where the music resolves from a cadence on
E major, not into A major, but via F# minor to F major.

**Example 28.**
(*a*). *Così fan tutte*, no. 29, bars 12–23

(b). No. 29, bars 25–8

(c). No. 29, bars 32–5

(d). No. 3, bars 10–13

Example 29.
(*a*). *Così fan tutte*, no. 29, bars 76–83

which falsehood is clothed in flat or subdominant keys. Moreover, the theme itself is of a purity that prefigures the profound emotion of *Die Zauberflöte*, comparable with the moment late in Act II when Pamina and Tamino meet after their separate trials (Example 29(*b*) ), or the beginning of the Priests' March. The second half of the 'larghetto' theme reappears shortly in the famous Canon of the Act II Finale (Example 29(*c*) ).

(*b*).  *Die Zauberflöte*, Act II Finale, bars 277–84

(*c*).  *Così fan tutte*, Act II Finale, bars 173–80

Fiordiligi is lost from the moment that Ferrando touches A major, although her anguished cries of 'giusto ciel, crudel' hint at the horror of her position. The tonality underlines the fact that Ferrando has shifted what was intended by both parties to be a flirtatious interlude on to a completely different emotional plane. Instead of offering a light diversion, Ferrando changes the basis of the exchange by demanding a deeper commitment. An exquisite oboe phrase announces Fiordiligi's surrender (bars 97–101), and the closing 'andante' completes the Duet almost as a formality, expressing little further passion (as if the characters have been drained by their battle of wills).

This Duet is both an emotional climax, and a perfect exemplar of the dramatic force of classical forms.[26] The substitution of C major for the dominant heralds a struggle which is articulated as much by modulation, rhythm, and dynamic as by the text. The placing of Ferrando's ultimate assault in A major accounts for Fiordiligi's defeat, since the power of this key lies in its consistent association with truth and sincerity. Yet the final enigma is unresolved. Ferrando may be expressing a true passion in the 'larghetto', addressing Fiordiligi with genuine ardour. Alternatively, he may be treacherously raising his attack on to a new level of emotional duplicity, spurred on by his own humiliation at the hands of Dorabella. Ferrando may only have assumed the cloak and language of passion, and may be ruthlessly exploiting the deepest musical foundations of feeling. In either case, the structure of the musical score, and the grand tonal design linking the diverse episodes of the story, have a transcendent dramatic relevance to Così fan tutte.

[26] It does not lessen one's admiration for Mozart's creative genius to point out that the format and structure of 'Fra gli amplessi' were modelled on the climactic duet 'Pianin, pianino' from L'arbore di Diana. In this work, Diana (a part which Adriana Ferrarese made her own) undertakes a similar emotional odyssey to that experienced by Fiordiligi. Diana is a woman who again resists love, rejecting the sensuous blandishments of others, until she finally succumbs in the Duet with Endimione. As in the Duet from Così fan tutte, 'Pianin, pianino' begins with a recitative accompagnato ('Misera! Dove son?') in which the heroine's soliloquy is interrupted by her lover. The Duet starts as an 'andantino' in C major, and moves through Eb major (precisely the same tonic–flat mediant relationship found in 'Fra gli amplessi') as Diana struggles with her feelings. It closes with a gentle faster-moving section in C major in which the lovers sing in thirds, reflecting their true harmony.

# Epilogue

I have argued in this book that Mozart's operas can only be understood within the social and musical context in which they were composed. Although Mozart's three collaborations with Da Ponte were written over a comparatively brief period (from the autumn of 1785 to the beginning of 1790), enormous changes took place both in the composer's personal life and in the society in which he lived. Each of the operas was produced with a particular situation and audience in mind.

The social context of the operas (detailed in earlier chapters) can perhaps be summarized as follows. *Le nozze di Figaro* was written for the sophisticated audience of a society in flux, one in which the conventions of the *ancien régime* coexisted with a new interest in egalitarianism. Enlightenment notions were propagated at the highest levels of the social structure, but continued to be viewed nervously by a hierarchy conditioned by centuries to consider itself sacrosanct. A whiff of scandal was attached to *Le nozze di Figaro*, and the audience expected to enjoy the *frisson* of contact with potentially inflammatory material. Mozart wrote the work during a period of high optimism, in which the success of the opera coupled with his popularity as a virtuoso performer were likely to establish him firmly in Vienna.

The conditions surrounding *Don Giovanni* were quite different. The hopes of 1785 and 1786 had not been fulfilled in Vienna, and Mozart found his position fragile. Ill health and the death of his father further disturbed his equilibrium. Against this background, Mozart and Da Ponte embarked on the risky venture of writing a Don Juan opera for Prague. The project was hazardous because although the story was still guaranteed to stimulate popular applause, more refined audiences were unlikely to be satisfied with the much-abused legend.[1] However, Mozart and Da Ponte gauged that the piece would be suitable for the musically intelligent but provincial and somewhat unsophisticated tastes of Prague. They appear not to have been optimistic about the success of the work in Vienna, and to some extent their fears were justified.

When *Così fan tutte* reached the stage early in 1790, the situation had changed yet again. If anything, Mozart's own circumstances were more

---

[1] This point has also been made by N. Pirrotta, 'The Traditions of Don Juan Plays and Comic Operas', *Proceedings of the Royal Musical Association*, 107 (1980–1), 60–70. Pirrotta suggests that Mozart and Da Ponte selected the story for Prague even before they knew about the success of the Gazzaniga/Bertati work.

desperate, since indecision and difficulty with musical composition were added to his material concerns. Society in Vienna had retreated from its flirtation with egalitarianism, and fear of revolution had led to the ascendancy of conservative elements. The commission of *Così fan tutte* must have appeared an unexpected boon to Mozart, and he responded by producing an opera specifically designed for his aristocratic audience. He perceived that they no longer wished to be challenged by notions of social upheaval, but would prefer an amusing exposition of more personal human foibles.

Musically, a progressive movement towards greater unity can be seen through the composition of these operas. This is reflected in the growing emphasis on tonal cohesion, linkage of disparate sections by thematic allusion, and the structural use of key. Ultimately, the purpose underlying these developments was to focus the drama in order to produce a more profound theatrical experience. Mozart employed the most elaborate means at his disposal within classical sonata style to achieve unity. Later composers elaborated those mechanisms still further, and found new ways of ensuring dramatic cohesion (such as reducing the pace of musical incident and composing on a grander scale). Unification in Mozart's work is confined by the premiss that individual musical units are self-contained. All Mozart's operas consist of a series of numbers that are complete in themselves, while fitting into the overall framework of the score. Later in the nineteenth-century, the structure itself was expanded, and sections of the score gain their significance through resonances across vast musical spans.[2]

These arguments concerning musical development do not imply that *Le nozze di Figaro* is an immature work, or that *Così fan tutte* is the finest. Rather, such trends reflect Mozart's evolving musical interests. Each of the collaborations with Da Ponte has perfections of its own, and embodies particular sets of ideas. At the risk of encapsulating these differences in almost banal brevity, one might describe *Le nozze di Figaro* as portraying the humanity and joy of human relationships, *Don Giovanni* as elaborating the profundities of human nature and existence, and *Così fan tutte* as distilling the essence of human emotion. All the operas however share a sense of tolerance and a lack of moralizing. Like Shakespeare and Goethe, Mozart rarely condemns even the most villanous, treacherous, or selfish individuals. Rather, he portrays them with sympathy and understanding. This Olympian poise is perhaps an added justi-

---

[2] These trends are exemplified most strikingly in the operas of Wagner and Berlioz, but are also apparent in later works by Strauss and the Italian *verismo* composers. A 5-minute extract from the operas of these composers (equivalent to a single number from a Mozart opera) is seldom satisfying in the absence of knowledge of the music that has gone before or will come afterwards, since each segment exists within a network of thematic, harmonic, and instrumental reference.

fication for describing Mozart as the quintessential 'classical' composer. It is one of the puzzles of human creativity that such omniscience should arise from a person with few pretensions in his private or intellectual life, and one whose universality emerged from an intense preoccupation with the mundane problems of survival and existence.

Mozart did however live in an age and intellectual milieu in which tolerance was considered to be one of the highest virtues. His ability to portray even the basest emotions with feeling and eloquence was perhaps also facilitated by the particular way in which dramatic expression was perceived by contemporary audiences. One of the most surprising facts about the eighteenth-century theatre audience is its degree of involvement in the drama. Despite the overpowering formality of social life, people were extravagant in their display of feelings in the theatre. They would cry, scream, or laugh as the occasion demanded. At death scenes, half the public would be in tears while the other half fainted. Nor was this pandemonium uncritical, for the vocal eighteenth-century audience was fiercely partisan. Men and women of the nobility and lower classes shouted as well as cheered, and disrupted the show by heckling when displeased with its progress. The paradoxical contrast with contemporary social rules is summarized by Richard Sennett as follows:

How can people whose lives are governed by impersonal and abstract convention be so spontaneous, so free to express themselves? All the complexity of the ancien régime city lies in that seeming paradox. Their spontaneity rebukes the notion that you must lay yourself bare in order to be expressive.[3]

This is even more surprising when the logistics of performance are recalled. The noise of the audience, the lighting in the theatre, the interpolation of ballets or comic distractions in serious works (and, in some theatres, the lounging of members of the audience on stage)—all these factors might be expected to militate against emotional involvement.

However, it is clear that a high level of engagement was not maintained throughout the performance. The audience was quite prepared to talk or play cards through dull passages, yet could rapidly be galvanized by the climactic moments on the stage. Hence the orientation of acting around a series of 'points' in each work: celebrated passages, individual lines, or even single words would elicit a massive response. They became the pivots of an interpretation. The entire reading of a part might be judged from a few moments (such as Hamlet's reaction on the first appearance of the Ghost). These important episodes were frequently demarcated by the performer moving downstage, stepping to the edge of the pit, and delivering the point directly to the audience. Baron Riesbeck described Mozart's

[3] R. Sennett, *The Fall of Public Man* (Cambridge, 1977), 73.

brother-in-law Joseph Lange using precisely this technique: 'When he is to speak a speech which he thinks will meet with applause, he comes as near to the pit as he can'.[4] A successful point would be vociferously applauded, and an encore demanded. Encores were not simply matters of graciousness or goodwill, for if the performer refused, the audience might stop the show and prevent any further progress until the point was repeated. In opera, pointing reached such a pitch that favourite phrases might be given in isolation at low-brow theatres.

The peculiar susceptibility of the eighteenth-century audience to instantaneous passion was coupled with a special attitude to displays of feeling in the theatre. The crucial element was the mode of emotional expression itself, and not its context, legitimacy, or relevance to the character. The self-contained expressive statement was paramount, and it did not matter that the circumstances might be incongruous. Such a 'point' 'led men to feel outraged at the actor or made them weep . . . because the gesture was absolutely believable in its own terms. It had no referent to the scene in which it occured'.[5] Hence it was immaterial to the audience whether the expression was put into the mouth of a dissembling villain or just hero. The depth of passion or sincerity of sentiment was secondary to the projection of the episode itself.[6] Seen in this light, the contradictions between passion and falsehood, and the 'wasting' of beautiful music on fickle or shallow sentiments, become irrelevant. Don Giovanni's seductiveness is not diminished by his duplicity, Elvira's anguish by her absurdity, or Dorabella and Guglielmo's amiable qualities by their superficiality. Ultimately, the expressive power of Mozart's music must be seen not only in the context of the operas themselves, but as a series of dramas of the moment, events isolated from the plot and judged by their own immediate effect. This is the manner in which the contemporary audience would 'read' the highpoints of the operas, and such considerations must also have influenced Mozart in the act of composition.

---

[4] J. C. Riesbeck, *Travels through Germany*, trans. Revd Mr Maty (London, 1787), i. 299.

[5] Sennett, *The Fall of Public Man*, p. 79.

[6] This emphasis on the moment is reflected in the elevation of performers in the eighteenth century to unprecedented heights, and the unbounded admiration given to individual actors and singers. The aesthetic experience of the performance was the audience's chief concern. One of the main frustrations in reading contemporary opera memoirs is their devotion to descriptions of particular singers, their abilities, strengths, and weaknesses, at the expense of any consideration of composers or other aspects of production (such as stage design, acting, or acoustics). Even Da Ponte described *Così fan tutte* as an opera he wrote for Adriana Ferrarese (see Introduction); the fact that Mozart was also involved came second in his mind.

# Appendix

## *LE NOZZE DI FIGARO,* 1786

### Cast of Characters
Count Almaviva, a Grandee of Spain
Countess Almaviva, his wife
Figaro, valet to the Count
Susanna, chambermaid to the Countess, and engaged to Figaro
Cherubino, page to the Count
Doctor Bartolo, a physician from Seville
Marcellina, his housekeeper
Don Basilio, music master
Antonio, gardener to the Count, and Susanna's uncle
Barbarina, Antonio's daughter
Don Curzio, a judge

### Synopsis
The action takes place in the castle and grounds of Aguas-Frescas, the country domain of Count Almaviva, near Seville. Several years have passed since the Count spirited his future wife Rosina away from the house of Dr Bartolo in Seville with the aid of the wily Figaro (in *Il barbieri di Siviglia*). The Count has now become bored with his wife, and his attentions are currently fixed on Susanna.

### *Act I*
**Scene i**: It is the morning of the day fixed for the marriage of Figaro and Susanna. The curtain opens on a half-furnished room, where Figaro is busy measuring the floor while Susanna tries on a hat (1). Figaro announces that the Count has given them the room, and explains how it conveniently lies midway between the apartments of the Count and the Countess. Susanna is less sanguine, pointing out how vulnerable she will be to the Count's advances if Figaro is absent (2). She describes how the Count has been trying to seduce her, using Basilio as his messenger. She is called away by a summons from the Countess.

**Scene ii**: Left alone, Figaro rages at the Count's iniquity, but vows to get the better of him (3). He leaves the room.

**Scene iii**: Don Bartolo and Marcellina enter. Despite her advanced years, Marcellina wishes to marry Figaro, and hopes to use the contract for a loan she previously gave Figaro to frustrate his marriage with Susanna. Bartolo promises to assist her, and swears vengeance on Figaro (4). He exits.

**Scene iv**: Susanna returns, and the two women quarrel (5). Marcellina comes off second best, and storms away in a fury.

**Scene v**: The page Cherubino enters and begs Susanna's help. The Count has just found him alone with Barbarina, and has dismissed him. He sighs with youthful passion for the Countess, and steals a ribbon of hers. He sings of his love for women in general (6).

**Scene vi**: The Count is heard outside, and Cherubino hides behind a chair. The Count comes in and declares his love for Susanna, but is himself interrupted by Basilio. The Count now hides behind the chair, but Cherubino quickly slips into the seat without being observed.

**Scene vii**: Basilio proclaims the Count's feeling for Susanna, but is angrily repulsed. He insinuates that Cherubino is in love with the Countess, at which the Count emerges from his hiding-place in a fury (7). He demonstrates how he discovered Cherubino in Barbarina's room, only to find the Page hidden in Susanna's chair. The Count now doubts Susanna's honesty, and calls for Figaro to see what has happened. She however boldly declares her innocence.

**Scene viii**: Figaro comes in with a chorus of peasants extolling the Count's goodness in abolishing the *Droit du Seigneur* (8). He asks the Count for his blessing on the marriage, but the latter prevaricates. The Count is nevertheless persuaded to forgive Cherubino, but appoints the Page to his regiment, ordering him to leave for Seville at once. Figaro secretly tells Cherubino to wait, and ends the Act extolling the joys and miseries of military life (9).

*Act II*

**Scene i**: The action moves to the Countess's apartment. The Countess is alone, bewailing the loss of her husband's love (10).

**Scene ii**: Susanna enters, and they discuss the Count's duplicity. Figaro joins them, and explains his plan. He has written an anonymous letter to the Count, suggesting that the Countess has arranged an assignation with a lover in the garden that evening. He hopes that the Count will be made so furious and suspicious that he will forget about trying to frustrate the marriage plan. Figaro suggests that Cherubino is dressed up as a woman and sent to the garden in the Countess's place, so as to cause the Count even greater embarrassment. The Countess and Susanna agree to the plot and Figaro leaves to make arrangements.

**Scene iii**: Cherubino enters the Countess's apartment and sings his *canzona* on love (11). The two women begin to dress Cherubino in women's clothes, and Susanna comments on the transformation (12). They discover that the ribbon stolen by Cherubino is tied round his arm to stop a small wound, and the Countess sends Susanna to fetch a bandage.

**Scene iv**: The scene is interrupted by a knock at the locked door. It is the Count, full of jealousy after receiving the anonymous letter. The Countess is terrified, and hides Cherubino in her dressing-room.

**Scene v**: The Count enters, suspicious at the Countess's delay in opening the door. Cherubino makes a noise in the dressing-room, and the Countess's demeanor betrays her. She claims that it is Susanna who is in the dressing-room, but the Count is unconvinced.

**Scene vi:** Meanwhile Susanna re-enters through another door, and overhears their quarrel (13). The Count wants to summon servants to break down the door, but the Countess dissuades him. The couple go off together to find tools to open the door themselves.

**Scene vii:** Susanna rushes into the apartment and releases Cherubino from the dressing-room (14). He escapes by jumping out of the window, and Susanna hides in his place.

**Scene viii:** The Count and Countess return. She warily admits that it is not Susanna but Cherubino who is in the dressing-room.

**Finale:** He is furious, orders Cherubino to come out, and disowns the Countess. However, when the door is opened, Susanna emerges. The Count and Countess are dumbfounded. The Count begs his wife's forgiveness, and this is eventually granted. The Countess and Susanna explain that the anonymous letter was a fiction concocted by Figaro. Figaro himself enters, and the Count sees an opportunity to regain the upper hand. He questions Figaro about the anonymous letter, but the latter denies all knowledge of it. They reach an impasse which is broken by the gardener Antonio who bursts in, angry that someone has jumped from the window and damaged his plants. Figaro, Susanna, and the Countess try to dismiss his claims as the ramblings of a drunkard. Finally Figaro admits that it was he who jumped from the window, and pretends to have a limp. Antonio produces a paper dropped by the fugitive. This is seized triumphantly by the Count, who believes that he has at last trapped Figaro. Antonio is dismissed, and Figaro struggles to 'remember' what he has dropped. Fortunately the Countess glimpses the document, and passes its contents secretly to Figaro via Susanna. It is Cherubino's commission to the regiment, and it lacks an official seal. Figaro victoriously proclaims the solution, and the Count is thwarted. However, Marcellina, Bartolo, and Basilio now rush in pleading for justice from the Count in Marcellina's case against Figaro. The Act ends in general uproar.

*Act III*

**Scene i:** The Act opens on a grand hall, decorated for the wedding ceremony. The Count paces up and down, musing on the events of the day.

**Scene ii:** The Countess and Susanna enter secretly in the background, and the Countess urges Susanna to make an assignation with the Count. Susanna approaches the Count, and gives him equivocal encouragement (16).

**Scene iii:** She is just about to leave when she bumps into Figaro. She tells him that they have won their case, and the couple leave.

**Scene iv:** The Count overhears their departing remarks, and realizes that he has been betrayed. He sings of his jealous fury against Figaro, and passion for Susanna (17), exiting at the end of the Aria.

**Scene v:** The Count, Marcellina, Figaro, Bartolo, and the judge Don Curzio enter to hear the case against Figaro. Don Curzio announces that Figaro must pay his debt or marry Marcellina. Figaro says that he cannot marry without the consent of his parents, and it emerges that he is actually the son of Bartolo and Marcellina, stolen at birth by bandits. Mother and son embrace while the other characters express astonishment (18). Susanna rushes in with money given by the Countess to pay the debt, only to find Figaro and Marcellina in each other's arms. Once the situation is explained, she too is delighted; only the Count is frustrated, and leaves with Don Curzio.

**Scene vi**: Bartolo agrees to marry Marcellina to make a double wedding-day, and the group leave the stage in delight.

**Scene vii**: Barbarina and Cherubino enter, and after a brief exchange go off to disguise the Page as a girl.

**Scene viii**: The Countess enters the chamber, brooding on the necessity of joining forces with her servants against her husband. She sings of her days of love that are past (19). She leaves the stage.

**Scene ix**: Antonio comes in with the Count, telling him about the plot to dress Cherubino as a girl. They go off to view the evidence in Barbarina's room.

**Scene x**: The Countess and Susanna discuss their plot to lure the Count to an assignation in the garden. The Countess dictates a letter to Susanna, telling the Count to come to the garden that evening (20).

**Scene xi**: Barbarina and the other village girls enter together with Cherubino dressed as a girl. They are carrying flowers which they offer to the Countess (21).

**Scene xii**: Antonio and the Count burst in and expose Cherubino. The Count rounds on the Countess, but his righteous indignation is checked when Barbarina reveals embarrassing intimacies.

**Scene xiii**: The scene is interrupted by Figaro, announcing that the wedding-party is ready. The Count questions Figaro further about the incidents of the morning, but is unable to extract an admission of guilt.

**Finale**: The music for the ceremony begins (22). The two brides, Susanna and Marcellina, are presented to the Count. Susanna uses the opportunity to pass her letter to the Count. Later there is dancing, and Figaro notices the Count pricking his finger on the pin used to close the letter. The Act ends with a chorus of celebration.

*Act IV*

**Scene i**; The scene represents a clearing in the palace gardens containing two pavilions. Barbarina is found searching for the pin that she has dropped (23).

**Scene ii**: She is interrupted by Figaro and Marcellina, and tells them that she is looking for the pin that the Count ordered her to return to Susanna. Figaro gives her a replacement, and she dances off.

**Scene iii**: Figaro turns to his mother in despair. He realizes that it is Susanna who made the assignation with the Count during the wedding-dance, and believes that he has been betrayed. He storms away.

**Scene iv**: Left alone, Marcellina determines to support Susanna and sings of the perfidy of men (24). She leaves the stage.

**Scene v**: Barbarina enters with some food that she has brought for Cherubino, who has told her that he will be hiding in the left-hand pavilion. She hears someone coming, and hides in the pavilion in fright.

**Scene vi**: It is Figaro, who has brought Basilio and Bartolo to witness Susanna's faithlessness. He leaves to lay further traps.

**Scene vii**: Basilio and Bartolo talk about the turn of events. Bartolo supports Figaro, but Basilio argues that Figaro should bear the shame, just as he himself has always done (25). They leave.

**Scene viii**: Figaro returns to keep watch alone. He sings of his love for Susanna and fury at her behaviour, warning all men never to trust women (26). He hides.

**Scene ix**: Marcellina brings Susanna and the Countess to the spot. Susanna is disguised as the Countess, and vice versa. Marcellina hides in the left-hand pavilion.

**Scene x**: Figaro overhears Susanna and the Countess talking. As the Countess goes into a pavilion, Susanna is determined to have fun at the expense of Figaro, and sings of her impatience for her lover (27).

**Scene xi**: As Figaro bemoans his fate, Cherubino enters and spies the Countess, whom he takes to be Susanna.

**Finale**: He flirts with the Countess, who is terrified that the Count will discover them. The Count enters in the background, and together with Figaro and Susanna, overhears the Page's conversation with the Countess. Cherubino attempts to kiss the Countess, but the Count intervenes and receives the kiss himself. Cherubino hides, and Figaro receives the blow that the Count has aimed at his Page.

The Count settles down to make love to the Countess, whom he believes to be Susanna. As they prepare to retire, Figaro intervenes, and the Countess slips away. The Count goes off into the darkness as well, leaving Figaro.

Susanna enters, and Figaro begins to denounce his bride. However, he soon recognizes Susanna despite her disguise. Thereupon he pretends to make love to the 'Countess'. Susanna, who does not realize that she has been discovered, is in her turn mortified. She slaps Figaro, but when he shows that he knows who she really is, the two are reconciled. They are in each other's arms when the Count enters, looking for 'Susanna'. He sees his wife making love with his servant, and explodes in rage at the dishonour. He calls for assistance, and manages to catch Figaro, although Susanna escapes. Servants enter with torches, together with Basilio, Bartolo, Antonio, and Don Curzio. One by one, Cherubino, Barbarina, Marcellina, and Susanna are dragged from their hiding-places. The Count denounces the 'Countess', and refuses to forgive her. Whereupon the real Countess appears. The Count is astonished and begs humbly for forgiveness himself. This is granted by the Countess, and the Opera ends in general rejoicing.

**Musical Outline**

*Act I*

1. Duettino (Figaro and Susanna): 'Cinque, dieci, venti, trenta'.
2. Duettino (Figaro and Susanna): 'Se a caso madama la notte ti chiama'.
3. Cavatina (Figaro): 'Se vuol ballare, signor Contino?'
4. Aria (Bartolo): 'La vendetta, oh, la vendetta'.
5. Duettino (Marcellina and Susanna): 'Via resti servita'.
6. Aria (Cherubino): 'Non sò più cosa son'.
7. Trio (Susanna, the Count, and Basilio): 'Cosa sento! Tosto andate'.
8. Chorus: 'Giovani lieti, fiori spargete'.
9. Aria (Figaro): 'Non più andrai farfallone amoroso'.

*Act II*

10. Cavatina (Countess): 'Porgi amor qualche ristoro'.
11. Canzona (Cherubino): 'Voi, che sapete che cosa è amor'.
12. Aria (Susanna): 'Venite, inginocchiatevi'.
13. Trio (Count, Countess, and Susanna): 'Susanna or via sortite?'
14. Duettino (Susanna and Cherubino): 'Aprite, presto aprite'.
15. Finale.

*Act III*

16. Duet (Count and Susanna): 'Crudel! perchè finora'.
17. Recitative and Aria (Count): 'Hai già vinta la causa!—Vendrò mentr'io sospiro'.
18. Sextet (Marcellina, Figaro, Bartolo, Don Curzio, Count, and Susanna): 'Riconosci in questo amplesso'.
19. Recitative and Aria (Countess): 'E Susanna non vien!—Dove sono i bei momenti'.
20. Duettino (Countess and Susanna): 'Che soave zefiretto'.
21. Chorus: 'Ricevete, o padroncina, queste rose e questi fior'.
22. Finale.

*Act IV*

23. Cavatina (Barbarina): 'L'ho perduta, me meschina'.
24. Aria (Marcellina): 'Il capro e la capretta son sempre, in amistà.
25. Aria (Basilio): 'In quegli anni, in cui val poco'.
26. Recitative and Aria (Figaro): 'Tutto è disposso—Aprite un pò que gl'occhi'.
27. Recitative and Aria (Susanna): 'Giunse al fin il momento—Deh, vieni non tardar'.
28. Finale.

DON GIOVANNI OR IL DISSOLUTO PUNITO, 1787

**Cast of Characters**

Don Giovanni, a licentious young nobleman
Commendatore, an elderly officer
Donna Anna, daughter of the Commendatore
Don Ottavio, a young nobleman, betrothed to Donna Anna
Donna Elvira, a lady from Burgos, abandoned by Don Giovanni
Leporello, Don Giovanni's servant
Zerlina, a young countrywoman
Masetto, a young countryman, betrothed to Zerlina

**Synopsis**

The action takes place in a Spanish city.

*Act I*

**Scene i:** The Opera opens outside the Commendatore's house. Leporello, wrapped in a cloak, is waiting impatiently for his master Don Giovanni, who has entered the house hoping to seduce Donna Anna (1). Leporello hears noises and hides as Don Giovanni enters with Donna Anna clinging to his arm. Don Giovanni refuses to reveal his identity to Anna. She calls for help, and her father comes out. The Commendatore and Don Giovanni argue, draw swords, and the Commendatore is killed.

**Scene ii:** Don Giovanni and Leporello make their escape.

**Scene iii:** Donna Anna returns hastily with Don Ottavio. They find the corpse of the Commendatore. Donna Anna is distraught, and insists that Ottavio swears an oath of vengeance (2).

**Scene iv:** The scene shifts to a street at night. Leporello upbraids Don Giovanni about his way of life, and is threatened for his pains. Their dispute is interrupted when Don Giovanni senses the presence of a woman.

**Scene v:** Donna Elvira enters, vowing revenge on her betrayer (3). Don Giovanni offers his assistance, only to discover that the woman is Donna Elvira, whom he seduced and abandoned after three days. Don Giovanni escapes, leaving Leporello to make his excuses to Elvira. Leporello explains by showing Donna Elvira the catalogue of his master's conquests (4). He leaves stealthily.

**Scene vi:** Elvira expresses her sense of outrage and distress.

**Scene vii:** It is now daytime, and a group of country people appear singing and dancing, and celebrating the marriage of Zerlina and Masetto (5).

**Scene viii:** Don Giovanni and Leporello enter. Giovanni is immediately attracted to Zerlina, and invites the whole group to his *palazzo*. Leporello is instructed to look after Masetto. Masetto is reluctant to leave Zerlina, but grudgingly obeys Don Giovanni (6).

**Scene ix:** Left alone with Zerlina, Don Giovanni soon charms her with flattery, promises of marriage, and tenderness (7).

**Scene x**: They are about to leave when Donna Elvira enters. She foils Don Giovanni's plan by warning Zerlina about him (8). Elvira and Zerlina leave together.

**Scene xi**: As Don Giovanni curses the failure of his schemes, Donna Anna and Ottavio come on the scene. Anna fails to recognize Don Giovanni, and she solicits his help.

**Scene xii**: Just as he is ingratiating himself with Anna and Ottavio, Elvira returns to denounce him once more. Anna and Ottavio are uncertain whether to believe Elvira's apparent sincerity, or Giovanni's claims that she is mad (9). Don Giovanni manages to hustle Elvira away. But in parting, he betrays himself to Donna Anna.

**Scene xiii**: Anna turns to Ottavio in anguish, and recounts the events of the previous night, when Don Giovanni attacked her in her room. She renews her demand that Don Ottavio takes revenge (10), before leaving the stage.

**Scene xiv**: Don Ottavio determines to find the truth in the matter. In the Aria (10*b*) interpolated into the first production in Vienna, he expresses his love for Donna Anna in soliloquy.

**Scene xv**: Leporello now enters, vowing that he must leave his dangerous master. He is joined by Don Giovanni, who is delighted that Leporello has prepared the entertainments for the peasants, and has managed to extricate Zerlina from Elvira's protection. Don Giovanni eagerly anticipates the evening's pleasures (11).

**Scene xvi**: The scene changes to the garden of Don Giovanni's *palazzo*. Zerlina manages with difficulty to calm Masetto's jealous suspicions (12). However, her work is undone by the approach of Don Giovanni.

**Finale**: Masetto hides, in order to see what will happen when Zerlina meets Don Giovanni. Giovanni enters giving orders to his servants and exhorting the peasants to enjoy themselves. They all depart, leaving Don Giovanni alone with Zerlina. He renews his advances, but is interrupted by Masetto. Diplomatically he scolds Masetto for leaving his bride alone, and leads the couple to the ballroom.

Don Ottavio, Donna Anna, and Donna Elvira enter the garden in masks, encouraging each other to bravery. Leporello spies them from a window, and is ordered by Don Giovanni to invite them to the festivities. They accept, and in an 'adagio' trio dwell on their mixed emotions.

A change of scene brings the ballroom of the *palazzo*, where the entertainment is in progress. The masked trio enter, and are greeted with dignity by Don Giovanni. They all proclaim a toast to freedom. A formal minuet is heard, and Ottavio dances with Anna. A second band begins a dance that Leporello joins with the reluctant Masetto. A third *contredanse* is played at the same time, and Don Giovanni takes Zerlina as his partner. He manoeuvres her out of the ballroom. The dancing is disbanded in confusion as the other characters hear Zerlina calling for help.

Don Giovanni steps out of the sideroom dragging Leporello onto the stage, accusing him of villainy. The others are not duped, however. Don Ottavio draws a pistol, and Giovanni is dumbfounded to discover who his masked guests are. The company rain curses on Don Giovanni, as he and Leporello try to gather their wits. The Act ends in uproar.

*Act II*

**Scene i**: Don Giovanni and Leporello are arguing in the street outside Donna Elvira's lodging (14). Leporello once again wishes to leave Giovanni's service, but is bribed to remain. Don Giovanni explains that he wishes to seduce Elvira's maid, and exhanges clothes with his servant so as not to appear to be a nobleman.

**Scene ii**: Donna Elvira appears at the window, singing of her unhappiness (15). While Don Giovanni expresses love for her from the shadows, Leporello acts his master's part.

**Scene iii**: Elvira is convinced and comes down. She leaves with Leporello dressed as the supposed Giovanni. Don Giovanni is now free to serenade Elvira's maid (16).

**Scene iv**: Unexpectedly, Masetto and a crowd of peasants arrive on the scene, brandishing weapons and threatening to kill Giovanni. In his guise as Leporello, Don Giovanni pretends to assist them, only to bewilder the group and send them off in confusion (17).

**Scene v**: Left alone with Masetto, Don Giovanni takes his weapons, then beats him with the flat of his sword. Don Giovanni escapes.

**Scene vi**: Zerlina enters and finds the wounded Masetto. She is soon able to cure him with tenderness (18).

**Scene vii**: The action moves to a dark courtyard near Donna Anna's house. Donna Elvira enters with Leporello still in disguise. He tries to find a way out, leaving her in the dark (19). Donna Anna and Ottavio enter. She sings of her grief and Ottavio tries to comfort her. The sextet (19) continues into the next scene.

**Scene viii**: As Leporello attempts to get away, he is caught by Zerlina and Masetto. All turn on Leporello, but Elvira defends him. Then Leporello reveals his true identity, and they are all astonished. Anna departs with her servants.

**Scene ix**: Each character has his or her quarrel with Leporello, and he attempts to mollify them all (20). Leporello quietly approaches the door, and escapes.

**Scene x**: The others are unable to catch him. Ottavio begs the other characters to comfort Donna Anna (21).

> **Scene x*b***: In the scenes composed for the Vienna production to replace Scene x, Zerlina recaptures Leporello and ties his hands. He begs for mercy (21*b*).
>
> **Scene x*c***: Zerlina leaves Leporello in the custody of a peasant, but he escapes.
>
> **Scene x*d***: Zerlina returns with Donna Elvira, and is amazed to find that Leporello has disappeared. She goes out to inform Don Ottavio.
>
> **Scene x*e***: Left alone, Elvira dwells on her ambivalent feelings for Don Giovanni, and her miserable situation (21c).

**Scene xi**: The scene is a lonely cemetery. Don Giovanni jumps over the wall, extricating himself from another adventure. He is shortly joined by Leporello, furious that his master's plots have put him at such risk. Don Giovanni gleefully recounts how his most recent conquest believed him to be Leporello. The latter is chilled by his master's heartlessness. Suddenly, they hear an unearthly voice prophecying Don Giovanni's end. They discover that they are near the monument to the late Commendatore. Don Giovanni jokes over the inscription, and blasphemously commands Leporello to invite the Commendatore to dinner (22). The terrified servant acquiesces, and both are astonished when the statue nods and replies in the affirmative.

**Scene xii**: The action moves to a room in Donna Anna's house. Ottavio pleads for her hand and accuses her of cruelty. She denies the charge, and begs him to be patient (23).

**Finale**: The Finale takes place in a banqueting-hall in Don Giovanni's *palazzo*. A table has been set for dinner, and Giovanni commands his musicians to play. As he indulges himself, Leporello looks on jealously, and surreptitiously purloins some of the food.

Elvira enters excitedly, and begs Don Giovanni to renounce his way of life. He stoutly refuses. As she leaves, Elvira screams in terror. Don Giovanni sends Leporello to investigate. He too screams in horror, and reports that the statue is at the door. A knock is heard, and the statue of the Commendatore is there.

In a voice of sepulchral grandeur, the Commendatore announces his presence, and asks Don Giovanni to dinner with him. Despite Leporello's warnings, Don Giovanni bravely accepts. He takes the Commendatore's hand, whereupon a deathly chill comes over him. The Commendatore urges Giovanni to repent, but he remains resolute. Flames appear and the earth trembles as ghostly voices describe Don Giovanni's dreadful fate. In an agony of pain and terror, he is engulfed and disappears from the stage.

The room returns to normal as Donna Anna, Elvira, Ottavio, Zerlina, and Masetto come in, accompanied by a minister of justice. Trembling, Leporello describes Don Giovanni's end, and the other characters are astounded. They consider their future plans. Ottavio begs Anna to marry him, but she requests a further year of mourning. Elvira announces that she will retire to a convent, Masetto and Zerlina decide to go home, while Leporello realizes that he must find another, better master. Together they moralize on the fate of all wrong-doers.

### Musical Outline

*Act I*

1. Introduzione (Leporello, Donna Anna, Don Giovanni, and the Commendatore): 'Notte e giorno faticar'.
2. Recitative and Duet (Donna Anna and Don Ottavio): 'Mà qual mai s'offre—Fuggi, crudele, fuggi'.
3. Aria (Donna Elvira with Don Giovanni and Leporello): 'Ah chi mi dice mai'.
4. Aria (Leporello): 'Madamina, il catalogo'.

5. Duet and Chorus (Zerlina and Masetto): 'Giovinette che fate all'amore'.
6. Aria (Masetto): 'Hò capito'.
7. Duettino (Don Giovanni and Zerlina): 'Là ci darem la mano'.
8. Aria (Donna Elvira): 'Ah fuggi il traditor'.
9. Quartet (Donna Anna, Donna Elvira, Don Ottavio, and Don Giovanni): 'Non ti fidar, o misera'.
10. Recitative (Donna Anna and Don Ottavio) and Aria (Donna Anna): 'Don Ottavio, son morta!—Or sai chi l'onore'.
10*b*. Aria (Don Ottavio): 'Dalla sue pace'.
11. Aria (Don Giovanni): 'Fin ch'han dal vino'.
12. Aria (Zerlina): 'Batti, batti, o bel Masetto'.
13. Finale.

*Act II*

14. Duet (Don Giovanni and Leporello): 'Eh via buffone'.
15. Trio (Donna Elvira, Don Giovanni, and Leporello): 'Ah taci, ingiusto core'.
16. Canzonetta (Don Giovanni): 'Deh vieni alla finestra'.
17. Aria (Don Giovanni): 'Metà di voi quà vadano'.
18. Aria (Zerlina): 'Vedrai, carino'.
19. Sextet (Leporello, Donna Elvira, Donna Anna, Don Ottavio, Zerlina, and Masetto): 'Sola, sola in bujo loco'.
20. Aria (Leporello): 'Ah pietà Signori miei'.
21. Aria (Don Ottavio): 'Il mio tesoro intanto'.
21*b*. Duet (Zerlina and Leporello): 'Per queste tue manine'.
21*c*. Recitative and Aria (Donna Elvira): 'In quali eccessi, o Numi—Mi tradì quell'alma ingrata'.
22. Duet (Don Giovanni and Leporello): 'O statua gentilissima'.
23. Recitative and Aria (Donna Anna): 'Crudele!—Ah no—Non mi dir, bell' idol mio'.
24. Finale.

### COSÌ FAN TUTTE OR LA SCUOLA DEGLI AMANTI 1790

**Cast of Characters**

Fiordiligi, a lady from Ferrara living in Naples
Dorabella, her sister
Guglielmo, an officer, engaged to Fiordiligi
Ferrando, an officer, engaged to Dorabella
Don Alfonso, an old bachelor
Despina, chambermaid to the two ladies

**Synopsis**

The opera is set in Naples.

*Act I*

**Scene i**: The curtain opens on a café, where Ferrando and Guglielmo are arguing with Don Alfonso (1). The two officers are hotly defending the fidelity and constancy of their ladies. They would like to fight Don Alfonso over the matter, but he refuses. Alfonso asserts that a faithful woman is like the phoenix (2). He offers to prove to the officers that Fiordiligi and Dorabella are like other women. Ferrando and Guglielmo propose a wager, and speculate about the ways in which they will spend their winnings (3).

**Scene ii**: The action shifts to a garden overlooking the sea. Fiordiligi and Dorabella are admiring the portraits of their lovers, hanging in lockets they wear, and sing of their happiness and love (4). They both hope to be married soon, and impatiently await the arrival of the men.

**Scene iii**: Unexpectedly, Don Alfonso enters, and shows by his demeanour that he has bad news (5). He tells the ladies that the regiment has been summoned to the front, and that Ferrando and Guglielmo must leave at once.

**Scene iv**: The two officers appear in travelling clothes, apparently full of sadness (6). The ladies bemoan the cruelty of fate, and announce that they wish to die. Ferrando and Guglielmo encourage them to be brave, and to look forward to the day when they will be reunited (7). A drum roll is heard, indicating that the time of departure is imminent.

**Scene v**: A march is heard in the distance, and a boat appears. Soldiers and their followers sing of the joys of military life (8). Don Alfonso tells the officers that they must go, and the lovers embrace. Fiordiligi and Dorabella beg the men to write every day and to remain faithful, while Alfonso has difficulty restraining his laughter (9). The chorus is repeated as the officers are borne away across the sea.

**Scene vi**: Fiordiligi, Dorabella, and Don Alfonso watch the boat disappearing into the distance. They pray for calm weather and gentle seas (10). The ladies retire indoors.

**Scene vii**: Left alone, Don Alfonso derides the sentimental indulgence of the lovers. He thinks any man foolish who would gamble money on the faith of a woman.

**Scene viii**: The scene changes to a room inside Fiordiligi and Dorabella's house. Their chambermaid Despina is complaining about her work.

**Scene ix**: She announces to Fiordiligi and Dorabella that their breakfast is prepared, but the two women are far to agitated to eat. Dorabella commands Despina to lock out light and air, and dilates on her misery and distress (11). Despina eventually discovers the cause of the ladies' sorrow and advises them to amuse themselves rather than die of grief. She expounds her own carefree philosophy (12). They all leave the stage.

**Scene x**: Don Alfonso enters, intending to enlist Despina in his plan. Despina comes in and is quickly bribed. Don Alfonso tells her that he has two rich friends who wish to 'console' Fiordiligi and Dorabella.

**Scene xi**: Ferrando and Guglielmo enter in absurd disguise. Don Alfonso introduces them to Despina, who is astonished at their appearance, and fails to recognize them (13). Fiordiligi and Dorabella appear, disturbed by the noise. Alfonso hides as the two officers declare their love. The ladies are outraged, while Ferrando and Guglielmo are secretly delighted by their response. Don Alfonso then re-enters, pretending to have just arrived, and 'recognizes' the officers as close friends. He asks them what they are doing in the house, giving them the opportunity to renew their suit. Fiordiligi rounds on them in indignation, and Despina flees the room. Fiordiligi proclaims her steadfastness, likening herself to a rock standing unmoved amid storm and tempest (14). The two ladies make to leave, but are detained by Guglielmo, who now proudly describes the physical attractions of Ferrando and himself (15). The ladies sweep out.

**Scene xii**: Ferrando and Guglielmo are convulsed with laughter, and Alfonso tries to restrain them (16). The two men are convinced that they will win the wager, but Alfonso insists that the plan should continue. Ferrando now sings of his love (17), then leaves with Guglielmo to await further instructions.

**Scene xiii**: Alfonso and Despina discuss the situation, and Despina is more than ever determined to assist the new lovers.

**Finale**: The scene shifts to the garden. The two sisters sing of the torment and uncertainty that has entered their lives.

Ferrando and Guglielmo rush in, carrying phials of 'arsenic' which they proceed to drain. They are closely pursued by Don Alfonso, who together with the two sisters expresses horror as the two officers collapse on the stage. Fiordiligi and Dorabella call for help, and Despina enters. She suggests that the ladies support the dying men while she and Alfonso go to fetch a doctor. Left alone with Ferrando and Guglielmo, the sisters gingerly approach them, finding their appearances rather more interesting than before. They express their pity, and the men are apprehensive about their greater tractability. Don Alfonso returns with Despina in the guise of a doctor. Despina bewilders them with her mock learning, and they describe the cause of the illness. She decides that the cure is a magnet, parodying the cure made famous by Mesmer. She instructs the ladies to hold the men up, and passes the magnet over them. Ferrando and Guglielmo revive. They pretend to believe that they are in heaven, and that Fiordiligi and Dorabella are angels. The ladies find their resistance severely tried. Then Ferrando and Guglielmo demand a kiss. This is too much for the sisters, whose indignation is revived. The Act ends with the ladies protesting furiously, while the others wonder whether their fire will turn to passion in due course.

## Act II

**Scene i**: The curtain opens on a room in the sisters' house. Despina is encouraging the two ladies to flirt with their new admirers. She describes the wiles that a woman needs to develop in order to succeed with men (19).

**Scene ii**: Despina leaves the sisters wondering what to do. They soon persuade each other that it would cause no harm to be courted by their strange suitors. They decide which man each should have (20). Dorabella prefers the dark one (Guglielmo) while Fiordiligi takes the blond (Ferrando).

**Scene iii**: Don Alfonso enters and tells the ladies that an entertainment has been arranged for them in the garden.

**Scene iv**: The action shifts to the garden by the seashore. A boat decorated with flowers is there, together with a band of musicians. Ferrando and Guglielmo serenade Fiordiligi and Dorabella (21).

The two officers and the ladies are embarrassed and unable to speak. Don Alfonso and Despina encourage them, and finally act for them. Don Alfonso apologizes for the men's earlier offences, and Despina forgives them on behalf of the sisters (22). Don Alfonso and Despina leave.

**Scene v**: The couples talk of commonplaces until Ferrando and Fiordiligi depart for a walk. After they have left, Guglielmo histrionically declares his love for Dorabella. After a show of resistance, Dorabella concedes, and they exchange lockets. The two sing of their love (23) before leaving the stage arm-in-arm.

**Scene vi**: Fiordiligi enters in consternation, pursued by Ferrando. She angrily rejects his advances, but he responds by singing of his feelings (24).

**Scene vii**: Ferrando leaves the stage to a troubled Fiordiligi. She reflects on her dilemma, and feels guilty to have strayed even as far as she has. She prays that her lover will pity and forgive her (25), before going off the stage.

**Scene viii**: Ferrando and Guglielmo come in. Ferrando believes that they have won the wager until Guglielmo breaks the news of Dorabella's inconstancy. He shows Ferrando the locket given him by Dorabella—it contains Ferrando's own portrait. Ferrando is outraged and vows vengeance. Guglielmo responds by addressing an aria to women in general, chiding them for convincing men of their fidelity (26). He leaves.

**Scene ix**: Left alone, Ferrando renews his lamentations. He is torn between resentment of Dorabella's behaviour and continued love for her (27).

Don Alfonso and Guglielmo overhear some of Ferrando's outburst. Guglielmo is complacently unsurprised that Dorabella has fallen while Fiordiligi remains constant; after all, who would lightly give up a man such as himself? Alfonso persuades them to continue with the charade.

**Scene x**: The scene moves to a room in the sisters' house. Despina and Dorabella are discussing the latter's change of heart. Fiordiligi comes in and admits her ambivalence. Dorabella encourages her to give in, and sings of the uncertainty of love (28). Dorabella and Despina leave.

**Scene xi**: Fiordiligi realizes that her sister and maid are conspiring against her, and stiffens her resolve. Guglielmo, Don Alfonso, and Ferrando appear at the door, unseen by Fiordiligi. Guglielmo is full of admiration for his lover. Fiordiligi decides to dress in one of the officers' uniforms and follow Guglielmo to the front. She instructs Despina to find the clothes.

**Scene xii**: As Fiordiligi prepares herself for departure, she joyfully anticipates her reunion with Guglielmo. But she is interrupted by the disguised Ferrando, who is more than ever determined to seduce her (29). Fiordiligi feels that she has been betrayed. Ferrando ardently promises true love, and she finally succumbs. As the two sing of their bliss, Don Alfonso restrains Guglielmo only with difficulty. Fiordiligi and Ferrando go off.

**Scene xiii**: Guglielmo gives way to fury and bitterness. Ferrando returns in triumph. Despina now enters, joyfully announcing that the ladies have agreed to marry their foreign suitors. She is proud of her part in the business. Don Alfonso reminds the officers that despite their humiliation, they still love the sisters. Together with Ferrando and Guglielmo, he excuses the ladies, declaring that all women behave thus (30).

**Finale**: The Finale opens on a festively decorated Hall. Despina is busy making preparations for the wedding. Don Alfonso enters and approves the arrangements.

The two couples enter in stately fashion, accompanied by a chorus of admiration. They proclaim themselves supremely happy, and toast each other. Only Guglielmo refuses to take part, muttering darkly under his breath.

Don Alfonso announces that the notary has arrived. Despina enters in disguise and reels off the contracts drawn up for Fiordiligi and Sempronio (Ferrando), and for Dorabella and Tizio (Guglielmo). The men are described as Albanian nobles. Just as the sisters sign the contracts, a military band is heard outside, and the chorus reiterate their Act I celebration of military life. Alfonso goes off to investigate, and returns thunderstruck to tell the party that Ferrando and Guglielmo have come back. In the confusion, the two men disappear, while Despina hides in a room. The sisters tremble in fear. Ferrando and Guglielmo enter, no longer in disguise, to be reunited with their faithful lovers. They are mystified by the silence of their ladies. Guglielmo enters the side room, only to discover the notary. However, Despina reveals herself, adding to the confusion of the ladies.

Don Alfonso contrives to drop the marriage contract, and it is picked up by Ferrando and Guglielmo. The enraged officers turn on the ladies, but they point to Don Alfonso. He directs them to the room in which the Albanians are supposedly hidden, and the women fear bloodshed as Ferrando and Guglielmo rush off. They, however, come back with the remnants of their disguises. The whole plot is now revealed. and the sisters are devastated. Even Despina is ashamed, realizing the way in which she has been duped into promoting the subterfuge. Fiordiligi and Dorabella round on Don Alfonso. He declares that it was all for the best, and that the lovers should embrace with true faith, now that they have all been undeceived. The officers forgive the sisters, and the original partnerships are restored. The opera ends with all the characters proclaiming the virtues of being guided by reason through the trials of life.

## Musical Outline

*Act I*

1. Trio (Ferrando, Guglielmo, and Don Alfonso): 'La mia Dorabella capace non è'.
2. Trio (Ferrando, Guglielmo, and Don Alfonso): È la fede delle femmine'.
3. Trio (Ferrando, Guglielmo, and Don Alfonso): 'Una bella serenata'.
4. Duet (Fiordiligi and Dorabella): 'Ah guarda sorella'.
5. Aria (Don Alfonso): 'Vorrei dir'.
6. Quintet (Fiordiligi, Dorabella, Ferrando, Guglielmo, and Don Alfonso): 'Sento, o Dio, che questo piede'.
7. Duettino (Ferrando and Guglielmo): 'Al fato dan legge quegli occhi'.

8. Chorus: 'Bella vita militar'.
9. Quintet (Fiordiligi, Dorabella, Ferrando, Guglielmo, and Don Alfonso): 'Di scrivermi ogni giorni'.
10. Trio (Fiordiligi, Dorabella, and Don Alfonso): 'Soave sia il vento'.
11. Recitative and Aria (Dorabella): 'Ah scostati—Smanie implacabili'.
12. Aria (Despina): 'In uomini, in soldati'.
13. Sextet: 'Alla bella Despinetta'.
14. Aria (Fiordiligi): 'Come scoglio immoto resta'.
15. Aria (Guglielmo): 'Non siate ritrosi'.
16. Trio (Ferrando, Guglielmo, and Don Alfonso): 'E voi ridete'.
17. Aria (Ferrando): 'Un'aura amorosa'.
18. Finale.

*Act II*

19. Aria (Despina): 'Una donna a quindici anni'.
20. Duet (Fiordiligi and Dorabella): 'Prenderò quel brunettino'.
21. Duet with Chorus (Ferrando and Guglielmo): 'Secondate aurette amiche'.
22. Quartet (Despina, Don Alfonso, Ferrando, and Guglielmo): 'La mano a me date'.
23. Duet (Dorabella and Guglielmo): 'Il core vi dono, bell'idolo mio'.
24. Aria (Ferrando): 'Ah lo veggio quell'anima bella'.
25. Recitative and Rondo (Fiordiligi): 'Ei parte . . . senti . . . ah no—Per pietà, ben mio'.
26. Aria (Guglielmo): 'Donne mie la fate a tanti'.
27. Recitative and Cavatina (Ferrando): 'In qual fiero contrasto . . . Tradito, schernito dal perfido cor'.
28. Aria (Dorabella): È amore un ladroncello'.
29. Duet (Fiordiligi and Ferrando): 'Fra gli amplessi'.
30. Andante (Don Alfonso, Ferrando, and Guglielmo): 'Tutti accusan le donne'.
31. Finale.

# Bibliography

Abert, A. A., 'Italian Opera', in E. Wellesz and F. Sternfeld (eds.), *The New Oxford History of Music, vii*, The Age of Enlightenment 1745–1790 (London, 1973).

Abert, H., *Mozart's Don Giovanni*, trans. P. Gellhorn (London, 1976).

Allanbrook, W. J., 'Pro Marcellina: The shape of "Figaro", Act IV', *Music and Letters*, 63 (1982), 69–84.

—— *Rhythmic Gesture in Mozart* (Chicago, 1983).

Anderson, E., *The Letters of Mozart and his Family*, 2nd edn. prepared by A. Hyatt King and M. Carolan (London, 1966).

Angermüller, R., *'Auf Ehre und Credit': Die Finanzen des W. A. Mozart* (Munich, 1983).

Ariosto, L., *Orlando Furioso*, trans. Sir John Harington (1591); Facs. edn. (Amsterdam, 1970).

Austen, J., *The Story of Don Juan: A Study of the Legend and the Hero* (London, 1939).

Badura-Skoda, E., 'The Influence of the Viennese Popular Comedy on Haydn and Mozart', *Proceedings of the Royal Musical Association*, 100 (1973–4), 185–99.

Bär, C., *Mozart: Krankheit, Tod, Begräbnis* (Kassel, 1966).

—— 'Er war . . . kein guter Wirth', *Acta Mozartiana*, 25 (1978), 30–53.

Batley, E. M., *A Preface to The Magic Flute* (London, 1969).

Baur-Heinhold, M., *Baroque Theatres* (London, 1967).

Beales, D., *Joseph II i, In the Shadow of Maria Theresa, 1740–1780* (Cambridge, 1987).

Beaumarchais, P., *The Marriage of Figaro*, trans. V. Luciani (Woodbury, NY, 1974)

Biba, O., 'Grundzüge des Konzertwesens in Wien zu Mozarts Zeit', *Mozart-Jahrbuch 1978–9*, 132–43.

Bitter, C., *Wandlungen in den Inszenierungsformen des Don Giovanni von 1787 bis 1928* (Regensburg, 1961).

Blom, E., *Mozart* (London, 1974).

Blume, F., 'Mozart's Style and Influence', in *The Mozart Companion*, ed. by H. C. Robbins Landon and D. Mitchell (London, 1965).

Boccaccio, G., *The Decameron*, trans. J. M. Rigg (London, 1963).

Branscombe, P., '*Die Zauberflöte*: Some Textual and Interpretative Problems', *Proceedings of the Royal Musical Association*, 92 (1965–6), 45–63.

Brion, M., *Daily Life in the Vienna of Mozart and Schubert*, trans. J. Stewart (London, 1961).

Brophy, B., *Mozart the Dramatist* (London, 1964).

—— 'Da Ponte and Mozart', *The Musical Times*, 122 (1981), 454–6.

Brown, J., *Letters upon the Poetry and Music of Italian Opera* (Edinburgh, 1789).

Bruford, W. H., *Theatre, Drama and Audience in Goethe's Germany* (London, 1950).

—— *Germany in the Eighteenth Century* (Cambridge, 1959).

Burney, C., *The Present State of Music in France and Italy*, 2nd edn. (London, 1773).

—— *A General History of Music*, ii (London, reprinted 1935).

Burney, F., *The Diary of Fanny Burney*, ed. L. Gibbs (London, 1940).

Bushee, A. H., *Three Centuries of Tirso De Molina* (Philadelphia, 1939).

Carse, A., *The Orchestra in the Eighteenth Century* (New York, 1969).

Carter, T., *W.A. Mozart: Le nozze di Figaro* (Cambridge, 1987).

Casanova, G., *The History of my Life*, v, trans. W. R. Trask (London, 1967).

Chailley, J., *The Magic Flute, Masonic Opera*, trans. H. Weinstock (London, 1972).

Chantavoine, J., *Mozart dans Mozart* (Paris, 1948).

Choderlos de Laclos, *Les Liaisons dangereuses*, trans. R. Aldington (London, 1946).

Citron, M. J., 'Corona Schröter: Singer, Composer, Actress', *Music and Letters*, 61 (1980), 15–27.

Cooke, D., *The Language of Music* (Oxford, 1959).

Cox, C., *The Real Figaro* (London, 1962).

Craft, R., *Current Convictions* (London, 1978).

Da Ponte, L., *Memoirs*, trans. E. Abbott (New York, 1967).

Davies, P., 'Mozart's Illnesses and Death', *Journal of the Royal Society of Medicine*, 76 (1983), 776–85.

—— 'Mozart's Illnesses and Death, 2: The Last Year and the Fatal Illness', *The Musical Times*, 125 (1984), 554–60.

Dent, E. J., *Mozart's Operas* (London, 1960).

—— *The Rise of Romantic Opera*, ed. W. Dean (London, 1976).

Deutsch, O. E., *Mozart, A Documentary Biography*, trans. E. Blom, P. Branscombe, and J. Noble (London, 1966).

Dickson, P. G. M., *Finance and Government under Maria Theresia 1740–1780*, ii (Oxford, 1987).

Dittersdorf, K, von, *Autobiography*, trans. A. D. Coleridge (London, 1896).

Eibl, J., 'Süssmayr and Constanze', *Mozart-Jahrbuch 1976–7*, 277–80.

Einstein, A., *Mozart: His Character—his Work*, trans. A. Mendel and N. Broder (London, 1971).

Elias, N., *The Civilising Process*, trans. E. Jephcott (Oxford, 1978).

Fischer, L., 'Mozarts "Musikalische Regie": Eine musicdramaturgische Analyse', in *Così fan tutte: Beiträge zur Wirkungsgeschichte von Mozarts Oper* ed. S. Vill (Bayreuth, 1978).

Fiske, R., *English Theatre Music in the Eighteenth Century* (London, 1973).

Ghislanzoni, A., *Giovanni Paisiello* (Rome, 1969).

Goethe, J. W. von, *Die Leiden des jungen Werthers*, trans. V. Lange as *The Sorrows of Young Werther* (New York, 1949).

—— *Die Wahlverwandtschaften*, trans. R. J. Hollingdale as *Elective Affinities* (London, 1971).

—— *Goethe: Conversations and Encounters* ed. and trans. by D. Luke and R. Pick (London, 1966).

Goldoni, C., *Memoirs*, trans. J. Black (London, 1938).

Gombrich, E. H., '*Così fan tutte* (Procris included)', *Journal of the Warburg and Courtauld Institutes*, 17 (1954), 260–87.

Gozzi, C., *Memorie Inutile* (Venice, 1797).

—— *Useless Memoirs*, trans. J. A. Symonds (London, 1962).

Hamann, H. W., 'Mozarts Schulerkreis', *Mozart-Jahrbuch 1962–3*, 115–39.

Hanslick, E., *Geschichte des Conzertwesens in Wien* (Vienna, 1869).

Heartz, D., 'The Creation of the *Buffo Finale* in Italian Opera', *Proceedings of the Royal Musical Association*, 104 (1977–8), 67–78.

—— 'Mozart and his Italian Contemporaries: *La Clemenza di Tito*', *Mozart-Jahrbuch 1978–9*, 275–93.

—— 'Nicholas Jadot and the Building of the Burgtheater' *Musical Quarterly*, 48 (1982), 1–31.

—— 'La Clemenza di Sarastro', *The Musical Times*, 124 (1983), 152–7.

—— 'Setting the Stage for Figaro', *The Musical Times*, 127 (1986), 256–60.

—— 'Constructing *Le nozze di Figaro*', *Journal of the Royal Musical Association*, 112 (1987), 77–98.

Hildesheimer, W., *Mozart*, trans. M. Faber (London, 1983).

Hodges, S., *Lorenzo Da Ponte* (London, 1985).

Hogan, C. B., *The London Stage 1776–1800: A Critical Introduction* (Carbondale, Ill. 1968).

Hogarth, G., *Memoirs of the Opera* (London, 1851).

Horanyi, M., *The Magnificence of Eszterháza*, trans. A. Deák (London, 1962).

Höslinger, C., 'Mozarts Opern in den Sonnleithner Regesten', *Mozart-Jahrbuch 1978–9*, 149–53.

Howitt, W., *The Rural and Domestic Life of Germany* (London, 1842).

Hunter, M., 'The Fusion and Juxtaposition of Genres in *Opera Buffa* 1770–1800: Anelli and Piccinni's *Griselda*', *Music and Letters*, 67 (1986), 363–80.

Jahn, O., *W. A. Mozart*, iv (Leipzig, 1859).

—— *The Life of Mozart*, trans. P. Townsend (London, 1882).

Kelly, M., *Reminiscences*, ed. R. Fiske (London, 1975).

Kerman, J., *Opera as Drama* (New York, 1956).

King, A. H., *Mozart in Retrospect* (London, 1955).

—— *A Mozart Legacy* (London, 1984).

Kingston Ward, M., 'Mozart's Clarinettist', *Monthly Musical Record*, 85 (1955), 8–14.

Kivy, P., *The Corded Shell* (Princeton, 1981).

Köchel, L. von, *Chronologisch-thematisches Verzeichnis sämtlichter Tonwerke Wolfgang Amadé Mozarts*, 6th edn. by F. Giegling, A. Weinmann, and G. Sievers (Wiesbaden, 1964).

Kraemer, U., 'Wer hat Mozart verhungern Lassen?', *Musica*, 30 (1976), 203–11.

Kramer, K., 'Da Ponte's *Così fan tutte*', *Nachrichten der Akademie des Wissenschaften in Göttingen*, Phil.-Hist. Klasse (1973).

Kristek, I., *Mozart's Don Giovanni in Prague* (Prague, 1987).

Kritsch, C. and Zeman, H., 'Das Rätsel eines genialen Opernentwurfs: Da Pontes Libretto zu Così fan tutti' und das literarische Umfeld des 18. Jahrhunderts', in *Die Österreichische Literatur: Ihr Profil an der Wende vom 18. zum 19. Jahrhundert (1750–1830)*, ed. H. Zeman, i (Graz, 1979).

Kunze, S., *Don Giovanni vor Mozart* (Munich, 1972).

Laslett, P., *Family Life and Illicit Love in Earlier Generations* (Cambridge, 1977).

Lavin, I., 'Cephalus and Procris: Transformations of an Ovidian Myth', *Journal of the Warburg and Courtauld Institutes*, 17 (1954), 260–87.

Lawrence, W. W., *Shakespeare's Problem Comedies* (London, 1969).

Leeson, D. and Whitwell, D., 'Mozart's Thematic Catalogue', *The Musical Times*, 114 (1973), 781–3.

Levarie, S., *Mozart's Le Nozze di Figaro: A Critical Analysis* (Chicago, 1952).

Lewes, G. H., *The Life of Goethe* (London, 1864).

Livermore, A., 'Così fan tutte: A Well-kept Secret', *Music and Letters*, 46 (1965), 316–21.

Macartney, C. A., *The Habsburg Empire 1790–1918* (London, 1968).

McGairl, P., 'The Vauxhall Jubilee, 1786', *The Musical Times*, 127 (1986), 611–5.

McLaren, A., *Birth Control in Nineteenth-Century England* (London, 1978).

Macpherson, J., *The Baths and Wells of Europe* (London, 1869).

Mandel, O., *The Theatre of Don Juan: A Collection of Plays and Views 1630–1963* (Lincoln, Nebr. 1963).

Mann, T., *Der Tod in Venedig*, trans. by H. T. Lowe-Porter as *Death in Venice* (London, 1955).

—— *Lotte in Weimar*, trans. H. T. Lowe-Porter (London, 1968).

Mann, W., *The Operas of Mozart* (London, 1977).

Michtner, O., *Das alte Burgtheater als Opernbühne von der Einführung des deutschen Singspiele (1778) bis zum Tod Kaiser Leopold II (1792)*. Theatergeschichte Österreichs (Vienna, 1970).

Moore, J., *A View of Society and Manners in France, Switzerland and Germany* (London, 1779).

Morehen, J., 'Masonic Instrumental Music of the Eighteenth Century: A Survey', *The Music Review*, 42 (1981), 215–24.

Morrow, M. S., 'Mozart and Viennese Concert Life', *The Musical Times*, 126 (1985), 453–4.

Mount Edgcumbe, *Musical Reminiscences* (London, 1827).

Nalbach, D., *The King's Theatre 1704–1867* (London, 1972).

Niemetschek, F. X., *The Life of Mozart*, trans. H. Mautner (London, 1956).

Noske, F., *The Signifier and the Signified* (The Hague, 1977).

*Nouveau Guide par Vienne* (Vienna, 1792).

Novello, V. and M., *A Mozart Pilgrimage*, ed. N. Medici, and R. Hughes (London, 1975).

Parke, W., *Musical Memoirs* (London, 1830).

Payer von Thurn, R., *Joseph II als Theaterdirektor* (Vienna, 1920).

Pestelli, G., *The Age of Mozart and Beethoven*, trans. E. Cross (Cambridge, 1984).

Piozzi, H. L., *Observations and Reflections made in the Course of a Journey through France, Italy and Germany* (London, 1789).

Pirrotta, N., 'The Traditions of Don Juan Plays and Comic Operas', *Proceedings of the Royal Musical Association*, 107 (1980–81), 60–70.

Plantinga, L., *Muzio Clementi: His Life and Music* (London, 1977).

Pollock, L., *Forgotten Children: Parent-Child Relations from 1500-1800* (Cambridge, 1983).

Restif de la Bretonne, *Monsieur Nicolas*, trans. and ed. R. Baldick (London, 1966).

Riesbeck, J. C., *Travels through Germany*, trans. Revd Mr Maty (London, 1787).

Robbins Landon, H. C., *Haydn Chronicle and Works*, ii (London, 1978).

—— *Mozart and the Masons* (London, 1982).

—— *Mozart's Last Year* (London, 1988).

Robinson, M. F., *Opera before Mozart* (London, 1978).

Rosen, C., *The Classical Style* (London, 1971).

—— *Sonata Forms* (New York, 1980).

Rusack, H. H., *Gozzi in Germany* (New York, 1930).

Rushton, J., *W. A. Mozart: Don Giovanni* (Cambridge, 1981).

Russell, C., 'The first Don Giovanni opera: *La privatà castigata* by Eustachio Bambini', *Mozart-Jahrbuch 1980-3*, 385–92.

Russo, J. L., *Lorenzo Da Ponte* (New York, 1922).

Ryle, G., *The Concept of Mind* (London, 1963).

Sadie, S., *The New Grove Mozart* (London, 1982).

Sagarra, E., *A Social History of Germany* (London, 1977).

Saint-Foix, G. de, *W. A. Mozart: Sa vie musicale et son œuvre*, v (Paris, 1946).

Salter, L., 'Footnotes to a Satire: Salieri's *Prima la musica, poi le parole*', *The Musical Times*, 126 (1985), 21–4.

Schmitdbauer, P., 'The Changing Household: Austrian Household Structure from the Seventeenth to the early Twentieth Century', in *Family Forms in Historic Europe*, ed. R. Wall (Cambridge, 1983).

Schorske, C. *Fin-de-siècle Vienna: Politics and Culture* (New York, 1980).

Schrade, L., *W. A. Mozart* (Bern, 1964).

Sennett, R., *The Fall of Public Man* (Cambridge, 1977).

Shamgar, B., 'On Locating the Retransition in Classic Sonata Form', *Music Review*, 42 (1981), 130–43.

Singer, I., *Mozart and Beethoven: The Concept of Love in their Operas* (Baltimore, 1977).

Smith, P. J., *The Tenth Muse* (London, 1971).

Smith, W. C., *The Italian Opera and Contemporary Ballet in London, 1789-1820* (London, 1955).

Solomon, M., *Beethoven* (London, 1978).

Steptoe, A., 'The Sources of *Così fan tutte*: A Reappraisal', *Music and Letters*, 62 (1981), 281–94.

—— 'Mozart, Joseph II and Social Sensitivity', *The Music Review*, 43 (1982), 109–20.

—— 'Mozart and Poverty: A Re-Examination of the Evidence', *The Musical Times*, 125 (1984), 196–201.

—— 'Mozart, Mesmer and *Così fan tutte*', *Music and Letters*, 67 (1986), 248–55.

Stevens, D., *Musicology* (London, 1980).

Stone, L., *The Family, Sex and Marriage in England 1500–1800* (London, 1977).

Swinburne, H., *The Courts of Europe at the Close of the Last Century* (London, 1841).

Tannahill, R. (ed.), *Paris in the Revolution* (London, 1966).

Thomson, K., *The Masonic Thread in Mozart* (London, 1977).

Tyson, A., 'A New Light on Mozart's Prussian Quartets', *The Musical Times*, 116 (1975), 126–30.

—— '*La clemenza di Tito* and its chronology', *The Musical Times*, 116 (1975), 221–7.

—— 'The Mozart Fragments in the Mozarteum, Salzburg: A Preliminary Study of their Chronology and Significance', *Journal of the American Musicological Association*, 34 (1981), 471–510.

—— 'Notes on the Composition of *Così fan tutte*', *Journal of the American Musicological Association*, 37 (1984), 356–401.

—— 'Some problems in the text of *Le nozze di Figaro*: did Mozart have a hand in them?' *Journal of the Royal Musical Association*, 112 (1987), 99–131.

Volek, T. and Macek, J., 'Beethoven's Rehearsals at the Lobkowitz's', *The Musical Times*, 127 (1986), 75–80.

Wallace, Lady G.M., *Letters of Distinguished Musicians* (London, 1867).

Wangermann, E., *From Joseph II to the Jacobin Trials* (London, 1959).

—— *The Austrian Achievement 1700–1800* (London, 1973).

Weston, P., *Clarinet Virtuosi of the Past* (London, 1971).

Williams, B., 'Don Giovanni as an Idea', in *W. A. Mozart: Don Giovanni* ed. J. Rushton (Cambridge, 1981).

Wlassak, E., *Chronik des K. K. Hof-Burgtheaters* (Vienna, 1876).

Wraxall, N., *Memoirs of the Courts of Berlin, Warsaw and Vienna* (Dublin, 1799).

Zaguri, P., 'Lettere inedite del patrizio Pietro Zaguri a Giacomo Casanova', ed. P. Molmenti *Atti del Reale Istituto Veneto di Scienze, Lettere ed Arti*, 70 (1910–11).

Zinzendorf, L and K., *Ihr Selbstbiographien* (Vienna, 1879).

Zobel, K. and Warner, F. E., 'The Old Burgtheater: A Structural History', *Theatre Studies*, 19 (1972–3), 19–53.

# Index of Mozart's Works

*The bold numbers in the left hand columns refer to Köchel numbers*

**87** *Mitridate, rè di Ponto* 155
**111** *Ascanio in Alba* 141
**175** Piano concerto in D 56, 143
**196** *La finta giardiniera* 5, 209
**219** Violin concerto in A 143
**261** Violin concerto movement 143
**299b** *Les petits riens* 135
**310** Piano sonata in A minor 192
**317** Mass in C (Coronation) 209, 225
**361** Serenade in B♭ 158
**365** Concerto for two pianos 216–7
**366** *Idomeneo* 81, 140
**382** Concerto rondo for piano 143
**384** *Die Entführung aus dem Serail* 40, 59, 68–9, 85, 87, 140, 144, 158, 164–5, 192
**385** Symphony in D (Haffner) 56
**406** String quintet in C minor 72
**413** Piano concerto in F 52
**414** Piano concerto in A 52
**415** Piano concerto in C 52, 56
**416** Soprano aria 56
**418** Soprano aria 135, 143, 149
**419** Soprano aria 135, 143, 149
**420** Tenor aria 135, 143
**422** *L'oca del Cairo* 1
**427** Mass in C minor 84
**430** *Lo sposo deluso* 1, 222
**446** Music to a pantomime 95
**466** Piano concerto in D minor 192, 198
**467** Piano concerto in C 198
**469** *Davidde Penitente* 56, 85
**471** *Die Maurerfreude* 20
**479** Vocal quartet 143
**480** Vocal trio 143
**482** Piano concerto in E♭ 2
**486** *Der Schauspieldirektor* 2, 59, 145, 222
**488** Piano concerto in A 2, 198
**491** Piano concerto in C minor 2, 59, 198
**492** *Le nozze di Figaro*
    composition 1–2
    harmonic structure 175, 190–1
    libretto 109–14
    orchestration 156, 176
    performances 3, 5, 47–8, 59, 103
    plot 247–51
    reception 3, 6, 183–4, 243
        'Aprite un pò que gl' occhi' 112, 191

        'Cosa sento! Tosto andate' 165–71
        'Deh vieni non tardar' 5
        Finale (Act 2) 110, 112, 174–83
        Finale (Act 4) 110
        'In quegli anni, in cui val poco' 172
        'La vendetta' 186
        'Non più andrai' 2
        'Non sò più cosa son' 211
        'Porgi amor qualche ristoro' 111, 157, 172
        'Riconosci in questo amplesso' 165
        'Vedrò mentr'io sospiro' 172
        'Venite, inginocchiatevi' 103, 172
        'Voi che sapete' 108
**503** Piano concerto in C 210
**505** Scena and rondo for soprano 147
**515** String quintet in C 72, 198
**516** String quintet in G minor 72, 192, 198, 210
**527** *Don Giovanni*
    characterisation 200–4
    composition 3–4
    libretto 117–20
    musical reminiscence 188–9
    orchestration 156–7, 211
    performances 5, 48, 59–60, 151
    plot 253–6
    precedents 115–6
    reception 4, 6, 155–7, 243
    revision for Vienna 4–5, 199–200
    tonal structure 187, 191–8, 204
        'Ah fuggi il traditor' 201
        'Ah taci, ingiusto core' 196, 203
        'Batti, batti, o bel Masetto 196
        'Dalla sua pace' 4
        Finale (Act 1) 26
        Finale (Act 2) 200, 203–6
        'Fuggi, crudele, fuggi' 187–8, 195
        Il mio tesoro' 4
        'In quali eccessi. . .Mi tradì' 5, 194
        *Introduzione* 186–9, 196, 202–3
        'Là ci darem la mano' 196, 202
        'Madamina, il catalogo' 108, 186, 201

'Metà di voi quà vadano' 194
'Non mi dir, bell' idol mio' 157
'Non ti fidar, o misera' 188–9,
196–7, 200
'Or sai chi l'onore' 156, 196
'Per queste tue manine' 5, 152
'Sola, sola in bujo loco' 187, 195
539 Song with orchestra 28
542 Piano trio in Eb 73
543 Symphony in Eb 73
550 Symphony in G minor 198
551 Symphony in C 189, 198, 210
553–562 Canons 73
566 Orchestration of *Acis and Galatea* 60
575 String quartet in D 59, 209–10
576 Piano sonata in D 209–10
577 Soprano aria 5, 103, 143, 222
579 Soprano aria 5, 103, 143
581 Clarinet quintet 157
582 Soprano aria 46, 143
583 Soprano aria 46, 143, 222
588 *Così fan tutte*
attitude to women 88, 90, 129, 131
borrowings 209–10
commission 41, 59, 244
composition 5–6
libretto 128–39
musical reminiscence 213–5
orchestration 156–8, 210–2
parody 221–30
performances 6, 47–8, 153
plot 257–61

reception 7, 243–4
sources 86–8, 121–7
total organisation 212, 232–7, 242
'Ah guarda sorella' 216, 234
'Ah lo veggio quell' anima bella'
211
'Come scoglio immoto resta'
209–10, 213, 221, 223–7
'Di scrivermi ogni giorni' 230–1
'Donne mie la fate a tanti' 235
Finale (Act 1) 216–7
Finale (Act 2) 210, 213, 225
'Fra gli amplessi' 213, 236–42
'Il core vi dono' 235
'Per pietà, ben mio' 221, 231,
235
'Prenderò quel brunettino' 217
'Sento, o Dio, che questo piede'
211, 213, 217–21, 229
'Smanie implacabili' 215–6,
.225–9
'Soave sia il vento' 230–2
'Tradito, schernito' 211, 236
'Una bella serenata' 219, 237
'Un'aura amorosa' 213, 232
589 String quartet in Bb 209
595 Piano concerto in Bb 62, 73
618 Motet 231
620 *Die Zauberflöte* 60, 62, 93, 139, 207,
210, 235, 240–1
621 *La clemenza di Tito* 60, 69, 189, 207
622 Clarinet concerto 157, 208
626 Requiem 59

# General Index

Adamberger, Valentin 135, 144
Albertarelli, Francesco 4
*All's Well that Ends Well* (Shakespeare) 67–8
Angermüller, Rudolf 64
Arco, Count Karl 54
Attwood, Thomas 55
Austrian Empire
    censorship 29, 31
    economics 15, 19, 28
    foreign policy 27–8
    reaction to Joseph II's reforms 28–9
    social structure 15–7, 81–2, 89–90

Bach, Johann Sebastian 210
Baden 24, 87–8
Banti, Birgitta 103, 148
Bär, Carl 66
Barisani, Sigmund 74
Bassi, Luigi 4, 148, 202
Beaumarchais, Pierre Augustin Caron de 112
Beethoven, Ludwig van 34
Benucci, Francesco 2–6, 43, 65, 151–3, 235–6
Berlin 40–1, 155–6
Bertati, Giovanni 3, 108, 116–8
Bondini, Caterina 4, 151
Bondini, Pasquale 3–4
Brown, John 50–1
Burgtheater
    company 103, 145–54
    management 43–4, 159
    repertoire 45–8
    structure 42, 146
Burney, Charles 101, 147, 158
Burney, Fanny 14, 21
Bussani, Dorotea 3, 6, 149–50, 233–4
Bussani, Francesco 3–4, 6, 150, 153

Calvesi, Vincenzio, 6, 154
Cannabich, Christian 60
Carse, Adam 156, 211
Casanova, Giacomo 102, 105, 207
Casti, Giambattista 47, 136
Cavalieri, Caterina 4, 144–5
Charlotte, Queen 21
Cimarosa, Domenico 47, 49, 150
Clementi, Muzio 36, 55–6
Cobenzl, Count Johann Philipp 80, 95
Colloredo, Count Hieronymus, Prince-
    Archbishop of Salzburg 3, 52–3, 79
Coltellini, Celesta 43–4
Concert profits 40, 58

Craft, Robert 8
*Cymbeline* (Shakespeare) 124–5

Da Ponte, Lorenzo
    Adriana Ferrarese 100–4
    Burgtheater 44, 100, 103–4, 138
    early life 98–100
    libretti 107, 122, 183–5
    literary influences 99
    opinion of libretti 106–7, 173
*Decameron* (Boccaccio) 123–4
Dent, Edward 8, 143
*Die Leiden des jungen Werthers* (Goethe) 53,
    130
Dittersdorf, Karl Ditters von 33, 35, 37,
    39–40, 48–9, 60, 68–9
*Doktor und Apotheker* (Dittersdorf) 49
Dresden 35–6, 49, 56
Dušek, Josepha 36, 58–9, 61

Education 19, 77, 83
Einstein, Alfred 63, 163, 232
Enlightenment 18–9, 79, 82–6, 243
Eszterháza 15, 25, 60

Ferrarese, Adriana (La Ferrarese) 5–6, 101–5,
    122, 138, 221–2
*Fidelio* (Beethoven) 232
Fischer, Ludwig 144
Fiske, Roger 153
Frederick William, King 40, 59, 208–9
Freemasonry 19–20, 31, 82–4
French revolution 29–30

Gassmann, Florian 223
George III, King 21
Gluck, Christoph Willibald von 60, 229
Goethe, Johann Wolfgang von 49, 53, 116,
    130
Goldoni, Carlo 105–6, 115–7, 130–1, 134
Gombrich, Sir Ernst 125, 138
Gozzi, Carlo 98–9, 107, 122, 136–7, 150, 159
Grimm, Baron Friedrich Melchior 62, 184
Guglielmi, Pietro 47, 49

*Hamlet* (Shakespeare) 9, 245
Handel, George Frederick 60, 210
Hasse, Johann Adolph 37
Haydn, Joseph 25, 34, 69, 97, 142–3
Herder, Johann Gottfried 30

Hildesheimer, Wolfgang 86
Hogarth, George 7

*Il barbiere di Siviglia* (Paisiello) 47, 142, 199
*Il burbero di buon cuore* (Martín y Soler) 46, 107, 222
*Il curioso indiscreto* (Anfossi) 135, 159
*Il matrimonio segreto* (Cimarosa) 150
*Il rè Teodoro* (Paisiello) 37, 41, 47–8, 108, 142

Jacquin, Gottfried van 3, 95, 117
*Job* (Dittersdorf) 40
Johnson, Samuel 14
Jomelli, Niccolò 37
Joseph II, Emperor
    *Così fan tutte* 121
    death 18, 30
    informality 20–2, 86
    *Le nozze di Figaro* 2, 113, 184
    opera 42–4, 51, 85, 102, 152, 154
    reforms 18–20
    reversal of policy 27–32

Kaunitz, Prince Anton Wenzel 25, 82
Kelly, Michael 2–3, 21–3, 25, 43, 45, 65, 94, 141, 154
Kerman, Joseph 129, 162

*La cifra* (Salieri) 5, 103, 107
*La fedeltà premiata* (Haydn) 229
*La grotta di Trofonio* (Salieri) 47–8, 135–6
*L'arbore di Diana* (Martín y Soler) 3, 47–8, 108–9, 122–3, 242
*La novela del curioso impertinente* (Cervantes) 127, 135
*La vendemmia* (Gazzaniga) 152–3
*La vilanella rapita* (Bianchi) 114
Lange (Weber), Aloisia 4–6, 56, 65, 86–7, 135, 145, 149
Lange, Joseph 20, 65, 74, 87, 95–6, 141, 246
Laschi (Mombelli), Luisa 3–4, 58, 151
Lawrence, William Witherle 9
*Le droghe d'amore* (Gozzi) 107, 123, 136–7
*Le Jeu de l'amour et du hasard* (Marivaux) 133–4
*Le mariage de Figaro* (Beaumarchais) 110–4, 184
Leopold II, Emperor 44, 61, 104
*Les liaisons dangereuses* (Choderlos de Laclos) 131–2
*L'infedeltà delusa* (Haydn) 113

Mandini, Stephano 3
Mann, Thomas 160, 185, 208
Mann, William 221
Maria Theresa, Empress 18, 22, 81

Marivaux, Pierre Carlet de 129, 132–4
Martín y Soler, Vicente 38, 46–8
Mazzolà, Catarino 100
*Measure for Measure* (Shakespeare) 129
Mesmerism 137–8
Metastasio, Pietro 14, 140, 223
Moore, John 16, 20, 22–3, 27
Mount Edgcumbe, Lord 103, 152
Mozart, Anna Maria 77
Mozart, Constanze 41, 63–6, 68, 72, 75, 78, 87–94
Mozart, Leopold 1, 35, 39, 58, 60, 62, 72, 77–8, 84, 89, 95, 97
Mozart, Maria Anna (Nannerl) 60, 72
Mozart, Wolfgang Amadeus
    acquaintances 64–5, 80–81
    attention to performers' style 142–5, 152
    attitudes to opera 1, 108, 140–2
    behaviour 41, 63, 92–3, 116
    beliefs 77, 79, 85
    children 71–3, 91–4
    concerts 55–8, 61–2
    debts 66–8, 73
    expenditure 60, 62–6
    health 66, 74–5
    Joseph II 18, 22, 85–6
    marriage 58, 78, 86–94
    musical style 160–5, 173, 210–2
    pattern of creative output 69–72, 75, 198, 208–9
    performance style 36, 52, 57
    popularity 46–9, 51–2, 55–9, 61
    publications 41, 59, 72
    residences in Vienna 13, 58, 60, 64, 72–3
    revenue 37, 41, 54–5, 58–61, 64
    teaching 54–5
    travel 35–6, 39, 42, 61, 90
    way of life 54, 58, 63–4, 74, 94–7

Niemetschek, Franz Xaver 63, 85, 121

*Orlando furioso* (Ariosto) 125–6
Opera
    organisation 37–8, 41–2, 152–3
    repertoires 49, 142
    standards of performance 44–5, 145–6, 155–6
*Opera buffa*
    conventions 105–6, 129, 170, 173, 206
    musical form 163–4
    *seria* parodies 107, 113, 221–3
*Opera seria* 43, 50–1
Orchestras in the 18th Century 155–6, 158

Paisiello, Giovanni 37–8, 45–8, 50, 59, 68
Pergen, Count Johann Anton 31–2, 104
Piccinni, Nicola 50

Piozzi, Hester Lynch (Mrs Thrale) 14, 23, 51, 117
Prague
    *Don Giovanni* 4, 117, 243
    opera company 4, 151, 156
    reception of *Le nozze di Figaro* 3
Puchberg, Michael 5, 52, 59, 66–7, 72–3, 81

Raaff, Anton 144
Religion 19, 77–8, 83–5
Riesbeck, Johann Caspar 17, 23–4, 96
Rosen, Charles 160, 163, 165
Ruskin, John 6
Ryle, Gilbert 11

Sadie, Stanley 59
St. Petersburg 37, 39
Salieri, Antonio 3, 6, 38, 46–8, 61, 134, 140, 144, 148, 223
Sarti, Giuseppe 38, 47, 52, 148
Schikaneder, Emanuel 43, 95–6, 184
Schiller, Friedrich von 49
*School for Scandal* (Sheridan) 135, 141
Schröder, Friedrich 7, 95, 141
Schröter, Corona 146
Schuster, Joseph 33
Shakespeare, William 9, 124, 129, 141
Singer, Irvin 207, 222
Sorabji, Kaikhosru Shapurji 8
Stadler, Anton 157–8
Stephanie, Gottlieb 95, 140–1
Storace, Nancy 3, 39, 43, 56, 65, 142, 146–8
Storace, Stephen 147, 154
Swieten, Gottfried van 20, 31, 59–60

Swinburne, Henry 35

*Tarare* (Salieri) 3, 46
*The West Indian* (Cumberland) 141
Theatre repertoires 49, 95
Teyber, Therese 56
Thun, Countess Wilhelmine 53, 79–80, 95
Tirso da Molina 107, 115
Tonkünstler-Societät 44, 53–4, 56
Trattner, Johann von 56, 81
Tyson, Alan 70, 209

*Una cosa rara* (Martín y Soler) 3, 38, 47, 109, 141, 155, 159, 199

Venice 98–100
Vienna
    appearance 13–4
    concert life 55–7
    cost of living 65–6, 68
    society 15–6, 22–7, 82, 85, 92
    taste in music 45–7, 117, 139, 141, 143, 184
Vocal style 146, 148–9, 153–4
Voltaire, François-Marie Arouet de 79

Wagner, Richard 7
Williams, Bernard 204
Wranitsky, Anton 33, 35
Wraxall, Nathaniel 23, 25
Wucherer, Georg 31

Zaguri, Pietro 102, 105
Zinzendorf, Count Karl 138, 147

Printed in the United States
19278LVS00004B/259-261